IMPORTANT

HERE IS YOUR REGISTRATION CODE TO ACCESS
MCGRAW-HILL *CONNECT LUCAS* ONLINE CONTENT

To access *Connect Lucas*, you need the registration code included on this card. Once the code is entered, you will be able to use the online resources for the length of your course.

Access is provided only if you have purchased a new book. If the registration code is missing from this registration card, please visit connectlucas.com to learn how to obtain a new code. Your registration code is nontransferable and can only be used once.

Connect Lucas is a revolutionary digital experience to accompany the tenth edition of Stephen E. Lucas' *The Art of Public Speaking*. *Connect Lucas* allows you to access the complete media and research library, study aids, speech preparation and assessment tools from a single place, connectlucas.com.

To Get Started

1. Go to connectlucas.com. Bookmark this site for future use. Click "Register."

2. Fill out the registration form including the registration code provided to the right.

3. Follow the on-screen instructions to login. You will need to use the login name and password you selected during the registration process.

Instructors: Please go to connectlucas.com and click Instructor Resources.

ISBN 978-0-07-726228-0
MHID 0-07-726228-X

EAN

90000

9 780077 262280

www.mhhe.com

connect for education

Powered by Connect for Education

IAYNIP

LUH2926FFFF06F

REGISTRATION CODE

The McGraw-Hill Companies

McGraw-Hill
Higher Education

The Art of
Public Speaking

TENTH EDITION

STEPHEN E. LUCAS
University of Wisconsin–Madison

Boston   Burr Ridge, IL   Dubuque, IA   Madison, WI   New York   San Francisco   St. Louis
Bangkok   Bogotá   Caracas   Kuala Lumpur   Lisbon   London   Madrid   Mexico City
Milan   Montreal   New Delhi   Santiago   Seoul   Singapore   Sydney   Taipei   Toronto

Mc Graw Hill **Higher Education**

Published by McGraw-Hill, an imprint of The McGraw-Hill Companies, Inc., 1221 Avenue of the Americas, New York, NY 10020. Copyright 2009, 2007, 2004, 2001, 1998, 1995, 1992, 1989, 1986, 1983 by Stephen E. Lucas. All rights reserved. No part of this publication may be reproduced or distributed in any form or by any means, or stored in a database or retrieval system, without the prior written consent of The McGraw-Hill Companies, Inc., including, but not limited to, in any network or other electronic storage or transmission, or broadcast for distance learning.

This book is printed on acid-free paper.

1 2 3 4 5 6 7 8 9 0 DOW / DOW 0 9 8

ISBN: 978-0-07-338515-0 (Student Edition)
MHID: 0-07-338515-8
ISBN: 978-0-07-726223-5 (Instructor's Edition)
MHID: 0-07-726223-9

Vice President and Editor in Chief: *Michael Ryan*
Publisher: *Frank Mortimer*
Executive Editor: *Katie Stevens*
Executive Marketing Manager: *Leslie Oberhuber*
Director of Development: *Rhona Robbin*
Freelance Editor: *Jessica Bodie Richards*
Editorial Assistant: *Erika Lake*
Production Editor: *Brett Coker*
Manuscript Editor: *Margaret Moore*
Design Manager: *Laurie Entringer*
Interior Designer: *Maureen McCutcheon*
Photo Editor: *Natalia Peschiera*
Photo Researcher: *Barbara Salz*
Senior Production Supervisor: *Richard DeVitto*
Digital Project Manager: *Sarah Hegarty*
Media Project Manager: *Ron Nelms*
Supplements Producer: *Louis Swaim*
Composition: *9.5/12 ITC Stone Serif Medium by Aptara® Inc., York, Pennsylvannia*
Printing: *45# Publisher's Matte Plus by R.R. Donnelley & Sons*

Credits: The credits section for this book begins on page C-1 and is considered an extension of the copyright page.

Library of Congress Cataloging-in-Publication Data

Lucas, Stephen, 1946—
    The art of public speaking / Stephen Lucas. – 10th ed.
        p. cm.
    Includes bibliographical references and index.
    ISBN-13: 978-0-07-338515-0 (alk. paper)
    ISBN-10: 0-07-338515-8 (alk. paper)
    1. Public speaking. I. Title.
    PN4129.15.L83 2008
    808.5'1–dc22

                                                2008036093

The Internet addresses listed in the text were accurate at the time of publication. The inclusion of a Web site does not indicate an endorsement by the authors or McGraw-Hill, and McGraw-Hill does not guarantee the accuracy of the information presented at these sites.

www.mhhe.com

About the Author

Stephen E. Lucas is Professor of Communication Arts and Evjue-Bascom Professor in the Humanities at the University of Wisconsin–Madison, where he has taught since 1972. He received his bachelor's degree from the University of California, Santa Barbara, and his master's and doctorate degrees from Penn State University.

Professor Lucas has been recognized for his work as both a scholar and a teacher. His first book, *Portents of Rebellion: Rhetoric and Revolution in Philadelphia, 1765–1776*, received the Golden Anniversary Award of the National Communication Association in 1977 and was nominated for a Pulitzer Prize. His major articles include "The Schism in Rhetorical Scholarship" (1981), "The Renaissance of American Public Address: Text and Context in Rhetorical Criticism" (1988), "The Stylistic Artistry of the Declaration of Independence" (1990), and "The Rhetorical Ancestry of the Declaration of Independence" (1998), for which he received the Golden Anniversary Monograph Award of the National Communication Association. His most recent book is *Words of a Century: The Top 100 American Speeches, 1900–1999* (2009).

Professor Lucas has received a number of teaching awards, including the Chancellor's Award for Excellence in Teaching at the University of Wisconsin and the National Communication Association's Donald Ecroyd Award for Outstanding Teaching in Higher Education. His lecture course on "The Rhetoric of Campaigns and Revolutions" is among the most popular on campus and has twice been selected for statewide broadcast in its entirety by Wisconsin Public Radio. Professor Lucas is featured in the Educational Video Group's program on the history of American public address, and he has appeared on the History Channel's documentary on the Declaration of Independence.

Professor Lucas has directed the introductory public speaking course at the University of Wisconsin–Madison since 1973. Over the years he has been responsible for numerous teaching innovations and has supervised the training of hundreds of graduate assistants. In addition to participating in public speaking workshops and colloquia at schools throughout the United States, he has served as a judge for the major national English-language public speaking competitions in China, has lectured at numerous Chinese universities, and has conducted workshops for Chinese instructors on teaching public speaking.

Stephen Lucas and his wife, Patty, live in Madison, Wisconsin, and have two sons, Jeff and Ryan. His interests include travel, sports, art, and photography.

Contents in Brief

Contents

CHAPTER 1

Speaking in Public 2

PART 1

SPEAKING AND LISTENING

CHAPTER 2

Ethics and Public Speaking   28

CHAPTER 3

Listening   46

Giving Your First Speech   63

Selecting a Topic and a Purpose   74

PART 2

SPEECH PREPARATION: GETTING STARTED

CHAPTER 5

Analyzing the Audience 94

CHAPTER 6

Gathering Materials 118

PART **3**

SPEECH PREPARATION: ORGANIZING AND OUTLINING

CHAPTER 9

Beginning and Ending the Speech 184

CHAPTER 10

Outlining the Speech 206

CHAPTER 11

Using Language 222

CHAPTER 12

Delivery 242

CHAPTER 13

Using Visual Aids   266

PART 5

VARIETIES OF PUBLIC SPEAKING

CHAPTER 15

Speaking to Persuade 322

CHAPTER 16

Methods of Persuasion 350

CHAPTER 17

Speaking on Special Occasions 380

CHAPTER 18

Speaking in Small Groups   392

APPENDIX

Speeches for Analysis and Discussion   A1

Preface

I could not have imagined when I wrote the first edition of *The Art of Public Speaking* the extraordinary response it would receive. As the book enters its tenth edition, I am deeply appreciative of the students and teachers who have made it the leading work on its subject at colleges and universities across the United States and around the globe.

In preparing this edition, I have retained what readers have identified as the main strengths of previous editions. The book continues to be informed by classical and contemporary theories of rhetoric but does not present theory for its own sake. Keeping a steady eye on the practical skills of public speaking, it offers full coverage of all major aspects of speech preparation and presentation.

As in previous editions, I have followed David Hume's advice that one "who would teach eloquence must do it chiefly by examples." Whenever possible, I have tried to *show* the principles of public speaking in action in addition to describing them. Thus you will find in the book a large number of narratives and extracts from speeches—set off from the text in a contrasting typeface. There are also many speech outlines and sample speeches. All these are provided so students can *see* how to formulate specific purpose statements, how to analyze and adapt to audiences, how to organize ideas and construct outlines, how to assess evidence and reasoning, how to use language effectively, and so forth.

Because the immediate task facing students is to present speeches in the classroom, I have relied heavily on examples that relate directly to students' classroom needs and experiences. The speech classroom, however, is a training ground where students develop skills that will serve them throughout life. Therefore, I have also included a large number of illustrations drawn from the kinds of speaking experiences students will face after they graduate—in their careers and in their communities.

I have also been guided by the belief that a book intended for students who want to speak more effectively should never lose sight of the fact that the most important part of speaking is thinking. The ability to think critically is vital to a world in which personality and image too often substitute for thought and substance. While helping students become capable, responsible speakers, *The Art of Public Speaking* also seeks to help them become capable, responsible thinkers.

Features of the Tenth Edition

Given the enthusiastic response to previous editions, I have kept the basic philosophy and approach of the book intact. At the same time, I have taken this edition as an opportunity to examine everything with a fresh eye. In addition to making content changes in response to advances in technology and the evolving needs of students and instructors, I have edited each chapter in the interest of economy, clarity, and precision. The result, in combination with a dynamic new design and a pathbreaking technology program, is a sleeker, more streamlined book that retains the comprehensive coverage and stylistic accessibility of its predecessors.

Other features include:

Developing Confidence

Stage fright is a universal phenomenon that has been studied by scholars in multiple academic disciplines, including communication, psychology, theatre and drama, sociology, and medicine. The research shows unequivocally that stage fright transcends cultural boundaries, age, sex, occupation, and socioeconomic standing. Everyone is affected by it to some degree or another. Consequently, one of the first tasks in any public speaking book is to help students develop a positive attitude toward the subject and confidence in their abilities to succeed as speakers.

I have always covered this subject in Chapter 1, but I have expanded and updated the discussion in this edition to help students understand both the universality of stage fright and the methods they can use to control it. I have also added a Checklist for Speaking with Confidence. Modeled on the checklists that were such a popular feature of the ninth edition, it is designed to help students as they move toward becoming more poised and confident speakers. Like all checklists for this edition, it is also available at connectlucas.com, which is explained on pages xx–xxii.

Internet Research

For all the time they spend on the Internet, many students do not understand how to use it systematically for research. There is a vast difference between browsing the Web and using it to conduct focused, efficient searches. Accordingly, in Chapter 6, I have thoroughly updated the treatment of Internet research to account for the changing capabilities of search engines, the consolidation of information-oriented Web sites, and the continuing growth of virtual libraries.

I have also expanded the section on Evaluating Internet Documents. The biggest challenge for many students is not finding information on the Internet, but thinking critically about the information they do find. To assist them, I discuss authorship, sponsorship, and recency as criteria for assessing the quality of Internet documents. In addition, I have added a Checklist for Evaluating Internet Documents.

Citing Sources Orally

The bibliography that students include with a speech outline identifies the sources they used in constructing the speech. But listeners do not have access to that outline. For them, the speaker needs to identify his or her sources orally during the speech. This is partly a matter of providing the information listeners need to gauge the quality and reliability of a speaker's sources. It is also a matter of blending citations skillfully into the texture of the speech. As with other aspects of speechmaking, the Internet poses special challenges here as well. Too often, students are inclined to say something like "As I found on the Web" or "As the Internet states."

In Chapter 7, I have added a new section titled Citing Sources Orally that helps students with all these challenges. It deals with both print and online sources, and it includes a checklist that students can apply as they construct their speeches. In addition, connectlucas.com includes a collection of sample oral citations that supplement those in the book.

PowerPoint

In the eighth edition, I added an appendix following Chapter 13 explaining how to use PowerPoint without either dominating a speech or enfeebling it. The response to this appendix has been extremely favorable, and I have updated it in this edition to keep pace with changes in PowerPoint. In addition, because PowerPoint is a visual medium, the DVD of student speeches that accompanies this edition includes several presentations that illustrate how to use PowerPoint to best advantage. Finally, for students who need more guidance than can be provided in the book, connectlucas.com includes step-by-step tutorials for PowerPoint 2003 and PowerPoint 2007.

Taken together, all these resources provide the most comprehensive set of teaching materials for PowerPoint available with any speech textbook. They give the kind of guidance students need to use PowerPoint effectively and responsibly—in the classroom and beyond.

Introductions, Conclusions, and Visual Aids DVD

Because speeches are performative acts, students need to be able to view speakers in action as well as read their words on the printed page. In conjunction with this edition, I have developed a new video program titled *Introductions, Conclusions, and Visual Aids*. Part One of this 30-minute DVD uses excerpts from a wide range of speeches to illustrate the principles of effective introductions and conclusions. Part Two contains examples of speakers using a variety of visual aids and presentation media.

Introductions, Conclusions, and Visual Aids is based on the principles of visual learning and provides an exciting resource that instructors can use to help students understand and apply the principles discussed in the book.

Student Speeches for Analysis and Discussion DVD

In addition to *Introductions, Conclusions, and Visual Aids*, this edition includes a DVD of 24 student speeches for analysis and discussion, all with an option for closed captioning. Eight of the speeches are new to this edition. All together, there are seven introductory speeches, eight informative speeches, five persuasive speeches, and four commemorative speeches. Thirteen of the speeches are printed in the book; texts of the others are available in the *Instructor's Manual*.

The speeches reflect the diversity of today's society and college classroom. They are presented by speakers of many backgrounds, deal with a wide range of topics, and employ several kinds of visual aids. All, however, are meant to illustrate the principles of organization, audience analysis, supporting materials, creativity, and language that are discussed throughout the book and that are central to effective public speaking in any context.

The DVD also includes three sets of paired Needs Improvement and Final Version speeches. In addition to "The Hidden World of Chili Peppers," which was so popular in the ninth edition, the new DVD includes a speech of self-introduction titled "Pot, Soil, Water" and an informative presentation on "Securing Yourself Online." In all three cases, the needs improvement version contains many of the flaws that typically appear in student presentations early in the term—inadequate preparation, underdevelopment of ideas, sloppy organization, ineffective use of visual aids, and the like. My aim is to show students—rather than just tell them—the things to avoid if they want to craft a successful speech. Once students have seen the needs improvement version, instructors can show the final version, in which the flaws have been corrected.

Connect Lucas

Although I find it a bit strange to write about a feature that has my name in the title, I could not be more pleased with the content of *Connect Lucas*. A revolutionary digital resource, it provides online access at a single site to all the teaching and learning materials available with *The Art of Public Speaking*. These materials incorporate everything that was on the Student CD-ROM in previous editions—plus a lot more. Specially marked icons in the book direct readers to appropriate items at connectlucas.com. Those items include:

- *Video Clips:* More than 60 clips demonstrate the principles of public speaking in action. Running from 20 seconds to a minute and a half in length and accompanied by a text introduction, each clip is fully integrated with the book, offers the option of closed captioning, and has been carefully chosen to illustrate a particular aspect of public speaking.

- *Full Speeches:* There are 21 full student presentations, including six introductory speeches, six informative speeches, five persuasive speeches, and four commemorative speeches—all with a closed-captioning option. Each is accompanied by an audio introduction and an outline of the speech, as well as by critical-thinking questions that can be used for classroom discussion or for out-of-class assignments.

- *Speech Outliner:* This innovative learning tool guides students systematically through the process of organizing and outlining their speeches. Tutorial screens explain the organizational methods involved in composing each part of the speech, and the outliner automatically formats the speech in accordance with proper outlining principles. It also allows students to save, revise, and print their work.

- *Interactive Outline Exercises:* Six exercises present scrambled outlines that students can rearrange in the correct order by using standard drag-and-drop procedures. As with other features at connectlucas.com, the aim of these exercises is to put online technology to the best possible pedagogical use.

- *Bibliography Formats and Bibliomaker:* Covering more than 30 types of source material—from books, essays, and newspaper articles to government publications, television programs, and Internet documents—the Bibliography Formats provide a comprehensive set of sample citations for both Modern Language Association (MLA) and American Psychological Association (APA) formats. The accompanying Bibliomaker automatically formats bibliographic entries according to the citation style chosen by the student.

- *Interactive Study Questions:* Entirely different from the questions in the *Test Bank*, the study questions are designed both to gauge students' knowledge and to help them learn. After students enter their answer for each question, they receive not just an indication of whether the answer is right or wrong, but *feedback* that explains the correct answer.

- *Interactive Key-Term Flashcards:* A set of electronic flashcards for each chapter helps students study key terms and concepts from the book. In addition to being fully interactive, the flashcards allow students to do a self-quiz that tests their comprehension of key terms.

- *Speech Preparation Checklists:* All 17 checklists in the book are also available at connectlucas.com. In addition to helping students keep on track as they prepare their speeches, the checklists can be printed or e-mailed in case instructors want students to submit them with their speeches.

- *Worksheets:* New to this edition, more than 20 worksheets deal with such topics as listening, audience analysis and adaptation, library and Internet research, informative and persuasive speech preparation, and out-of-class speech observations. Students can print the worksheets or complete them electronically and e-mail them to their instructor.

- *Speech Self-Assessments:* Also new to this edition, self-assessment forms for the introductory, informative, persuasive, and commemorative speeches direct students in reflecting on their presentations and what they need to work on in the future. Like other elements of *Connect Lucas*, the self-assessments are designed for online courses as well as for traditional classrooms.

- *Speech Capture:* This cutting-edge tool lets students upload video recordings of their speeches, which instructors can watch and grade online. Instructors can insert comments at any point in the video, thereby allowing for precise, pinpointed feedback. The Speech Capture tool can also be used for peer review and in conjunction with the student self-assessment forms discussed above.

- *Top 100 Speeches:* Available in the online Research Library at connectlucas. com, texts of the top 100 American speeches of the 20th century provide another valuable resource. When possible, audio or video links are also provided. The speeches can be incorporated into class by having each student give an informative presentation about one of the top 100. Students often find this a fascinating assignment that broadens their horizons beyond the classroom.

- *Audio Abridgement:* This highly popular "book on tape" is now available online. Each chapter runs about 20 minutes, focuses on key concepts, and allows listeners to review when commuting, working out, or just sitting down to study. As with other audio and video resources at connectlucas.com, the audio abridgement can be downloaded to iPods, iPhones, and other MP3 and MP4 players.

- *Course Management System:* Another advantage of *Connect Lucas* is that it allows instructors to create, administer, and grade assignments completely online. It also provides a single site for posting syllabi, course announcements, assignments, grades, and discussion forums.

The only way to gain a full appreciation of all the resources provided at connectlucas.com is to visit the site and explore it yourself. But I hope this summary has made clear why I am so excited about it. Firmly grounded in the principles of speech pedagogy and taking full advantage of advances in instructional technology, it is a 21st-century resource that far surpasses what is available with any other public speaking textbook.

Connect Lucas Plus

Connect Lucas Plus contains everything available with *Connect Lucas*, but goes beyond it to provide a media-rich electronic version of the textbook itself. Identical in content to the print version of *The Art of Public Speaking*, it embeds in the text all the teaching and learning resources discussed on the preceding pages as part of *Connect Lucas*. Rather than switching between the printed page and *Connect Lucas*, students can read the book online and link instantly to everything available at connectlucas.com.

Given the traditional image of online books as one dreary PDF page after another, it is important to stress that the electronic version of *The Art of Public Speaking* has been created specifically for the online environment. Colorful, dynamic, and visually appealing, it draws students into the book by using the same innovative technology and design techniques as high-quality sites across the Web.

Although designed primarily to meet the needs of students and instructors in online courses, the electronic *Art of Public Speaking* is also perfectly suitable for use in traditional classes. Students can choose the print version or the electronic version based on their personal preferences. In either case, they will receive the same content and the same access to all the resources integral to this edition.

Resources for Instructors

The Art of Public Speaking has an exceptional set of instructional resources. Some are found in the book itself; others are supplemental to it. Taken together, they provide a fully integrated teaching and learning system. In addition to those described in the sections on *Connect Lucas* and *Connect Lucas Plus*, they include the following:

Annotated Instructor's Edition

The *Annotated Instructor's Edition* provides a wealth of teaching aids for each chapter in the book. These aids include video resources, speech assignments, instructional strategies, class activities, discussion questions, and related readings. The *Annotated Instructor's Edition* is also cross-referenced with *Connect Lucas*, the *Instructor's Manual*, the Instructor's Resource CD-ROM, and other supplements that accompany *The Art of Public Speaking*.

Instructor's Manual

Running close to 500 pages, the *Instructor's Manual* provides a comprehensive guide to teaching from *The Art of Public Speaking*. It contains outlines for each chapter of the book; discusses the end-of chapter exercises; furnishes supplementary exercises and classroom activities; offers suggested course outlines and speaking assignments; and provides 37 additional speeches for discussion and analysis.

Test Bank

The *Test Bank* furnishes 2,236 examination questions based on *The Art of Public Speaking*; 289 questions are new to this edition. As a special feature, the *Test Bank* offers preconstructed true-false quizzes for each chapter in the book, as well as three complete final examinations. The quizzes are also available with *Connect Lucas* and *Connect Lucas Plus*, where they can be assigned and graded

The *Test Bank* is also available electronically in McGraw-Hill's EZ Test program. In addition to reproducing questions from the *Test Bank*, this program allows instructors to add their own questions, to create multiple versions of a single exam, and to export exams for use with course management systems such as WebCT or BlackBoard. An EZ Test Online service helps instructors administer online exams and quizzes that have been created with EZ Test.

PowerPoint Slides with Video Clips

There is also a collection of 480 slides for instructors who use PowerPoint in their lectures and discussions. Fully revised for this edition, the slides include photographs, illustrations, and video clips as well as text. Instructors can use the slides just as they are, or they can modify them to fit the special needs of individual classes. The slides can be found on the Instructor's Resource CD-ROM described below, as well as at connectlucas.com.

Instructor's Resource CD-ROM

For the convenience of instructors, the *Instructor's Manual*, *Test Bank*, and PowerPoint slides are all available on the Instructor's Resource CD-ROM. The CD also includes *Selections from the Communication Teacher*, *Teaching Public Speaking*, *Teaching Public Speaking Online*, and the *Handbook for Teachers of Non-Native Speakers of English*—all of which are described below.

- *Selections from the Communication Teacher:* Over the years, I have compiled six volumes of selections from the *Communication Teacher* to accompany *The Art of Public Speaking*. All six are available on the Instructor's Resource CD-ROM. They cover a host of topics related to the teaching of public speaking, including audience analysis, critical thinking, diversity and multiculturalism, informative speaking, persuasion, and general instructional methods. Taken together, they reprint more than 380 brief articles that offer a wealth of practical ideas for classroom use.

- *Teaching Public Speaking:* Written primarily for beginning instructors, *Teaching Public Speaking* reprints my essay of the same title from *Teaching Communication: Theory, Research, and Methods* (Lawrence Erlbaum Associates). This essay presents an overview of the pedagogical philosophy behind *The Art of Public Speaking* and discusses a number of practical classroom issues.

- *Teaching Public Speaking Online:* Written by Professor Jennifer Cochrane of Indiana University and Purdue University at Indianapolis, *Teaching Public*

Speaking Online has been fully updated for the tenth edition. It is available on the Instructor's Resource CD-ROM and at connectlucas.com, and it provides a wealth of practical guidance for instructors who are using *The Art of Public Speaking* in an online course. It draws upon Professor Cochrane's pioneering experience with online instruction to explore how one can teach an intellectually rich, practically rewarding public speaking course via the Web.

- *Handbook for Teachers of Non-Native Speakers of English:* Developed for instructors who have ESL students in their public speaking classes, this 60-page handbook focuses on the central issues that should be considered when working with students from different linguistic and cultural backgrounds. It is available on the Instructor's Resource CD-ROM.

Video Introduction to *The Art of Public Speaking*

In this new 25-minute DVD, I provide an overview of the tenth edition and explain how instructors can integrate its many features—print and electronic alike—into their courses.

Acknowledgments

"'Tis the good reader," said Ralph Waldo Emerson, "that makes the good book." I have been fortunate to have very good readers indeed, and I would like to thank the reviewers and symposium participants whose names appear on page xxvi for their many helpful comments and suggestions.

In addition, I would like to express my gratitude to the students at the University of Wisconsin whose speeches provided the material for so many of the examples in the text; to Erik Goddard, who assisted with the research for this edition; to Jim Ferris, who provided a valuable sounding board on numerous issues; and to members of the Communication Arts 100 teaching staff at the University of Wisconsin, who helped me by collecting sample speeches and by identifying rough spots in the ninth edition.

Special thanks go to Amy Slagell for doing a marvelous job generating new questions for the *Test Bank;* to Jennifer Cochrane for her splendid supplement on using *The Art of Public Speaking* in an online course; and to Sue Vander Hook for her expert formatting of the *Instructor's Manual, Test Bank,* and *Student Workbook.* Above all, I am indebted to Paul Stob, who worked with me throughout the revision process. It is because of him that the book is appearing on schedule, despite the fact that I was out of commission for two months with a broken elbow.

I am grateful to Carl Burgchardt for his contributions to the appendix on "Giving Your First Speech"; to Randy Fitzgerald and Paul Porterfield for helping me secure the videotape of Sajjid Zahir Chinoy's "Questions of Culture"; and to Nie Lisheng, Editor-in-Chief of *21st Century,* for permission to use video excerpts from speeches presented at China's national English-language public speaking competition sponsored by *China Daily* and *21st Century.*

I also owe many thanks to *The Art of Public Speaking* team at McGraw-Hill. It was once again my privilege to work with Rhona Robbin, whose expertise, professionalism, and unflagging commitment to the book have helped sustain it through four editions. Leslie Oberhuber is in her third edition as the book's marketing manager, and she deserves no small share of credit for its success during that span. Publisher Frank Mortimer and Executive Editor Katie Stevens joined the book in this edition. Both have a strong commitment to excellence, and both have been indispensable to keeping *The Art of Public Speaking* fresh and creative.

Anyone who has worked with online projects knows that they are exceedingly complex. After taking time to begin a family, Jessica Bodie Richards returned to the book on this edition, and I cannot imagine anyone else being as successful in coordinating the myriad details involved in the development of *Connect Lucas*. Aoife Dempsey and Sarah Hegarty have also been indispensable. Their vision of the possibilities of online learning, combined with their extraordinary work translating that vision into reality, have helped make *Connect Lucas* and *Connect Lucas Plus* benchmarks for the use of instructional technology in college publishing.

Brett Coker was another key member of the book team. As project manager for this edition, he did a spectacular job getting the book through production on the tightest of schedules, notwithstanding vicissitudes that might have driven someone of lesser ability (and patience) into another profession. Laurie Entringer oversaw the design with skill and imagination, Barbara Salz did a superb job of photo research, and Erika Lake helped in numerous ways. Rich DeVitto, Louis Swaim, and Ron Nelms helped steer the book and supplements through the final stages of production. I would be remiss if I did not also thank Mike Ryan, Steve Debow, and Ed Stanford, all of whom helped drive the innovative spirit of this edition.

As always, my biggest debt is to my wife, Patty, whose love and support have sustained me through the years.

Stephen E. Lucas
Madison, Wisconsin

Reviewers and Symposium Participants

Donna Acerra
Northampton Community College

Richard N. Armstrong
Wichita State University

Nancy Arnett
Brevard Community College

Gretchen Arthur
International Academy of Design and Technology–Detroit

Leonard Assante
Volunteer State Community College

Jennifer Becker
University of Missouri–Columbia

Shirene Bell
Salt Lake Community College

Kimberly Berry
Ozarks Technical Community College

Patrick Breslin
Santa Fe Community College

Christa Brown
Minnesota State University

Ferald Bryan
Northern Illinois University

Dana Burnside
Lehigh Carbon Community College

Richard Capp
Hill College

Nick Carty
Dalton State College

Crystal Church
Cisco Junior College

Jennifer Cochrane
Indiana University–Purdue University, Indianapolis

Sandra Pensoneau–Conway
Wayne State University

Shirley Lerch Crum
Coastal Carolina Community College

Amy Darnell
Columbia College

Belle A. Edson
Arizona State University

Tracy Fairless
University of Central Oklahoma

Bryan Fisher
Francis Marion University

Kevin M. Gillen
Indiana University

Donna Gotch
California State University, San Bernardino

Jo Anna Grant
California State University, San Bernardino

Omar Guevara
Weber State University

Karen A. Hamburg
Camden County College

Kenneth Harris
Palo Alto College

Tina M. Harris
University of Georgia

Delwyn Jones
Moraine Valley Community College

Susan Kilgard
Anne Arundel Community College

Patricia King
McHenry County College

Linda Kurz
University of Missouri–Kansas City

Jerri Lynn Kyle
Missouri State University

Kathleen LeBesco
Marymount Manhattan College

Mark Lewis
Riverside Community College

Libby McGlone
Columbus State Community College

Nicki L. Michalski
Lamar University

Marjorie Keeshan Nadler
Miami University

April Wallace Nunn
Calhoun Community College

Kekeli Nuviadenu
Bethune-Cookman University

Jean Perry
Glendale Community College

The Art of
Public Speaking

Speaking in Public

G rowing up in rural Tennessee, Van Jones had no intention of becoming a public speaker. Studying journalism at the University of Tennessee at Martin, he hoped one day to report the news, not to make it. Nevertheless, he soon found himself drawn to campus politics, and he became a vocal member of the student body.

After attending law school, Jones joined the San Francisco–based Lawyers Committee for Human Rights to work on problems confronting inner-city communities. A few years later he established the Ella Baker Center for Human Rights, a nonprofit organization dedicated to promoting opportunity in urban America.

But Jones didn't stop there. Over the years, he combined human rights initiatives with his interest in environmental justice. Today, he is president of Green for All, which focuses on creating green-collar jobs throughout America. In 2007 he worked with members of the U.S. House of Representatives to pass the Green Jobs Act, which approved $125 million to train environmentally conscious workers.

How has Jones achieved all this? Partly through his legal training and dauntless spirit. But just as important is his ability to communicate with people through public speaking, which has been the primary vehicle for spreading his message. He has been described as "one of the most powerful and inspiring prophetic voices of our time." Audiences are moved "by his heart, inspired by his commitment, and rocked by his eloquence."

If you had asked Van Jones early in his life, "Do you see yourself as a major public speaker?" he probably would have laughed at the idea. Yet today he gives more than 100 presentations a year. Along the way, he has lectured at Harvard and Columbia and has addressed the U.S. Conference of Mayors, the National Symposium on Climate Change, and the World Economic Forum. More than a few pundits have suggested that elective office might be in his future.

The Power of Public Speaking

connectlucas.com
View John F. Kennedy, Martin Luther King, Ronald Reagan, Barbara Jordan, and other speakers in the online Media Library for this chapter (Video Clip 1.1)

Throughout history people have used public speaking as a vital means of communication. What the Greek leader Pericles said more than 2,500 years ago is still true today: "One who forms a judgment on any point but cannot explain" it clearly "might as well never have thought at all on the subject."[1] Public speaking, as its name implies, is a way of making your ideas public—of sharing them with other people and of influencing other people.

During modern times many women and men around the globe have spread their ideas and influence through public speaking. In the United States, the list includes Franklin Roosevelt, Billy Graham, Cesar Chavez, Barbara Jordan, Ronald Reagan, Martin Luther King, Hillary Clinton, and Barack Obama. In other countries, we see the power of public speaking employed by such people as former British Prime Minister Margaret Thatcher, South African leader Nelson Mandela, Burmese democracy champion Aung San Suu Kyi, and Kenyan environmentalist and Nobel Prize winner Wangari Maathai.

As you read these names, you may think to yourself, "That's fine. Good for them. But what does that have to do with me? I don't plan to be a president or a preacher or a crusader for any cause." Nevertheless, the need for public speaking will almost certainly touch you sometime in your life—maybe tomorrow, maybe not for five years. Can you imagine yourself in any of these situations?

You are one of seven management trainees in a large corporation. One of you will get the lower-management job that has just opened. There is to be a large staff meeting at which each of the trainees will discuss the project he or she has been developing. One by one your colleagues make their presentations. They have no experience in public speaking and are intimidated by the higher-ranking managers present. Their speeches are stumbling and awkward. You, however, call upon all the skills you learned in your public speaking course. You deliver an informative talk that is clear, well reasoned, and articulate. You get the job.

One of your children has a learning disability. You hear that your local school board has decided, for budget reasons, to eliminate the special teacher who has been helping your child. At an open meeting of the school board, you stand up and deliver a thoughtful, compelling speech on the necessity for keeping the special teacher. The school board changes its mind.

You are the assistant manager in a branch office of a national company. Your immediate superior, the branch manager, is about to retire, and there will be a retirement dinner. All the executives from the home office will attend. As his close working associate, you are asked to give a farewell toast at the party. You prepare and deliver a speech that is both witty and touching—a perfect tribute to your boss. After the speech, everyone applauds enthusiastically, and a few people have tears in their eyes. The following week you are named branch manager.

connectlucas.com
To read the words of famous speakers, log on to the Top 100 American Speeches of the 20th Century in the online Research Library.

Fantasies? Not really. Any of these situations could occur. In a survey of 480 companies and public organizations, communication skills—including public speaking—were ranked first among the personal qualities of college graduates sought by employers. In another survey, college graduates in the work force were asked to rank the skills most essential to their career development. What was at the top of their list? Oral communication.[2]

The importance of such skill is true across the board—for accountants and architects, teachers and technicians, scientists and stockbrokers. Even in highly specialized fields such as civil and mechanical engineering, employers consistently rank the ability to communicate above technical knowledge when deciding whom to hire and whom to promote. The ability to speak effectively is so prized that college graduates are increasingly being asked to give a presentation as part of their job interview.

Nor has the growth of the Internet and other new technologies reduced the need for public speaking. As one communication consultant states, "There are more avenues to reach people than ever before, but there's no substitute for face-to-face communication." To be successful, says business leader Midge Costanza, you must have "the ability to stand on your feet, either on a one-to-one basis or before a group, and make a presentation that is convincing and believable."[3]

The same is true in community life. Public speaking is a vital means of civic engagement. It is a way to express your ideas and to have an impact on issues that matter in society. As a form of empowerment, it can—and often does—make a difference in things people care about very much. The key phrase here is "make a difference." This is what most of us want to do in life—to make a difference, to change the world in some small way. Public speaking offers you an opportunity to make a difference in something you care about very much.

The Tradition of Public Speaking

Given the importance of public speaking, it's not surprising that it has been taught and studied around the globe for thousands of years. Almost all cultures have an equivalent of the English word "orator" to designate someone with special skills in public speaking. The oldest known handbook on effective speech was written on papyrus in Egypt some 4,500 years ago. Eloquence was highly prized in ancient India, Africa, and China, as well as among the Aztecs and other pre-European cultures of North and South America.[4]

In classical Greece and Rome, public speaking played a central role in education and civic life. It was also studied extensively. Aristotle's *Rhetoric*, composed during the third century B.C.E., is still considered the most important work on its subject, and many of its principles are followed by speakers (and writers) today. The great Roman leader Cicero used his speeches to defend liberty and wrote several works about oratory in general.

Over the centuries, many other notable thinkers have dealt with issues of rhetoric, speech, and language—including the Roman educator Quintilian, the Christian preacher St. Augustine, the medieval writer Christine de Pizan, the British philosopher Francis Bacon, and the American critic Kenneth Burke.[5] In recent years, communication researchers have provided an increasingly scientific basis for understanding the methods and strategies of effective speech.

Your immediate objective is to apply those methods and strategies in your classroom speeches. What you learn, however, will be applicable long after you leave college. The principles of public speaking are derived from a long tradition and have been confirmed by a substantial body of research. The more you know about those principles, the more effective you will be in your own speeches—and the more effective you will be in listening to the speeches of other people.

Similarities Between Public Speaking and Conversation

How much time do you spend each day talking to other people? The average adult spends about 30 percent of her or his waking hours in conversation. By the time you read this book, you will have spent much of your life perfecting the art of conversation. You may not realize it, but you already employ a wide range of skills when talking to people. These skills include the following:

1. *Organizing your thoughts logically.* Suppose you were giving someone directions to get to your house. You wouldn't do it this way:

When you turn off the highway, you'll see a big diner on the left. But before that, stay on the highway to Exit 67. Usually a couple of the neighbors' dogs are in the street, so go slow after you turn at the blinking light. Coming from your house you get on the highway through Maple Street. If you pass the taco stand, you've gone too far. The house is blue.

Instead, you would take your listener systematically, step by step, from his or her house to your house. You would organize your message.

2. *Tailoring your message to your audience.* You are a geology major. Two people ask you how pearls are formed. One is your roommate; the other is your nine-year-old niece. You answer as follows:

To your roommate: "When any irritant, say a grain of sand, gets inside the oyster's shell, the oyster automatically secretes a substance called nacre, which is principally calcium

Many skills used in conversation also apply in public speaking. As you learn to speak more effectively, you may also learn to communicate more effectively in other situations.

carbonate and is the same material that lines the oyster's shell. The nacre accumulates in layers around the irritant core to form the pearl."

To your niece: "Imagine you're an oyster on the ocean floor. A grain of sand gets inside your shell and makes you uncomfortable. So you decide to cover it up. You cover it with a material called mother-of-pearl. The covering builds up around the grain of sand to make a pearl."

3. *Telling a story for maximum impact.* Suppose you are telling a friend about a funny incident at last week's football game. You don't begin with the punch line ("Keisha fell out of the stands right onto the field. Here's how it started. . . ."). Instead, you carefully build up your story, adjusting your words and tone of voice to get the best effect.

4. *Adapting to listener feedback.* Whenever you talk with someone, you are aware of that person's verbal, facial, and physical reactions. For example:

You are explaining an interesting point that came up in biology class. Your listener begins to look confused, puts up a hand as though to stop you, and says "Huh?" You go back and explain more clearly.

A friend has asked you to listen while she practices a speech. At the end you tell her, "There's just one part I really don't like—that quotation from the attorney general." Your friend looks very hurt and says, "That was my favorite part!" So you say, "But if you just worked the quotation in a little differently, it would be wonderful."

Each day, in casual conversation, you do all these things many times without thinking about them. You already possess these communication skills. And these are among the most important skills you will need for public speaking.

To illustrate, let's return briefly to one of the hypothetical situations at the beginning of this chapter. When addressing the school board about the need for a special teacher:

- You *organize* your ideas to present them in the most persuasive manner. You steadily build up a compelling case about how the teacher benefits the school.

- You *tailor your message* to your audience. This is no time to launch an impassioned defense of special education in the United States. You must show how the issue is important to the people in that very room—to their children and to the school.

- You tell your story for *maximum impact.* Perhaps you relate an anecdote to demonstrate how much your child has improved. You also have statistics to show how many other children have been helped.

- You *adapt to listener feedback.* When you mention the cost of the special teacher, you notice sour looks on the faces of the school board members. So you patiently explain how small that cost is in relation to the overall school budget.

In many ways, then, public speaking requires the same skills used in ordinary conversation. Most people who communicate well in daily talk can learn to communicate just as well in public speaking. By the same token, training in public speaking can make you a more adept communicator in a variety of situations, such as conversations, classroom discussions, business meetings, and interviews.

Differences Between Public Speaking and Conversation

Despite their similarities, public speaking and everyday conversation are not identical. Imagine that you are telling a story to a friend. Then imagine yourself telling the story to a group of seven or eight friends. Now imagine telling the same story to 20 or 30 people. As the size of your audience grows, you will find yourself adapting to three major differences between conversation and public speaking:

1. *Public speaking is more highly structured.* It usually imposes strict time limitations on the speaker. In most cases, the situation does not allow listeners to interrupt with questions or commentary. The speaker must accomplish her or his purpose in the speech itself. In preparing the speech, the speaker must anticipate questions that might arise in the minds of listeners and answer them. Consequently, public speaking demands much more detailed planning and preparation than ordinary conversation.

2. *Public speaking requires more formal language.* Slang, jargon, and bad grammar have little place in public speeches. As angry as he is about industrial pollution, when Van Jones speaks to a congressional committee, he doesn't say, "We've damn well got to stop the greedy creeps who pollute low-income communities just to make a few more bucks." Listeners usually react negatively to speakers who do not elevate and polish their language when addressing an audience. A speech should be "special."

3. *Public speaking requires a different method of delivery.* When conversing informally, most people talk quietly, interject stock phrases such as "like" and "you know," adopt a casual posture, and use what are called vocalized pauses ("uh," "er," "um"). Effective public speakers, however, adjust their voices to be heard clearly throughout the audience. They assume a more erect posture. They avoid distracting mannerisms and verbal habits.

With study and practice, you will be able to master these differences and expand your conversational skills into speechmaking. Your speech class will provide the opportunity for this study and practice.

Developing Confidence: Your Speech Class

One of the major concerns of students in any speech class is stage fright. We may as well face the issue squarely. Many people who converse easily in all kinds of everyday situations become frightened at the idea of standing up before a group to make a speech.

If you are worried about stage fright, you may feel better knowing that you are not alone. A 2001 Gallup Poll asked Americans to list their greatest fears. Forty percent identified speaking before a group as their top fear, exceeded only by the 51 percent who said they were afraid of snakes. A 2005 survey produced similar results, with 42 percent of respondents being terrified by the prospect of speaking in public. In comparison, only 28 percent said they were afraid of dying.[6]

In a different study, researchers concentrated on social situations and, again, asked their subjects to list their greatest fears. Here is how they answered:[7]

stage fright
Anxiety over the prospect of giving a speech in front of an audience.

Greatest Fear	Percent Naming
A party with strangers	74
Giving a speech	70
Asked personal questions in public	65
Meeting a date's parents	59
First day on a new job	59
Victim of a practical joke	56
Talking with someone in authority	53
Job interview	46

Again, speechmaking ranks near the top in provoking anxiety.

NERVOUSNESS IS NORMAL

If you feel nervous about giving a speech, you are in very good company. Some of the greatest public speakers in history have suffered from stage fright, including Abraham Lincoln, Margaret Sanger, and Winston Churchill. The famous Roman orator Cicero said: "I turn pale at the outset of a speech and quake in every limb and in my soul."[8] Oprah Winfrey, Conan O'Brien, and Jay Leno all report being anxious about speaking in public. Early in his career, Leonardo DiCaprio was so nervous about giving an acceptance speech that he hoped he would not win the Academy Award for which he had been nominated. Eighty-one percent of business executives say public speaking is the most nerve-wracking experience they face.[9] What comedian Jerry Seinfeld said in jest sometimes seems literally true: "Given a choice, at a funeral most of us would rather be the one in the coffin than the one giving the eulogy."

Actually, most people tend to be anxious before doing something important in public. Actors are nervous before a play, politicians are nervous before a campaign speech, athletes are nervous before a big game. The ones who succeed have learned to use their nervousness to their advantage. Listen to American gymnast Shawn Johnson speaking after her balance beam routine in the women's apparatus finals at the 2008 Olympic Games in Beijing: "I was so nervous I couldn't get anything right in warm ups. But I wanted to do my best and end on a good note." Putting her butterflies to good use, Johnson ended on a good note, indeed, by scoring 16.225 points to win the gold medal.

Much the same thing happens in speechmaking. Most experienced speakers have stage fright before taking the floor, but their nervousness is a healthy sign that they are getting "psyched up" for a good effort. Novelist and lecturer I. A. R. Wylie explains, "Now after many years of practice I am, I suppose, really a 'practiced speaker.' But I rarely rise to my feet without a throat constricted with terror and a furiously thumping heart. When, for some reason, I *am* cool and self-assured, the speech is always a failure."[10]

In other words, it is perfectly normal—even desirable—to be nervous at the start of a speech. Your body is responding as it would to any stressful situation—by producing extra *adrenaline*. This sudden shot of adrenaline is what makes your heart race, your hands shake, your knees knock, and your skin perspire. Every public speaker experiences all these reactions to some extent. The question is: How can you control your nervousness and make it work for you rather than against you?

DEALING WITH NERVOUSNESS

Rather than trying to eliminate every trace of stage fright, you should aim at transforming it from a negative force into what one expert calls *positive nervousness*—"a zesty, enthusiastic, lively feeling with a slight edge to it. . . . It's still nervousness, but it feels different. You're no longer victimized by it; instead, you're vitalized by it. You're in control of it."[11]

Don't think of yourself as having stage fright. Instead, think of it as "stage excitement" or "stage enthusiasm."[12] It can help you get focused and energized in the same way that it helps athletes, musicians, and others get primed for a game or a concert. Think of it as a normal part of giving a successful speech.

Here are six time-tested ways you can turn your nervousness from a negative force into a positive one.

Acquire Speaking Experience

You have already taken the first step. You are enrolled in a public speaking course, where you will learn about speechmaking and gain speaking experience. Think back to your first day at kindergarten, your first date, your first day

adrenaline
A hormone released into the bloodstream in response to physical or mental stress.

positive nervousness
Controlled nervousness that helps energize a speaker for her or his presentation.

The need for public speaking arises in many situations. Here Dr. Jim Thomas explains the surgical procedures used in a pioneering operation at Children's Medical Center in Dallas, Texas.

at a new job. You were probably nervous in each situation because you were facing something new and unknown. Once you became accustomed to the situation, it was no longer threatening. So it is with public speaking. For most students, the biggest part of stage fright is fear of the unknown. The more you learn about public speaking and the more speeches you give, the less threatening speechmaking will become.

Of course, the road to confidence will sometimes be bumpy. Learning to give a speech is not much different from learning any other skill—it proceeds by trial and error. The purpose of your speech class is to shorten the process, to minimize the errors, to give you a nonthreatening arena—a sort of laboratory—in which to undertake the "trial."

Your teacher recognizes that you are a novice and is trained to give the kind of guidance you need to get started. In your fellow students you have a highly sympathetic audience who will provide valuable feedback to help you improve your speaking skills. As the class goes on, your fears about public speaking will gradually recede until they are replaced by only a healthy nervousness before you rise to speak.[13]

Prepare, Prepare, Prepare

Another key to gaining confidence is to pick speech topics you truly care about—and then to prepare your speeches so thoroughly that you cannot help but be successful. Here's how one student combined enthusiasm for his topic with thorough preparation to score a triumph in speech class:

Jesse Young was concerned about taking a speech class. Not having any experience as a public speaker, he got butterflies in his stomach just thinking about talking in front of an audience. But when the time came for Jesse's first speech, he was determined to make it a success.

Jesse chose Habitat for Humanity as the topic for his speech. He had been a volunteer for the past three years, and he believed deeply in the organization and its mission. The purpose of his speech was to explain the origins, philosophy, and activities of Habitat for Humanity.

As Jesse spoke, it became clear that he was enthusiastic about his subject and genuinely wanted his classmates to share his enthusiasm. Because he was intent on communicating with his audience, he forgot to be nervous. He spoke clearly, fluently, and dynamically. Soon the entire class was engrossed in his speech.

Afterward Jesse admitted that he had surprised even himself. "It was amazing," he said. "Once I passed the first minute or so, all I thought about were those people out there listening. I could tell that I was really getting through to them."

How much time should you devote to preparing your speeches? A standard rule of thumb is that each minute of speaking time requires one to two hours of preparation time—perhaps more, depending on the amount of research needed for the speech. This may seem like a lot of time, but the rewards are well worth it. One professional speech consultant estimates that proper preparation can reduce stage fright by up to 75 percent.[14]

If you follow the techniques suggested by your teacher and in the rest of this book, you will stand up for every speech fully prepared. Imagine that the day for your first speech has arrived. You have studied your audience and selected a topic you know will interest them. You have researched the speech thoroughly and practiced it several times until it feels absolutely comfortable. You have even tried it out before two or three trusted friends. How can you help but be confident of success?

Think Positively

Confidence is mostly the well-known power of positive thinking. If you think you can do it, you usually can. On the other hand, if you predict disaster and doom, that is almost always what you will get. This is especially true when it comes to public speaking. Speakers who think negatively about themselves and the speech experience are much more likely to be overcome by stage fright than are speakers who think positively. Here are some ways you can transform negative thoughts into positive ones as you work on your speeches:

Negative Thought	Positive Thought
I wish I didn't have to give this speech.	This speech is a chance for me to share my ideas and gain experience as a speaker.
I'm not a great public speaker.	No one's perfect, but I'm getting better with each speech I give.
I'm always nervous when I give a speech.	Everyone's nervous. If other people can handle it, I can too.
No one will be interested in what I have to say.	I have a good topic and I'm fully prepared. Of course they'll be interested.

Many psychologists believe that the ratio of positive to negative thoughts in regard to stressful activities such as speechmaking should be at least five to one. That is, for each negative thought, you should counter with a minimum of five positive ones. Doing so will not make your nerves go away completely, but it will help keep them under control so you can concentrate on communicating your ideas rather than on brooding about your fears and anxieties.

Use the Power of Visualization

Visualization is closely related to positive thinking. It is used by athletes, musicians, actors, speakers, and others to enhance their performance in stressful situations. How does it work? Listen to long-distance runner Vicki Huber:

> Right before a big race, I'll picture myself running, and I will try and put all of the other competitors in the race into my mind. Then I will try and imagine every possible situation I might find myself in . . . behind someone, being boxed in, pushed, shoved or cajoled, different positions on the track, laps to go, and, of course, the final stretch. And I always picture myself winning the race, no matter what happens during the event.

Of course, Huber doesn't win every race she runs, but research has shown that the kind of mental imaging she describes can significantly increase athletic performance.[15] It has also shown that visualization can help speakers control their stage fright.[16]

The key to visualization is creating a vivid mental blueprint in which you see yourself succeeding in your speech. Picture yourself in your classroom rising to speak. See yourself at the lectern, poised and self-assured, making eye contact with your audience and delivering your introduction in a firm, clear voice. Feel your confidence growing as your listeners get more and more caught up in what you are saying. Imagine your sense of achievement as you conclude the speech knowing you have done your very best.

As you create these images in your mind's eye, be realistic but stay focused on the positive aspects of your speech. Don't allow negative images to eclipse the positive ones. Acknowledge your nervousness, but picture yourself overcoming it to give a vibrant, articulate presentation. If one part of the speech always seems to give you trouble, visualize yourself getting through it without any hitches. And be specific. The more lucid your mental pictures, the more successful you are likely to be.

As with your physical rehearsal of the speech, this kind of mental rehearsal of the speech should be repeated several times in the days before you speak. It doesn't guarantee that every speech will turn out exactly the way you envision it—and it certainly is no substitute for thorough preparation. But used in conjunction with the other methods of combating stage fright, it is a proven way to help control your nerves and to craft a successful presentation.

Know That Most Nervousness Is Not Visible

Many novice speakers are worried about appearing nervous to the audience. It's hard to speak with poise and assurance if you think you look tense and insecure. One of the most valuable lessons you will learn as your speech class proceeds is that only a fraction of the turmoil you feel inside is visible on the outside. "Your nervous system may be giving you a thousand shocks," says one experienced speaker, "but the viewer can see only a few of them."[17]

Even though your palms are sweating and your heart is pounding, your listeners probably won't realize how tense you are—especially if you do your best to act cool and confident on the outside. Most of the time when students confess after a speech, "I was so nervous I thought I was going to

visualization
Mental imaging in which a speaker vividly pictures himself or herself giving a successful presentation.

die," their classmates are surprised. To them the speaker looked calm and assured.

Knowing this should make it easier for you to face your listeners with confidence. As one student stated after watching a videotape of her first classroom speech, "I was amazed at how calm I looked. I assumed everyone would be able to see how scared I was, but now that I know they can't, I won't be nearly so nervous in the future. It really helps to know that you look in control even though you may not feel that way."

Don't Expect Perfection

It may also help to know that there is no such thing as a perfect speech. At some point in every presentation, every speaker says or does something that does not come across exactly as he or she had planned. Fortunately, such moments are usually not evident to the audience. Why? Because the audience does not know what the speaker *plans* to say. It hears only what the speaker *does* say. If you momentarily lose your place, reverse the order of a couple statements, or forget to pause at a certain spot, no one need be the wiser. When such moments occur, just proceed as if nothing happened.

One of the biggest reasons people are concerned about making a mistake in a speech is that they view speechmaking as a performance rather than an act of communication. They feel the audience is judging them against a scale of absolute perfection in which every misstated word or awkward gesture will count against them. But speech audiences are not like judges in a violin recital or an ice-skating contest. They are not looking for a virtuoso performance, but for a well-thought-out address that communicates the speaker's ideas clearly and directly. Sometimes an error or two can actually enhance a speaker's appeal by making her or him seem more human.[18]

As you work on your speeches, make sure you prepare thoroughly and do all you can to get your message across to your listeners. But don't panic about being perfect or about what will happen if you make a mistake. Once you free your mind of these burdens, you will find it much easier to approach your speeches with confidence and even with enthusiasm.

Besides stressing the six points just discussed, your teacher will probably give you several tips for dealing with nervousness in your first speeches. They may include:

- Be at your best physically and mentally. It's not a good idea to stay up until 2:00 A.M. partying with friends or cramming for an exam the night before your speech. A good night's sleep will serve you better.

- As you are waiting to speak, quietly tighten and relax your leg muscles, or squeeze your hands together and then release them. Such actions help reduce tension by providing an outlet for your extra adrenaline.

- Take a couple slow, deep breaths before you start to speak. Most people, when they are tense, take short, shallow breaths, which only reinforces their anxiety. Deep breathing breaks this cycle of tension and helps calm your nerves.

- Work especially hard on your introduction. Research has shown that a speaker's anxiety level begins to drop significantly after the first 30 to 60

Terrified early in his career by the prospect of giving a public speech, today Leonardo DiCaprio is an accomplished speaker who confidently addresses audiences around the globe.

seconds of a presentation.[19] Once you get through the introduction, you should find smoother sailing the rest of the way.

- Make eye contact with members of your audience. Remember that they are individual people, not a blur of faces. And they are your friends.

- Concentrate on communicating with your audience rather than on worrying about your stage fright. If you get caught up in your speech, your audience will too.

- Use visual aids. They create interest, draw attention away from you, and make you feel less self-conscious.

If you are like most students, you will find your speech class to be a very positive experience. As one student wrote on her course evaluation at the end of the class:

I was really dreading this class. The idea of giving all those speeches scared me half to death. But I'm glad now that I stuck with it. It's a small class, and I got to know a lot of the students. Besides, this is one class in which I got to express *my* ideas, instead of spending the whole time listening to the teacher talk. I even came to enjoy giving the speeches. I could tell at times that the audience was really with me, and that's a great feeling.

Over the years thousands of students have developed confidence in their speechmaking abilities. As your confidence grows, you will be better able to stand before other people and tell them what you think and feel and know—and to make them think and feel and know those same things. The best part about confidence is that it nurtures itself. After you score your first triumph, you will be that much more confident the next time. And as you become a more confident public speaker, you will likely become more confident in other areas of your life as well.

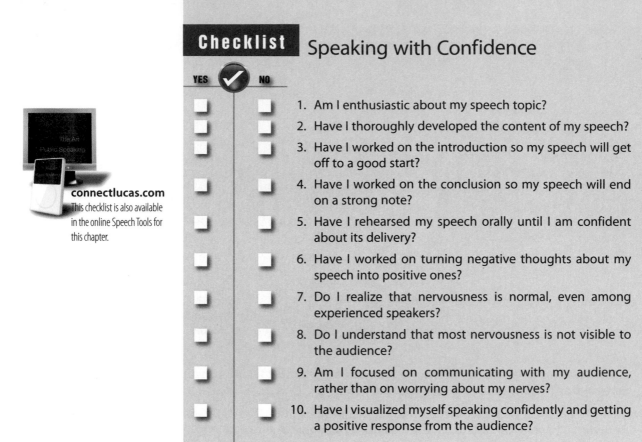

Checklist Speaking with Confidence

YES ✓ NO

1. Am I enthusiastic about my speech topic?
2. Have I thoroughly developed the content of my speech?
3. Have I worked on the introduction so my speech will get off to a good start?
4. Have I worked on the conclusion so my speech will end on a strong note?
5. Have I rehearsed my speech orally until I am confident about its delivery?
6. Have I worked on turning negative thoughts about my speech into positive ones?
7. Do I realize that nervousness is normal, even among experienced speakers?
8. Do I understand that most nervousness is not visible to the audience?
9. Am I focused on communicating with my audience, rather than on worrying about my nerves?
10. Have I visualized myself speaking confidently and getting a positive response from the audience?

Public Speaking and Critical Thinking

That guy at the party last night really owned me when we were talking about the economy. I know my information is right, and I'm sure his argument didn't make sense, but I can't put my finger on the problem.

I worked really hard on my term paper, but it's just not right. It doesn't seem to hang together, and I can't figure out what's wrong.

Political speeches are so one-sided. The candidates sound good, but they all talk in slogans and generalities. It's really hard to decide who has the best stands on the issues.

critical thinking

Focused, organized thinking about such things as the logical relationships among ideas, the soundness of evidence, and the differences between fact and opinion.

Have you ever found yourself in similar situations? If so, you may find help in your speech class. Besides building confidence, a course in public speaking can develop your skills as a critical thinker. Those skills can make the difference between the articulate debater and the pushover, the A student and the C student, the thoughtful voter and the coin tosser.

What is critical thinking? To some extent, it's a matter of logic—of being able to spot weaknesses in other people's arguments and to avoid them in your own. It also involves related skills such as distinguishing fact from opinion, judging the credibility of statements, and assessing the soundness of evidence. In the broadest sense, critical thinking is focused, organized thinking—the ability to see clearly the relationships among ideas.[20]

If you are wondering what this has to do with your public speaking class, the answer is quite a lot. As the class proceeds, you will probably spend a good deal of time organizing your speeches. While this may seem like a purely mechanical exercise, it is closely interwoven with critical thinking. If the structure of your speech is disjointed and confused, odds are that your thinking is also disjointed and confused. If, on the other hand, the structure is clear and cohesive, there is a good chance your thinking is too. Organizing a speech is not just a matter of arranging the ideas you already have. Rather, it is an important part of shaping the ideas themselves.

What is true of organization is true of many aspects of public speaking. The skills you learn in your speech class can help you become a more effective thinker in a number of ways. As you work on expressing your ideas in clear, accurate language, you will enhance your ability to think clearly and accurately. As you study the role of evidence and reasoning in speechmaking, you will see how they can be used in other forms of communication as well. As you learn to listen critically to speeches in class, you will be better able to assess the ideas of speakers (and writers) in a variety of situations.[21]

To return to the examples at the beginning of this section:

The guy at the party last night—would well-honed critical thinking skills help you find the holes in his argument?

The term paper—would better organization and a clear outline help pull it together?

Political speeches—once you get past the slogans, are the candidates drawing valid conclusions from sound evidence?

If you take full advantage of your speech class, you will be able to enhance your skills as a critical thinker in many circumstances. This is one reason public speaking has been regarded as a vital part of education since the days of ancient Greece.

The Speech Communication Process
••

As you begin your first speeches, you may find it helpful to understand what goes on when one person talks to another. Regardless of the kind of speech communication involved, there are seven elements—speaker, message, channel, listener, feedback, interference, and situation. Here we shall focus on how these elements interact when a public speaker addresses an audience.

SPEAKER

Speech communication begins with a speaker. If you pick up the telephone and call a friend, you are acting as a speaker. (Of course, you will also act as a listener when your friend is talking.) In public speaking, you will usually present your entire speech without interruption.

Your success as a speaker depends on *you*—on your personal credibility, your knowledge of the subject, your preparation of the speech, your manner of speaking, your sensitivity to the audience and the occasion. But successful speaking also requires enthusiasm. You can't expect people to be interested in what you say unless you are interested yourself. If you are truly excited about

speaker
The person who is presenting an oral message to a listener.

your subject, your audience is almost sure to get excited along with you. You can learn all the techniques of effective speechmaking, but before they can be of much use, you must first have something to say—something that sparks your own enthusiasm.

MESSAGE

message
Whatever a speaker communicates to someone else.

The message is whatever a speaker communicates to someone else. If you are calling a friend, you might say, "I'll be a little late picking you up tonight." That is the message. But it may not be the only message. Perhaps there is a certain tone in your voice that suggests reluctance, hesitation. The underlying message might be "I really don't want to go to that party. You talked me into it, but I'm going to put it off as long as I can."

Your goal in public speaking is to have your *intended* message be the message that is *actually* communicated. Achieving this depends both on what you say (the verbal message) and on how you say it (the nonverbal message).

Getting the verbal message just right requires work. You must narrow your topic down to something you can discuss adequately in the time allowed for the speech. You must do research and choose supporting details to make your ideas clear and convincing. You must organize your ideas so listeners can follow them without getting lost. And you must express your message in words that are accurate, clear, vivid, and appropriate.

Besides the message you send with words, you send a message with your tone of voice, appearance, gestures, facial expression, and eye contact. Imagine that one of your classmates gets up to speak about student loans. Throughout her speech she slumps behind the lectern, takes long pauses to remember what she wants to say, stares at the ceiling, and fumbles with her visual aids. Her intended message is "We must make more money available for student loans." But the message she actually communicates is "I haven't prepared very well for this speech." One of your jobs as a speaker is to make sure your nonverbal message does not distract from your verbal message.

CHANNEL

channel
The means by which a message is communicated.

The channel is the means by which a message is communicated. When you pick up the phone to call a friend, the telephone is the channel. Public speakers may use one or more of several channels, each of which will affect the message received by the audience.

Consider a speech to Congress by the President of the United States. The speech is carried to the nation by the channels of radio and television. For the radio audience the message is conveyed entirely by the President's voice. For the television audience the message is conveyed by both the President's voice and the televised image. The people in Congress have a more direct channel. They not only hear the President's voice as amplified through a microphone, but they also see him and the setting firsthand.

In a public speaking class your channel is the most direct of all. Your classmates will see you and hear you without any electronic intervention.

LISTENER

listener
The person who receives the speaker's message.

The listener is the person who receives the communicated message. Without a listener, there is no communication. When you talk to a friend on the phone, you have one listener. In public speaking you will have many listeners.

The critical thinking skills you develop in researching and organizing your speeches can be applied in many forms of communication, including meetings and group projects.

Everything a speaker says is filtered through a listener's *frame of reference*— the total of his or her knowledge, experience, goals, values, and attitudes. Because a speaker and a listener are different people, they can never have exactly the same frame of reference. And because a listener's frame of reference can never be exactly the same as a speaker's, the meaning of a message will never be exactly the same to a listener as to a speaker.

You can easily test the impact of different frames of reference. Ask each of your classmates to describe a chair. If you have 20 classmates, you'll probably get 20 different descriptions. One student might picture a large, overstuffed easy chair, another an elegant straight-backed chair, yet another an office chair, a fourth a rocking chair, and so on. Even if two or more envision the same general type—say, a rocking chair—their mental images of the chair could still be different. One might be thinking of an early American rocker, another of a modern Scandinavian rocker—the possibilities are unlimited. And "chair" is a fairly simple concept. What about "patriotism" or "freedom"?

Because people have different frames of reference, a public speaker must take great care to adapt the message to the particular audience being addressed. To be an effective speaker, you must be *audience-centered.* You will quickly lose your listeners' attention if your presentation is either too basic or too sophisticated. You will also lose your audience if you do not relate to their experience, interests, knowledge, and values. When you make a speech that causes listeners to say "That is important to *me,*" you will almost always be successful.

FEEDBACK

When the President addresses the nation on television, he is engaged in one-way communication. You can talk back to the television set, but the President won't hear you. Most situations, however, involve *two-way* communication. Your listeners don't simply absorb your message like human sponges. They send back messages of their own. These messages are called feedback.

frame of reference
The sum of a person's knowledge, experience, goals, values, and attitudes. No two people can have exactly the same frame of reference.

feedback
The messages, usually nonverbal, sent from a listener to a speaker.

In public speaking there is plenty of feedback to let you know how your message is being received. Do your listeners lean forward in their seats, as if paying close attention? Do they applaud in approval? Do they laugh at your jokes? Do they have quizzical looks on their faces? Do they shuffle their feet and gaze at the clock? The message sent by these reactions could be "I am fascinated," "I am bored," "I agree with you," "I don't agree with you," or any number of others. As a speaker, you need to be alert to these reactions and adjust your message accordingly.

Like any kind of communication, feedback is affected by one's frame of reference. How would you feel if, immediately after your speech, all your classmates started to rap their knuckles on the desks? Would you run out of the room in despair? Not if you were in a European university. In many parts of Europe, students rap their knuckles on their desks to show admiration for a classroom lecture. You must understand the feedback to be able to deal with it.

INTERFERENCE

Interference is anything that impedes the communication of a message. When you talk on the telephone, sometimes there is static, or wires get crossed so that two different conversations are going on at once. That is a kind of interference.

interference
Anything that impedes the communication of a message. Interference can be external or internal to listeners.

In public speaking there are two kinds of interference. One, like the static or crossed wires in a phone conversation, is *external* to the audience. Many classrooms are subject to this kind of interference—from traffic outside the building, the clatter of a radiator, students conversing in the hall, a room that is stifling hot or freezing cold. Any of these can distract listeners from what you are saying.

A second kind of interference is *internal* and comes from within your audience. Perhaps one of your listeners has a toothache. She may be so distracted by the pain that she doesn't pay attention to your speech. Another listener could be worrying about a test in the next class period. Yet another could be brooding about an argument with his girlfriend.

As a speaker, you must try to hold your listeners' attention despite these various kinds of interference. In the chapters that follow you will find many ways to do this.

SITUATION

The situation is the time and place in which speech communication occurs. Conversation always takes place in a certain situation. Sometimes the situation helps—as when you propose marriage over an intimate candlelight dinner. Other times it may hurt—as when you try to speak words of love in competition with a blaring stereo. When you have to talk with someone about a touchy issue, you usually wait until the situation is just right.

situation
The time and place in which speech communication occurs.

Public speakers must also be alert to the situation. Certain occasions—funerals, church services, graduation ceremonies—require certain kinds of speeches. Physical setting is also important. It makes a great deal of difference whether a speech is presented indoors or out, in a small classroom or in a gymnasium, to a densely packed crowd or to a handful of scattered souls. When you adjust to the situation of a public speech, you are only doing on a larger scale what you do every day in conversation.

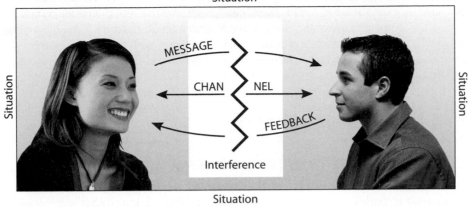

• FIGURE 1.1

Now let us look at a complete model of the speech communication process, as shown in Figure 1.1 above.[22]

THE SPEECH COMMUNICATION PROCESS: EXAMPLE WITH COMMENTARY

The following example shows how the various components of the speech communication process interact:

Situation	It was 5:15 P.M., and the fall sales conference of OmniBrands, Inc., had been going on all day. A series of new-product presentations to buyers from the company's largest customers had taken much longer than expected.
Speaker	Alyson Kaufman was worried. As a marketing manager for fragrances, she was the last speaker of the day. When Alyson rose to address the audience, she knew she faced a difficult situation. She had been allotted 45 minutes to introduce her products, and the meeting was scheduled to end in 15 minutes. What's more, holiday sales of her entire product line depended in large part on this presentation.
Channel *Interference*	Alyson stepped to the microphone and began to speak. She could see members of the audience looking at their watches, and she knew they were eager to get to dinner after a long day of presentations.
Adapting to *Interference*	"Good afternoon," Alyson said, "and thanks for your attention. I know everyone is ready for dinner—I certainly am. I was given 45 minutes for my presentation—okay, everybody groan—but with your kind cooperation, I'll do my best to finish in under half an hour. I think you'll find the time well worth your while, because the products I am going to tell you about will seriously boost your holiday sales." Alyson was relieved to see several people smiling as they settled back in their seats.
Message	Now that she had the audience's attention, Alyson presented each new product as briefly as she could. She streamlined her planned presentation to emphasize the features that would be most appealing to the buyers and the ones they would be most likely to remember. She ended by handing out samples of the products and promising to contact anyone who needed more information. She quickly added her e-mail address to her PowerPoint slides and was encouraged to see people writing it down.

As promised, Alyson finished in under half an hour. "And that wraps it up!" she concluded. "Let's eat!" Later, the marketing director complimented Alyson on dealing so well with a tough situation. "You did a great job," the marketing director said. "Next year, we'll try to make all the presentations as concise and efficient as yours."

Public Speaking in a Multicultural World

CULTURAL DIVERSITY IN THE MODERN WORLD

The United States has always been a diverse society. In 1673 a visitor to what is now New York City was astonished to find that 18 languages were spoken among the city's 8,000 inhabitants. By the middle of the 19th century, so many people from so many lands had come to the United States that novelist Herman Melville exclaimed, "You cannot spill a drop of American blood without spilling the blood of the whole world."[23]

One can only imagine what Melville would say today! The United States has become the most diverse society on earth. For more than a century, most immigrants to the U.S. were Europeans—Irish, Germans, English, Scandinavians, Greeks, Poles, Italians, and others. Together with African Americans, they made America the "melting pot" of the world.[24] Today another great wave of immigration—mostly from Asia and Latin America—has transformed the United States into what one writer calls "the first universal nation," a multicultural society of unmatched diversity.[25]

The diversity of life in the United States can be seen in cities and towns, schools and businesses, community groups, and houses of worship all across the land. Consider the following:

- There are 195 nations in the world, and every one of them has someone living in the United States.

- Houston has two radio stations that broadcast solely in Vietnamese and a daily newspaper that prints in Chinese.

- Nearly 60 percent of the people in Miami were born outside the United States.

- More than 47 million people in the U.S. speak a language other than English at home.

These kinds of developments are not limited to the United States. We live in an age of international multiculturalism. The Internet allows for instant communication everywhere around the world. CNN is broadcast to more than 1 billion people globally. International air travel has made national boundaries almost meaningless. All nations are becoming part of a vast global village. For example:

- There are 77,000 transnational corporations around the world, and they account for more than 30 percent of the world's economic output.

- McDonald's sells twice as many hamburgers and French fries abroad than it does in the United States; Nike makes 63 percent of its sales through exports.

- France has as many Muslims as practicing Catholics; radio CHIN in Toronto, Canada, broadcasts in 31 languages.

- In Geneva, Switzerland, there are so many people from around the world that nearly 60 percent of the school population is non-Swiss.

CULTURAL DIVERSITY AND PUBLIC SPEAKING

Diversity and multiculturalism are such basic facts of life that they can play a role in almost any speech you give. Consider the following situations: A business manager briefing employees of a multinational corporation. A minister sermonizing to a culturally diverse congregation. An international student explaining the customs of his land to students at a U.S. university. A teacher addressing parents at a multiethnic urban school. These are only a few of the countless speaking situations affected by the cultural diversity of modern life.

Speechmaking becomes more complex as cultural diversity increases. Part of the complexity stems from the differences in language from culture to culture. Nothing separates one culture from another more than language. Language and culture are so closely bound that "we communicate the way we do because we are raised in a particular culture and learn its language, rules, and norms."[26]

The meanings attached to gestures, facial expressions, and other nonverbal signals also vary from culture to culture. Even the gestures for such basic messages as "hello" and "goodbye" are culturally based. The North American "goodbye" wave is interpreted in many parts of Europe and South America as the motion for "no," while the Italian and Greek gesture for "goodbye" is the same as the U.S. signal for "come here."[27]

Many stories have been told about the fate of public speakers who fail to take into account cultural differences between themselves and their audiences. Consider the following scenario:[28]

The sales manager of a U.S. electronics firm is in Brazil to negotiate a large purchase of computers by a South American corporation. After three days of negotiations, the sales manager holds a gala reception for all the major executives to build goodwill between the companies.

As is the custom on such occasions, time is set aside during the reception for an exchange of toasts. When it is the sales manager's turn to speak, he praises the Brazilian firm for its many achievements and talks eloquently of his respect for its president and other executives. The words are perfect, and the sales manager can see his audience smiling in approval.

And then—disaster. As the sales manager closes his speech, he raises his hand and flashes the classic U.S. "OK" sign to signal his pleasure at the progress of the negotiations. Instantly the festive mood is replaced with stony silence; smiles turn to icy stares. The sales manager has given his Brazilian audience a gesture with roughly the same meaning as an extended middle finger in the United States.

The next day the Brazilian firm announces it will buy its computers from another company.

As this story illustrates, public speakers can ill afford to overlook their listeners' cultural values and customs. The methods of effective speech explained throughout this book will be helpful to you in speaking to culturally diverse audiences. Here we need to stress the importance of avoiding the ethnocentrism

Public speaking is a vital mode of communication in most cultures around the world. Here French finance minister Christine Lagarde addresses the World Economic Forum in Davos, Switzerland.

that often blocks communication between speakers and listeners of different cultural backgrounds.

AVOIDING ETHNOCENTRISM

ethnocentrism
The belief that one's own group or culture is superior to all other groups or cultures.

Ethnocentrism is the belief that our own group or culture—whatever it may be—is superior to all other groups or cultures. Because of ethnocentrism, we identify with our group or culture and see its values, beliefs, and customs as "right" or "natural"—in comparison to the values, beliefs, and customs of other groups or cultures, which we tend to think of as "wrong" or "unnatural."[29]

Ethnocentrism is part of every culture, and it can play a positive role in creating group pride and loyalty. But it can also lead to prejudice and hostility toward different racial, ethnic, or cultural groups. To be an effective public speaker in a multicultural world, you need to keep in mind that all people have their special beliefs and customs.

Avoiding ethnocentrism does not mean you must agree with the values and practices of all groups and cultures. At times you might try to convince people of different cultures to change their traditional ways of doing things—as speakers from the United Nations seek to persuade farmers in Africa to adopt more productive methods of agriculture, or as delegates from the U.S. and China attempt to influence the other country's trade policies.

If such speakers are to be successful, however, they must show respect for the cultures of the people they address. They need to adapt their message to the cultural values and expectations of their listeners.

When you work on your speeches, be alert to how cultural factors might affect the way listeners respond. As we shall see in Chapter 5, for classroom speeches you can use audience-analysis questionnaires to learn about the backgrounds and opinions of your classmates. For speeches outside the classroom, the person who invites you to speak can usually provide information about the audience.

Internet Connection
www.connectlucas.com

Once you know about any cultural factors that might affect your listeners' response, try to put yourself in their place and to hear your message through their ears. If there is a language difference, avoid words or phrases that might cause misunderstanding. When researching the speech, keep an eye out for supporting materials that will relate to a wide range of listeners. Also, consider using visual aids. As we shall see in Chapter 13, they can be especially helpful in bridging a gap in language or cultural background.

When delivering your speech, be alert to feedback that might indicate the audience is having trouble grasping your ideas. If you see puzzled expressions, restate your point to make sure it is understood. With some audiences, you can encourage feedback by asking, "Am I making myself clear?" or "Did I explain this point fully enough?"

If you pose such questions, however, be aware that listeners from different cultures may respond quite differently. Most Arabs, North Americans, and Europeans will give you fairly direct feedback if you ask for it. Listeners from Asian and Caribbean countries, on the other hand, may not respond, out of concern that doing so will show disrespect for the speaker. (See Chapter 5 for a full discussion of audience analysis and adaptation.)

Finally, we should note the importance of avoiding ethnocentrism when listening to speeches. As we shall see in Chapters 2 and 3, speech audiences have a responsibility to listen courteously and attentively. When you listen to a speaker from a different cultural background, be on guard against the temptation to judge the speaker on the basis of his or her appearance or manner of delivery. Too often we form opinions about people by the way they look or speak rather than by what they *say*. No matter what the cultural background of the speaker, you should listen to her or him as attentively as you would want your audience to listen to you.[30]

SUMMARY

Public speaking has been a vital means of personal empowerment and civic engagement throughout history. The need for effective public speaking will almost certainly touch you sometime in your life. Your speech class will give you training in researching topics, organizing your ideas, and presenting yourself skillfully. This training is invaluable for every type of communication.

There are many similarities between public speaking and daily conversation, but public speaking is also different from conversation. First, it usually imposes strict time limitations and requires more detailed preparation than does ordinary conversation.

Second, it requires more formal language. Listeners react negatively to speeches loaded with slang, jargon, and bad grammar. Third, public speaking demands a different method of delivery. Effective speakers adjust their voices to the larger audience and work at avoiding distracting physical mannerisms and verbal habits.

One of the major concerns of students in any speech class is stage fright. Your class will give you an opportunity to gain confidence and make your nervousness work for you rather than against you. You will take a big step toward overcoming stage fright if you think positively, prepare thoroughly, visualize yourself giving a successful speech, keep in mind that most nervousness is not visible to the audience, and think of your speech as communication rather than as a performance in which you must do everything perfectly.

A course in public speaking can also help develop your skills as a critical thinker. Critical thinking helps you organize your ideas, spot weaknesses in other people's reasoning, and avoid them in your own.

The speech communication process includes seven elements—speaker, message, channel, listener, feedback, interference, and situation. The speaker is the person who initiates a speech transaction. Whatever the speaker communicates is the message, which is sent by means of a particular channel. The listener receives the communicated message and provides feedback to the speaker. Interference is anything that impedes the communication of a message, and the situation is the time and place in which speech communication occurs. The interaction of these seven elements determines the outcome in any instance of speech communication.

Because of the diversity of modern life, many—perhaps most—of the audiences you address will include people of different cultural backgrounds. When you work on your speeches, be alert to how such factors might affect the responses of your listeners and adapt your message accordingly. Above all, avoid the ethnocentric belief that your own culture or group is superior to all others. Also keep in mind the importance of avoiding ethnocentrism when listening to speeches. Accord every speaker the same courtesy and attentiveness you would want from your listeners.

KEY TERMS

stage fright *(9)*

adrenaline *(10)*

positive nervousness *(10)*

visualization *(13)*

critical thinking *(16)*

speaker *(17)*

message *(18)*

channel *(18)*

listener *(18)*

frame of reference *(19)*

feedback *(19)*

interference *(20)*

situation *(20)*

ethnocentrism *(24)*

REVIEW QUESTIONS

connectlucas.com
For further review, go to the Study Questions in the online Study Aids for this chapter.

After reading this chapter, you should be able to answer the following questions:

1. In what ways is public speaking likely to make a difference in your life?

2. How is public speaking similar to everyday conversation?

3. How is public speaking different from everyday conversation?

4. Why is it normal—even desirable—to be nervous at the start of a speech?

5. How can you control your nervousness and make it work for you in your speeches?

6. What are the seven elements of the speech communication process? How do they interact to determine the success or failure of a speech?

7. What is ethnocentrism? Why do public speakers need to avoid ethnocentrism when addressing audiences with diverse cultural, racial, or ethnic backgrounds?

EXERCISES FOR CRITICAL THINKING

1. Think back on an important conversation you had recently in which you wanted to achieve a particular result. (*Examples:* Asking your employer to change your work schedule; explaining to a friend how to change the oil and filter in a car; attempting to talk your spouse or partner into buying the computer you like rather than the one he or she prefers.) Work up a brief analysis of the conversation.

   In your analysis, explain the following: (1) your purpose in the conversation and the message strategy you chose to achieve your purpose; (2) the communication channels used during the conversation and how they affected the outcome; (3) the interference—internal or external—you encountered during the conversation; (4) the steps you took to adjust to feedback; (5) the strategic changes you would make in preparing for and carrying out the conversation if you had it to do over again.

2. Divide a sheet of paper into two columns. Label one column "Characteristics of an Effective Public Speaker." Label the other column "Characteristics of an Ineffective Public Speaker." In the columns, list and briefly explain what you believe to be the five most important characteristics of effective and ineffective speakers. Be prepared to discuss your ideas in class.

3. On the basis of the lists you developed for Exercise 2, candidly evaluate your own strengths and weaknesses as a speaker. Identify the three primary aspects of speechmaking you most want to improve.

Applying *the* **Power** *of* **Public Speaking**

It's been three years since you graduated from college. After gaining experience as an administrative assistant at a major office equipment manufacturer, you've just been promoted to marketing manager for office copiers. Though you have occasionally given brief reports to other members of your work team, you're now facing your first speech to a large audience. At your company's annual sales meeting, you will address the sales force about the company's new multifunction printer/copiers, and how to sell them to dealers such as Office Depot and OfficeMax.

You're pleased to have this opportunity and you know it shows the company's faith in your abilities. Yet the closer you get to the day of the speech, the harder it is to control the butterflies in your stomach. There will be 200 people in your audience, including all the sales managers and regional managers, in addition to the sales force. All eyes will be on you. It's important that you come across as confident and well informed, but you're afraid your stage fright will send the opposite message. What strategies will you use to control your nerves and make them work for you?

Ethics and Public Speaking

The Importance of Ethics

Guidelines for Ethical Speaking
  Make Sure Your Goals Are Ethically Sound
  Be Fully Prepared for Each Speech
  Be Honest in What You Say
  Avoid Name-Calling and Other Forms of Abusive
    Language
  Put Ethical Principles into Practice

Plagiarism
  Global Plagiarism
  Patchwork Plagiarism
  Incremental Plagiarism
  Plagiarism and the Internet

Guidelines for Ethical Listening
  Be Courteous and Attentive
  Avoid Prejudging the Speaker
  Maintain the Free and Open Expression of Ideas

SaveDarfur.org

When the rumors started, Suzanne Smart, chief financial officer for Pharmatronic, Inc., called a press conference. Dozens of print and TV reporters showed up. Smart looked directly into the cameras and said, "I can assure you that no one at Pharmatronic has used insider information to make money for themselves or to manipulate the company's stock price. In addition to being illegal, insider trading is a serious breach of trust and I would never let it happen at my company."

Suzanne's presentation was highly convincing and for a time it quieted the rumors about financial improprieties. Unfortunately, however, her statements were false, and only three weeks later, she was indicted by the federal government for insider trading.

At the trial, it became clear that Suzanne was guilty of manipulating the company's stock price to benefit herself at the expense of other investors. In fact, on the very day that Smart had faced the TV cameras to deny any wrongdoing, she had secretly sold over 1,000 shares of Pharmatronic stock based on information about the company's failure to win approval for a new anticancer drug. As a result, she made hundreds of thousands of dollars, while ordinary investors suffered huge losses.

When the judge sentenced Smart to a stiff prison sentence, he made clear that he was influenced partly by her brazen lies at the press conference. Had she told the truth, her pleas for leniency might have been better received.

This is not a happy story, but it shows why public speaking needs to be guided by a strong sense of integrity. Suzanne Smart was persuasive when speaking to the press, but she was unethical in lying to cover her illegal activities. As a result, she injured thousands of investors, destroyed her reputation, and ended up with a long jail sentence. Perhaps if she had confessed before the cameras that day, she would have received a fine and a reprimand instead of the harshest jail sentence the judge could impose.

The goal of public speaking is to gain a desired response from listeners—but not at any cost. Speechmaking is a form of power and therefore carries with it heavy ethical responsibilities. As the Roman rhetorician Quintilian stated 2,000 years ago, the ideal of speechmaking is the good person speaking well. In this chapter, we explore that ideal by looking at the importance of ethics in public speaking, the ethical obligations of speakers and listeners, and the practical problem of plagiarism and how to avoid it.

The Importance of Ethics

ethics
The branch of philosophy that deals with issues of right and wrong in human affairs.

Ethics is the branch of philosophy that deals with issues of right and wrong in human affairs. Questions of ethics arise whenever we ask whether a course of action is moral or immoral, fair or unfair, just or unjust, honest or dishonest.

We face such questions daily in almost every part of our lives. The parent must decide how to deal with a child who has been sent home from school for unruly behavior. The researcher must decide whether to shade her data "just a bit" in order to gain credit for an important scientific breakthrough. The shopper must decide what to do with the $5 extra change mistakenly given by the clerk at the grocery store. The student must decide whether to say anything about a friend he has seen cheating on a final exam.

Questions of ethics also come into play whenever a public speaker faces an audience. In an ideal world, as the Greek philosopher Plato noted, all public speakers would be truthful and devoted to the good of society. Yet history tells us that the power of speech is often abused—sometimes with disastrous results.

Adolf Hitler was unquestionably a persuasive speaker. His oratory galvanized the German people, but his aims were horrifying and his tactics despicable. He remains to this day the ultimate example of why the power of the spoken word needs to be guided by a strong sense of ethical integrity.

As a public speaker, you will face ethical issues at every stage of the speechmaking process—from the initial decision to speak through the final presentation of the message. And the answers will not always be easy. Consider the following example:

Felicia Robinson is running for school board in a large eastern city. Her opponent is conducting what Felicia regards as a highly unethical campaign. In addition to twisting the facts about school taxes, the opponent is pandering to racial prejudice by raising resentment against African Americans and newly arrived immigrants.

Five days before the election, Felicia, who is slightly behind in the polls, learns that the district attorney is preparing to indict her opponent for shady business practices. But the indictment will not be formally issued until after the election. Nor can it be taken as evidence that her opponent is guilty—like all citizens, he has the right to be presumed innocent until proven otherwise.

Still, news of the indictment could be enough to throw the election Felicia's way, and her advisers urge her to make it an issue in her remaining campaign speeches. Should Felicia follow their advice?

There are creditable arguments to be made on both sides of the ethical dilemma faced by Felicia Robinson. She has tried to run an honest campaign, and she is troubled by the possibility of unfairly attacking her opponent— despite the fact that he has shown no such scruples himself. Yet she knows that the impending indictment may be her last chance to win the election, and she is convinced that a victory for her opponent will spell disaster for the city's school system. Torn between her commitment to fair play, her desire to be elected, and her concern for the good of the community, she faces the age-old ethical dilemma of whether the ends justify the means.

"So," you may be asking yourself, "what is the answer to Felicia Robinson's dilemma?" But in complex cases such as hers there are no cut-and-dried answers. As the leading book on communication ethics states, "We should formulate meaningful ethical guidelines, not inflexible rules."[1] Your ethical decisions will be guided by your values, your conscience, your sense of right and wrong.

But this does not mean such decisions are simply a matter of personal whim or fancy. Sound ethical decisions involve weighing a potential course of action against a set of ethical standards or guidelines. Just as there are guidelines for ethical behavior in other areas of life, so are there guidelines for ethical conduct in public speaking. These guidelines will not automatically solve every ethical quandary you face as a speaker, but knowing them will provide a reliable compass to help you find your way.

ethical decisions
Sound ethical decisions involve weighing a potential course of action against a set of ethical standards or guidelines.

Guidelines for Ethical Speaking

MAKE SURE YOUR GOALS ARE ETHICALLY SOUND

Not long ago, I spoke with a former student—we'll call her Melissa—who had turned down a job in the public relations department of the American Tobacco Institute. Why? Because the job would have required her to lobby on behalf of the cigarette industry. Melissa did not believe she could ethically promote a product that she saw as responsible for thousands of deaths and illnesses each year.

Given Melissa's view of the dangers of cigarette smoking, there can be no doubt that she made an ethically informed decision. On the other side of the coin, someone with a different view of cigarette smoking could make an ethically informed decision to *take* the job. The point of this example is not to judge the rightness or wrongness of Melissa's decision (or of cigarette smoking), but to illustrate how ethical considerations can affect a speaker's choice of goals.

Your first responsibility as a speaker is to ask whether your goals are ethically sound. During World War II, Hitler stirred the German people to condone war, invasion, and genocide. More recently, we have seen politicians who betray the public trust for personal gain, business leaders who defraud investors of millions of dollars, preachers who lead lavish lifestyles at the expense of their religious duties. There can be no doubt that these are not worthy goals.

But think back for a moment to the examples of speechmaking given in Chapter 1. What do the speakers hope to accomplish? Report on a business project. Improve the quality of education. Pay tribute to a fellow worker. Protect communities against industrial pollution. Support Habitat for Humanity. Few people would question that these goals are ethically sound.

As with other ethical issues, there can be gray areas when it comes to assessing a speaker's goals—areas in which reasonable people with well-defined standards of right and wrong can legitimately disagree. But this is not a reason to avoid asking ethical questions. If you are to be a responsible public speaker, you cannot escape assessing the ethical soundness of your goals.

BE FULLY PREPARED FOR EACH SPEECH

"A speech," as Jenkin Lloyd Jones states, "is a solemn responsibility." You have an obligation—to yourself and to your listeners—to prepare fully every time you stand in front of an audience. The obligation to yourself is obvious: The better you prepare, the better your speech will be. But the obligation to your listeners is no less important. Think of it this way: The person who makes a bad 30-minute speech to an audience of 200 people wastes only a half hour of her or his own time. But that same speaker wastes 100 hours of the audience's time—more than four full days. This, Jones exclaimed, "should be a hanging offense!"

At this stage of your speaking career, of course, you will probably not be facing many audiences of 200 people. And you will probably not be giving many speeches in which the audience has come for the sole purpose of listening to you. But neither the size nor the composition of your audience changes your ethical responsibility to be fully prepared. Your speech classmates are as worthy of your best effort as if you were addressing a jury or a business meeting, a union conference or a church congregation, the local Rotary club or even the United States Senate.

Being prepared for a speech involves everything from analyzing your audience to creating visual aids, organizing your ideas to rehearsing your delivery. Most crucial from an ethical standpoint, though, is being fully informed about your subject. Why is this so important? Consider the following story:

Among current public speakers, Nobel Peace Prize winner and human rights activist Elie Wiesel is highly regarded for his ethically sound goals and powerful persuasive appeal.

Victoria Nuñez, a student at a large state university, gave a classroom speech on suicide prevention. Victoria had learned about the topic from her mother, a volunteer on a suicide-prevention hotline, but she also consulted her psychology textbook as well as several magazine articles on the warning signs of suicide. She also interviewed a crisis-intervention counselor at the campus health service.

In addition to her research, Victoria gave a lot of thought to planning and delivering her speech. She even prepared a handout for the class listing signs that a person might attempt suicide and providing contact information for local mental-health resources. On the day of her speech, Victoria was thoroughly prepared—and she gave an excellent presentation.

Only a few days later, one of Victoria's classmates, Paul Nichols, had a conversation with his roommate that raised a warning flag about whether the roommate might be depressed and in danger of suicide. Based on the information in Victoria's speech, Paul spoke to his roommate, got him to talk about his worries, and convinced him to seek counseling. Paul might have saved his roommate's life, thanks to Victoria's speech.

This is an especially dramatic case, but it demonstrates how your speeches can have a genuine impact on your listeners. As a speaker, you have an ethical responsibility to consider that impact and to make sure you prepare fully so as not to communicate erroneous information or misleading advice. If Victoria had not done such a thorough job researching her speech, she might have given her classmates faulty information—information that might have had tragic results.

No matter what the topic, no matter who the audience, you need to explore your speech topic as thoroughly as possible. Investigate the whole story; learn about all sides of an issue; seek out competing viewpoints; get the facts right. Not only will you give a better speech, you will also fulfill one of your major ethical obligations.

BE HONEST IN WHAT YOU SAY

Nothing is more important to ethical speechmaking than honesty. Public speaking rests on the unspoken assumption that "words can be trusted and people will be truthful."[2] Without this assumption, there is no basis for communication, no reason for one person to believe anything that another person says.

Does this mean *every* speaker must *always* tell "the truth, the whole truth, and nothing but the truth"? We can all think of situations in which this is impossible (because we do not know the whole truth) or inadvisable (because it would be tactless or imprudent). Consider a parent who tells his two-year-old daughter that her screeching violin solo is "beautiful." Or a speaker who tells a falsehood in circumstances when disclosing the truth might touch off mob violence. Few people would find these actions unethical.[3]

In contrast, think back to the case of Suzanne Smart at the start of this chapter. Suzanne knew she had used insider information to profit from the sale of her company's stock. Yet she denied that she had done so, and she profited at the expense of other investors. There is no way to excuse Suzanne's behavior. She told a flat-out lie without regard for its consequences on other people.

Such blatant contempt for the truth is one kind of dishonesty in public speaking. But more subtle forms of dishonesty are just as unethical. They include juggling statistics, quoting out of context, misrepresenting sources, painting tentative findings as firm conclusions, portraying a few details as the whole story, citing unusual cases as typical examples, and substituting innuendo and half-truths for evidence and proof. All of these violate the speaker's duty to be accurate and fair in presenting information.

While on the subject of honesty in speechmaking, we should also note that ethically responsible speakers do not present other people's words as their own. They do not plagiarize their speeches. This subject is so important that we devote a separate section to it later in this chapter.

AVOID NAME-CALLING AND OTHER FORMS OF ABUSIVE LANGUAGE

"Sticks and stones can break my bones, but words can never hurt me." This popular children's chant could not be more wrong. Words may not literally break people's bones, but they can leave psychological scars as surely as sticks and stones can leave physical scars. As one writer explains, "Our identities, who and what we are, how others see us, are greatly affected by the names we are called and the words with which we are labeled."[4] This is why almost all communication ethicists warn public speakers to avoid name-calling and other forms of abusive language.

Name-Calling and Personal Dignity

name-calling
The use of language to defame, demean, or degrade individuals or groups.

Name-calling is the use of language to defame, demean, or degrade individuals or groups. When applied to various groups in America, it includes such epithets as "fag," "kike," "nigger," "honkey," "wop," "jap," "chink," and "spic." Such terms have been used to debase people because of their sexual orientation, religious beliefs, or ethnic background. These words dehumanize the groups they are directed against and imply that they do not deserve to be treated with dignity and respect.

Internet Connection

www.connectlucas.com

In Chapter 11 we will look at ways you can avoid biased language in your speeches. For now, the point to remember is that, contrary to what some people claim, avoiding racist, sexist, and other kinds of abusive language is not simply a matter of political correctness. Such language is ethically suspect because it devalues and stereotypes the people in question.

Such language is also a destructive social force. When used repeatedly and systematically over time, it helps reinforce attitudes that encourage prejudice, hate crimes, and civil rights violations.[5] The issue is not one of politics, but of respecting the dignity of the diverse groups in contemporary society.

Name-Calling and Free Speech

Name-calling and abusive language also pose ethical problems in public speaking when they are used to silence opposing voices. A democratic society depends upon the free and open expression of ideas. In the United States, all citizens have the right to join in the never-ending dialogue of democracy. As a public speaker, you have an ethical obligation to help preserve that right by avoiding tactics such as name-calling that inherently impugn the accuracy or respectability of public statements made by groups or individuals who voice opinions different from yours.

This obligation is the same regardless of whether you are black or white, Christian or Muslim, male or female, gay or straight, liberal or conservative. A pro-environmentalist office seeker who castigated everyone opposed to her ideas as an "enemy of wildlife" would be on as thin ice ethically as a politician who labeled all his adversaries "tax-and-spend liberals."

Like other ethical questions in public speaking, name-calling raises some thorny issues. Although name-calling can be hazardous to free speech, it is still protected under the free-speech clause of the Bill of Rights. This is why the American Civil Liberties Union, a major defender of constitutional rights, has opposed broadly worded codes against abusive speech on college campuses. Such codes usually prohibit threatening or insulting speech against racial or religious minorities, women, gays and lesbians, and people with physical disabilities. To date, these codes have not survived legal challenges, and many schools have subsequently developed more sharply focused regulations that they hope will stand up in court.[6]

But whatever the legal outcome may be, it will not alter the ethical responsibility of public speakers—on or off campus—to avoid name-calling and other kinds of abusive language. Legality and ethics, though related, are not identical. There is nothing illegal about falsifying statistics in a speech, but there is no doubt that it is unethical. The same is true of name-calling. It

Bill of Rights

The first 10 amendments to the United States Constitution.

may not be illegal to cast racial, sexual, or religious slurs at people in a speech, but it is still unethical. Not only does it demean the dignity of the groups or individuals being attacked, but it undermines the right of all groups in the U.S. to be fairly heard.

PUT ETHICAL PRINCIPLES INTO PRACTICE

It is easy to pay lip service to the importance of ethics. It is much harder to act ethically. Yet that is just what the responsible public speaker must do. As one popular book on ethics states, "Being ethical means behaving ethically *all the time*—not only when it's convenient."[7]

As you work on your speeches, you will ask yourself such questions as "Is my choice of topic suitable for the audience?" "Are my supporting materials clear and convincing?" "How can I phrase my ideas to give them more punch?" These are *strategic* questions. As you answer them, you will try to make your speech as informative, as persuasive, or as entertaining as possible.

But you will also face moments of *ethical* decision—similar, perhaps, to those faced by Suzanne Smart, Felicia Robinson, and the other speakers in this chapter. When those moments arrive, don't simply brush them aside and go on your way. Keep in mind the guidelines for ethical speechmaking we have discussed and do your best to follow them through thick and thin. Make sure you can answer yes to all the questions on the Checklist for Ethical Public Speaking (Figure 2.1, p. 37).

Questions of ethics arise whenever a speaker faces an audience. Of all the ethical obligations facing speakers, none is more important than honesty in order to maintain the bond of trust with listeners.

Plagiarism

plagiarism
Presenting another person's language or ideas as one's own.

"Plagiarism" comes from *plagiarius,* the Latin word for kidnapper. To plagiarize means to present another person's language or ideas as your own—to give the impression you have written or thought something yourself when you have actually taken it from someone else.[8] We often think of plagiarism as an ethical issue in the classroom, but it can have repercussions in other situations:

Joanne Calabro was in her second year as school superintendent in the northern New Jersey town of Fort Lee. In May 2007, she spoke at a ceremony for students being inducted into the National Honor Society. It was a brief speech—only six minutes—but the repercussions would last much, much longer.

One of the students at the ceremony recognized some of Calabro's passages and decided to check them online. He discovered that she had lifted the entire speech from a sample induction address posted on About.com. Further evidence came from a videotape of Calabro delivering the speech.

Ethical Public Speaking ▐ Checklist

	YES ✓	NO
1. Have I examined my goals to make sure they are ethically sound?	☐	☐
a. Can I defend my goals on ethical grounds if they are questioned or challenged?		
b. Would I want other people to know my true motives in presenting this speech?		
2. Have I fulfilled my ethical obligation to prepare fully for the speech?	☐	☐
a. Have I done a thorough job of studying and researching the topic?		
b. Have I prepared diligently so as not to communicate erroneous or misleading information to my listeners?		
3. Is the speech free of plagiarism?	☐	☐
a. Can I vouch that the speech represents my own work, my own thinking, my own language?		
b. Do I cite the sources of all quotations and paraphrases?		
4. Am I honest in what I say in the speech?	☐	☐
a. Is the speech free of any false or deliberately deceptive statements?		
b. Does the speech present statistics, testimony, and other kinds of evidence fairly and accurately?		
c. Does the speech contain valid reasoning?		
d. If the speech includes visual aids, do they present facts honestly and reliably?		
5. Do I use the power of language ethically?	☐	☐
a. Do I avoid name-calling and other forms of abusive language?		
b. Does my language show respect for the right of free speech and expression?		
6. All in all, have I made a conscious effort to put ethical principles into practice in preparing my speech?	☐	☐

connectlucas.com
This checklist is also available in the online Speech Tools for this chapter.

• FIGURE 2.1

When confronted with the facts, Calabro admitted to an error in judgment but insisted she had done nothing illegal. In fact, the speech on About.com was protected by copyright law, and Calabro might have been liable to legal action had the Web firm been so inclined. What she could not escape were the ethical consequences. Facing severe criticism within the school district and from the press, she had little choice but to resign her post as superintendent.[9]

As this story shows, plagiarism is a serious matter. If you are caught plagiarizing a speech in class, the punishment can range from a failing grade to expulsion from school. If you are caught plagiarizing outside the classroom, you stand to forfeit your good name, to damage your career, or, if you are sued, to lose a large amount of money. It is worth your while, then, to make sure you know what plagiarism is and how to avoid it.

GLOBAL PLAGIARISM

global plagiarism
Stealing a speech entirely from a single source and passing it off as one's own.

Global plagiarism is stealing your speech entirely from another source and passing it off as your own. The most blatant—and unforgivable—kind of plagiarism, it is grossly unethical.

Global plagiarism in a college classroom usually occurs because a student puts off the assignment until the last minute. Then, in an act of desperation, the student downloads a speech from the Internet or gets one written by a friend and delivers it as his or her own.

The best way to avoid this, of course, is not to leave your speech until the last minute. Most teachers explain speech assignments far enough in advance that you should have no trouble getting an early start. By starting early, you will give yourself plenty of time to prepare a first-rate speech—a speech of your own.

If, for some reason, you fail to get your speech ready on time, do not succumb to the lure of plagiarism. Whatever penalty you suffer from being late will pale in comparison with the consequences if you are caught plagiarizing.

PATCHWORK PLAGIARISM

patchwork plagiarism
Stealing ideas or language from two or three sources and passing them off as one's own.

Unlike global plagiarism, in which a speaker pirates an entire speech from a single source, patchwork plagiarism occurs when a speaker pilfers from two or three sources. Here's an example:

Daniel Fine chose "Recent Discoveries About Dinosaurs" as the topic for his informative speech. In his research, Daniel found three especially helpful sources. The first was a printed guide to a recent museum exhibition about new dinosaur discoveries in North and South America. The second was Wikipedia, and the third was Montana State University's Web site about its dinosaur research program.

Unfortunately, instead of using these materials creatively to write a speech in his own words, Daniel lifted long passages from the museum guide, Wikipedia, and the university Web site and patched them together with a few transitions. When he was finished, he had a speech that sounded wonderful—but it was composed almost entirely of other people's words.

As it turned out, Daniel's teacher had been to the same exhibit and thought parts of the speech sounded familiar. After checking her copy of the museum guide, her suspicions were confirmed. Fearful that Daniel might have filched from more than one source, she looked for Web sites with information about dinosaurs. She quickly found both of the sites Daniel had used. He was caught red-handed.

This story illustrates an important point about plagiarism. Daniel did not take his speech from a single source. He even did a little research. But copying from a few sources is no less plagiarism than is copying from a single source. When you give a speech, you declare that it is your work—that it is the product of your thinking, your beliefs, your language. Daniel's speech did not contain any of these. Instead, it was cut and pasted wholly from other people's ideas, other people's words.

"But," you may be thinking, "not many students are experts on their speech topics. Why should they be expected to come up with new ideas that

Speakers who begin work on their speeches early and consult a wide range of sources are less likely to fall into the trap of plagiarism than are speakers who procrastinate and rely on a limited number of sources.

even the experts haven't thought of?" The answer is they aren't. The key is not whether you have something absolutely original to say, but whether you do enough research and thinking to come up with your own slant on the topic.

As with global plagiarism, one key to averting patchwork plagiarism is to start working on your speech as soon as possible. The longer you work on it, the more apt you are to come up with your own approach. It is also vital to consult a large number of sources in your research. If you have only two or three sources, you are far more likely to fall into the trap of patchwork plagiarism than if you consult a wide range of research materials.

INCREMENTAL PLAGIARISM

In global plagiarism and patchwork plagiarism, the entire speech is cribbed more or less verbatim from a single source or a few sources. But plagiarism can exist even when the speech as a whole is not pirated. This is called incremental plagiarism. It occurs when the speaker fails to give credit for particular parts—increments—of the speech that are borrowed from other people. The most important of these increments are quotations and paraphrases.

incremental plagiarism
Failing to give credit for particular parts of a speech that are borrowed from other people.

Quotations

Whenever you quote someone directly, you must attribute the words to that person. Suppose you are giving a speech on Malcolm X, the famous African-American leader of the 1960s. While doing your research, you run across the following passage from Bruce Perry's acclaimed biography, *Malcolm: The Life of the Man Who Changed Black America:*

Malcolm X fathered no legislation. He engineered no stunning Supreme Court victories or political campaigns. He scored no major electoral triumphs. Yet because of the way he articulated his followers' grievances and anger, the impact he had upon the body politic was enormous.[10]

This is a fine quotation that summarizes the nature and importance of Malcolm's impact on American politics. It would make a strong addition to your speech—as long as you acknowledge Perry as the author. The way to avoid plagiarism in this instance is to introduce Perry's statement by saying something like:

In *Malcolm: The Life of the Man Who Changed Black America,* historian Bruce Perry says the following about Malcolm's impact on American politics. . . .

Or,

According to historian Bruce Perry in his book *Malcolm: The Life of the Man Who Changed Black America.* . . .

Now you have clearly identified Perry and given him credit for his words rather than presenting them as your own.

Paraphrases

paraphrase
To restate or summarize an author's ideas in one's own words.

When you paraphrase an author, you restate or summarize her or his ideas in your own words. Suppose, once again, that your topic is Malcolm X. But this time you decide to paraphrase the statement from Bruce Perry's biography rather than quoting it. You might say:

Malcolm X was not a politician. He did not pass any laws, or win any Supreme Court victories, or get elected to any office. But he stated the grievances and anger of his followers so powerfully that the whole nation took notice.

Even though you do not quote Perry directly, you still appropriate the structure of his ideas and a fair amount of his language. Thus you still need to give him credit—just as if you were repeating his words verbatim.

It is especially important in this case to acknowledge Perry because you are borrowing his opinion—his judgment—about Malcolm X. If you simply recount basic facts about Malcolm's life—he was born in Omaha, Nebraska, converted to the Nation of Islam while in prison, traveled to Mecca toward the end of his life, was assassinated in February 1965—you do not have to report the source of your information. These facts are well known and can be found in any standard reference work.

On the other hand, there is still considerable debate about Malcolm's views of other African-American leaders, the circumstances surrounding his death, and what he might have done had he lived. If you were to cite Perry's views on any of these matters—regardless of whether you quoted or paraphrased—you would need to acknowledge him as your source.

As more than one speaker (and writer) has discovered, it is possible to commit incremental plagiarism quite by accident. This is less offensive than deliberate plagiarism, but it is plagiarism nonetheless. There are two ways to guard against incremental plagiarism. The first is to be careful when taking research notes to distinguish among direct quotations, paraphrased material, and your own comments. (See Chapter 6 for a full discussion of research methods.) The second way to avoid incremental plagiarism is to err on the side of caution. In other words, when in doubt, cite your source.

PLAGIARISM AND THE INTERNET

When it comes to plagiarism, no subject poses more confusion—or more temptation—than the Internet. Because it's so easy to copy information from the Web, many people are not aware of the need to cite sources when they use Internet materials in their speeches. If you don't cite Internet sources, you are just as guilty of plagiarism as if you take information from print sources without proper citation.

One way to avoid patchwork plagiarism or incremental plagiarism when working with the Internet is to take careful research notes. Make sure you keep a record of the following: (1) the title of the Internet document, (2) the author or organization responsible for the document, (3) the date on which the document was last updated, (4) the date on which you accessed the site. You will need all this information for your speech bibliography.

You will also need to identify your Internet sources when you present the speech. It's not enough to say "As I found on the Web" or "According to the Internet." You need to specify the author and the Web site. In Chapter 7, we'll look more closely at how to cite Internet documents. For now, keep in mind that providing such citations is another of your ethical responsibilities as a public speaker.

Another problem with regard to the Internet is the large number of Web sites that sell entire speeches or papers. In addition to being highly unethical, using material from one of these sites is extremely risky. The same technology that makes it easy to plagiarize from the Web makes it easy for teachers to locate material that has been plagiarized and the exact source from which it has been taken.

You should also know that almost all the speeches (and papers) offered for sale on the Web are of very low quality. If you are ever tempted to purchase one, keep in mind there is a good chance you will waste your money and get caught in the process. Here, as in other aspects of life, honesty is the best policy.

Guidelines for Ethical Listening

So far in this chapter we have focused on the ethical duties of public speakers. But speechmaking is not a one-way street. Listeners also have ethical obligations. They are (1) to listen courteously and attentively; (2) to avoid prejudging the speaker; and (3) to maintain the free and open expression of ideas. Let us look at each.

BE COURTEOUS AND ATTENTIVE

Imagine that you are giving your first classroom speech. You have put a great deal of time into writing the speech, and you have practiced your delivery until you are confident you can do well—especially once you get over the initial rush of stage fright.

You have worked hard on your introduction, and your speech gets off to a fine start. Most of your classmates are paying close attention, but some are not. One appears to be doing homework for another class. Another keeps sneaking glances at the school newspaper. Two or three are gazing out the window, and one is leaning back in his chair with his eyes shut!

You try to block them out of your mind—especially since the rest of the class seems interested in what you are saying—but the longer you speak, the more concerned you become. "What am I doing wrong?" you wonder to yourself. "How can I get these people to pay attention?" The more you think about this, the more your confidence and concentration waver.

When you momentarily lose your place halfway through the speech, you start to panic. Your nerves, which you have held in check so far, take the upper hand. Your major thought now becomes "How can I get this over as fast as possible?" Flustered and distracted, you rush through the rest of your speech and sit down.

Just as public speakers have an ethical obligation to prepare fully for each speech, so listeners have a responsibility to be courteous and attentive during the speech. This responsibility—which is a matter of civility in any circumstance—is especially important in speech class. You and your classmates are in a learning situation in which you need to support one another.

When you listen to speeches in class, give your fellow students the same courtesy and attention you want from them. Come to class prepared to listen to—and to learn from—your classmates' speeches. As you listen, be conscious of the feedback you are sending the speaker. Sit up in your chair rather than slouching; maintain eye contact with the speaker; show support and encouragement in your facial expressions. Keep in mind the power you have as a listener over the speaker's confidence and composure, and exercise that power with a strong sense of ethical responsibility.

AVOID PREJUDGING THE SPEAKER

We have all heard that you can't judge a book by its cover. The same is true of speeches. You can't judge a speech by the name, race, lifestyle, appearance, or reputation of the speaker. As the National Communication Association states in its Credo for Ethical Communication, listeners should "strive to understand and respect" speakers "before evaluating and responding to their messages."[11]

This does not mean you must agree with every speaker you hear. Your aim is to listen carefully to the speaker's ideas, to assess the evidence and reasoning offered in support of those ideas, and to reach an intelligent judgment about the speech. In Chapter 3, we will discuss specific steps you can take to improve your listening skills. For now it is enough to know that if you prejudge a speaker—either positively or negatively—you will fail in one of your ethical responsibilities as a listener.

MAINTAIN THE FREE AND OPEN EXPRESSION OF IDEAS

As we saw earlier in this chapter, a democratic society depends on the free and open expression of ideas. The right of free expression is so important that it is protected by the First Amendment to the U.S. Constitution, which declares, in part, that "Congress shall make no law . . . abridging the freedom of speech." Just as public speakers need to avoid name-calling and other tactics that can undermine free speech, so listeners have an obligation to maintain the right of speakers to be heard.

As with other ethical issues, the extent of this obligation is open to debate. Disputes over the meaning and scope of the First Amendment arise almost daily in connection with issues such as terrorism, pornography, and hate

It is vital for a democratic society to maintain the free and open expression of ideas. Here U.S. Senator Daniel Akaka explains the dangers that hate speech poses to democratic ideals.

speech. The question underlying such disputes is whether *all* speakers have a right to be heard.

There are some kinds of speech that are not protected under the First Amendment—including defamatory falsehoods that destroy a person's reputation, threats against the life of the President, and inciting an audience to illegal action in circumstances where the audience is likely to carry out the action. Otherwise, the Supreme Court has held—and most experts in communication ethics have agreed—that public speakers have an almost unlimited right of free expression.

In contrast to this view, it has been argued that some ideas are so dangerous, so misguided, or so offensive that society has a duty to suppress them. But who is to determine which ideas are too dangerous, misguided, or offensive to be uttered? Who is to decide which speakers are to be heard and which are to be silenced? As Edward Kennedy explained in his acclaimed speech "Tolerance and Truth in America," once we succumb to the temptation of censoring ideas with which we disagree, "we step onto a slippery slope where everyone's freedom is at risk."

No matter how well intentioned they may be, efforts to "protect" society by restricting free speech usually end up repressing minority viewpoints and unpopular opinions. In U.S. history such efforts were used to keep women off the public platform until the 1840s, to stop abolitionist orators from exposing the evils of slavery before the Civil War, to muzzle labor organizers during the 1890s, and to impede civil rights leaders in the 1960s. Imagine what American society might be like if these speakers had been silenced!

It is important to keep in mind that ensuring a person's freedom to express her or his ideas does not imply agreement with those ideas. You can disagree entirely with the message but still support the speaker's right to express it. As the National Communication Association states in its Credo for Ethical Communication, "freedom of expression, diversity of perspective, and tolerance of dissent" are vital to "the informed decision making fundamental to a civil society."[12]

SUMMARY

Because public speaking is a form of power, it carries with it heavy ethical responsibilities. Today, as for the past 2,000 years, the good person speaking well remains the ideal of commendable speechmaking.

There are five basic guidelines for ethical public speaking. The first is to make sure your goals are ethically sound—that they are consistent with the welfare of society and your audience. The second is to be fully prepared for each speech. The third is to be honest in what you say. Responsible speakers do not distort the truth for personal gain. They are accurate and fair in their message and in their methods.

The fourth guideline for ethical speaking is to avoid name-calling and other forms of abusive language. Name-calling is ethically suspect because it demeans the dignity of the people being attacked and because it can undermine the right of all groups to be fairly heard. The final guideline is to put ethical principles into practice at all times.

Of all the ethical lapses a speaker can commit, few are more serious than plagiarism. Global plagiarism is lifting a speech entirely from a single source. Patchwork plagiarism involves stitching a speech together by copying from a few sources. Incremental plagiarism occurs when a speaker fails to give credit for specific quotations and paraphrases that are borrowed from other people.

In addition to your ethical responsibilities as a speaker, you have ethical obligations as a listener. The first is to listen courteously and attentively. The second is to avoid prejudging the speaker. The third is to support the free and open expression of ideas. In all these ways, your speech class will offer a good testing ground for questions of ethical responsibility.

KEY TERMS

ethics *(30)*

ethical decisions *(31)*

name-calling *(34)*

Bill of Rights *(35)*

plagiarism *(36)*

global plagiarism *(38)*

patchwork plagiarism *(38)*

incremental plagiarism *(39)*

paraphrase *(40)*

REVIEW QUESTIONS

connectlucas.com
For further review, go to the Study Questions in the online Study Aids for this chapter.

After reading this chapter, you should be able to answer the following questions:

1. What is ethics? Why is a strong sense of ethical responsibility vital for public speakers?

2. What are the five guidelines for ethical speechmaking discussed in this chapter?

3. What is the difference between global plagiarism and patchwork plagiarism? What are the best ways to avoid these two kinds of plagiarism?

4. What is incremental plagiarism? How can you steer clear of it when dealing with quotations and paraphrases?

5. What are the three basic guidelines for ethical listening discussed in this chapter?

1. Look back at the story of Felicia Robinson on page 31. Evaluate her dilemma in light of the guidelines for ethical speechmaking presented in this chapter. Explain what you believe would be the most ethical course of action in her case.

2. The issue of insulting and abusive speech—especially slurs directed against people on the basis of race, religion, gender, or sexual orientation—is extremely controversial. Do you believe society should punish such speech with criminal penalties? To what degree are colleges and universities justified in trying to discipline students who engage in such speech? Do you feel it is proper to place any boundaries on free expression in order to prohibit insulting and abusive speech? Why or why not? Be prepared to explain your ideas in class.

3. All the following situations could arise in your speech class. Identify the ethical issues in each and explain what, as a responsible speaker or listener, your course of action would be.

   a. You are speaking on the topic of prison reform. In your research, you run across two public opinion polls. One of them, an independent survey by the Gallup Organization, shows that a majority of people in your state oppose your position. The other poll, suspect in its methods and conducted by a partisan organization, says a majority of people in your state support your position. Which poll do you cite in your speech? If you cite the second poll, do you point out its shortcomings?

   b. When listening to an informative speech by one of your classmates, you realize that much of it is plagiarized from a magazine article you read a couple weeks earlier. What do you do? Do you say something when your instructor asks for comments about the speech? Do you mention your concern to the instructor after class? Do you talk with the speaker? Do you remain silent?

   c. While researching your persuasive speech, you find a quotation from an article by a highly respected expert that will nail down one of your most important points. But as you read the rest of the article, you realize the author does not in fact support the policy you are advocating. Should you still include the quotation in your speech?

Applying *the* Power *of* Public Speaking

Having graduated with a degree in public administration and hoping to pursue a career in politics, you have been fortunate to receive a staff position with one of the leading senators in your state legislature. Since your arrival two months ago, you have answered phones, ordered lunch, made copies, stapled mailings, and stuffed envelopes. Finally you have been asked to look over a speech the senator will deliver at your alma mater. Surely, you think, this will be the first of many important assignments once your value is recognized.

After reading the speech, however, your enthusiasm is dampened. You agree wholeheartedly with its support of a bill to fund scholarships for low-income students, but you're dismayed by its attack on opponents of the bill as "elitist bigots who would deny a college education to those who need it most." You haven't been asked to comment on the ethics of the speech, and you certainly don't want to jeopardize your position on the senator's staff. At the same time, you think his use of name-calling may actually arouse sympathy for the opposition. The senator would like your comments in two hours. What will you tell him?

Listening

It was a hot afternoon in May. The professor of ancient history was lecturing on the fall of the Roman Empire. She began: "Yesterday we discussed the political and social conditions that weakened the empire from within. Today we will talk about the invasions that attacked the empire from the outside—the Visigoths from the northwest, the Ostrogoths from the northeast, the Vandals from the south, the Huns from the west, and Homer Simpson from the southeast."

Nobody batted an eye. Nobody looked up. The classroom was quiet, except for the scratch of pens as the students took notes—presumably recording Homer Simpson as an invader of the Roman Empire.

hearing
The vibration of sound waves on the eardrums and the firing of electrochemical impulses in the brain.

listening
Paying close attention to, and making sense of, what we hear.

This story illustrates what one research study after another has revealed—most people are shockingly poor listeners. We fake paying attention. We can look right at someone, appear interested in what that person says, even nod our head or smile at the appropriate moments—all without really listening.

Not listening doesn't mean we don't hear. *Hearing* is a physiological process, involving the vibration of sound waves on our eardrums and the firing of electrochemical impulses from the inner ear to the central auditory system of the brain. But *listening* involves paying close attention to, and making sense of, what we hear. Even when we think we are listening carefully, we usually grasp only 50 percent of what we hear. After 24 hours we can remember only 10 percent of the original message.[1] It's little wonder that listening has been called a lost art.[2]

Listening Is Important

Although most people listen poorly, there are exceptions. Top-flight business executives, successful politicians, brilliant teachers—nearly all are excellent listeners.[3] So much of what they do depends on absorbing information that is given verbally—and absorbing it quickly and accurately. If you had an interview with the president of a major corporation, you might be shocked (and flattered) to see how closely that person listened to your words.

In our communication-oriented age, listening is more important than ever. This is why, in most companies, effective listeners hold higher positions and are promoted more often than ineffective listeners.[4] When business managers are asked to rank-order the communication skills most crucial to their jobs, they usually rank listening number one.[5] Listening is so important that in one survey of America's Fortune 500 companies, almost 60 percent of the respondents said they provide some kind of listening training for their employees.[6]

Even if you don't plan to be a corporate executive, the art of listening can be helpful in almost every part of your life. This is not surprising when you realize that people spend more time listening than doing any other communicative activity—more than reading, more than writing, more even than speaking.

Think for a moment about your own life as a college student. Close to 90 percent of class time in U.S. colleges and universities is spent listening to discussions and lectures. A number of studies have shown a strong correlation between listening and academic success. Students with the highest grades are usually those with the strongest listening skills. The reverse is also true—students with the lowest grades are usually those with the weakest listening skills.[7]

There is plenty of reason, then, to take listening seriously. Employers and employees, parents and children, wives and husbands, doctors and patients, students and teachers—all depend on the apparently simple skill of listening. Regardless of your profession or walk of life, you never escape the need for a well-trained ear.

Listening is also important to you as a speaker. It is probably the way you get most of your ideas and information—from television, radio, conversation, and lectures. If you do not listen well, you will not understand what you hear and may pass along your misunderstanding to others.

Besides, in class—as in life—you will listen to many more speeches than you give. It is only fair to pay close attention to your classmates' speeches; after all, you want them to listen carefully to *your* speeches. An excellent way to improve your own speeches is to listen attentively to the speeches of other people. Over and over, teachers find that the best speakers are usually the best listeners.

A side benefit of your speech class is that it offers an ideal opportunity to work on the art of listening. During the 95 percent of the time when you are not speaking, you have nothing else to do but listen and learn. You can sit there like a stone—or you can use the time profitably to master a skill that will serve you in a thousand ways.

Listening and Critical Thinking

One of the ways listening can serve you is by enhancing your skills as a critical thinker. We can identify four kinds of listening:[8]

- *Appreciative listening*—listening for pleasure or enjoyment, as when we listen to music, to a comedy routine, or to an entertaining speech.

- *Empathic listening*—listening to provide emotional support for the speaker, as when a psychiatrist listens to a patient or when we lend a sympathetic ear to a friend in distress.

- *Comprehensive listening*—listening to understand the message of a speaker, as when we attend a classroom lecture or listen to directions for finding a friend's house.

- *Critical listening*—listening to evaluate a message for purposes of accepting or rejecting it, as when we listen to the sales pitch of a used-car dealer or the campaign speech of a political candidate.

appreciative listening
Listening for pleasure or enjoyment.

empathic listening
Listening to provide emotional support for a speaker.

comprehensive listening
Listening to understand the message of a speaker.

critical listening
Listening to evaluate a message for purposes of accepting or rejecting it.

Although all four kinds of listening are important, this chapter deals primarily with comprehensive listening and critical listening. They are the kinds of listening you will use most often when listening to speeches in class, when taking lecture notes in other courses, when communicating at work, and when responding to the barrage of commercials, political messages, and other persuasive appeals you face every day. They are also the kinds of listening that are most closely tied to critical thinking.

As we saw in Chapter 1, critical thinking involves a number of skills. Some of those skills—summarizing information, recalling facts, distinguishing main points from minor points—are central to comprehensive listening. Other skills of critical thinking—separating fact from opinion, spotting weaknesses in reasoning, judging the soundness of evidence—are especially important in critical listening. When you engage in comprehensive listening or critical listening, you must use your mind as well as your ears. When your mind is not actively involved, you may be hearing, but you are not *listening*. In fact, listening and critical thinking are so closely allied that training in listening is also training in how to think.[9]

At the end of this chapter, we'll discuss steps you can take to improve your skills in comprehensive and critical listening. If you follow these steps, you may also become a better critical thinker.

Four Causes of Poor Listening

NOT CONCENTRATING

spare "brain time"
The difference between the rate at which most people talk (120 to 150 words a minute) and the rate at which the brain can process language (400 to 800 words a minute).

The brain is incredibly efficient. Although we talk at a rate of 120 to 150 words a minute, the brain can process 400 to 800 words a minute.[10] This would seem to make listening very easy, but actually it has the opposite effect. Because we can process a speaker's words and still have plenty of spare "brain time," we are tempted to interrupt our listening by thinking about other things. Here's what happens:

Elena Kim works in the public communications department of a large financial services company. She attends regular staff meetings with the communications director. The meetings provide necessary information, but sometimes they seem to go on forever.

This morning the director is talking about tax-exempt college savings accounts and how to publicize them more effectively. "We've succeeded in reaching parents, so our next target market is grandparents who want to put away money for their grandchildren's education...."

"Grandparents," Elena thinks. "It was always great to see my grandparents when I was growing up. When I spoke to them over the weekend, Grandma didn't sound very good. I have to call them more often. . . ."

Elena snaps herself back to the meeting. The director is talking about the company's new executive vice president, who has just moved to headquarters from a regional firm in Florida. "Mr. Fernandez has never worked in a company this size, but his experience in Florida . . ."

"Florida," Elena dreams. "Sun, endless beaches, and the club scene in South Beach. Maybe I can snatch a few days' vacation in January. . . ."

Sternly, Elena pulls her attention back to the meeting. The communications director is now discussing the company's latest plan for public-service announcements. Elena is not involved in the plan, and her attention wanders once more.

That morning she had another argument with her roommate about cleaning the kitchen and taking out the garbage. Maybe it's time to decide if she can afford to live without a roommate. It sure would make for fewer hassles.

". . . an area Elena has researched extensively," the director is saying. Uh oh! *What* area does the director mean? Everyone looks at Elena, as she frantically tries to recall the last words said at the meeting.

It's not that Elena *meant* to lose track of the discussion. But there comes a point at which it's so easy to let your thoughts wander rather than to concentrate on what is being said. After all, concentrating is hard work. Louis Nizer, the famous trial lawyer, says, "So complete is this concentration that at the end

People spend more time listening than in any other communicative activity. One benefit of your speech class is that it can improve your listening skills in a variety of situations.

of a court day in which I have only listened, I find myself wringing wet despite a calm and casual manner."[11]

Later in this chapter, we will look at some things you can do to concentrate better on what you hear.

LISTENING TOO HARD

Until now we have been talking about not paying close attention to what we hear. But sometimes we listen *too* hard. We turn into human sponges, soaking up a speaker's every word as if every word were equally important. We try to remember all the names, all the dates, all the places. In the process we often miss the speaker's main point. What is worse, we may end up confusing the facts as well.

Shortly after graduating from college, Erik Waldman landed an excellent job at a graphics design firm. Knowing he had never been good at budgeting his money, he was determined to begin thinking about his long-range economic future. When his employer circulated an e-mail announcing a financial planning workshop, Erik signed up right away.

The first session was about retirement planning. Simone Fisher, who was conducting the workshop, explained that 7 of 10 Americans between the ages of 22 and 35 do not have either a monthly budget or a regular savings plan. Erik wrote down every number Simone mentioned.

"If you want to have a retirement income equal to 75 percent of your current salary," Simone continued, "you will need to invest at least 6 percent of your present earnings, and beyond that you need to figure in future inflation rates. We have set aside time this afternoon to meet with you personally to calculate your individual savings needs. In the meantime, I want to stress that the most important thing is to start saving now."

Erik wrote furiously to record all the statistics Simone cited. When she opened the floor for questions, Erik raised his hand and said, "I have two questions. When is the best time to start saving for retirement? And how am I supposed to figure out my savings target if I don't know what inflation rates will be in the future?"

This is a typical example of losing the speaker's point by concentrating on details. Erik had fixed his mind on remembering all the statistics in Simone's presentation, but he blocked out the main message—that it is best to start saving now and that he would get help developing an individual plan.

Rather than trying to remember everything a speaker says, efficient listeners usually concentrate on main ideas and evidence. We'll discuss these things more thoroughly later in the chapter.

JUMPING TO CONCLUSIONS

Renee Collins, a recent college graduate, took a job as an editorial assistant in the research department of a regional magazine. Shortly after Renee arrived, the editor in charge of the research department left the magazine for another job. For the next two months, Renee struggled to handle the work of the research department by herself. She often felt in over her head, but she knew this was a good opportunity to learn, and she hated to give up her new responsibilities.

One day Duane Perkins, the editor in chief of the magazine, comes into Renee's office to talk. The following conversation takes place:

Duane: You've done a great job these last two months, Renee. But you know we really need a new editor. So we've decided to make some changes.

Renee: I'm not surprised. I know I've made my share of mistakes.

Duane: Everyone makes mistakes when they're starting out. And you've been carrying a lot of responsibility. Too much. That's why . . .

Renee: That's okay. I'm grateful to have had a chance to try my hand at this. I know I'm inexperienced, and this is an important department.

Duane: Yes, it is. And it's not an easy job. We really need an editor and an assistant to handle all the work. That's why I wanted to tell you . . .

Renee: You're right, of course. I hope you've found somebody good to be the new editor.

Duane: I think so. But, Renee, I don't think you understand . . .

Renee: No, I understand. I knew all along that I was just filling in.

Duane: Renee, you're not listening.

Renee: Yes, I am. You're trying to be nice, but you're here to tell me that you've hired a new editor and I'll be going back to my old job.

Duane: No, that's not it at all. I think you've done a fine job under difficult circumstances. You've proved yourself, and I intend to make *you* the editor. But I think you'll need an assistant to help you.

Why is there so much confusion here? Clearly, Renee is unsure about her future at the magazine. So when Duane starts to talk about making some changes, Renee jumps to a conclusion and assumes the worst. The misunderstanding could have been avoided if, when Duane had said, "We've decided to make some changes," Renee had asked, "What changes?"—and then *listened.*

This is one form of jumping to conclusions—putting words into a speaker's mouth. It is one reason why we sometimes communicate so poorly with people we are closest to. Because we're so sure we know what they mean, we don't listen to what they actually say.

Another way of jumping to conclusions is prematurely rejecting a speaker's ideas as boring or misguided. We may decide early on that a speaker has nothing valuable to say. Suppose you think fraternities and sororities are a valuable addition to a college's social and civic life, but a speaker's announced topic is "The Greek System: An Institution Whose Time Is Past?" You may decide in advance not to listen to the speaker. That would be a mistake. You might pick up information that could strengthen or modify your thinking. In another situation, you might jump to the conclusion that a topic is boring. Let's say the announced topic is "Architecture and History." It sounds dull. So you tune out—and miss a fascinating discussion filled with human-interest stories about buildings and other structures from the ancient pyramids to the latest skyscrapers.

Nearly every speech has something to offer you—whether it be information, point of view, or technique. You are cheating yourself if you prejudge and choose not to listen.

FOCUSING ON DELIVERY AND PERSONAL APPEARANCE

Avid readers of American history, Greg and Marissa were thrilled when they saw a poster at their local bookstore advertising a lecture by the author of a new book on the Battle of Gettysburg. The book had received good reviews, and Greg and Marissa made plans to attend the lecture.

Arriving at the bookstore, they took their seats and listened while the speaker discussed his research and major findings. "That was great," Marissa exclaimed when they got back to the car. But Greg was scowling. "What's wrong?" Marissa asked.

"I know you're going to think this is stupid," Greg began. "The guy was a decent speaker, and he seemed to know his stuff. But did you see the sport coat he was wearing? It's so retro—and his tie was atrocious. No matter how I tried, I couldn't stop thinking I was watching someone from *That '70s Show*."

This story illustrates a common problem. Sometimes we judge people by the way they look or speak and don't listen to what they say. It's easy to become distracted by a speaker's accent, personal appearance, or vocal mannerisms and lose sight of the message. Focusing on a speaker's delivery or personal appearance is one of the major sources of interference in the speech communication process, and it is something we always need to guard against.

How to Become a Better Listener

TAKE LISTENING SERIOUSLY

The first step toward becoming a better listener is to accord listening the seriousness it deserves. Good listeners are not born that way. They have *worked* at learning how to listen effectively. Good listening does not go hand in hand with intelligence, education, or social standing. Like any other skill, it comes from practice and self-discipline. Check your current skills as a listener by completing the Listening Self-Evaluation Worksheet on page 54 (Figure 3.1).[12] Once you have identified your shortcomings as a listener, make a serious effort to overcome them.

LISTENING SELF-EVALUATION

How often do you indulge in the following 10 bad listening habits? Check yourself carefully in each one.

HABIT	FREQUENCY					SCORE
	Almost Always	Usually	Sometimes	Seldom	Almost never	
1. Giving in to mental distractions	_____	_____	_____	_____	_____	_____
2. Giving in to physical distractions	_____	_____	_____	_____	_____	
3. Trying to recall everything a speaker says	_____	_____	_____	_____	_____	
4. Rejecting a topic as uninteresting before hearing the speaker	_____	_____	_____	_____	_____	
5. Faking paying attention	_____	_____	_____	_____	_____	
6. Jumping to conclusions about a speaker's meaning	_____	_____	_____	_____	_____	
7. Deciding a speaker is wrong before hearing everything she or he has to say	_____	_____	_____	_____	_____	
8. Judging a speaker on personal appearance	_____	_____	_____	_____	_____	
9. Not paying attention to a speaker's evidence	_____	_____	_____	_____	_____	
10. Focusing on delivery rather than on what the speaker says	_____	_____	_____	_____	_____	
					TOTAL	_____

How to score:

For every "almost always" checked, give yourself a score of	2
For every "usually" checked, give yourself a score of	4
For every "sometimes" checked, give yourself a score of	6
For every "seldom" checked, give yourself a score of	8
For every "almost never" checked, give yourself a score of	10

Total score interpretation:

Below 70	You need lots of training in listening.
From 71–90	You listen well.
Above 90	You listen exceptionally well.

• **FIGURE 3.1**

BE AN ACTIVE LISTENER

So many aspects of modern life encourage us to listen passively. We listen to our iPods while studying. Parents listen to their children while fixing dinner. Television reporters listen to a politician's speech while walking around the auditorium looking for their next interview.

This type of passive listening is a habit—but so is active listening. Active listeners give their undivided attention to the speaker in a genuine effort to understand his or her point of view. In conversation, they do not interrupt the speaker or finish his or her sentences. When listening to a speech, they do not allow themselves to be distracted by internal or external interference, and they do not prejudge the speaker. They take listening seriously and do the best they can to stay focused on the speaker and his or her message.

There are a number of steps you can take to improve your skills of active listening. They include resisting distractions, not allowing yourself to be diverted by a speaker's appearance or delivery, suspending judgment until you have heard the speaker out, focusing your listening, and developing note-taking skills. We'll discuss each of these in turn.

active listening
Giving undivided attention to a speaker in a genuine effort to understand the speaker's point of view.

RESIST DISTRACTIONS

In an ideal world, we could eliminate all physical and mental distractions. In the real world, however, we cannot. Because we think so much faster than a speaker can talk, it's easy to let our attention wander. Sometimes it's very easy—when the room is too hot, when construction machinery is operating right outside the window, when the speaker is tedious. But our attention can stray even in the best of circumstances—if for no other reason than a failure to stay alert and make ourselves concentrate.

Whenever you find this happening, make a conscious effort to pull your mind back to what the speaker is saying. Then force it to stay there. One way to do this is to think ahead of the speaker—try to anticipate what will come next. This is not the same as jumping to conclusions. When you jump to conclusions, you put words into the speaker's mouth and don't listen to what is said. In this case you *will* listen—and measure what the speaker says against what you had anticipated.

connectlucas.com
The Listening Self-Evaluation Worksheet is available in the online Speech Tools for this chapter.

Another way to keep your mind on a speech is to review mentally what the speaker has already said and make sure you understand it. Yet another is to listen between the lines and assess what a speaker implies verbally or says nonverbally with body language. Suppose a speaker is introducing someone to an audience. The speaker says, "It gives me great pleasure to present to you my very dear friend, Nadine Zussman." But the speaker doesn't shake hands with Nadine. He doesn't even look at her—just turns his back and leaves the podium. Is Nadine really his "very dear friend"? Certainly not.

Attentive listeners can pick up all kinds of clues to a speaker's real message. At first you may find it difficult to listen so intently. If you work at it, however, your concentration is bound to improve.

DON'T BE DIVERTED BY APPEARANCE OR DELIVERY

If you had attended Abraham Lincoln's momentous Cooper Union speech of 1860, this is what you would have seen:

The long, ungainly figure upon which hung clothes that, while new for this trip, were evidently the work of an unskilled tailor; the large feet and clumsy hands, of which, at the outset, at least, the orator seemed to be unduly conscious; the long, gaunt head, capped by a shock of hair that seemed not to have been thoroughly brushed out, made a picture which did not fit in with New York's conception of a finished statesman.[13]

But although he seemed awkward and uncultivated, Lincoln had a powerful message about the moral evils of slavery. Fortunately, the audience at Cooper Union did not let his appearance stand in the way of his words.

Similarly, you must be willing to set aside preconceived judgments based on a person's looks or manner of speech. Gandhi was an unimpressive-looking man who often spoke dressed in a simple white cotton cloth. Renowned physicist Stephen Hawking is severely disabled and can speak only with the aid of a voice synthesizer. Yet imagine how much poorer the world would be if no one listened to them. Even though it may tax your tolerance, patience, and concentration, don't let negative feelings about a speaker's appearance or delivery keep you from listening to the message.

On the other hand, try not to be misled if the speaker has an unusually attractive appearance. It's all too easy to assume that because someone is good-looking and has a polished delivery, he or she is speaking eloquently. Some of the most unscrupulous speakers in history have been handsome people with hypnotic delivery skills. Again, be sure you respond to the message, not to the package it comes in.

SUSPEND JUDGMENT

Unless we listen only to people who think exactly as we do, we are going to hear things with which we disagree. When this happens, our natural inclination is to argue mentally with the speaker or to dismiss everything she or he says. But neither response is fair, and in both cases we blot out any chance of learning or being persuaded.

Does this mean you must agree with everything you hear? Not at all. It means you should hear people out *before* reaching a final judgment. Try to understand their point of view. Listen to their ideas, examine their evidence, assess their reasoning. *Then* make up your mind. The aim of active listening is to set aside "one's own prejudices, frames of reference and desires so as to experience as far as possible the speaker's world from the inside."[14] It has been said more than once that a closed mind is an empty mind.

FOCUS YOUR LISTENING

As we have seen, skilled listeners do not try to absorb a speaker's every word. Rather, they focus on specific things in a speech. Here are three suggestions to help you focus your listening.

Listen for Main Points

Most speeches contain from two to four main points. Here, for example, are the main points of a recent speech on controlling the cost of health care delivered by pharmaceuticals executive Robert Ingram:[15]

1. The first priority in reducing the cost of health care is preventing disease.

2. The second priority is providing accurate diagnosis and appropriate treatment.

3. The third priority is being innovative in tackling health problems.

These three main points are the heart of Ingram's message. As with any speech, they are the most important things to listen for.

Unless a speaker is terribly scatterbrained, you should be able to detect his or her main points with little difficulty. Often a speaker will give some idea at the outset of the main points to be discussed in the speech. For example, at the end of his introduction, Ingram said: "I would submit that the solution comes in the form of three very simple, but very important, basic principles." Noticing this, a sharp listener would have been prepared for a speech with three main points. Ingram also gave a preview statement identifying each of the main points before he started the body of his speech. As the speech progressed, he enumerated each point. After this, only the most inattentive of listeners could have missed his main points.

Listen for Evidence

Identifying a speaker's main points, however, is not enough. You must also listen for supporting evidence. By themselves, Ingram's main points are only assertions. You may be inclined to believe them just because they come from a major business executive. Yet a careful listener will be concerned about evidence no matter who is speaking. Had you been listening to Ingram's speech, you would have heard him support his claims with a mass of verifiable evidence. Here is an excerpt:

Seventy-five percent of the total amount we spend in this country on health care is spent on the 45 percent of our population that have one or more chronic diseases. . . .

We need to look at health care spending holistically, recognizing that the biggest slice of the health care pie goes to hospitals at about 31 percent, followed by doctors and clinics at 22 percent, while spending on prescription drug therapy, including the pharmacist's dispensing fee, accounts for 11 percent of the overall health care bill, which, by the way, is the same percentage that it has been for over forty years.

Payers who cut medicine budgets in isolation—even if they cut their pharmacy spending by half—do nothing to lower the over 90 percent of costs that make up the total health care bill.

There are four basic questions to ask about a speaker's evidence:

Is it *accurate*?

Is it taken from *objective* sources?

Is it *relevant* to the speaker's claims?

Is it *sufficient* to support the speaker's point?

In Ingram's case, the answer to each question is yes. His figures about the amount of money spent on health care in the United States and where that money goes are well established in the public record and can be verified by independent sources. The figures are clearly relevant to Ingram's claim that the cost of prescription drugs is only a small part of total spending on health care, and they are sufficient to support that claim. If Ingram's evidence were inaccurate, biased, irrelevant, or insufficient, you should be wary of accepting his claim.

We shall discuss these—and other—tests of evidence in detail in Chapters 7 and 16. For now, it's enough to know that you should be on guard against unfounded assertions and sweeping generalizations. Keep an eye out for the speaker's evidence and for its accuracy, objectivity, relevance, and sufficiency.

Listen for Technique

We said earlier that you should not let a speaker's delivery distract you from the message, and this is true. However, if you want to become an effective speaker, you should study the methods other people use to speak effectively.

Analyze the introduction: What methods does the speaker use to gain attention, to relate to the audience, to establish credibility and goodwill? Assess the organization of the speech: Is it clear and easy to follow? Can you pick out the speaker's main points? Can you follow when the speaker moves from one point to another?

Study the speaker's language: Is it accurate, clear, vivid, appropriate? Does the speaker adapt well to the audience and occasion? Finally, diagnose the speaker's delivery: Is it fluent, dynamic, convincing? Does it strengthen or weaken the impact of the speaker's ideas? How well does the speaker use eye contact, gestures, and visual aids?

As you listen, focus on the speaker's strengths and weaknesses. If the speaker is not effective, try to determine why. If he or she is effective, try to pick out techniques you can use in your own speeches. If you listen in this way, you will be surprised how much you can learn about successful speaking.

DEVELOP NOTE-TAKING SKILLS

Speech students are often amazed at how easily their teacher can pick out a speaker's main points, evidence, and techniques. Of course, the teacher knows what to listen for and has had plenty of practice. But the next time you get an opportunity, watch your teacher during a speech. Chances are she or he will be listening with pen and paper. When note taking is done properly, it is a surefire way to improve your concentration and keep track of a speaker's ideas.

Research confirms that listening carefully and taking effective notes are vital skills for success in college. They will also benefit you in countless situations throughout life.

The key words here are *when done properly.* Unfortunately, many people don't take notes effectively. Some try to write down everything a speaker says. They view note taking as a race, pitting their handwriting agility against the speaker's rate of speech. As the speaker starts to talk, the note taker starts to write. But soon the speaker is winning the race. In a desperate effort to keep up, the note taker slips into a scribbled writing style with incomplete sentences and abbreviated words. Even this is not enough. The speaker pulls so far ahead that the note taker can never catch up.[16]

Some people go to the opposite extreme. They arrive armed with pen, notebook, and the best of intentions. They know they can't write down everything, so they wait for the speaker to say something that grabs their attention. Every once in a while the speaker rewards them with a joke, a dramatic story, or a startling fact. Then the note taker seizes pen, jots down a few words, and leans back to await the next fascinating tidbit. By the end of the lecture the note taker has a set of tidbits—and little or no record of the speaker's important ideas.

As these examples illustrate, most inefficient note takers suffer from one or both of two problems: They don't know *what* to listen for, and they don't know *how* to record what they do listen for.[17] The solution to the first problem is to focus on a speaker's main points and evidence. But once you know what to listen for, you still need a sound method of note taking.

Although there are a number of systems, most students find the *key-word outline* best for listening to classroom lectures and formal speeches. As its name suggests, this method briefly notes a speaker's main points and supporting evidence in rough outline form. Suppose a speaker says:

key-word outline
An outline that briefly notes a speaker's main points and supporting evidence in rough outline form.

Hospitals in the United States are facing a serious shortage of nurses. According to the American Hospital Association, the nurse shortage nationwide has reached an alarming total of 120,000. The National Association of Nurse Recruiters reports that the average hospital has 47 full-time nursing positions vacant. Hospitals in major cities such as New York, Los Angeles, and Miami have had to reduce services because of a lack of nurses.

There are four major causes for this shortage of nurses. One cause is that there are not enough faculty members at nursing schools to train the number of nurses needed by hospitals. A second cause is that nurses can find employment at medical facilities other than hospitals. A third cause is that many nurses are reluctant to stay on the job because of poor working hours that include nights, holidays, and weekends. A fourth cause is that nurses are burdened with excessive paperwork.

A key-word note taker would record something like this:

> Serious nurse shortage
> > Total of 120,000
> > Average 47 per hospital
> > Reduced services at hospitals
>
> Four major causes
> > Low faculty at nursing schools
> > Employment available beyond hospitals
> > Poor working hours
> > Excessive paperwork

Notice how brief the notes are. Yet they accurately summarize the speaker's ideas. They are also very clear. By separating main points from subpoints and evidence, the outline format shows the relationships among the speaker's ideas.

Perfecting this—or any other—system of note taking requires practice. But with a little effort you should see results soon. As you become a better note taker, you will become a better listener. There is also a good chance you will become a better student. Research confirms that students who take effective notes usually receive higher grades than those who do not.[18]

SUMMARY

Most people are poor listeners. Even when we think we are listening carefully, we usually grasp only half of what we hear, and we retain even less. Improving your listening skills can be helpful in every part of your life, including speechmaking.

The most important cause of poor listening is giving in to distractions and letting our thoughts wander. Sometimes, however, we listen too hard. We try to remember every word a speaker says, and we lose the main message by concentrating on details. In other situations, we may jump to conclusions and prejudge a speaker without hearing out the message. Finally, we often judge people by their appearance or speaking manner instead of listening to what they say.

You can overcome these poor listening habits by taking several steps. First, take listening seriously and commit yourself to becoming a better listener. Second, work at being an active listener. Give your undivided attention to the speaker in a genuine effort to understand her or his ideas. Third, resist distractions. Make a conscious effort to keep your mind on what the speaker is saying. Fourth, try not to be diverted by appearance or delivery. Set aside preconceived judgments based on a person's looks or manner of speech.

Fifth, suspend judgment until you have heard the speaker's entire message. Sixth, focus your listening by paying attention to main points, to evidence, and to the speaker's techniques. Finally, develop your note-taking skills. When done properly, note taking is an excellent way to improve your concentration and to keep track of a speaker's ideas.

hearing *(48)*

listening *(48)*

appreciative listening *(49)*

empathic listening *(49)*

comprehensive listening *(49)*

critical listening *(49)*

spare "brain time" *(50)*

active listening *(55)*

key-word outline *(59)*

REVIEW QUESTIONS

After reading this chapter, you should be able to answer the following questions:

1. What is the difference between hearing and listening?
2. How is listening connected with critical thinking?
3. Why is it important to develop strong listening skills?
4. What are the four main causes of poor listening?
5. What are seven ways to become a better listener?

connectlucas.com
For further review, go to the
Study Questions in the online
Study Aids for this chapter.

EXERCISES FOR CRITICAL THINKING

1. Which of the four causes of poor listening do you consider the most important? Choose a specific case of poor listening in which you were involved. Explain what went wrong.

2. Using the Listening Self Evaluation Worksheet on page 54, undertake a candid evaluation of your major strengths and weaknesses as a listener. Explain what steps you need to take to become a better listener.

3. Watch the lead story this week on *60 Minutes, 20/20,* or another newsmagazine program. Using the key-word outline method of note taking, record the main ideas of the story.

4. Choose a lecture in one of your other classes. Analyze what the lecturer does most effectively. Identify three things the lecturer could do better to help students keep track of the lecture.

Members of your public speaking class have begun making their introductory speeches. You've already given yours and can now relax and watch your fellow students. The first speaker this morning is Nadira, a classmate you don't yet know. She steps confidently to the front of the room, wearing her *Hijab,* the traditional Muslim head scarf.

"Today," Nadira begins, "I would like to tell you about the path that took my family from Egypt to America and me to school at this university. . . ." Soon you realize that you've been thinking about Nadira's clothing, rather than focusing on what she is saying. You pull your attention back, grab your pencil, and try to pick up what she is saying. What else can you do to ensure that you listen effectively to the rest of her presentation?

Giving Your
First Speech

You may be surprised to learn that one of your first assignments is to give a speech. You say to yourself, "What am I going to do? I have barely started this course, yet I'm supposed to stand up in front of the whole class and give a speech! I've only read a few pages in the textbook, and I don't know much about public speaking. Where do I begin?"

If these are your thoughts, you aren't alone. Most beginning speech students have a similar reaction. Fortunately, giving your first speech sounds a lot harder than it is. The purpose of this appendix is to help you get started on preparing and delivering your speech.

Preparing Your Speech

Usually a brief, simple presentation, the first assignment is often called an ice breaker speech because it is designed to "break the ice" by getting students up in front of the class as soon as possible. This is an important step because much of the anxiety associated with public speaking comes from lack of experience giving speeches. Once you have broken the ice by giving a speech, you will feel less anxious and will have taken the first step on the road to confidence.

DEVELOPING THE SPEECH

There are a number of possible assignments for the first speech. One is a speech of self-introduction that provides insight into the speaker's background, personality, beliefs, or goals. In other cases, students are asked to introduce a classmate, rather than themselves. Some instructors require yet a different kind of speech. No matter which you are assigned, be sure to focus your presentation sharply so it conforms to the assigned time limit. One of the most common mistakes students make on their first speech is trying to cover too much material. You should select a limited number of points and illustrate them clearly.

It would be impossible, for example, to tell your audience everything about your life in a two- or three-minute speech. A better approach would be to focus on one or two events that have helped define who you are—competing in the state track meet, tutoring disadvantaged children, getting your first job, and the like. This allows you to make a few well-developed points about a clearly defined subject.

On the other hand, avoid the temptation to narrow the focus of your topic too much. Few listeners would be pleased to hear a two- or three-minute discussion of advanced trumpet-playing techniques. Such a speech would be too specialized for most classroom audiences.

Once you have a topic for your speech, be creative in developing it. Think of ways to make your presentation mysterious or suspenseful. Suppose you are telling the audience about meeting a celebrity, visiting a famous place, or participating in a newsworthy event. Rather than identifying the celebrity at the outset, you might save his or her name for the end of your speech. As your story unfolds, tantalize your classmates with clues about your celebrity's gender, physical characteristics, special talents, and the like, but keep the name secret until the last moment.

In addition to mystery and suspense, audiences are naturally interested in dangerous situations, adventure, and drama. If your task is to introduce a fellow student, find out if she or he has ever been in danger. Suppose your classmate was caught in a flood or spent a year in Africa with the Peace Corps. The details would make excellent material for a speech.

If you think about it, every person has faced risk, done the unusual, or triumphed over hardship. Try to find ways to include such fascinating experiences in your speech.

You can also make your speech interesting by using colorful, descriptive language. One speaker used this technique when introducing a fellow student, named Alexa, to the class. The speaker began by saying:

> The spotlight shines. The music blares. The crowd cheers. The colors, bright and vibrant, bleed together as Alexa and her partner sail around the dance floor. Her partner touches her hand and her waist, but only briefly. He then spins her away, and she glides across the floor in what seems like a single motion. Alexa has worked many weeks for this moment. Alexa, you see, is a championship ballroom dancer.

connectlucas.com
View the introduction from "Gotta Dance" in the online Media Library for this appendix (Video Clip A1.1).

The speaker could have said, "Alexa is a terrific ballroom dancer and finds it quite exciting." Instead, the speaker painted a word picture so listeners could visualize the dance floor, the rhythm of the music, the brilliant colors of the costumes, the excitement of the competition as Alexa and her partner performed in perfect symmetry. Colorful and concrete illustrations like this are always more interesting than dull language and abstract generalizations.

You might wonder whether you should use humor to make your first speech entertaining. Audiences love witty remarks, jokes, and funny situations, but like anything else, humor is effective only when done well. It should flow naturally out of the speech content rather than being contrived. If you are not normally a funny person, you are better off giving a sincere, enthusiastic speech and leaving out the jokes. In no case should you include humor that involves obscenity, embarrasses individuals, or negatively stereotypes groups of people. The best kind of humor gently pokes fun at ourselves or at universal human foibles.

ORGANIZING THE SPEECH

Regardless of your topic, your speech will have three main parts—an introduction, a body, and a conclusion. Your first job in the introduction is to get the attention and interest of the audience. You can do this by posing a question, telling a story, making a startling statement, or opening with a quotation. The purpose of all these methods is to create a dramatic, colorful opening that will make your audience want to hear more.

connectlucas.com
View the beginning of "Kiyomi and Me" in the online Media Library for this appendix (Video Clip A1.2).

For an excellent example, look at the speech excerpt on Video Clip A1.2 in the online Media Library for this Appendix. The speaker's assignment was to present a narrative about a significant experience in her life. This is how she began:

> Her name was Kiyomi. She was a mysterious Japanese dancer. Last autumn I got to meet her. How, you ask. Well, actually, she was a character in a play. I met her the day I became her. That day was one of the happiest days of my life. I wanted that part so desperately it was all I could think about. Being Kiyomi was one of the most memorable experiences of my life.

After this introduction, the speaker's classmates were eager to hear more about Kiyomi and her role in the speaker's life.

In addition to gaining attention and interest, the introduction should orient your listeners toward the subject matter of your speech. In the longer speeches you will give later in the term, you will usually need to provide an explicit preview statement that identifies the main points to be discussed in the body of your speech. (For example, "Today I will inform you about the symptoms, causes, and treatment of hepatitis C.")

Because your introductory speech is so short, you may not need a detailed preview statement. But you still need to give your audience a clear sense of your topic and purpose. Look back for a moment at the introduction about Kiyomi quoted earlier. Notice how it moves from arousing curiosity to letting the audience know what the rest of the speech will focus on. By the end of the introduction, there is no doubt about the topic of the speech. (Be sure to check with your instructor to see what kind of preview statement he or she prefers for the introductory speech.)

After getting the audience's attention and revealing your topic, you are ready to move into the body of your speech. In some speeches, the body seems to organize itself. If you have been assigned to tell a story about a significant experience in your life, you will relate the events chronologically, in the order they occurred.

But not all speeches follow such a format. Suppose you have been asked to give a presentation introducing a classmate. You could organize the most important biographical facts about your subject in chronological order, but this might result in a dull, superficial speech: "In 1990 Alicia was born in Cleveland, attended King Elementary School from 1995 to 2002, and graduated from South High School in 2008."

A better way of structuring your remarks might be to discuss three of the most important aspects of Alicia's life, such as hobbies, career goals, and family. This is called the topical method of organization, which subdivides the speech topic into its natural, logical, or conventional parts. Although there are many other ways to organize a speech, your first presentation will probably use either chronological or topical order.

Regardless of the method of organization you use, remember to limit the number of main points in the body of your speech. In a two-minute presentation, you won't have time to develop more than two or three main points.

Once you have selected those points, make sure each one focuses on a single aspect of the topic. For example, if your first point concerns your classmate's hometown, don't introduce irrelevant information about her job or favorite music. Save this material for a separate point, or cut it.

Try to make your main points stand out by introducing each with a transition statement. In a speech introducing a classmate, you might begin the first main point by saying:

Rico's family moved a great deal throughout his childhood.

When you reach the second point, you might introduce it like this:

Moving a lot led to Rico's outgoing nature and confidence in making friends. In fact, he has friends all around the world with whom he corresponds regularly over e-mail.

You have now let your audience know that the first main point is over and that you are starting the second one. The third main point might begin as follows:

Corresponding with people all over the world is more than just a hobby for Rico, since he is majoring in international relations.

Transition statements such as these will help your audience keep track of your main ideas.

When you finish discussing your final point, you will be ready to move into your conclusion. You need to accomplish two tasks in this part of the speech: let the audience know you are about to finish and reinforce your major theme.

If possible, end on a dramatic, clever, or thought-provoking note. For example, in the speech about Kiyomi, the student devoted the body of her speech to explaining how she won the role and what happened when she performed it on stage. Then, in her conclusion, she wrapped up by saying:

connectlucas.com
View the ending of "Kiyomi and Me" in the online Media Library for this appendix (Video Clip A1.3).

I needed this experience to appreciate who I was. I realized that I should be myself and not long to be someone else. So what if I'm not the most graceful or feminine person? So what if I don't possess all the wonderful characteristics of Kiyomi? I am still me—not a character in a play. Yet by playing that character, I learned one of the most important lessons of my life. I learned that by becoming a woman who never was, I became proud of who I am.

The final lines bring the speech to a dramatic close and underscore why the experience of playing Kiyomi was so important to the speaker.

Delivering Your Speech

Once you have selected a subject and organized the content into a clear structure, it is time to work on the delivery of your speech. Because this is your first speech of the term, no one expects you to give a perfectly polished presentation. Your aim is to do as well as possible while also laying a foundation you can build upon in later speeches. With this is mind, we'll look briefly at the extemporaneous method of speech delivery, the importance of rehearsing your speech, and some of the major factors to consider when speech day arrives.

SPEAKING EXTEMPORANEOUSLY

You might be inclined, as are many beginning speakers, to write out your speech like an essay and read it word for word to your listeners. The other extreme is to prepare very little for the speech—to wing it by trusting to your wits and the inspiration of the moment. Neither approach is appropriate.

Most experts recommend speaking extemporaneously, which combines the careful preparation and structure of a manuscript presentation with the spontaneity and enthusiasm of an unrehearsed talk. Your aim in an extemporaneous speech is to plan your major points and supporting material without trying to memorize the precise language you will use on the day of the speech.

The extemporaneous method requires you to know the content of your speech quite well. In fact, when you use this method properly, you become so familiar with the substance of your talk that you need only a few brief notes to remind you of the points you intend to cover. The notes should consist of key words or phrases, rather than complete sentences and paragraphs. This way, when you are in front of the audience, you will tell them what you know about the topic in your own words.

Prepare your notes by writing or printing key terms and phrases on index cards or sheets of paper. Some instructors require students to use index cards because they are small and unobtrusive, don't rustle or flop over, and can be held in one hand, which allows the speaker to gesture more easily. Other teachers recommend sheets of paper because you can get more information on them and because it is easier to print out computer files on paper. If you are unsure what your instructor prefers, ask well before your speech is due.

Whether you use index cards or sheets of paper, your notes should be large enough to read clearly at arm's length. Many experienced speakers double- or triple-space their notes because this makes them easier to see at a glance. Write or print on only one side of the index card or paper, and use the fewest notes you can manage and still present the speech fluently and confidently.

connectlucas.com
View an excerpt from "A Heart Worn on My Hand" in the online Media Library for this appendix (Video Clip A1.4).

You can see an example of extemporaneous delivery on Video Clip A1.4 in the online Media Library for this appendix. The student is giving a speech of self-introduction using a personal object—in this case, a softball glove—to explain something important about herself. As you view the excerpt, notice that even though the speaker's points are well planned, she is not tied to a manuscript. When talking about her glove, she sets down her notes and points to things on the glove that reflect different aspects of her life. All the while, she speaks directly to her classmates and makes strong eye contact with them.

At first, it may seem very demanding to deliver a speech extemporaneously. In fact, though, you use the extemporaneous method in everyday conversation. Do you read from a manuscript when you tell your friends an amusing story? Of course not. You recall the essential details of your story and tell the tale to different friends, on different occasions, using somewhat different language each time. You feel relaxed and confident with your friends, so you just tell them what is on your mind in a conversational tone. Try to do the same thing in your speech.

REHEARSING THE SPEECH

When you watch a truly effective extemporaneous speaker, the speech comes out so smoothly that it seems almost effortless. In fact, that smooth delivery is the result of a great deal of practice. As your speech course progresses, you will gain more experience and will become more comfortable delivering your speeches extemporaneously.

The first time you rehearse your introductory speech, however, you will probably struggle. Words may not come easily, and you may forget some things you planned to say. Don't become discouraged. Keep going and complete the speech as well as you can. Concentrate on gaining control of the ideas rather than on trying to learn the speech word for word. You will improve every time you practice.

For this approach to work, you must rehearse the speech out loud. Looking silently over your notes is not enough. Speaking the words aloud will help you master the content of your talk. Once you have a fairly good grasp of the speech, ask friends or family members to listen and to give constructive feedback. Don't be shy about asking. Most people love to give their opinion about something, and it's crucial that you rehearse with a live audience before presenting the speech in class.

As you practice, time your speech to make sure it is neither too long nor too short. Because of nerves, most people talk faster during their first speech than when they practice it. When you rehearse at home, make certain your speech runs slightly longer than the minimum time limit. That way, if your speaking rate increases when you get in front of your classmates, your speech won't end up being too short.

PRESENTING THE SPEECH

When it is your turn to speak, move to the front of the room and face the audience. Assume a relaxed but upright posture. Plant your feet a bit less than shoulder-width apart and allow your arms to hang loosely by your side. Arrange your notes before you start to speak. Then take a moment to look over your audience and to smile. This will help you establish rapport with your classmates from the start.

Once you are into the speech, feel free to use your hands to gesture, but don't try to plan all your gestures ahead of time. If you don't normally use your hands expressively during informal conversation, then you shouldn't feel compelled to gesture a lot during your speech. Whatever gestures you do use should flow naturally from your feelings.

Above all, don't let your gestures or bodily actions distract listeners from your message. Do your best to avoid nervous mannerisms such as twisting your hair, wringing your hands, shifting your weight from one foot to the other, rocking back and forth, or tapping your fingers on the lectern. No matter how nervous you feel, try to appear calm and relaxed.

During your talk, look at your classmates as often as you can. One of the major reasons for speaking extemporaneously is to maintain eye contact with your audience. In your own experience, you know how much more impressive a speaker is when she or he looks at the audience while speaking.

If you have practiced the extemporaneous method of delivery and prepared your notes properly, you should be able to maintain eye contact with your audience most of the time. Be sure to look to the left and right of the room, as well as the center, and avoid the temptation to speak exclusively to one or two sympathetic individuals. When you are finished speaking, your classmates should have the impression that you established a personal connection with each of them.

Try to use your voice as expressively as you would in normal conversation. Concentrate on projecting to the back of the room and, despite your nerves, fight the temptation to race through your speech. If you make a conscious effort to speak up, slow down, and project clearly, you will be on the right track to an effective presentation.

Look, for example, at Video Clip A1.5 in the online Media Library for this appendix, which presents excerpts from two ice breaker speeches. Neither speaker had taken a public speaking class before, yet both rose to the occasion by focusing on the basic elements of delivery we have just discussed. As you watch the video, notice how both—despite their nervousness—convey a sense of poise and confidence, establish strong eye contact with their classmates, and use the extemporaneous method of delivery. Work on doing the same in your first speech.

Finally, as we saw in Chapter 1, remember that it's normal to be nervous before delivering a speech. You can deal with your nerves by preparing thoroughly, thinking positively, and visualizing yourself giving a successful

connectlucas.com
View excerpts from "Rhymes with Orange" and "My Life from Toe to Head" in the online Media Library for this appendix (Video Clip A1.5).

speech. If you have butterflies in your stomach before delivering your speech, sit quietly in your chair and take several slow, deep breaths. You can also help reduce your tension by tightening and relaxing your leg muscles, or by squeezing your hands together and then releasing them. Keep in mind that while you may be anxious about giving your speech, usually your nervousness will not be visible to your audience.

All the topics discussed in this appendix are developed in much more detail in the rest of this book. For now, keep your introductory assignment in perspective. Remember that neither your audience nor your instructor expects perfection. You are not a professional speaker, and this is the first speech of the class. Do your best on the assignment and have fun with it. Plan what you want to say, organize the material clearly, practice thoroughly, and use the extemporaneous method of delivery. You may be surprised by how much you enjoy giving your first speech.

Sample Speeches with Commentary

connectlucas.com
View "Pot, Soil, Water" and "Brooklyn Roads" in the online Media Library for this appendix (Video Clips A1.6 and A1.7).

The following presentations were prepared by students in beginning speech classes at the University of Wisconsin. The first is a speech of self-introduction; the second is a speech introducing a classmate. As you read the speeches, notice how clearly they are organized and how creatively they are developed. You can watch the delivery of both speeches in the online Media Library for this appendix.

Pot, Soil, Water

COMMENTARY	SPEECH
The introduction captures attention and reveals the topic. By referring to a houseplant and the elements it needs to grow, the speaker provides a creative touch that runs through the entire speech. She ends the introduction by linking the plant's pot, soil, and water to her family, friends, and interests, the three main points she will discuss in the body.	Those of you with a green thumb know that a healthy houseplant like this one needs a number of things to grow, including a good pot, rich soil, and adequate water. The pot is the plant's home, the comforting place where it grows up. The soil gives the plant nutrients and helps its roots expand. Water is the basis of all life and allows the plant to thrive. Like this plant and the pot, soil, and water it requires to grow, you can get a sense of my growth by looking at my family, my friends, and my interests.

Each main point in the body is clearly stated and discussed. As you can see from the online video, the speaker communicates sincerely and with excellent eye contact.

The assignment for this speech required students to use an object to introduce themselves to the class. As the speech proceeds, notice how the speaker does not focus on describing the object in this case, her houseplant—but on how the plant provides insight into the speaker herself.

The speaker completes the body by mentioning some of her interests. This kind of information is almost always part of a speech of self-introduction. It is effective here because of the inventive way it is woven into the overall theme of the speech.

The speaker summarizes the main points of her speech and completes the comparison with her houseplant by stating that she is not finished growing. The final sentence ties everything together and ends the speech on a positive note.

The pot represents my family. A pot holds the plant together just like my family holds me together. My mom and dad not only gave me life but a loving home to grow up in. If I ever had a bad day, they kept me from falling apart. As the plant protects the roots and the soil, my family protected me as I grew through my childhood.

The soil represents my friends, who have supported me as I branched out into new experiences. Here on campus, my three best friends have helped me adjust to college by showing me around, by introducing me to new people, and by helping me with my assignments. They encourage me to follow my dreams and are always willing to offer advice. As the nutrients from the soil feed the plant, my friends have helped me grow and develop.

The water represents my interests. Without water, this plant would turn brown and dull, but with water, the plant is bright and full of life. Like water for this plant, my interests help me flourish rather than wilt. I have a broad range of interests, including music, art, swimming, and watching movies. My interests make my personal colors more vibrant and allow me to bloom.

I wouldn't be who I am today without my family, my friends, and my interests. But like this plant, I still have some growing to do—more things to learn and more things to experience. Luckily, because of my own pot, soil, and water, I'm confident I will bloom into the person I want to be.

Brooklyn Roads

COMMENTARY	SPEECH
This paragraph serves as the speaker's introduction. The opening quotation gains attention, while the second sentence identifies the central idea that will be developed in the rest of the speech.	As the poet E. E. Cummings once said, "To be nobody but yourself in a world which is doing its best, day and night, to make you everybody else means to fight the hardest battle which any human being can fight." As a young boy, your classmate Danny made a promise to himself to fight for his individuality, and to this day he has not given up on that promise.
The body of this speech contains three main points, each of which deals with an aspect of Danny's individuality. The first focuses on his background and early education, culminating with his desire to be the first in his family to attend college.	Growing up in a poverty-stricken Brooklyn neighborhood, Danny had hopes of making his individual mark in the world. He saw the struggles his parents endured because they didn't have the same opportunities as kids today. With his parents' support, he ventured outside Brooklyn to Manhattan, where he attended grammar school and high school. While in high school, Danny decided that he wanted to attend college, something that neither of his parents had the chance to do.

The second main point deals with Danny's decision to attend the University of Wisconsin. The figure of 812 miles adds specificity and is more memorable than saying "Danny has traveled several hundred miles."

Now the speaker moves to his third main point, which deals with other ways in which Danny has shown his individuality. The ideas are presented clearly and concisely. As is evident from the online video, the speaker presents his ideas extemporaneously. He has strong eye contact, excellent vocal variety, and a personable manner of delivery.

The speaker concludes by restating the central theme of his speech. The final words pose a serious question that reinforces the importance of maintaining one's individuality.

When choosing a school, Danny again showed his individuality. While most of his friends and classmates stayed in their comfort zone by attending college close to home, Danny has traveled 812 miles to attend the University of Wisconsin, where he hopes to study engineering.

Danny shows his individuality in other ways as well. He started playing billiards in high school, and it's been a hobby of his ever since. Unlike pool, which is based on shooting balls into pockets, billiards has no pockets and is much more challenging than pool. Danny also plays handball, another game with a loyal following but definitely outside the football-basketball-baseball mainstream. Then there was Danny's decision to ignore the instant popularity of iPods. Instead, he checked out all the options and bought a ZEN mp3 player. If you have the time, Danny will gladly tell you all of the virtues of ZEN.

For Danny, being an individual in a world of trends hasn't been the easiest of battles. But, he says, it's worth the effort. After all, would you want to lose what makes you who you are?

Selecting a Topic and a Purpose

Choosing a Topic
  Topics You Know a Lot About
  Topics You Want to Know More About
  Brainstorming for Topics

Determining the General Purpose

Determining the Specific Purpose
  Tips for Formulating the Specific Purpose Statement
  Questions to Ask About Your Specific Purpose

Phrasing the Central Idea
  What Is the Central Idea?
  Guidelines for the Central Idea

As you read through this book, you will find examples of hundreds of speeches that were delivered in classrooms, in the political arena, in community and business situations. Here is a very small sample of the topics they cover:

aromatherapy	Native American casinos
breast cancer	obsessive compulsive disorder
Cesar Chavez	Pilates
driving age	Quebec
election reform	robotics
free trade	study abroad
genetic engineering	Title IX
Habitat for Humanity	Underground Railroad
identity theft	volunteering
Judaism	women's gymnastics
Koran	x-rays
laser surgery	Yangtze River
Martin Luther King	zoos

Undoubtedly you noticed that the list runs from A to Z. This array of topics wasn't planned. It happened naturally in the course of presenting many different kinds of speeches. The list is given here simply to show you that there are literally endless possibilities for speech topics—from A to Z.

Choosing a Topic

topic
The subject of a speech.

The first step in speechmaking is choosing a topic. For speeches outside the classroom this is seldom a problem. Usually the speech topic is determined by the occasion, the audience, and the speaker's qualifications. When Condoleezza Rice lectures on a college campus, she is invited to speak about foreign policy and current events. Christine Amanpour will discuss women and journalism. Richard Roeper might share his views about the latest in filmmaking. The same is true of ordinary citizens. The doctor is asked to inform high-school athletes and their parents about sport injuries, the head of a neighborhood coalition speaks about zoning regulations, the florist discusses how to grow thriving houseplants.

In a public speaking class the situation is different. Students generally have great leeway in selecting topics. This would appear to be an advantage, since it allows you to talk about matters of personal interest. Yet there may be no facet of speech preparation that causes more gnashing of teeth than selecting a topic.

It is a constant source of amazement to teachers that students who regularly chat with their friends about almost any subject under the sun become mentally paralyzed when faced with the task of deciding what to talk about in their speech class. Fortunately, once you get over this initial paralysis, you should have little trouble choosing a good topic.

When you look for a speech topic, keep in mind special expertise you may have or sports, hobbies, travel, and other personal experiences that would make for an interesting presentation.

There are two broad categories of potential topics for your classroom speeches: (1) subjects you know a lot about and (2) subjects you want to know more about. Let's start with the first.

TOPICS YOU KNOW A LOT ABOUT

Most people speak best about subjects with which they are most familiar. When thinking about a topic, draw on your own knowledge and experience. Everyone knows things or has done things that can be used in a speech.

Think for a moment about unusual experiences you may have had or special expertise you may have acquired. One student, who grew up in Pakistan, presented a fascinating speech about daily life in that country. Another used her knowledge as a jewelry store salesperson to prepare a speech on how to judge the value of cut diamonds. A third student, who had lived through a tornado, gave a gripping speech about that terrifying experience.

Too dramatic? Nothing in your life is as interesting? Yet another student, who described herself as "just a housewife who is returning to school to finish the education she started 20 years ago," delivered a witty speech on the adjustments she had to make in coming back to college—sitting in class with students young enough to be her children, balancing her academic work against her family commitments, and the satisfaction of completing the education she had begun years earlier.

Here are a few more examples of speech topics based largely on the students' personal knowledge and experience:

The Basics of Backpacking

Making a Difference: The Peace Corps

A Tour of Old Jerusalem

Performing with the Native American Dance Troupe

How to Have a Successful Job Interview

TOPICS YOU WANT TO KNOW MORE ABOUT

On the other hand, you may decide to make your speech a learning experience for yourself as well as for your audience. You may choose a subject about which you already have some knowledge or expertise but not enough to prepare a speech without doing additional research. You may even select a topic that you want to explore for the first time. Say, for example, you've always been interested in extrasensory perception but never knew much about it. This would be a perfect opportunity to research a fascinating subject and turn it into a fascinating speech.

Or suppose you run across a subject in one of your other classes that catches your fancy. Why not investigate it further for your speech class? One student used this approach to develop a speech on a valuable natural resource known as coltan, which commands huge prices and is used in electronic devices such as laptops, cell phones, and pagers. After hearing about the subject in his electrical engineering class, the student researched the topic further. In the process, he learned that coltan has also become an object of warfare in Central Africa. Using what he learned in his research, he put together a captivating speech that kept everyone's attention from beginning to end.

Still another possibility—especially for persuasive speeches—is to think of subjects about which you hold strong opinions and beliefs. They may include national or international concerns such as gun control or global warming. Or perhaps you are closely involved in a local issue such as a teachers' strike or a proposal to increase tuition. Not all such topics must be "political." They can deal with anything from graduation requirements to helping people with physical disabilities, from dormitory regulations to building a church recreation center.

BRAINSTORMING FOR TOPICS

connectlucas.com
View an excerpt from "Coltan: Money, Guns, and Cell Phones" in the online Media Library for this chapter (Video Clip 4.1).

After all this, you may still be thinking, "I *don't* care about coltan. I've *never* been to Pakistan. I'm *not* active in politics. WHAT am I going to talk about?" If you are having trouble selecting a topic, there are a number of brainstorming procedures you can follow to get started.

Personal Inventory

First, make a quick inventory of your experiences, interests, hobbies, skills, beliefs, and so forth. Jot down anything that comes to mind, no matter how silly or irrelevant it may seem. From this list may come a general subject area out of which you can fashion a specific topic. This method has worked for many students.

Clustering

If the first method doesn't work, try a technique called clustering. Take a sheet of paper and divide it into nine columns as follows: People, Places, Things, Events, Processes, Concepts, Natural Phenomena, Problems, and Plans and Policies. Then list in each column the first five or six items that come to mind. The result might look like this:

brainstorming
A method of generating ideas for speech topics by free association of words and ideas.

People	Places	Things
Barack Obama	Iraq	iPod
John McCain	Grand Canyon	Blackberry
Hillary Clinton	the moon	television

People	Places	Things
Lorena Ochoa	Paris	robots
my family	my hometown	scientists

Events	Processes
graduation	learning CPR
Passover	cooking Thai food
Chinese New Year	avoiding credit card debt
Cinco de Mayo	taking photographs
World Cup	writing a job resumé

Concepts	Natural Phenomena
business ethics	lightning
conservatism	hurricanes
free-speech theories	coastal erosion
Buddhism	earthquakes
creationism	tidal waves

Problems	Plans and Policies
global warming	universal health care
terrorism	nuclear power
election fraud	domestic partner benefits
campus crime	homeschooling
domestic abuse	needle-exchange programs

Very likely, several items on your lists will strike you as potential topics. If not, take the items you find most intriguing and compose sublists for each. Try to free-associate. Write down a word or idea. What does that trigger in your mind? Whatever it is, write that down next, and keep going until you have five or six ideas on your list. For example, working from the lists printed above, one student composed sublists for television, campus crime, and lightning:

Television	Campus Crime	Lightning
movies	police	thunder
Academy Awards	fingerprints	noise
prizes	hands	traffic
lotteries	gloves	air pollution
gambling	cold weather	gasoline

Can you follow her trail of association? In the first column, television made her think of movies. Movies suggest the Academy Awards. The Academy Awards are prizes. Prizes reminded her of lotteries. Lotteries are a form of gambling. Suddenly, this student remembered an article she had read on the problem of gambling addiction in America. The idea clicked in her mind. After considerable research she developed an excellent speech titled "Gambling Addiction: Why You Can't Beat the Odds."

That's a far cry from television! If you started out free-associating from cartoons, you would doubtless end up somewhere completely different. This is what clustering is all about.

Reference Search

By clustering, most people come up with a topic rather quickly. But if you are still stymied, don't despair. There is a third technique you can use. Browse through an encyclopedia, a periodical database, or some other reference work until you come across what might be a good speech topic. As an experiment, one student scanned *The American Heritage Dictionary,* limiting herself to the letter *b*. Within 10 minutes she had come up with these potential topics:

Bible	bonsai	Baja California	bar mitzvah
backpacking	blackjack	Braille	backgammon
Bill of Rights	bioethics	bicycle	butterflies
ballet	Beethoven	Beijing	beer
beta-carotene	birthstones	botulism	Buddhism

With proper research and development, any one of these could make an excellent speech.

Internet Search

Yet another possibility is to connect to a subject-based search engine such as Yahoo! Directory (dir.yahoo.com) or the Librarians' Index to the Internet (www.lii.org). Both begin with a dozen or so major categories, such as Media, Education, Science, Recreation, Business, Government, and Society and Culture. If you click on one of the categories, you will see a group of subcategories, any of which might get you closer to a speech topic.

One of the advantages of using the Internet in this way is that you can make your search more and more specific until you find just the right subject. Suppose, for example, that you are looking under Health in Yahoo! Directory and your attention is grabbed by Nutrition. If you click on this link, you will see a screen with a detailed list of subheadings, one of which is Vegetarianism. Clicking on that link will yield sites on particular aspects of vegetarianism. If nothing grabs your attention along the way, you can start over with another broad subject area and proceed until you find just what you are looking for.

Whatever the means you use for selecting a topic, *start early*. The major reason students have difficulty choosing speech topics is that, like most people, they tend to procrastinate—to put off starting projects for as long as possible.

Start thinking about your topic as soon as each assignment is announced. Pay attention to interesting subjects in class and conversation, on the Internet, radio, and television, in newspapers and magazines. Jot down ideas for topics as they occur to you. Having an inventory of possible topics to choose from is much better than having to rack your brain for one at the last minute.

If you get an early start on choosing a topic, you will have plenty of time to pick just the right one and prepare a first-rate speech.

Determining the General Purpose

Along with choosing a topic, you need to determine the general purpose of your speech. Usually it will fall into one of two overlapping categories—to inform or to persuade.

When your general purpose is to inform, you act as a teacher or lecturer. Your goal is to convey information clearly, accurately, and interestingly. If you describe how to lift weights, narrate the major events of the latest Middle East crisis, or report on your sorority's financial position, you are speaking to inform. Your aim is to enhance the knowledge and understanding of your listeners—to give them information they did not have before.

general purpose
The broad goal of a speech.

When your general purpose is to persuade, you act as an advocate or a partisan. You go beyond giving information to espousing a cause. You want to *change* or *structure* the attitudes or actions of your audience. If you try to convince your listeners that they should start a regular program of weight lifting, that the United States should modify its policy in the Middle East, or that your sorority should start a fund-raising drive to balance its budget, then you are speaking to persuade. In doing so, you cannot help but give information; but your primary goal is to win over your listeners to your point of view—to get them to believe something or do something as a result of your speech.

In speech classes, the general purpose is usually specified as part of the speech assignment. For speeches outside the classroom, however, you have to make sure of your general purpose yourself. Usually this is easy to do. Are you going to explain, report, or demonstrate something? Then your general purpose is to inform. Are you going to sell, advocate, or defend something? Then your general purpose is to persuade. But no matter what the situation, you must be certain of exactly what you hope to achieve by speaking.

Determining the Specific Purpose

Once you have chosen a topic and a general purpose, you must narrow your choices to determine the specific purpose of your speech. The specific purpose should focus on one aspect of a topic. You should be able to state your specific purpose in a single infinitive phrase (to inform my audience about . . . ; to persuade my audience to . . .) that indicates *precisely* what you hope to accomplish with your speech.

specific purpose
A single infinitive phrase that states precisely what a speaker hopes to accomplish in his or her speech.

For example, Duane Winfield, a student at a large state university, decided to give his first classroom speech on a topic from his personal experience. For the past two years, he had volunteered his time to perform music for patients in mental hospitals, nursing homes, and residences for disabled adults. He had seen how enthusiastically the patients responded to music, even when they remained unmoved by other kinds of stimuli. Duane's experience had given him a better understanding of the benefits of music therapy, and he wanted to share this understanding with his classmates. This gave him a topic and a general purpose, which he stated like this:

Topic: Music therapy

General Purpose: To inform

So far, so good. But what aspect of his topic would Duane discuss? The kinds of facilities in which he had worked? His specific role as a performer? The evidence that music therapy can improve patients' mental health? The needs of patients with different kinds of illnesses? He had to choose something interesting that he could cover in a six-minute speech. Finally, he settled on describing his most memorable experiences with patients to show how music affected them. He stated his specific purpose this way:

Specific Purpose: To inform my audience about the benefits of music therapy for people with psychological or cognitive disabilities.

This turned out to be an excellent choice, and Duane's speech was among the best in the class.

Notice how clear the specific purpose statement is. Notice also how it relates the topic directly to the audience. That is, it states not only what the *speaker* wants to *say* but also what the speaker wants the *audience* to *know* as a result of the speech. This is very important, for it helps keep the audience at the center of your attention as you prepare your speech.

Look what happens when the specific purpose statement does not include the audience.

Specific Purpose: To explain the benefits of music therapy for people with psychological or cognitive disabilities.

Explain to whom? To musicians? To medical students? To social workers? Those would be three different speeches. The musicians would want to know about the kinds of music Duane played. The medical students would want to hear about research on the benefits of music therapy. The social workers would want to learn how to implement a music program. Communicating effectively with each group would require preparing a different speech.

When the audience slips out of the specific purpose, it may slip out of the speaker's consciousness. You may begin to think your task is the general one of preparing "an informative speech," when in fact your task is the specific one of informing a particular group of people. As we shall see in the next chapter, it is almost impossible to prepare a good speech without keeping constantly in mind the *people* for whom it is intended.

TIPS FOR FORMULATING THE SPECIFIC PURPOSE STATEMENT

Formulating a specific purpose is the most important early step in developing a successful speech. When writing your purpose statement, follow the general principles outlined on the following pages.

Internet Connection

www.connectlucas.com

Write the Purpose Statement as a Full Infinitive Phrase, Not as a Fragment

Ineffective: Calendars.

More Effective: To inform my audience about the four major kinds of calendars used in the world today.

The ineffective statement is adequate as an announcement of the speech topic, but it is not thought out fully enough to indicate the specific purpose.

Express Your Purpose as a Statement, Not as a Question

Ineffective: What is Día de los Muertos?

More Effective: To inform my audience about the history of Mexico's Día de los Muertos celebration.

The question might arouse the curiosity of an audience, but it is not effective as a specific purpose statement. It gives no indication about what direction the speech will take or what the speaker hopes to accomplish.

Avoid Figurative Language in Your Purpose Statement

Ineffective: To persuade my audience that the campus policy on student parking really stinks.

More Effective: To persuade my audience that the campus policy on student parking should be revised to provide more spaces for students before 5 p.m.

Although the ineffective statement indicates something of the speaker's viewpoint, it does not state concisely what he or she hopes to achieve. Figurative language can reinforce ideas within a speech, but it is too ambiguous for a specific purpose statement.

Limit Your Purpose Statement to One Distinct Idea

Ineffective: To persuade my audience to become literacy tutors and to donate time to the Special Olympics.

This purpose statement expresses two unrelated ideas, either of which could be the subject of a speech. The easiest remedy is to select one or the other as a focus for your presentation.

Think of opinions you hold when looking for speech topics. One student spoke on the specific purpose "To persuade my audience that stronger measures should be taken to protect African elephants."

More Effective: To persuade my audience to become literacy tutors.

Or:

More Effective: To persuade my audience to donate time to the Special Olympics.

Does this mean you can never use the word "and" in your specific purpose statement? Not at all. Suppose your specific purpose is "To inform my audience about the causes and effects of epilepsy." In this case, "and" is appropriate because it connects two related parts of a unified topic. What you need to avoid is not simply the word "and," but a specific purpose statement that contains two unrelated ideas, either of which could be developed into a speech in its own right.

Make Sure Your Specific Purpose Is Not Too Vague or General

Ineffective: To persuade my audience that something should be done about medical care.

More Effective: To persuade my audience that the federal government should adopt a system of national health insurance for all people in the United States.

The ineffective purpose statement falls into one of the most common traps—it is too broad and ill-defined. It gives no clues about what the speaker believes should be done about medical care. The more effective purpose statement is sharp and concise. It reveals clearly what the speaker plans to discuss.

The more precise your specific purpose, the easier it will be to prepare your speech. Consider this topic and specific purpose:

Topic: Hot-air balloons.

Specific Purpose: To inform my audience about hot-air balloons.

With such a hazy purpose, you have no systematic way of limiting your research or of deciding what to include in the speech and what to exclude. The origins of hot-air balloons, how they work, their current popularity—all could be equally relevant to a speech designed "to inform my audience about hot-air balloons."

In contrast, look at this topic and specific purpose:

Topic: Hot-air balloons.

Specific Purpose: To inform my audience about the scientific uses of hot-air balloons.

Now it is easy to decide what is germane and what is not. The origins of hot-air balloons, how they work, their popularity for recreation—all are interesting, but none is essential to the specific purpose of explaining "the scientific uses of hot-air balloons." Thus you need not worry about researching these matters or about explaining them in your speech. You can spend your preparation time efficiently.

QUESTIONS TO ASK ABOUT YOUR SPECIFIC PURPOSE

Sometimes you will arrive at your specific purpose almost immediately after choosing your topic. At other times you may do quite a bit of research before deciding on a specific purpose. Much will depend on how familiar you are with the topic, as well as on any special demands imposed by the assignment, the audience, or the occasion. But whenever you settle on your specific purpose, ask yourself the following questions about it.

Does My Purpose Meet the Assignment?

Students occasionally stumble over this question. Be sure you understand your assignment and shape your specific purpose to meet it. If you have questions, check with your instructor.

Can I Accomplish My Purpose in the Time Allotted?

Most classroom speeches are quite short, ranging from four to ten minutes. That may seem like a lot of time, but you will quickly find what generations of students have discovered—time flies when you are giving a speech! Most people speak at an average rate of 120 to 150 words a minute. This means that a six-minute speech will consist of roughly 720 to 900 words. That is not long enough to develop a highly complex topic. Here are some specific purpose statements that would defy being handled well in the time normally allotted for classroom speeches:

> To inform my audience about the rise and fall of ancient Rome.
>
> To inform my audience about the role of technology in human history.
>
> To persuade my audience to convert to Buddhism.

You are much better off with a limited purpose that you have some reasonable hope of achieving in the short span of four to ten minutes.

Is the Purpose Relevant to My Audience?

The price of retirement homes in Palm Springs might be an engrossing topic for older citizens who are in the market for such dwellings. And the quality of hot lunches in the elementary schools is of great concern to the students who

Checklist | Specific Purpose

YES ✓ **NO**

1. Is the specific purpose written as a full infinitive phrase?
2. Does the specific purpose include a reference to the audience?
3. Is the specific purpose phrased as a statement rather than a question?
4. Is the specific purpose free of figurative language?
5. Is the specific purpose limited to one distinct subject?
6. Does the specific purpose indicate precisely what I plan to accomplish in the speech?
7. Does the specific purpose meet the requirements of the assignment?
8. Can the specific purpose be accomplished in the time allotted for the speech?
9. Is the specific purpose relevant to my audience?
10. Does the specific purpose deal with a nontrivial subject?
11. Is the specific purpose suitable for a nontechnical audience?

connectlucas.com
This checklist is also available in the online Study Tools for this chapter.

eat them and the parents who pay for them. But neither subject has much relevance for an audience of college students. No matter how well you construct your speeches, they are likely to fall flat unless you speak about matters of interest to your listeners.

This is not to say you must select only topics that pertain directly to the college student's daily experience. Most students have wide-ranging backgrounds, interests, ideas, and values. And most of them are intellectually curious. They can get involved in an astonishing variety of subjects. Follow your common sense and make sure *you* are truly interested in the topic. Also, when speaking on a subject that is not obviously relevant to your listeners, find a way to tie it in with their goals, values, interests, and well-being. We'll discuss how to do this in the next chapter.

Is the Purpose Too Trivial for My Audience?

Just as you need to avoid speech topics that are too broad or complicated, so you need to steer clear of topics that are too superficial. How to build a fire without matches might absorb a group of Cub Scouts, but your classmates would probably consider it frivolous. Unfortunately, there is no absolute rule for determining what is trivial to an audience and what is not. Here are some examples of specific purposes that most people would find too trivial for classroom speeches:

To inform my audience about the parts of a backpack.

To inform my audience how to tie a bow tie.

To persuade my audience that espresso is better than cappuccino.

Is the Purpose Too Technical for My Audience?

Nothing puts an audience to sleep faster than a dry and technical speech. Beware of topics that are inherently technical and of treating ordinary subjects in a technical fashion. Although you may be familiar with the principles and vocabulary of international finance or clinical psychology, most of your classmates probably are not. There are aspects of these and similar subjects that can be treated clearly, with a minimum of jargon. But if you find that you can't fulfill your specific purpose without relying on technical words and concepts, you should reconsider your purpose.

Here are some examples of specific purposes that are overly technical for most classroom speeches:

To inform my audience about the solution to Fermat's Last Theorem.

To inform my audience about the principles of neutrino physics.

To inform my audience about the methods of encryption technology.

We shall discuss the details of audience analysis and adaptation in Chapter 5. For the moment, remember to make sure that your specific purpose is appropriate for your listeners. If you have doubts, ask your instructor, or circulate a questionnaire among your classmates (see pages 109–112).

Phrasing the Central Idea

WHAT IS THE CENTRAL IDEA?

The specific purpose of a speech is what you hope to accomplish. The *central idea* is a concise statement of what you *expect to say*. Sometimes it is called the thesis statement, the subject sentence, or the major thought. Whatever the term, the central idea is usually expressed as a simple, declarative sentence that refines and sharpens the specific purpose statement.

Imagine you run into a friend on your way to speech class. She says, "I have to dash to my history lecture, but I hear you're giving a speech today. Can you tell me the gist of it in one sentence?" "Sure," you reply. "America's prison system suffers from three major problems—overcrowding of inmates, lack of effective rehabilitation programs, and high expense to taxpayers."

Your answer is the central idea of your speech. It is more precise than your topic (America's prison system) or your specific purpose statement ("To inform my audience of the three major problems facing America's prison system"). By stating exactly what the three major problems are, the central idea sums up your speech in a single sentence.

Another way to think of the central idea is as your *residual message*—what you want your audience to remember after they have forgotten everything else in the speech. Most of the time the central idea will encapsulate the main points to be developed in the body of the speech. To show how this works, let's take a few of the examples we saw earlier in this chapter and develop them from the topic, general purpose, and specific purpose to the central idea.

We can start with the speech about music therapy.

Topic: Music therapy.

General Purpose: To inform.

central idea
A one-sentence statement that sums up or encapsulates the major ideas of a speech.

residual message
What a speaker wants the audience to remember after it has forgotten everything else in a speech.

Specific Purpose:	To explain the benefits of music therapy for people with psychological or cognitive disabilities.
Central Idea:	Music therapy developed as a formal mode of treatment during the twentieth century, utilizes a number of methods, and is explained by several theories that account for its success.

connectlucas.com
View the introduction from "The Benefits of Music Therapy" in the online Media Library for this chapter (Video Clip 4.2).

Look carefully at this example. It shows how the speaker might start with a broad subject (music therapy) that becomes narrower and narrower as the speaker moves from the general purpose to the specific purpose to the central idea. Notice also how much more the central idea suggests about the content of the speech. From it we can expect the speaker to address three main points—the first summarizing the development of music therapy, the second looking at methods of music therapy, and the third exploring theories that account for the success of music therapy.

This sharpening of focus as one proceeds to the central idea is crucial. Here is another example:

Topic:	Día de los Muertos.
General Purpose:	To inform.
Specific Purpose:	To inform my audience about the history of Mexico's Día de los Muertos celebration.
Central Idea:	Día de los Muertos can be traced to the Aztecs, was moved from summer to fall by Spanish priests, and today is celebrated in a number of ways in different regions of Mexico.

This central idea is especially well worded. We can assume from it that the body of the speech will contain three main points: (1) on the Aztec origins of Día de los Muertos, (2) on how it was changed by the Spanish, and (3) on the ways it is celebrated today.

Notice in each of these examples how much more the central idea reveals about the content of the speech than does the specific purpose. This is not accidental. Often you can settle on a specific purpose statement early in preparing your speech. The central idea, however, usually emerges later—after you have done your research and have decided on the main points of the speech. The process may work like this:

As an environmental science major, Marcia Esposito had learned that many experts fear the world may face a severe water shortage by the year 2025. She decided this would make a good topic for her informative speech. Tentatively, she adopted the following specific purpose statement: "To inform my audience about the seriousness of the growing international water crisis." Then Marcia started her research.

An article in *Newsweek*, which she located through LexisNexis, explained how the population in countries such as China, India, and Palestine is outstripping the available supply of fresh water. According to the article, 400 million Chinese do not have access to suitable drinking water, and two-thirds of India's 1.1 billion people lack the water they need.

Next Marcia found a report on the United Nations Web site about the impact of pollution on the water supply. The report stated that in developing countries "more than 90 percent of sewage and 70 percent of industrial wastewater is dumped untreated into surface water."

Unlike the specific purpose, which you need to settle on early in the speech preparation process, the central idea usually takes shape later, as a result of your research and analysis of the topic.

Then Marcia hit upon the idea of interviewing one of her environmental science professors. In addition to confirming Marcia's research about the impact of population growth and pollution, the professor mentioned the problems caused by mismanagement of water supplies. Around the world 65 to 70 percent of the water people use is lost to waste, evaporation, and other inefficiencies; the rate in the United States is about 50 percent.

Marcia digested all this information. Now she was ready to formulate her central idea: "Population growth, pollution, and mismanagement are creating a serious shortage of fresh water in many parts of the world."

GUIDELINES FOR THE CENTRAL IDEA

What makes a well-worded central idea? Essentially the same things that make a well-worded specific purpose statement. The central idea (1) should be expressed in a full sentence, (2) should not be in the form of a question, (3) should avoid figurative language, and (4) should not be vague or overly general.

Here, for example, are four poorly written central ideas. See if you can identify the problem with each and figure out how each might be phrased more effectively:

Ineffective: Paying college athletes a monthly salary is a good idea.

Ineffective: Problems of fad diets.

Ineffective: What are nanorobots?

Ineffective: Mexico's Yucatán Peninsula is an awesome place for a vacation.

The first is too general. To say that paying college athletes a monthly salary is a "good idea" does not convey the speaker's viewpoint sharply and clearly. What does the speaker mean by a "good idea"? A revised central idea for this speech might be:

Checklist — Central Idea

YES	✓	NO	
☐		☐	1. Is the central idea written as a complete sentence?
☐		☐	2. Is the central idea phrased as a statement rather than a question?
☐		☐	3. Is the central idea free of figurative language?
☐		☐	4. Does the central idea clearly encapsulate the main points to be discussed in the body of the speech?
☐		☐	5. Can the central idea be adequately discussed in the time allotted for the speech?
☐		☐	6. Is the central idea relevant to the audience?
☐		☐	7. Is the central idea appropriate for a nontechnical audience?

More Effective: Because college athletes in revenue-producing sports such as football and basketball generate millions of dollars in revenue for their schools, the NCAA should allow such athletes to receive a $300 monthly salary as part of their scholarships.

The second ineffective central idea is also too general, but it suffers further from not being written as a complete sentence. "Problems of fad diets" does not reveal enough about the content of the speech to serve as the central idea. It should be rewritten as a full sentence that identifies the problems of fad diets to be discussed in the speech:

More Effective: Although fad diets produce quick weight loss, they can lead to serious health problems by creating deficiencies in vitamins and minerals and by breaking down muscle tissue as well as fat.

The third poorly written central idea is phrased as a question rather than as a full declarative sentence. Asking "What are nanorobots?" might be a good way to catch the attention of listeners, but it does not encapsulate the main points to be developed in the speech. A more effective central idea would be:

More Effective: Microscopic in size, nanorobots are being developed for use in medicine, weaponry, and daily life.

The final ineffective central idea is flawed by its use of figurative language. To say that the Yucatán Peninsula is an "awesome" place for a vacation does not indicate what characteristics of the Yucatán Peninsula the speaker intends to discuss. A better central idea might be:

More Effective: Mexico's Yucatán Peninsula has many attractions for vacationers, including a warm climate, excellent food, and extensive Mayan ruins.

Notice that in all these examples the more effective central idea sums up the main points of the speech in a single sentence. If you are having trouble phrasing your central idea, the reason may be that you do not yet have a firm grasp on the main points of your speech. Do not worry too much about your central idea until after you have developed the body of your speech (see Chapter 8). If, at that point, you still can't come up with a clear, concise central idea, your speech itself may not be clear or concise. Keep working on the speech until you can compose a central idea that fits the criteria just discussed. The result will be a sharper central idea and a tighter, more coherent speech.

SUMMARY

The first step in speechmaking is choosing a topic. For classroom speeches, you can choose a subject you know well or one you research especially for the speech. If you have trouble picking a topic, you can use one of four brainstorming procedures. First, make an inventory of your hobbies, interests, skills, beliefs, and so forth. Second, use clustering to list the first topics that come to mind in several categories. Third, check a reference work for ideas. Fourth, use an Internet subject directory to help you scan possible topics.

The general purpose of your speech will usually be to inform or to persuade. When your general purpose is to inform, your goal is to communicate information clearly, accurately, and interestingly. When your general purpose is to persuade, your goal is to win listeners over to your point of view.

Once you know your topic and general purpose, you must focus on a specific purpose statement that indicates precisely what your speech seeks to achieve. The specific purpose statement should (1) be a full infinitive phrase; (2) be worded as a statement, not a question; (3) avoid figurative language; (4) concentrate on one distinct idea; (5) not be vague or general.

Keep several questions in mind as you formulate your specific purpose statement: Does my purpose meet the assignment? Can I accomplish my purpose in the time allotted? Is the purpose relevant to my audience? Is the purpose too trivial or too technical for my audience?

The central idea refines and sharpens your specific purpose. It is a concise statement of what you will say in your speech, and it usually crystallizes in your thinking after you have done your research and have decided on the main points of your speech. The central idea usually encapsulates the main points to be developed in the body of your speech.

KEY TERMS

topic *(76)*

brainstorming *(78)*

general purpose *(81)*

specific purpose *(81)*

central idea *(87)*

residual message *(87)*

REVIEW QUESTIONS

connectlucas.com
For further review, go to the Study Questions in the online Study Aids for this chapter.

After reading this chapter, you should be able to answer the following questions:

1. What four brainstorming methods can you follow if you are having trouble choosing a topic for your speech?

2. What are the two general purposes of most classroom speeches? How do they differ?

3. Why is determining the specific purpose such an important early step in speech preparation? Why is it important to include the audience in the specific purpose statement?

4. What are five tips for formulating your specific purpose?

5. What are five questions to ask about your specific purpose?

6. What is the difference between the specific purpose and the central idea of a speech? What are four guidelines for an effective central idea?

EXERCISES FOR CRITICAL THINKING

1. Using one of the four brainstorming methods described in this chapter, come up with three topics you might like to deal with in your next classroom speech. For each topic, devise two possible specific purpose statements suitable for the speech assignment. Make sure the specific purpose statements fit the guidelines discussed in the chapter.

2. Below is a list of nine topics. Choose three, and for each of the three compose two specific purpose statements—one suitable for an informative speech and one suitable for a persuasive speech.

   Example

   Topic: School buses

   Informative: To inform my audience of the dangerous conditions of many school buses in the United States.

   Persuasive: To persuade my audience that the federal government should impose stronger safety standards for school buses in the United States.

education	technology	crime
sports	politics	prejudice
science	music	health

3. Here are several specific purpose statements for classroom speeches. Identify the problem with each, and rewrite the statement to correct the problem.

   To inform my audience how to sign up for Facebook.

   To persuade my audience that the U.S. government should increase funding for stem cell research and support the development of hydrogen-fuel vehicles.

   What is an individual retirement account?

   To inform my audience why square grooves are superior to U-shaped grooves on golf clubs.

   To inform my audience about Vietnam.

   Donate blood.

   To persuade my audience that something has to be done about the problem of antibiotic-resistant bacteria.

4. Below are three sets of main points for speeches. For each set, supply the general purpose, specific purpose, and central idea.

General Purpose:

Specific Purpose:

Central Idea:

Main Points:
  I. You should study abroad because it will enhance your personal development.
  II. You should study abroad because it will enhance your academic development.
  III. You should study abroad because it will enhance your career development.

General Purpose:

Specific Purpose;

Central Idea:

Main Points:
  I. The first step in getting a tattoo is shaving and sterilizing the skin.
  II. The second step in getting a tattoo is outlining the design.
  III. The third step in getting a tattoo is applying pigments to the design.
  IV. The fourth step in getting a tattoo is sterilizing and bandaging the tattoo.

General Purpose:

Specific Purpose:

Central Idea:

Main Points:
  I. As a writer, Thomas Jefferson penned the Declaration of Independence and *Notes on the State of Virginia*.
  II. As President, Thomas Jefferson negotiated the Louisiana Purchase and approved the Lewis and Clark expedition.
  III. As an architect, Thomas Jefferson designed Monticello and the University of Virginia.

Applying *the* **Power** *of* **Public Speaking**

Your communication degree has helped you land a job as spokesperson for the mayor of a medium-sized city on the West Coast. A year after starting the job, you are selected to organize an information campaign explaining the benefits of a new youth center proposed by the mayor.

To launch this campaign, you've decided to hold a news briefing at the end of the week. To open the briefing, you will present a short set of comments on the mayor's initiative. You decide to focus on four benefits of the youth center: (1) It will offer a range of activities—from sports to the arts—in a safe environment; (2) It will provide social networks for youths from all walks of life; (3) It will operate most hours of the day and night; (4) It will be free and open to everyone.

Following the format used in this chapter, state the general purpose, specific purpose, central idea, and main points of your comments.

Analyzing the Audie

In the midst of the heated 2008 campaign for the Democratic presidential nomination, Barack Obama faced one of the biggest challenges of his political career. His former minister, Jeremiah Wright, had made controversial, racially charged comments that circulated widely in the national media. Suddenly, Obama was forced to deal with Wright's remarks, the issue of race in America, and the future of his presidential campaign. In doing so, he had to address multiple audiences, including the white community, the black community, his supporters, backers of rival Hillary Clinton, undecided voters, and the nation in general.

On March 18, 2008, Obama spoke on national television from Philadelphia, the birthplace of the American republic. Well aware of the situation he faced, he crafted a speech that dealt thoughtfully with the concerns of his various audiences while stressing the fundamental unity of the American people. Only by working together, he said, can we "move beyond some of our old racial wounds and . . . continue on the path of a more perfect union."

The speech garnered almost universal praise across the political spectrum. Obama was hailed for his capacity to "lead public opinion" by explaining issues "so both sides can see each other's point of view." He pushed the nation "to move beyond race and gender, beyond Democrat and Republican, beyond politics and into reviving the spirit of the nation itself." It was, by any measure, a striking achievement.

connectlucas.com
View an excerpt from Barack Obama's "A More Perfect Union" in the online Media Library for this chapter (Video Clip 5.1).

Audience-Centeredness

audience-centeredness
Keeping the audience foremost in mind at every step of speech preparation and presentation.

Obama's speech points up an important fact: Good public speakers are *audience-centered*. They know the primary purpose of speechmaking is not to browbeat the audience or to blow off steam. Rather, it is to gain a *desired response* from listeners. Barack Obama's purpose in his speech was to gain a favorable response from the major groups in his audience. He did that by presenting himself and his ideas in ways that connected with the audience's goals, values, and beliefs.

Being audience-centered does not involve compromising your beliefs to get a favorable response. Nor does it mean using devious, unethical tactics to achieve your goal. As did Barack Obama, you can remain true to yourself and speak ethically while adapting your message to the needs of your listeners.

To be audience-centered, you need to keep several questions in mind when you work on your speeches:

To whom am I speaking?

What do I want them to know, believe, or do as a result of my speech?

What is the most effective way of composing and presenting my speech to accomplish that aim?

The answers to these questions will influence every decision you make along the way—selecting a topic, determining a specific purpose, settling on your main points and supporting materials, organizing the message, and, finally, delivering the speech.

In many ways, adapting to an audience during a public speech is not much different from what you do in your daily social contacts. Few people would walk into a party and announce, "You know those people protesting at the administration building are way over the edge!"

People usually prefer to open controversial topics with a fairly noncommittal position. You might say, "What's going on at the administration building?"

Then when you have heard and processed your companion's response, you can present your position accordingly. (You don't have to *agree* with a viewpoint different from your own, but neither do you have to hit your listeners over the head with your own opinion.)

Effective speakers seek to create a bond with their listeners by emphasizing common values, goals, and experiences. Communication scholars call this process *identification.* Barack Obama created identification with his audience by showing how his personal experience reflected both America's troubled racial history and the promise of a brighter tomorrow. "We may not look the same and we may not have come from the same place," he stated, "but we all want to move in the same direction—towards a better future for our children and our grandchildren."

When you make a speech, either in class or in some other forum, keep in mind the need to be audience-centered. Think in advance about your listeners' background and interests, about their level of knowledge regarding the speech topic, and about their attitudes regarding your stance on the topic. As you develop the speech, work on explaining your ideas so they will be clear, interesting, and persuasive to the audience.

At this point, you may be nodding your head and saying, "Of course, everyone knows that. It's only common sense." But knowing a precept and putting it into practice are two different matters. The aim of this chapter is to introduce the basic principles of audience analysis and adaption. Chapters 14–16 will deal with those features of audience analysis unique to informative and persuasive speaking.

identification

A process in which speakers seek to create a bond with the audience by emphasizing common values, goals, and experiences.

Your Classmates as an Audience

There is a tendency—among students and teachers alike—to view the classroom as an artificial speaking situation. In a way, it is. Your speech class is a testing ground where you can develop your communication skills before applying them outside the classroom. The most serious measure of success or failure is your grade, and that is determined ultimately by your teacher.

Because of this, it is easy to lose sight of your fellow students as an authentic audience. But each of your classmates is a real person with real ideas, attitudes, and feelings. Your speech class offers an enormous opportunity to inform and persuade other people. As one student wrote on her evaluation form at the end of her speech class, "I thought the speeches would all be phony, but they weren't. I've not only learned a lot about speaking—I've learned a lot about other things from listening to the speeches in class."

The best classroom speeches are those that take the classroom audience as seriously as a lawyer, a politician, a minister, or an advertiser takes an audience. You should consider every audience—inside the classroom and out—as worthy of your best efforts to communicate your knowledge or convictions. At the least you show respect for your listeners. At the most you could make a real difference in their lives. The following story demonstrates the latter:

Crystal Watkins gave an informative speech on the subject of small claims court, where ordinary people can press lawsuits involving up to $3,000 without lawyers. Part of her speech went like this: "It's two weeks after you have moved into a new apartment. A letter arrives from your old landlord. Expecting to get back your $600 security deposit, you joyfully tear open the envelope. Inside is a form letter explaining why your security deposit is not being refunded. What can you do about it? Nothing, right? Wrong! You can file a claim in small claims court."

Lee Callaway, one of Crystal's classmates, paid close attention. At the end of the previous term, he had run into a situation just like the one Crystal described. Not having money to hire a lawyer, he assumed he would have to forfeit his security deposit. But now, as he listened to Crystal's speech, Lee decided he would try to get his money back in small claims court. He filed suit the next week, and within a month he had his money back—thanks in part to his classmate's speech!

Most of your classroom speeches won't have this much immediate impact. Nevertheless, any topic that you handle conscientiously can influence your listeners—can enrich their experience, broaden their knowledge, perhaps change their views about something important.[1]

The Psychology of Audiences

What do you do when you listen to a speech? Sometimes you pay close attention; at other times you let your thoughts wander. People may be compelled to attend a speech, but no one can make them listen. The speaker must make the audience *choose* to pay attention.

Even when people do pay attention, they don't process a speaker's message exactly as the speaker intends. Auditory perception is always selective. Every speech contains two messages—the one sent by the speaker and the one received by the listener. As we saw in Chapter 1, what a speaker says is filtered through a listener's frame of reference—the sum of her or his needs, interests, expectations, knowledge, and experience. As a result, we listen and respond to speeches not as they are, but as we are. Or, to borrow from Paul Simon's classic song "The Boxer," people hear what they want to hear and disregard the rest.

egocentrism
The tendency of people to be concerned above all with their own values, beliefs, and well-being.

What do people want to hear? Very simply, they usually want to hear about things that are meaningful to them. People are *egocentric*. They pay closest attention to messages that affect their own values, beliefs, and well-being. Listeners approach speeches with one question uppermost in mind: "Why is this important to *me*?" As Harry Emerson Fosdick, the great preacher, once said: "There is nothing that people are so interested in as themselves, their own problems, and the way to solve them. That fact is . . . the primary starting point of all successful public speaking."[2]

What do these psychological principles mean to you as a speaker? First, they mean your listeners will hear and judge what you say on the basis of what they already know and believe. Second, they mean you must relate your message to your listeners—show how it pertains to them, explain why they should care about it as much as you do. Here's an example:

A recent graduate of a large state university, Naomi Springer is now an admissions counselor for the same school. Part of her job is to travel to high schools around the state and encourage students to apply to the university.

Recently Naomi addressed a group of potential students and their parents at West Rock High School, 150 miles north of campus. As usual, she explained the university's

Good speakers are audience-centered. Whether speaking formally or informally, they look for creative ways to communicate their ideas and keep their audience's attention.

world-class computer facilities, prestigious faculty, and well-funded libraries. Her audience, however, seemed restless and less attentive than usual. When she opened the floor for questions, immediately one of the parents raised his hand. "Your facilities all seem impressive," he said, "but what are you doing to keep our kids healthy?"

Naomi knew what the parent was talking about. A month earlier, three students in the dorms had contracted bacterial meningitis. The illnesses received national media attention and sparked debate over student health and the university's responsibilities. Naomi assured her audience that the university was taking all appropriate measures to deal with the situation, but she knew she would need to make some changes before her next presentation.

A week later, at another high school, Naomi began her speech by tackling the student-health issue head-on: "For now," she said, "I'm going to rush past our world-class computer facilities, prestigious faculty, and second-to-none libraries and get right to what I know is on all of your minds. Let me begin by describing what happened last month, and then I'll explain what we're doing to keep students healthy and safe." In a few moments, she had everyone's attention and her speech was off to a great start.

As Naomi's experience shows, you need some grasp of what your listeners know, believe, and care about. As Saul Alinksy, the noted community organizer, advises, "People only understand things in terms of their experience," which means that to communicate with them, "you must get inside their experience."[3]

Of course, you can't actually get inside another person's experience. But you can learn enough about your audience to know what you should do to make your ideas clear and meaningful. How you can do this is our next topic.

Demographic Audience Analysis

demographic audience analysis
Audience analysis that focuses on demographic factors such as age, gender, religion, sexual orientation, group membership, and racial, ethnic, or cultural background.

One of the ways speakers analyze audiences is by looking at demographic traits such as age; gender; sexual orientation; religion; group membership; racial, ethnic, or cultural background; and the like. This is called *demographic audience analysis*. It consists of two steps: (1) identifying the general demographic features of your audience, and (2) gauging the importance of those features to a particular speaking situation.

While demographic audience analysis can be a useful tool in understanding your audience, like all tools, it can be used improperly. When analyzing demographic information about your audience, it is essential that you avoid stereotyping. Stereotyping involves creating an oversimplified image of a particular group of people, usually by assuming that all members of the group are alike. Examples of stereotyping include the erroneous notions that all African Americans are athletic or that all Asians excel in science. Looking at demographic factors can provide important clues about your audience, but you must use those factors prudently and responsibly.

stereotyping
Creating an oversimplified image of a particular group of people, usually by assuming that all members of the group are alike.

In addition, as we shall see later in this chapter, you should always combine your demographic audience analysis with situational audience analysis. The importance of any given demographic factor will vary from audience to audience depending on the occasion and the speech topic. If you keep this in mind, demographic analysis can be a valuable starting point in gauging your audience's background, interests, values, and beliefs. Here are a few of the major demographic factors you should consider.

AGE

Are you a member of Generation X? Generation Y? Generation 2K? Are you twenty-something or thirty-something? To some extent, of course, these are merely labels. There is no generation in which everyone thinks alike, buys the same products, or votes for the same political candidates. Yet as Aristotle noted almost 2,500 years ago and as researchers have confirmed many times since, few things affect a person's outlook more than his or her age. Each generation has more or less common values and experiences that set it apart from other generations. Whatever your age, you are a product of your world.

You can see what this means for your speeches. Suppose you address an audience of older people. If you refer to Kayne West, Lil Wayne, or Rihanna, your audience may have no idea who you mean. Similarly, if you speak to an audience of young adults and casually mention the Tet offensive (an important campaign of the Vietnam War), they may not know what you are talking about. Even if younger listeners do recognize the name, it will not produce the same emotional associations as in people who lived through the war in Vietnam.

Depending on the composition of your speech class, you may face an audience that is mostly in their late teens and early twenties. If so, you can assume a common level of age experience. On the other hand, 40 percent of college students today are age 25 or older, and many classrooms include students in their thirties, forties, fifties, and beyond. You may then have to tackle two or three generations. This will give you good practice for speeches outside the classroom, where age is usually a major factor in audience analysis.

GENDER

Ben Appleby was sure he had done well in his interviews for a position as a sales representative with a major pharmaceutical company. The hiring committee thought so, too, and they invited him back for a final interview, where he would present a three-minute speech explaining why he was the best person for the job. If Ben was going to sell the company's products, the committee knew, he would need strong presentation skills.

During his speech, Ben talked about his qualifications, his work ethic, and why he would be a valuable addition to the company. In concluding, he said: "My aim will be to make sure physicians are thoroughly informed about the benefits of our products. The doctor will have all the information he needs to make sure his patients get the best medications available. It would be an honor to work for this company and to know I am making a small contribution to helping the doctor do the best he can for his patients."

When he finished, the committee applauded, but a couple members seemed less enthusiastic than Ben had hoped. The following week he found out why. The chair of the committee called to tell him that he got the job. But she added a word of caution: "We loved your presentation, but we want to remind you to be careful about how you refer to our customers. More than 35 percent of all doctors are women, and in fields such as pediatrics the number is over 50 percent. The female doctors you'll be calling on would be very surprised to be referred to as *he*."

As Ben realized, he was fortunate that the hiring committee thought enough of him to give him the job despite his gaffe. Vocational distinctions between the sexes have been eroding for many years. Women work as doctors, run corporations, enlist in the armed forces, and serve as college athletic directors. Men work as receptionists, nurses, flight attendants, and day-care attendants. In addition, the "typical" composition of audiences has changed. At one time, civic groups such as Kiwanis and Rotary clubs were all-male. Today most have sizable contingents of women. Parent associations, which were once composed almost solely of women, now include plenty of interested fathers. Speakers who fail to take account of such factors are almost certain to provoke negative reactions among some listeners, male and female alike.

At the same time, it is important to recognize that men and women are not alike in all their values and beliefs. When it comes to politics, for instance, American women tend to be more concerned about issues such as education, health care, and social justice, whereas men tend to stress economics and national security. But keep in mind that these are generalizations. There are lots of women who believe that national security comes first, just as there are plenty of men who give priority to social issues. An astute speaker will be equally attuned to the differences *and* the similarities between the sexes.[4]

SEXUAL ORIENTATION

Philip Ward, president of a major engineering firm, was hosting his annual awards banquet to recognize outstanding employees. After presenting all the plaques and checks, he said: "Now that we have honored these fine people for their career and community accomplishments, I would like to take a moment to recognize the spouses and partners who have supported their exceptional efforts." The room filled with applause.

After the ceremony, Ward made his way around the room shaking hands and chatting with award winners. "I want to congratulate you again on your superior design for the Houston water project," he said to Joanne Fitzpatrick.

"Thank you for the award," Joanne replied. "And I also want to thank you for being sensitive to the fact that many of us are supported by partners as well as by spouses. It really meant a lot to Julie and me to feel recognized and included."

As an experienced speaker and successful businessperson, Philip Ward is well aware of the need in contemporary society to adapt to his audience on the basis of sexual orientation. By mentioning "partners" as well as "spouses," he took an inclusive stance acknowledging the fact that couples can be same-sex or opposite-sex, married or unmarried. No matter what one's attitude toward gays, lesbians, or heterosexuals, audience-centered speakers are alert to how their messages will be received by people of various sexual orientations.

When you work on your speeches, keep an eye out for language, examples, and other elements that may unintentionally exclude listeners with same-sex partners. For example, in a speech about financial planning, rather than saying "most of us hope to graduate, find a good job, and get married," you could say "most of us hope to graduate, get a good job, and find a life partner."

You should also be alert to subtle uses of language with regard to sexual orientation. The label "homosexual," for example, is considered derogatory by lesbians and gay men. So are references to a gay or lesbian "lifestyle." Such references are also inaccurate because they imply that all gays and lesbians live the same way. Just as there is no single heterosexual lifestyle, there is no single lesbian or gay lifestyle.

You may be inclined to dismiss these suggestions as merely another form of political correctness, but just as audiences often include people of varying ages, races, and religions, so too do they contain people of different sexual orientations. Effective public speakers take all these demographic factors into account when preparing their remarks.

RACIAL, ETHNIC, AND CULTURAL BACKGROUND

As we saw in Chapter 1, the United States has long been a multicultural society. Populated originally by Native Americans and then by immigrants from all over the world, it is today a multiracial, multiethnic country of unmatched diversity. The majority of Americans support this diversity as a positive development in today's globalized world. Attitudes about race and ethnicity are quite different from what they were even a few decades ago.

Understanding those attitudes is crucial for speakers whether they are addressing a mixed-race audience or one with little apparent racial diversity,

Demographic audience analysis is vital to successful public speaking in any situation. Here U.S. Secretary of the Treasury Henry M. Paulson Jr. addresses a business audience in the United Arab Emirates.

whether they are delivering public speeches or simply making a few off-the-cuff remarks to a reporter. Consider, for example, the case of Geraldine Ferraro:

After serving three terms in the U.S. Congress, Geraldine Ferraro earned a permanent place in history in 1984 when the Democratic National Convention made her the first woman to be nominated by a major party for Vice President of the United States. Although she and her running mate, Walter Mondale, lost the election, she remained an important figure in the Democratic Party and subsequently sat on the United Nations Committee on Human Rights.

In 2008, Ferraro served on Hillary Clinton's finance committee during her campaign against Barack Obama for the Democratic presidential nomination. In March of that year, Ferraro made a speech at a cultural center in Torrance, California. Afterward, she granted an interview to a reporter from a local newspaper, in which she commented: "If Obama was a white man, he would not be in this position. And if he was a woman of any color, he would not be in this position. He happens to be very lucky to be who he is."

Within days, the national press had picked up the story. Obama called Ferraro's remarks "divisive," and Clinton said it was "regrettable that any of our supporters . . . say things that kind of veer off into the personal." Ferraro was unapologetic, claiming that her remarks were a simple statement of fact. They were interpreted, however, as meaning that Obama was winning the campaign not because of his achievements, but because of his race. Notwithstanding Ferraro's long record as a supporter of equal rights for African Americans, she was forced to resign her role in the Clinton campaign.

Ferraro's fate illustrates how important it is for speakers to be sensitive to issues of race, ethnicity, and cultural background. Whatever Ferraro meant by her remarks, they damaged her reputation and struck some observers as "a cynical effort to make Obama's race an issue" in the campaign.[5]

In addition to keeping in mind general attitudes about race and ethnicity, public speakers need to consider how racial, ethnic, and cultural differences among audience members might affect their reactions to a speech. Despite their similarities as Americans, people of European descent, blacks, Latinos,

Asians, and many others have different customs and beliefs that may bear upon your speech topic. Because we live in an age of globalization, you may also find yourself addressing listeners from countries other than your own.

The first step to being successful in such situations is to recognize that some of your listeners may indeed have racial, ethnic, or cultural perspectives that will affect their attitudes toward your speech topic. The second step is to try to determine what those perspectives are and how they are likely to affect the audience's response to your message. The third step is to adjust your speech so it will be as clear, suitable, and convincing as possible. No matter who the speaker, no matter what the occasion, adapting to people of diverse racial, ethnic, and cultural backgrounds is a vital aspect of the art of public speaking.

RELIGION

Russell Middleton, the director of the town's public library, was delighted to be invited to address his local civic association. He needed volunteers to help paint the reading rooms, and he felt sure he could recruit some from the association.

On the evening of his speech, Russell explained the painting project, making special mention of the fact that anyone who volunteered would help the library save money for more books and better programs. "Most of our work will be on Saturdays," he said. "We might also work in the evening, or maybe on a Sunday afternoon. But don't worry. We won't work on Sunday morning because that's when everyone will be at church." He finished by asking volunteers to sign up on a clipboard near the door.

At the end of the evening, Russell was pleased to see plenty of names on his clipboard, but he also found the following note. "Mr. Middleton," it began, "your project seems excellent, and I will be pleased to help. But I think you should remember that there are people in this community who do not go to church or worship on Sunday morning. I am Muslim, and some of the people sitting near me are Jewish. Fortunately, I had a chance to hear about your project before the comment about attending church on Sunday. If I hadn't, I might have concluded that you were not interested in my help. Please give me a call when you are ready to start the painting. Hamid Shakir."

As this story illustrates, you cannot assume that your views on religion—whatever they may be—are shared by your listeners. As current events around the world demonstrate, religious views are among the most emotionally charged and passionately defended of all human concerns. Even your small speech class might include a wide range of faiths, as well as atheists and agnostics.

As the United States has become more diverse culturally, it has also become more diverse religiously. The traditional mix of Protestantism, Catholicism, and Judaism has been enriched by growing numbers of Buddhists, Muslims, Hindus, Sikhs, Russian Orthodox, and others. One leading scholar on the subject says the United States is now "the most religiously diverse nation in the world."[6]

There is also great diversity within different faiths. You cannot assume that all Catholics support the official view of their church on birth control or women in the priesthood, that all Baptists are being born-again, or that all Muslims favor a subservient status for women. In matters of religion, the United States is truly a nation of many faiths, many voices, many views.

Whenever you speak on a topic with religious dimensions, then, be sure to consider the religious orientations of your listeners. Doing so can help you avoid potentially embarrassing pitfalls; in some cases, it may make the difference between an unsuccessful speech and a successful one.

GROUP MEMBERSHIP

"Tell me thy company," says Don Quixote, "and I'll tell thee what thou art." For all our talk about rugged individualism, Americans are very group-oriented. Workers belong to unions, businesspeople to chambers of commerce. Hunters join the National Rifle Association, environmentalists the Sierra Club, feminists the National Organization for Women. Doctors enroll in the American Medical Association, lawyers in the American Bar Association. There are thousands of such voluntary organizations in the United States.

Similar groups abound on campus. Some of your classmates may belong to fraternities or sororities, some to Campus Crusade for Christ, some to the Young Republicans, some to the film society, some to the ski club, and so forth. For speeches in the classroom, as well as for those outside the classroom, the group affiliations of your audience may provide excellent clues about your listeners' interests and attitudes.

Age; gender; sexual orientation; religion; racial, ethnic, and cultural background; group membership—these are just a few of the variables to consider in demographic audience analysis. Others include occupation, economic position, social standing, education, intelligence, and place of residence. Indeed, *anything* characteristic of a given audience is potentially important to a speaker addressing that audience. For your classroom speeches, you may want to learn about your classmates' academic majors, years in school, extracurricular activities, living arrangements, and job aspirations.

Perhaps the most important thing to keep in mind about demographic audience analysis is that it is not an end in itself. Your aim is not just to list the major traits of your listeners but to find in those traits clues about how your listeners will respond to your speech. Once you have done that, you are ready to move on to the next stage of audience analysis.

Situational Audience Analysis
●●

Situational audience analysis usually builds on demographic analysis. It identifies traits of the audience unique to the speaking situation at hand. These traits include the size of the audience, the physical setting, and the disposition of the audience toward the subject, the speaker, and the occasion.

situational audience analysis
Audience analysis that focuses on situational factors such as the size of the audience, the physical setting for the speech, and the disposition of the audience toward the topic, the speaker, and the occasion.

SIZE

Outside the classroom, the size of an audience can, with the aid of television and radio, range in the millions. Most speech classes, however, consist of between 20 and 30 people—a small- to medium-sized audience. This is a good size for beginning speakers, most of whom are terrified at the prospect of addressing a huge crowd. As you gain more experience, though, you may welcome the challenge of speaking to larger groups. Some speakers actually prefer a large audience to a small one.

No matter what size group you are addressing, bear in mind one basic principle: The larger the audience, the more formal your presentation must be. Audience size may also affect your language, choice of appeals, and use of visual aids.

PHYSICAL SETTING

Which of the following would you rather address?

An audience assembled immediately after lunch, crammed into an overheated room with inadequate seating

An audience assembled at 10:00 in the morning, comfortably seated in an airy, well-lighted room

Undoubtedly you chose the second option. Any of the adverse conditions listed in the first could seriously impair your audience's willingness to accept your ideas or even listen to you at all.

When you face any speaking situation, it is important to know in advance if there will be any difficulties with the physical setting. For classroom speeches, of course, you already do know. But speeches outside the classroom can present unpleasant surprises unless you do your homework beforehand.

When you are invited to speak, don't be shy about asking questions of the person who arranged the speech. If possible, look over the room a few days in advance, or else arrive early on the day of your speech to inspect the room. If it is too warm or too cold, see about adjusting the thermostat. Check the seating arrangements and the location of the lectern to be sure your audience can see you. In short, do everything you can to control the influence of physical setting on your audience.

What about circumstances you can't control? Your speech *is* scheduled directly after lunch or dinner. The room *is* too small for the audience expected. The heat *cannot* be regulated. Then you are simply going to have to work harder to adapt to these aspects of your listeners' discomfort. When faced with an audience that is potentially hot, sleepy, and cross, do your best to make the speech as interesting and lively as you can. Above all, don't be influenced *yourself* by the poor physical setting. If your audience sees that you are energetic, alert, and involved with your topic, chances are they will forget their discomfort and come right along with you.

DISPOSITION TOWARD THE TOPIC

As we saw in Chapter 4, you should keep your audience in mind when choosing a topic. Ideally, you will pick a topic that suits them as well as it suits you. Once you have your topic, however, you must consider in more detail their interest in the topic, knowledge about it, and attitudes toward it.

Interest

Outside the classroom, people do not often expend the time and effort to attend a speech unless they are interested in the topic. But the members of your speech class are a captive audience. Sometimes they will be deeply interested in your topic, particularly if it relates directly to them. Most of the time they will range from fairly interested to mildly curious to downright indifferent.

One of your tasks will be to assess their interest in advance and to adjust your speech accordingly. Most important, if your topic is not likely to generate great interest, you must take special steps to get your classmates involved. Here is a brief example of how to do this:

Sharon wanted to persuade her classmates to vote on a regular basis. She started by saying: "Suppose a total stranger was responsible for making life-or-death decisions about your life. You'd want to have a say in who that person was, wouldn't you? Well, total strangers do make decisions that affect you every single day—those total strangers are called members of Congress, Senators, and the President. And you can help choose all those people by doing one simple thing—voting on election day."

In the chapters that follow, we'll look closely at all the ways you can develop interest in your topic—by an arresting introduction, provocative supporting materials, vivid language, dynamic delivery, visual aids, and so forth.

Knowledge

There is often a strong correlation between interest in a topic and knowledge about it. People tend to be interested in what they know about. Likewise, they are inclined to learn about subjects that interest them. But there are exceptions. Few students know much about handwriting analysis, yet most would find it an absorbing topic. On the other hand, almost all know a lot about checking books out of the library, but few would find it a fascinating subject for a speech.

Your listeners' knowledge about your topic will to a large extent determine what you can say in your speech. If your listeners know little about your topic—whether or not they find it interesting—you will have to talk at a more elementary level. If they are reasonably well informed, you can take a more technical and detailed approach.

Attitude

The attitude of your listeners toward your topic can be extremely important in determining how you handle the material. If you know in advance the prevailing attitude among members of your audience, you can adjust your speech to address their concerns or to answer their objections. Consider the experiences of the following two students—one who did not account for listener attitude and one who did:

> Jen Salerno spoke about family-leave policies in the workplace. On the basis of her research, she believed there was evidence that such policies unfairly benefited a few parents at the expense of other employees, such as single people and childless couples. Unfortunately, rather than citing her sources and acknowledging that her point of view was controversial, Jen presented her material as though it were general knowledge.
>
> The speech was not well received. As one student commented, "You may be right in what you say, but I have trouble believing it. We've heard so much about the need for businesses to be family-friendly—can it all be wrong? I think you would have been more persuasive if you had looked at both sides of the issue rather than just your own."

Had Jen taken the skepticism of her audience into account and established the credibility of her sources, she might have made her arguments more convincing to her audience.

Compare the approach of Peter Kovals, who also espoused a controversial viewpoint:

> A firm opponent of steroids and other performance-enhancing drugs, Peter decided to give a persuasive speech calling for mandatory drug testing of high-school athletes. After distributing an audience-analysis questionnaire among his classmates, Peter found that three-fourths of them opposed his plan. They gave two major reasons. First, they did not believe it was necessary. Second, they saw it as an invasion of privacy.

connectlucas.com
View the beginning of "Make Your Voice Heard: Get Out and Vote" in the online Media Library for this chapter (Video Clip 5.2).

attitude
A frame of mind in favor of or opposed to a person, policy, belief, institution, etc.

connectlucas.com
View an excerpt from "Keeping Steroids Out of High-School Sports" in the online Media Library for this chapter (Video Clip 5.3).

Although Peter disagreed with those beliefs, he realized he could neither ignore them nor insult his classmates for holding them. He knew he would have to discuss these points logically and with hard evidence if he were to have any chance of persuading his audience.

As it turned out, Peter did convince some members of the class to reconsider their beliefs. He could not have done so without first investigating what those beliefs were and then adapting his message to them.[7]

DISPOSITION TOWARD THE SPEAKER

Let's return for a moment to Jen's speech about family leave. Jen was a first-year student with no special background in workplace issues. It's not surprising that her classmates took her statements with a large grain of salt. But suppose Jen had been a recognized expert who had conducted research on the impact of family leave on employee attitudes and business productivity. Then her listeners would have found her much more believable. Why? Because an audience's response to a message is invariably colored by their perception of the speaker.

The more competent listeners believe a speaker to be, the more likely they are to accept what he or she says. Likewise, the more listeners believe that a speaker has their best interests at heart, the more likely they are to respond positively to the speaker's message.

We will come back to this subject in detail when we deal with strategies for persuasive speaking in Chapter 16. For now, keep in mind that your listeners will always have *some* set of attitudes toward you as a speaker. Estimating what those attitudes are and how they will affect your speech is a crucial part of situational audience analysis.

DISPOSITION TOWARD THE OCCASION

It was Commencement Day at Dos Pueblos High School. The mood was festive as the valedictorian spoke eloquently about the special memories of the graduating class. There was laughter when the principal recounted a well-known prank from the class picnic.

Then Tim Harrington, the mayor, rose to say a few words. "What a pleasure it is to be here," he said. "I'm so proud of you, the graduates, and you, the parents who raised such a terrific group of kids." He continued in this vein for a couple minutes, interrupted by applause as he heaped praise on the students, their parents, their teachers, and their community.

The listeners' enthusiasm faded as Harrington began talking about the town's growth in recent years. He spoke glowingly about the condominiums, shopping centers, and office buildings that had risen on formerly unused land. He implied that citizens who wanted to slow the pace of growth were shortsighted and backward looking. When he concluded, he was met with grudging applause and quite a few hostile glares.

On other occasions, Harrington's remarks would not have touched off such a negative response. But graduation day was understood by the audience to be a celebratory occasion that focused on the students and their achievements. The last thing anyone expected to hear was a political speech. What angered the audience was not what the mayor said, but that he exploited the occasion for his own purposes.

No matter what the situation, listeners have fairly definite ideas about the speeches they consider appropriate. Speakers who seriously violate those expectations can almost always count on infuriating the audience.

Situational audience analysis provides crucial information that a speaker can use when preparing the speech and when adapting to developments during the speech.

Perhaps most important, the occasion will dictate how long a speech should be. When you are invited to speak, the chairperson will usually say how much time you have for your talk. If not, be sure to ask. And once you know, pare down your speech so it fits easily within the allotted time. Do not exceed that time under any circumstances, for you are likely to see your audience dwindle as you drone on. (This is one reason why most teachers insist that classroom speeches be kept within the designated time limit. It provides crucial training for speeches you will give outside the classroom.)

There are other audience expectations that apply to your classroom situation. One is that speeches will conform to the assignment. Another is that speakers will observe appropriate standards of taste and decorum. Failure to adhere to these expectations may disturb your classmates and will almost certainly damage your grade.

Getting Information About the Audience

Now that you know *what* to learn about an audience, the next question is, *how* do you learn it? A person running for high political office can rely on hired professional pollsters. If, as is more likely, you are invited sometime to address a particular group—say a meeting of the local Rotary club—the person who invites you can usually provide a good sketch of the audience. Ask your contact where you can find out more about the group's history and purpose. Best of all, if you know someone who has spoken to the same group, be sure to sound out that person.

What about your classmates as an audience? You can learn a lot about them just by observation and conversation. Still, you probably will need to know more about their backgrounds and opinions in relation to specific speech topics. Some teachers require students to do a formal audience-analysis questionnaire for at least one of their speeches.

Constructing questionnaires is not something you can be expected to master in a speech class. By following a few basic guidelines, however, you can learn to develop a good questionnaire for analyzing your classroom audience.

There are three major types of questions to choose from: fixed-alternative questions, scale questions, and open-ended questions.

fixed-alternative questions
Questions that offer a fixed choice between two or more alternatives.

Fixed-alternative questions, as their name implies, offer a fixed choice between two or more responses. For example:

Do you know what the insanity plea is in the U.S. legal system?

Yes _____

No _____

Not sure _____

By limiting the possible responses, such questions produce clear, unambiguous answers. They also tend to yield superficial answers. Other techniques are needed to get beneath the surface.

scale questions
Questions that require responses at fixed intervals along a scale of answers.

Scale questions resemble fixed-alternative questions, but they allow more leeway in responding. For example:

How often do you believe the insanity plea is used in U.S. court cases?

Very seldom ————————|————————|————————|————————|———————— Very often

Questions like these are especially useful for getting at the strength of a respondent's attitudes.

open-ended questions
Questions that allow respondents to answer however they want.

Open-ended questions give maximum leeway in responding. For example:

What is your opinion about the insanity plea in U.S. court cases?

Under what circumstances do you think the insanity plea is legitimate in a criminal trial?

Although open-ended questions invite more detailed responses than the other two types of questions, they also increase the likelihood of getting answers that do not give the kind of information you need.

Because each type of question has its advantages and disadvantages, many questionnaires contain all three types. Figure 5.1 (page 111) shows a questionnaire that was distributed before a classroom speech on volunteering. By using all three types of questions, the speaker did two things—elicited specific information about the audience and probed more deeply into their attitudes toward the speech topic. The results broke down as follows:

1. Roughly half of the class had participated as a volunteer. Therefore, the speaker knew she would have to explain clearly what was involved in this kind of work.

2. Five students knew someone close to them who had benefited from volunteer work by a community, religious, or charitable organization; most said they were not sure. Thus the speaker could not depend on a high degree of personal involvement among the audience.

Two fixed-alternative questions establish the listeners' level of knowledge about and degree of involvement with the topic.

1. Have you ever engaged in volunteer work for a community, religious, or charitable organization?

   Yes ______

   No ______

2. Have you or anyone close to you ever benefited from the volunteer work of a community, religious, or charitable organization?

   Yes ______

   No ______

   Not sure ______

This scale question is designed to show the attitudes of listeners who have participated in volunteer work.

3. If you have engaged in volunteer work, how would you rate the experience?

   ☐ Very rewarding
   ☐ Somewhat rewarding
   ☐ Neutral
   ☐ Somewhat unrewarding
   ☐ Very unrewarding

Another scale question gauges the listeners' sense of social obligation.

4. Do you agree or disagree with the following statement? To the extent possible, people have an obligation to help those in less fortunate circumstances.

   ☐ Strongly agree
   ☐ Mildly agree
   ☐ Undecided
   ☐ Mildly disagree
   ☐ Strongly disagree

Two open-ended questions help gauge the listeners' disposition toward volunteer work. The last question is especially important. It probes the specific issues the speaker needs to address for listeners who have not engaged in volunteer work.

5. If you have worked as a volunteer, do you plan to do so again? Why or why not?

6. If you have not worked as a volunteer, what is your major reason for not doing so? Please explain.

• FIGURE 5.1
Sample Questionnaire.

3. All but one of the students who had engaged in volunteer work rated it "very rewarding" or "somewhat rewarding." Not only would this portion of the audience be inclined to support the speaker's position, but the speaker could point to their attitude as proof that work as a volunteer is a rewarding experience.

4. Nearly 75 percent of the respondents either "strongly agreed" or "mildly agreed" that people have an obligation to help those in less fortunate circumstances. The speaker could therefore depend on an audience favorably inclined to the basic premise underlying volunteer work.

5. Answers to the fifth question—"If you have worked as a volunteer, do you plan to do so again? Why or why not?"—were interesting. All the respondents indicated that they planned to engage in volunteer work again, but most

said they were not likely to do so while in college because they were too busy with other activities.

6. Nearly 90 percent of the students who had not engaged in volunteer work stated that their major reason for not doing so was a lack of time. In combination with the answers to question 5, these responses showed that the speaker would have to deal persuasively with the time issue if she were to be successful in convincing people to volunteer while they were enrolled in school.

This questionnaire revealed a great deal about the listeners' knowledge, attitudes, and concerns. In putting together your own questionnaire, keep the following principles in mind:

1. Plan the questionnaire carefully to elicit precisely the information you need.

2. Use all three types of questions—fixed-alternative, scale, and open-ended.

3. Make sure the questions are clear and unambiguous.

4. Keep the questionnaire relatively brief.

connectlucas.com
You can create your own class survey by using the Questionnaire Maker in the online Speech Tools for this chapter.

Adapting to the Audience

Once you have completed the audience analysis, you should have a pretty clear picture of your listeners. But this does not guarantee a successful speech. The key is how well you *use* what you know in preparing and presenting the speech.

This point deserves special attention because it poses one of the hardest tasks facing novice speakers. Most people can identify the major characteristics of their audience, but many have trouble *adapting* their ideas to the audience. There are two major stages in the process of audience adaptation. The first occurs before the speech, as part of your preparation and rehearsal. The second occurs during the presentation of the speech itself.

connectlucas.com
View how the speakers in Video Clips 5.2 and 5.3 used audience-analysis questionnaires in their speeches (Video Clip 5.4 in the online Media Library for this chapter).

AUDIENCE ADAPTATION BEFORE THE SPEECH

As we have seen, you must keep your audience in mind at every stage of speech preparation. This involves more than simply remembering who your listeners will be. Above all, it means two things: (1) assessing how your audience is likely to respond to what you say in your speech, and (2) adjusting what you say to make it as clear, appropriate, and convincing as possible.

This is not always easy to do. We are all so wrapped up in our own ideas and concerns that we have trouble seeing things from other people's perspective—especially if their perspective is quite different from ours. To step outside your own frame of reference and see things from another person's point of view is a real achievement.

Yet this is what a successful speaker eventually learns to do. You must submerge your own views so completely that you can adopt, temporarily, those of your listeners. When you do this, you will begin to hear your speech through the ears of your audience and to adjust it accordingly. Try to imagine what they

In political campaigns, poll-taking helps the candidates keep track of public opinion. For classroom speeches, you can use an audience-analysis questionnaire to gauge the knowledge and opinions of your listeners.

will like, what they will dislike, where they will have doubts or questions, whether they will need more details here or fewer there, what will interest them and what will not.

At every point you must *anticipate* how your audience will respond. How will they react to your introduction and conclusion? Will they find your examples clear and convincing? Will your visual aids help them grasp your ideas? How will they respond to your language and manner of delivery? As you answer these questions, consciously identify with your listeners. Put yourself in their place and respond to your speech as they would.

Here is how one student worked out his problems of audience adaptation:

Juan Ruiz, a junior geology major, decided to give an informative speech about how earthquakes occur. From his audience analysis he learned that only two or three of his classmates knew much of anything about geology. To most of them, a tectonic plate would be found on a dinner table rather than below the surface of the earth. Juan realized, then, that he must present his speech at an elementary level and with a minimum of scientific language.

As he prepared the speech, Juan kept asking himself, "How can I make this clear and meaningful to someone who knows nothing about earthquakes or geological principles?" Since he was speaking in the Midwest, he decided to begin by noting that the most severe earthquake in American history took place not in California or Alaska, but at New Madrid, Missouri, in 1811. If such an earthquake happened today, it would be felt from the Rocky Mountains to the Atlantic Ocean and would flatten most of the cities in the Mississippi Valley. That, he figured, should get his classmates' attention.

Throughout the body of the speech, Juan dealt only with the basic mechanics of earthquakes and carefully avoided technical terms such as "asthenosphere," "lithosphere," and "subduction zones." He also prepared visual aids diagramming fault lines so his classmates wouldn't get confused.

To be absolutely safe, Juan asked his roommate—who was not a geology major—to listen to the speech. "Stop me," he said, "anytime I say something you don't understand." Juan's roommate stopped him four times, and at each spot Juan worked out a way to make his point more clearly. Finally, he had a speech that was interesting and perfectly understandable to his audience.

As you work on your speeches, try to keep your listeners constantly in mind. Anticipate how they will respond to your ideas. Be creative in thinking about ways to adapt your message to them. Like Juan, you will give a much better speech.

AUDIENCE ADAPTATION DURING THE SPEECH

No matter how hard you prepare ahead of time, things may not go exactly as planned on the day of your speech. For speeches in the classroom you may find that the projector for your visual aids is not available or that another student has the same topic as you. For speeches outside the classroom you might learn that the room for your speech has been changed, that the audience will be much larger (or smaller) than you had anticipated, or even that the amount of time available for your speech has been cut in half because a previous speaker has droned on for too long.

If something like this happens to you, don't panic. Find another way to present your visual aids. Modify your introduction to mention the other student's speech on your topic. Adjust your delivery to the changed audience size. If you find you have less time than you had planned, condense your speech to its most essential points and present them in the time available. Your listeners will sympathize with your predicament and will appreciate your regard for their time. This will more than compensate for your lost speaking time.

Finally, be sure to keep an eye out during your speech for audience feedback. If your listeners are sitting forward in their chairs, looking at you with interest, and nodding their heads in approval, you can assume things are going well. But suppose you find them frowning or responding with quizzical looks. Then you may need to back up and go over your point again, as in this example:

Myla Hanson, an economics major, had worked diligently to make sure her speech on the U.S. trade deficit was not too technical for her classmates. She explained everything from the ground up, prepared two excellent visual aids, and practiced giving the speech to her best friend, a music major and self-confessed "economics imbecile."

On the day of Myla's speech, everything went well until she got to her second main point, when she noticed that several of her classmates seemed puzzled by the relationship between international trade deficits and the U.S. cost of living. Knowing they would be lost for the rest of the speech if they didn't understand that relationship, Myla paused and said, "I can see some of you are confused by my explanation. Let me try it again from a different angle."

As Myla went through the material again, she could see her classmates nodding their heads in understanding. She could now go on with her speech, confident that her audience was ready to go with her.

Adapting to your audience is one of the most important keys to successful public speaking. Like other aspects of speechmaking, it is sometimes easier said than done. But once you master it, you'll see that it pays dividends in more personal facets of your life—when you adapt to an audience of one.

SUMMARY

Good speakers are audience-centered. They know that the aim of speechmaking is to gain a desired response from listeners. When working on your speeches, keep three questions in mind: To whom am I speaking? What do I want them to know, believe, or do as a result of my speech? What is the most effective way of composing and presenting my speech to accomplish that aim?

To be an effective speaker, you should know something about the psychology of audiences. People are egocentric. They typically approach speeches with one question uppermost in mind: "Why is this important to *me*?" Therefore, you need to study your audience and adapt your speech directly to their beliefs and interests.

The first stage in learning about your audience is to identify demographic traits such as age, gender, sexual orientation, religion, group membership, and racial, ethnic, or cultural background. The second stage is identifying traits of the audience unique to the speaking situation. These traits include the size of the audience, attitudes influenced by the physical setting, and your listeners' disposition toward the topic, toward you as a speaker, and toward the occasion.

For speeches outside the classroom, you can best get information about the audience by asking the person who invites you to speak. For classroom speeches, you can learn about your audience by observation and conversation. You also can circulate an audience-analysis questionnaire.

Once you complete the audience analysis, you must adapt your speech so it will be clear and convincing to your listeners. Put yourself in their place. Try to hear the speech as they will. Anticipate questions and objections, and try to answer them in advance. When you deliver your speech, keep an eye out for audience feedback and adjust your remarks in response.

KEY TERMS

audience-centeredness *(96)*

identification *(97)*

egocentrism *(98)*

demographic audience analysis *(100)*

stereotyping *(100)*

situational audience analysis *(105)*

attitude *(107)*

fixed-alternative questions *(110)*

scale questions *(110)*

open-ended questions *(110)*

REVIEW QUESTIONS

After reading this chapter, you should be able to answer the following questions:

1. Why must a public speaker be audience-centered?

2. What does it mean to say that people are egocentric? What implications does the egocentrism of audiences hold for you as a public speaker?

connectlucas.com

For further review, go to the Study Questions in the online Study Aids for this chapter.

3. What are the six demographic traits of audiences discussed in this chapter? Why is each important to audience analysis?

4. What is situational audience analysis? What factors do you need to consider in situational audience analysis?

5. How can you get information about an audience?

6. What are the three kinds of questions used in questionnaires? Why is it a good idea to use all three in audience analysis?

7. What methods can you use to adapt your speech to your audience before the speech? During the speech?

EXERCISES FOR CRITICAL THINKING

1. Advertisers are usually very conscious of their audience. Choose an issue of a popular magazine such as *Time, Newsweek, Sports Illustrated, Cosmopolitan,* or the like. From that issue select five advertisements to analyze. Try to determine the audience being appealed to in each advertisement, and analyze the appeals (verbal and visual) used to persuade buyers. How might the appeals differ if the ads were designed to persuade a different audience?

2. Below are three general speech topics and, for each, two hypothetical audiences to which a speech might be delivered. For each topic, write a brief paragraph explaining how you might adjust your specific purpose and message according to the demographic characteristics of the audience.

   a. *Topic:*   "Data Encryption"

       Audience #1:   50% computer science majors, 30% physics majors, 20% fine arts majors

       Audience #2:   40% business majors, 40% history majors, 20% computer science majors

   b. *Topic:*   "Sexual Assault: The Biggest Campus Crime"

       Audience #1:   80% female, 20% male

       Audience #2:   80% male, 20% female

   c. *Topic:*   "The Fall of the Berlin Wall"

       Audience #1:   Day class: 70% age 18 to 22, 30% age 23 and over

       Audience #2:   Evening class: 50% age 35 and over, 30% age 23 to 34, 20% age 18 to 22

3. For your next speech, design and circulate among your classmates an audience-analysis questionnaire like that discussed on pages 109–112. Use all three kinds of questions explained in the text: fixed-alternative, scale, and open-ended. After you have tabulated the results of the questionnaire, write an analysis explaining what the questionnaire reveals about your audience and what steps you must take to adapt your speech to the audience.

As an economics professor, your research, writing, and teaching on the Social Security system has attracted media attention. People seem particularly interested in your scholarly opinion because you support proposals that would allow workers to invest part of their Social Security contributions in personal retirement accounts. Aware of your perspective, the local Rotary club has invited you to speak on the subject at the club's weekly meeting.

Having taken a public speaking class in college, you know how important it is to analyze the audience you will be addressing. To prepare for your speech, you have arranged a telephone interview with the club's president to find out more about your audience. List (1) the two most important questions you want to ask the president about the demographics of your audience, and (2) the two most important questions you want to ask about the situational traits of your audience. Be specific in your questions and be prepared, if necessary, to explain your choice of questions.

Gathering Materials

uppose you are planning a trip to Spain. You want to know the major sites so you can work out an itinerary. You also need to know what things will cost, where the hostels are located, and how the train and bus systems work. How do you go about gathering all this information?

You can talk to people who have traveled in Spain and get ideas from them. You can consult guidebooks. You can search the Internet for information. If you have traveled to Europe before, you can draw on that experience. Since you want your trip to be a success, you gather as much information as you can before you leave.

Gathering materials for a speech is like gathering information for any project. There are many resources available if you take advantage of them. You can interview people with specialized knowledge. You can do research on the Internet or in the library. Sometimes you can use yourself as a resource—whenever you have personal experience or above-average knowledge about a subject. Let's turn first to the resource of your own experience.

Using Your Own Knowledge and Experience

Everybody is an expert on something, whether it is video games, child care, or backpacking. As we saw in Chapter 4, we often speak best about subjects with which we are familiar. This is why teachers encourage students to capitalize on their own knowledge and experience in developing speech topics.

When you choose a topic from your own experience, you may be tempted to depersonalize it by relying solely on facts and figures from books. Such outside information is almost always necessary. But supplementing it with the personal touch can really bring your speeches to life.

One student, afflicted with diabetes, chose to explain how a person can live with the disease on a daily basis. He cited statistics on the incidence of diabetes in the United States, identified symptoms of the disease, and related how it is treated. Along the way he illustrated his points by talking about his personal experiences. Here is part of what he said:

Being a diabetic presents a challenge one cannot afford to lose. On a personal note, I have tried not to let my diabetes affect my lifestyle. Last year I spent nine months traveling in Central and South America. The trip was very memorable, but I had one particularly frightening experience that quickly makes you realize just how vulnerable a diabetic is. On the fifth day of a two-week excursion down the Amazon River in Brazil, our canoe tipped, dumping everything into the river.

Although I recovered my pack, part of its contents—including my insulin—were swallowed up by the river. Without insulin I could not eat any food, for if I did, my blood sugar level would become too high and I could eventually go into convulsions, slip into a coma, and die. We returned back up the Amazon and traveled three days until we reached the first village and I could radio for more medicine. I was hot and hungry, but alive.

This speech has color and emotion. By drawing on his own experience, the speaker conveyed his point much more meaningfully than he could have in any other way.

Even if your life stories are not that dramatic, you can still put them to work for you. By thinking over your past experiences—gathering material from yourself—you can find many supporting details for your speeches.

Even in this age of the Internet, you will get some of the information for your speeches from the library. It contains many resources to help you find what you need, including librarians, the catalogue, periodical databases, newspapers, and reference works. We'll look at each in turn.

LIBRARIANS

Too often students waste their time wandering aimlessly in the library because they are afraid to ask for assistance. They don't want to appear stupid or to "bother" anyone. But would you be as sensitive about asking a doctor for help with a medical problem? Librarians are experts in their own field, trained in library use and research methods. If you have a question, don't hesitate to ask a librarian. He or she can help you find your way, locate sources, even track down a specific piece of information.

catalogue
A listing of all the books, periodicals, and other resources owned by a library.

THE CATALOGUE

The catalogue lists all the books, periodicals, and other resources owned by the library. Although there are many different computer systems for library catalogues, most allow you to search for books by author, title, subject, or keyword. The catalogue also tells you whether the book you want is available or is already checked out.

Figure 6.1 below shows a sample catalogue entry for a book. The key to finding the book on the shelves is the *call number*. Once you have the call number, all you have to do is find the right section of the shelves (or stacks, as they are called in some libraries) and retrieve your book.

call number
A number used in libraries to classify books and periodicals and to indicate where they can be found on the shelves.

PERIODICAL DATABASES

Periodical databases allow you to locate magazine or journal articles. Type the subject on which you want information in the database's search box, and citations of articles on your subject will appear on screen. You can then call up the full text of the articles.

periodical database
A research aid that catalogues articles from a large number of journals or magazines.

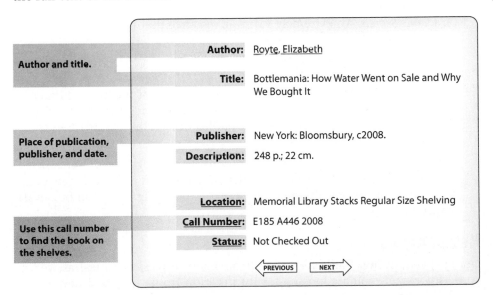

Author and title.

Author: Royte, Elizabeth

Title: Bottlemania: How Water Went on Sale and Why We Bought It

Place of publication, publisher, and date.

Publisher: New York: Bloomsbury, c2008.

Description: 248 p.; 22 cm.

Location: Memorial Library Stacks Regular Size Shelving

Use this call number to find the book on the shelves.

Call Number: E185 A446 2008

Status: Not Checked Out

PREVIOUS   NEXT

• FIGURE 6.1
Sample Catalogue Entry for a Book.

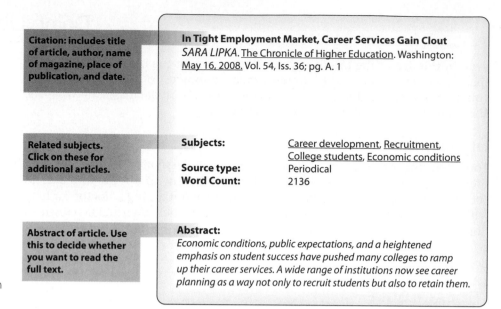

Citation: includes title of article, author, name of magazine, place of publication, and date.

In Tight Employment Market, Career Services Gain Clout
SARA LIPKA. <u>The Chronicle of Higher Education</u>. Washington: <u>May 16, 2008.</u> Vol. 54, Iss. 36; pg. A. 1

Related subjects. Click on these for additional articles.

Subjects: <u>Career development</u>, <u>Recruitment</u>, <u>College students</u>, <u>Economic conditions</u>
Source type: Periodical
Word Count: 2136

Abstract of article. Use this to decide whether you want to read the full text.

Abstract:
Economic conditions, public expectations, and a heightened emphasis on student success have pushed many colleges to ramp up their career services. A wide range of institutions now see career planning as a way not only to recruit students but also to retain them.

• **FIGURE 6.2**

Sample Periodical Entry from ProQuest Research Library.

abstract

A summary of a magazine or journal article, written by someone other than the original author.

In some cases, you may get an *abstract* of the article in addition to—or instead of—the full text. Keep in mind, however, that the abstract is only a summary of the article. You should never cite an article in your speech on the basis of the abstract alone. Always consult the full article.

The exact databases you can use will depend on what is available in your library. Here are four of the major, all-purpose databases. Odds are that your library will have at least one of them.

ProQuest Research Library. An excellent database that indexes more than 4,000 general-interest periodicals and academic journals and provides the full text of articles from more than half of them. Dates vary, but many of the full-text articles go back to 1988. Figure 6.2 shows a sample screen from ProQuest Research Library with a magazine citation and abstract.

Academic Search. An extremely valuable resource that provides the full text of articles from thousands of periodicals, popular and scholarly alike. It also indexes articles from *The New York Times, The Wall Street Journal,* and *The Christian Science Monitor.*

Reader's Guide Full Text. The electronic counterpart of the printed *Reader's Guide to Periodical Literature,* this database indexes and abstracts articles from more than 500 general-interest publications. Full-text articles are provided for over 300 periodicals.

Lexis/Nexis Academic. Composed of roughly 40,000 legal, news, reference, and business sources, this powerful database provides full-text access to a wide range of periodicals and other sources, including television broadcast transcripts.

NEWSPAPERS

Newspapers are invaluable for research on many topics, historical as well as contemporary. If you are looking for information from your local newspaper,

Library research is vital for most speeches. Knowing the resources available in your library and how to use them efficiently will make the research process much more productive.

your library will probably have current issues in the periodicals room. Back issues may be available on microfilm.

For national and international newspapers, consult one of the following databases:

ProQuest Newspapers. Indexes articles from more than 700 U.S. and international newspapers. Includes full-text articles for many newspapers back to 1985.

Lexis/Nexis Academic. In addition to magazine articles, Lexis/Nexis furnishes full-text articles from more than 500 U.S. and international newspapers, as well as daily updates from news services such as Reuters and the Associated Press.

Global NewsBank. Provides full-text articles from more than 1,600 international sources, including newspapers.

REFERENCE WORKS

Reference works are usually kept in a part of the library called the reference section. The right reference work can save you hours of time by putting at your fingertips a wealth of information that might be difficult to locate through a database or the library catalogue. The major kinds of reference works you are likely to use for your speeches are encyclopedias, yearbooks, quotation books, and biographical aids.

reference work
A work that synthesizes a large amount of related information for easy access by researchers.

Encyclopedias

We are all familiar with general encyclopedias such as the *Encyclopaedia Britannica* and the *Encyclopedia Americana*. They seek to provide accurate, objective information about all branches of human knowledge and can be an excellent place to begin your research. Many general encyclopedias can also be accessed online.

general encyclopedia
A comprehensive reference work that provides information about all branches of human knowledge.

In addition to general encyclopedias, there are special encyclopedias that cover their fields in much more depth than do general encyclopedias. Some of the most frequently used special encyclopedias are

special encyclopedia
A comprehensive reference work devoted to a specific subject such as religion, art, law, science, music, etc.

African American Encyclopedia

Asian American Encyclopedia

Dictionary of Art

Encyclopedia of Religion

Latino Encyclopedia

McGraw-Hill Encyclopedia of Science and Technology

Yearbooks

yearbook
A reference work published annually that contains information about the previous year.

As the name implies, yearbooks are published annually. They contain an amazing amount of current information that would otherwise be all but impossible to track down. Here are two of the most valuable:

World Almanac and Book of Facts. The *World Almanac* is a treasure trove of information. Among the things you can discover in it are the most-watched television shows of the previous year, professional and collegiate sports records, the literacy rate in Afghanistan, and the natural resources of Peru.

Facts on File. Available in both print and online versions, *Facts on File* is a weekly digest of national and foreign news events. At the end of the year, all the weekly issues are published together as *Facts on File Yearbook*.

Quotation Books

The best-known collection of quotations is *Bartlett's Familiar Quotations*. With more than 25,000 quotations from historical and contemporary figures, it has long been regarded as an indispensable source for speakers and writers alike. Other excellent quotation books include

Oxford Dictionary of Quotations

The New Quotable Woman

My Soul Looks Back, 'Less I Forget: A Collection of Quotations by People of Color

Ancient Echoes: Native American Words of Wisdom

Fire in Our Souls: Quotations of Wisdom and Inspiration by Latino Americans

A Treasury of Jewish Quotations

Biographical Aids

biographical aid
A reference work that provides information about people.

When you need information about people in the news, you can turn to one of the many reference works that contain brief life and career facts about contemporary men and women. They include

International Who's Who

Who's Who in America

Who's Who of American Women
Contemporary Black Biography
Dictionary of Hispanic Biography
Who's Who Among Asian Americans

Searching the Internet ● ●

The Internet has been called the world's biggest library. Unlike a library, however, the Internet has no central information desk, no librarians, no catalogue, and no reference section. Nor does it have a person or department in charge of determining whether materials are of high quality. You can unearth a great deal of information on the Internet, but you cannot always find the same range and depth as in a good library. This is why experts advise that you use the Internet to supplement, not to replace, library research.

In this section, we will look at ways you can go beyond browsing the Web and turn it into a powerful research tool for your speeches. After discussing search engines and other resources for conducting efficient, focused inquiries, we'll explain how to evaluate the reliability and objectivity of the research materials you find on the Web.

SEARCH ENGINES

Search engines are the key to finding materials on the Internet. There are numerous search engines, but the most widely used by far is Google. In addition to providing access to billions of Web pages, it has specialized search tools devoted to images, video, news, blogs, and finance. The question is: How can you use Google and other search engines *systematically* to find what you need? The answer is: Develop a search strategy that will allow you to zero in precisely on the information required for your speech.

Suppose you are using Google to look for information about sports injuries among college cheerleaders. If you simply enter the word *cheerleading* in the search box, you will get a list of every document catalogued by Google that contains the word *cheerleading*—more than 17 million in all. Some will deal with sports injuries among college cheerleaders, but the vast majority will not. Scanning through everything to find what you need would be a daunting task.

How do you limit your search to get more manageable results? If you type *college cheerleading* in Google's search box, you will still come up with more than a million citations. However, if you type "college cheerleading" in quotation marks, you will get only documents that contain the exact phrase "college cheerleading"—46,700 in all.

This is much better, but it's still far too many to go through one by one. So you narrow your search still further. This time you type the following entry into Google's search box:

"college cheerleading" + "sports injury"

The + sign limits the search to items that contain both sets of keywords, "college cheerleading" and "sports injury." This time you get a list of 110 documents, all of which deal specifically with sports injuries among college cheerleaders.

If you were using a search engine other than Google, you might enter different commands. But the basic principles for doing precise, pinpointed searches are similar from search engine to search engine. If you understand those principles, you will greatly increase your odds of finding exactly what you need for your speeches.

SPECIALIZED RESEARCH RESOURCES

Search aids are extremely helpful, but they are not the only vehicles for finding information online. Because the Internet is so vast, it is helpful to have a list of premium Web sites that you can turn to with confidence. In compiling the following list, I have concentrated on sites that are most likely to be helpful to you as you work on your speeches.

Virtual Libraries

virtual library
A search engine that combines Internet technology with traditional library methods of cataloguing and assessing data.

Search engines help you find what's on the Internet, but they don't evaluate the quality of the sources they retrieve. Librarians and other information specialists are working to make it easier to locate reliable, high-quality Web resources. One result of their efforts is virtual libraries—search engines that combine Internet technology with traditional library methods of assessing data. Here are two of the best:

Librarians' Internet Index (www.lii.org). Contains more than 20,000 entries organized into 14 main topics, including arts and humanities, health, law, business, media, science, and recreation.

Internet Public Library (www.ipl.org). In addition to subject collections that range from business to social science, it has links to a large number of reference sources as well as to a wide range of constantly evolving special collections.

Government Resources

One of the great strengths of the Internet as a research tool is the access it provides to government documents and publications. Whether you are looking for information from the federal government or from a state or local agency, chances are you can find it by starting your search at one of these Web sites:

USA.gov (www.usa.gov). One-stop shopping for all U.S. government information on the Internet. Provides links to more than 250 million Web pages from federal, state, local, and tribal governments.

Statistical Abstract (www.census.gov/compendia/statab/). The standard reference source for numerical information on social, political, and economic aspects of American life. Compiled by the Census Bureau, its incredible array of facts are organized in table form.

World Factbook (www.cia.gov/library/publications/the-world-factbook/). Published annually by the Central Intelligence Agency, the *World Factbook* is a rich compendium of information on every country in the world. Topics include people, government, economy, communication, transportation, and transnational issues.

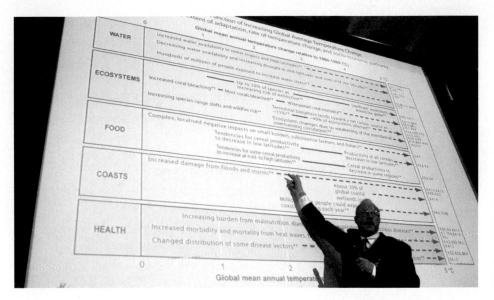

Research gives speakers facts and figures to support their ideas. Here European Union official Martin Parry reports at an intergovernmental meeting on global climate change.

Multicultural Resources

The Internet is a global phenomenon, and it mirrors the internationalism and diversity of our time. If you are speaking on a topic with multicultural dimensions, you may find help at one of the following sites:

Yahoo! Regional (http://dir.yahoo.com/Regional/). A great starting point that offers links to scores of countries and regions around the world, as well as to all 50 states of the U.S.

WWW Virtual Library: American Indians (www.hanksville.org/NAresources). Comprehensive resource with hundreds of links to sites dealing with Native American history, language, culture, education, health, art, and the like.

Princeton University Library Asian-American Studies (http://firestone.princeton. edu/asianamerican/). Provides links to scores of Web sites that feature topics, writings, and organizations of special interest to Asian Americans.

Latino/Hispanic Resources (www-rcf.usc.edu/~cmmr/Latino.html). Maintained by the University of Southern California's Center for Multilingual, Multicultural Research, this outstanding site provides links to a treasure trove of resources devoted to Latino- and Latina-related issues.

African American Web Connection (www.aawc.com). Award-winning Web site that deals with all aspects of African-American life. Also provides links to organizations such as the National Urban League, the Congressional Black Caucus, and the NAACP.

Of course, there are thousands of other useful Web sites. But the ones discussed above, in conjunction with a good search engine, should help get your research off to a good start.[1]

connectlucas.com
You can link to the Web sites identified on pp. 126–127 through the online Research Library for this chapter.

EVALUATING INTERNET DOCUMENTS

When you do research in a library, everything you find has been evaluated in one way or another before it gets to you. Books, magazines, and journals have

Checklist — Evaluating Internet Documents

YES ✓ NO

1. Is the author of the document clearly identified?
2. If the author is identified, is he or she an expert on the topic?
3. If the author is not an expert, can his or her opinions be accepted as objective and unbiased?
4. If the author is not identified, can the sponsoring organization be determined?
5. Is the sponsoring organization a government agency, an educational institution, or a nonprofit group?
6. Does the sponsoring organization have a reputation for expertise and objectivity?
7. Does the document include a copyright date, publication date, or date of last revision?
8. If a date is included, is the document recent enough to cite in my speech?

editorial procedures to determine whether a given work should or should not be published. Once a work is published, it has to be approved by the acquisitions staff for inclusion in the library.

The Internet, of course, is a very different story. The most trusted resources on the Web are those derived from printed works—government records, newspaper articles, research reports, and the like. But most Web documents exist only in electronic form. Of these, few have gone through the kind of editorial review that is designed to ensure a basic level of reliability in printed works. Anyone with a computer and access to the Internet can share his or her opinions with a discussion group, publish an electronic newsletter, or create a personal Web page. Never has the adage been more true than when applied to the Internet: "Don't believe everything you read."

In Chapter 7, we will discuss how to judge the soundness of supporting materials in general. Here we look at three criteria you can use to help distinguish between the jewels and the junk on the Internet.[2]

Authorship

Is the author of the Web document you are assessing clearly identified? If so, what are his or her qualifications? Is the author an expert on the topic? Can her or his data and opinions be accepted as objective and unbiased? Just as you should not cite a book or magazine article without identifying the author and his or her credentials, so you should not cite an electronic work in the absence of this information.

In a book or magazine article, information about the author is usually fairly easy to find. Too often, however, this is not true on the Internet. If you can't find information about the author in the document itself, look for a link to the author's homepage or to another site that explains the author's credentials.

Often you can learn about an author by typing her or his name in the Google search box. If the author is an accepted authority on the subject, there's a good chance Google will turn up information about credentials, publications, and affiliation. If that doesn't work, try checking one of the biographical aids listed earlier in this chapter (pages 124–125).

Sponsorship

Many Web documents are published by businesses, government agencies, public-interest groups, and the like rather than by individual authors. In such cases, you must judge whether the sponsoring organization is impartial enough to cite in your speech. Is the organization objective in its research and fair-minded in its statements? Is it economically unbiased with regard to the issue under discussion? Does it have a history of accuracy and nonpartisanship?

Over the years, some organizations have developed strong reputations for their expertise and objectivity. Many of these are public-interest groups such as Consumers Union, Common Cause, and the American Cancer Society. Others include the National Archives, the Centers for Disease Control, and similar government agencies. Private think tanks such as RAND, the Cato Institute, and the Brookings Institution often have definite political leanings but are usually well respected for the quality and substance of their research.

One way to gauge the credibility of a Web site is to look at the last three letters of its URL. The letters .gov and .edu are reserved for government agencies and educational institutions, respectively. It used to be that .org was used primarily by nonprofit organizations, with .com being used by businesses. Today, however, .org and .com are used by commerical and noncommercial groups alike.

You can also check the "About" link on the sponsoring organization's homepage. Often the resulting screen will identify the site's founders, purpose, or philosophy. If the homepage does not contain an "About" link, this may be a sign that the sponsoring organization is less than forthright and does not meet the necessary standards of objectivity and expertise.

What if you can't verify the credentials of an author or identify a credible sponsoring organization for an Internet document? The answer is easy: Don't use the document in your speech!

sponsoring organization
An organization that, in the absence of a clearly identified author, is responsible for the content of a document on the Internet.

Recency

One of the advantages of using the Internet for research is that it often has more recent information than you can find in print sources. But just because a document is on the Internet does not mean its facts and figures are up-to-the-minute.

The best way to determine the recency of an Internet document is to look for a copyright date, publication date, or date of last revision at the top or bottom of the document. If you are using a source located through a virtual library, you can usually be confident of its currency, as well as its objectivity and reliability. Government and academic sites usually include the date on which the site was last updated.

Once you know the date of the document, you can determine whether it is current enough to use in your speech. This is especially important with regard to statistics, which you should never cite from an undated source, whether in print or on the Internet. If you can't find the date on which a Web document was created or last modified, search for another work whose recency you can verify.

Interviewing

research interview
An interview conducted to gather information for a speech.

Most people think of interviewing in terms of job interviews or conversations with celebrities. But there is another kind of interview—the research (or investigative) interview. Among journalists it is a time-honored way to collect information. It is also an excellent way to gather materials for speeches.

When done well, interviewing (like many things) looks deceptively easy. In practice, it is a complex and demanding art. So before you dash off to conduct your interviews à la Larry King or Barbara Walters, you should understand a few basic principles of effective interviewing. They fall into three groups— what to do before the interview, what to do during the interview, and what to do after the interview.

To illustrate, we'll follow the entire interview process for a hypothetical speech about current issues in college athletics.

BEFORE THE INTERVIEW

The outcome of most interviews is decided by how well the interviewer prepares. Here are five steps you should take ahead of time to help ensure a successful outcome.

Define the Purpose of the Interview

You have done Internet and library research about current issues in college athletics and have a good grasp of the major points of view. But you still have many questions about the situation at your school. You decide the only way to get answers is to interview someone associated with the athletic program. In that decision you have begun to formulate a purpose for the interview.

Decide Whom to Interview

There are several possibilities, but you elect to start at the top—with the athletic director. That may seem a bit presumptuous, but in dealing with administrative organizations, it is usually best to go to the leaders first. They are likely to have a broad understanding of the issues. And if you need more specific information, they can get it for you or put you in touch with the right person.

Arrange the Interview

Because the athletic director is a busy person, you work out a plan for setting up the interview. Knowing that it's easier to brush someone off over e-mail or the telephone than in person, you go to the athletic office to request the interview. The athletic director agrees, and you set up the interview for three days later.

Decide Whether to Record the Interview

The major advantage of recording an interview is that it gives you an exact record you can check later for direct quotes and important facts. Even if you use a recorder, however, you should still take notes by hand in case the recorder malfunctions.

If the athletic director does not want the interview recorded, you will need to rely solely on your handwritten notes. Whatever you do, never smuggle a recorder in without the knowledge or consent of the person being interviewed. Not only is it unethical to do so, but the interviewee is bound to find out and you will only cause yourself trouble.

Prepare Your Questions

You now face the most important of your preinterview tasks—working out the questions you will ask. You should devise questions that are sensible, intelligent, and meaningful. Here are some types of questions to *avoid:*

- Questions you can answer without the interview. (How many sports does your school offer? What is the size of its athletic budget?) Queries like these just waste the subject's time and make you look foolish. Research this information before the interview.

- Leading questions. (Opinion polls show that most Americans believe athletics today have little relation to the academic purposes of a college education. You *do* think it's a problem, too, *don't you?*)

- Hostile, loaded questions. (I think it's disgraceful that many schools spend gobs of money on salaries for football and basketball coaches. Don't you think good teachers for all students are more important than coaches for a few athletes? What do you say to *that,* hmmm?)

You need not shy away from tough questions; just phrase them as neutrally as possible and save them until near the end of the interview. That way, if your interviewee becomes irritated or uncooperative, you'll still get most of the information you want.

When you are finished preparing, you should have a set of direct, specific, reasonable questions, such as the following:

- Recent studies have shown that most colleges—large and small—lose money on athletics. You were quoted last month as saying that our athletic department faces a potential deficit next year. What plans are there to deal with it?

- Do you agree with those who say that college sports are too commercialized? If so, what do you think should be done to solve the problem?

- Maintaining gender equity is a major issue in college athletics. How do you think large schools will fund programs for women if there is a reduced emphasis on revenue-producing sports such as football and basketball?

- In an ideal world, what do you believe should be the role of athletics on a college campus? Do you think we will be closer to that ideal in 10 years than we are today?

Although some experienced journalists conduct interviews with only a few key-word notes on the areas to be covered, you want to be sure not to forget anything during the interview. So you arrange your questions in the order you want to ask them and take the list with you to the interview.

DURING THE INTERVIEW

Every interview is unique. Because the session will seldom go exactly as you plan, you need to be alert and flexible. Here are several steps you can take to help make things proceed smoothly.

Dress Appropriately and Be on Time

The athletic director has a busy schedule and is doing you a favor by agreeing to an interview, so you show up on time. Since the interview is a special occasion, you dress appropriately. This is one way of confirming that you regard the interview as serious business.

Repeat the Purpose of the Interview

The athletic director invites you into the office; you exchange a few introductory remarks. Now, before you plunge into your questions, you take a moment to restate the purpose of the interview. You are more likely to get clear, helpful answers if your subject knows why you are following a certain line of questioning.

Set Up the Recorder, If You Are Using One

If your subject has agreed to being recorded, keep one principle in mind: The recorder should be as casual and inconspicuous as possible. Don't thrust the microphone into your subject's face. Don't fiddle endlessly with the machine. Set it up, turn it on, and then try to ignore it. With luck, your subject will ignore it too.

Keep the Interview on Track

Your goal in the interview is to get answers to the questions you have prepared. Suppose, however, that in answering one of your questions, the athletic director brings up an important point that is not covered on your list of questions. Rather than ignoring the point, you decide to pursue the new issue. You pose a couple questions about it, get helpful answers, then return to your prepared questions.

Throughout the interview, you pursue new leads when they appear, improvise follow-up questions when called for, then move on again in an orderly fashion. When the interview is over, you have answers to all your prepared questions—and a lot more.

Listen Carefully

During the interview, you listen attentively to the athletic director's answers. When you don't understand something, you ask for clarification. If you are not using a recorder and hear a statement you want to quote directly, you ask the athletic director to repeat it to make sure you get it exactly right. Chances are the athletic director will have been misquoted more than once in the press, so he or she will be happy to oblige.

Don't Overstay Your Welcome

Keep within the stipulated time period for the interview, unless your subject clearly wants to prolong the session. When the interview is over, you thank the athletic director for taking the time to talk with you.

Interviewing people with expertise on your speech topic can provide valuable information. When conducting an interview, be sure to listen attentively and to take accurate notes.

AFTER THE INTERVIEW

Although the interview is over, the interviewing process is not. You must now review and transcribe your notes.

Review Your Notes as Soon as Possible

When you leave the athletic director's office, the interview is fresh in your mind. You know what the cryptic comments and scrawls in your notes mean. But as time passes, the details will become hazy. Don't let something like this true story happen to you:

Years ago, a prominent woman—writer and diplomat—was being interviewed by a young reporter. Among other things, the reporter asked about hobbies and leisure activities. The woman replied that she enjoyed skeet shooting and raised Siamese cats. The reporter scribbled in her notes "shoots" and "cats"—but didn't bother to put a comma or a dash between the words. The interview was published. And ever since, that prominent woman has been trying to live down the reputation that she "shoots cats."

In reviewing your notes, try to concentrate on two things—discovering the main points that emerged during the interview and pulling out specific information that might be useful in your speech. If something is unclear, call the athletic director to make sure you have the facts right.

Transcribe Your Notes

Once you settle on the most important ideas and information from the interview, you should transcribe that material so it is in the same format as the rest of your research notes (see pages 134–137). By putting all your research notes in a consistent format, you can arrange and rearrange them easily when you start to organize your speech.[3]

Tips for Doing Research

Few people regard doing research as one of life's great joys. There are ways, however, to make it less tedious and more productive. Here are four ways that are guaranteed to help.

START EARLY

The biggest mistake students make when faced with a research project is waiting too long to begin. The longer you wait, the more problems you will encounter. You may find that a vital book has been checked out of the library or that you no longer have time to arrange a crucial interview. No matter what kind of research you do, you can be sure of one thing. It will *always* take longer than you expect.

Starting early also gives you plenty of time to think about what you find. In researching, you will collect much more material than you will actually use. Preparing a speech is a little like constructing a jigsaw puzzle. Once you gather the pieces, you have to decide how they fit together. The more time you give yourself, the more likely you are to get the pieces to fit just right.

MAKE A PRELIMINARY BIBLIOGRAPHY

In your research, you will run across the titles of books, magazine articles, Internet documents, and so on that look as if they might contain helpful information about your speech topic. Enter *each* item you find in your preliminary bibliography, even though you don't know whether you will use it in your speech. As a result, you may have 15 or 20 works in your preliminary bibliography. But remember that you have not yet examined all those works. Of the 15 or 20 preliminary sources, only 7 or 8 are likely to be of much use. Those final sources will be listed on the bibliography you turn in with your speech outline (see Chapter 10, page 211).

There are two major formats for citing documents in a bibliography. One comes from the Modern Language Association (MLA), the other from the American Psychological Association (APA). Both are widely used by communication scholars; ask your instructor which he or she prefers.

Whichever format you adopt, make sure your bibliography is clear, accurate, and consistent. Figure 6.3 (page 135) lists sample MLA and APA citations for 10 kinds of sources that are cited most frequently in student speeches. You can find a complete set of more than 30 MLA and APA sample citations in the Bibliography Formats in the online Speech Tools for this chapter at connectlucas.com. Once you have the correct information for each of your sources, you can enter it in the BiblioMaker, also available in the online Speech Tools, and it will automatically format your bibliography according to MLA or APA standards.

TAKE NOTES EFFICIENTLY

Asia Marshall started her speech preparation with the best of intentions. She was excited about her topic, "Great Women of Jazz," and she logged on to the Internet to begin researching the same day the assignment was announced. She found several interesting sources and took some notes about them. That evening she checked out a fascinating book about Billie Holiday and read it straight through. She didn't bother taking notes because she was sure she'd remember it all. The next day she looked through the *Encyclopedia of Jazz* and jotted a few notes on the back of her speech syllabus.

Then Asia remembered she had a test in another class. Somewhat panicked, she put aside her speech research to study. When she got back to the speech, the deadline was only

<aside>

preliminary bibliography

A list compiled early in the research process of works that look as if they might contain helpful information about a speech topic.

connectlucas.com
For a complete set of APA and MLA sample citations, check the Bibliography Formats in the online Speech Tools for this chapter.

</aside>

Book: Single author.	**MLA:**	Royte, Elizabeth. *Bottlemania: How Water Went on Sale and Why We Bought It.* New York: Bloomsbury, 2008. Print.
	APA:	Royte, E. (2008). *Bottlemania: How water went on sale and why we bought it.* New York: Bloomsbury.
Signed magazine article.	**MLA:**	Carr, Nicholas. "Is Google Making Us Stupid? What the Internet Is Doing to Our Brains." *Atlantic* July–Aug. 2008: 56–63. Print.
	APA:	Carr, N. (2008, July/August). Is Google making us stupid? What the Internet is doing to our brains. *The Atlantic, 302,* 56–63.
Signed newspaper article.	**MLA:**	Witt, Howard. "Hispanics Lead Pace in Diverse Nation." *Chicago Tribune* 1 May 2008, south-southwest ed., sec. 1: 4. Print.
	APA:	Witt, H. (2008, May 1). Hispanics lead pace in diverse nation. *Chicago Tribune,* section 1, p. 4.
Signed article in reference work.	**MLA:**	Roppolo, Kimberly. "Sweat Lodges." *Encyclopedia of American Indian History.* Eds. Bruce E. Johansen and Barry M. Pritzker. 4 vols. Santa Barbara, CA: ABC-CLIO, 2008. Print.
	APA:	Roppolo, K. (2008). Sweat lodges. In B. Johansen and B. Pritzker (Eds.), *Encyclopedia of American Indian history* (Vol. 2, pp, 473–474). Santa Barbara, CA: ABC-CLIO.
Personal interview.	**MLA:**	Rodriquez, James. Personal interview. 15 Oct. 2008.
	APA:	J. Rodriquez (personal communication, October 15, 2008)
Speech or lecture.	**MLA:**	Hassenzahl, David. "Industrialization and Climate." Environmental Studies 206: Introduction to Climate Change. University of Nevada, Las Vegas. 16 Sept. 2008. Lecture.
	APA:	Hassenzahl, D. (2008, September). Industrialization and climate. Lecture presented in Environmental Studies 206: Introduction to climate change. University of Nevada, Las Vegas.
Television program.	**MLA:**	"The Medicated Child." Narr. Will Lyman. *Frontline.* PBS, WGBH, Boston. 8 Jan. 2008. Television.
	APA:	Gaviria, M. (Writer and Director). (2008). The medicated child [Television series episode]. In R. Aronson-Rath (Senior Producer), *Frontline.* New York and Washington, D.C.: Public Broadcasting Service.
Online government publication.	**MLA:**	United States. Dept. of Health and Human Services. National Institute of Mental Health. *Panic Disorder.* 2 Apr. 2008. *National Institute of Mental Health.* Web. 7 July 2008.
	APA:	National Institute of Mental Health (2008, April). *Panic disorder.* Retrieved from http://www.nimh.nih.gov/health/topics/index.shtml
Online newspaper article.	**MLA:**	Daley, Beth. "Not As Green As They Claim To Be." *Boston Globe* 14 May 2008. *Boston.com.* Web. 5 June 2008.
	APA:	Daley, B. (2008, May 14). Not as green as they claim to be. *Boston Globe.* Retrieved from http://www.boston.com
Online magazine article.	**MLA:**	Ripley, Amanda. "How to Survive a Disaster." *Time* 29 May 2008. *Time.com.* Web. 6 June 2008.
	APA:	Ripley, A. (2008, May 29). How to survive a disaster. *Time.* Retrieved from http://www.time.com

• **FIGURE 6.3** Sample Bibliography Formats.

four days away. She dug out her notes, but what did they mean? One said, "Medford—*important!!!*" But who or what was Medford? Asia had thought she'd remember all about the Billie Holiday book, but without notes it was mostly a blur by now. With a sense of doom, she faced up to the fact that she would have to start over—and finish in four days.

Sound familiar? This has happened to almost everyone at least once. But once is enough. There is a better way to take research notes. Here is a method that has worked well for many students:

Take Plenty of Notes

Few things are more aggravating than trying to recall some bit of information you ran across in your research but neglected to record. The moral of Asia Marshall's story is clear: If there is even an outside chance that you may need a piece of information, make a note of it. This will take a little extra time in the short run, but in the long run it can save you much grief.

Record Notes in a Consistent Format

You should use the same format for all your research notes, whether they come from Internet sources, library documents, or personal interviews. In each case, record the note, the source of the note, and a heading indicating the subject of the note (see Figure 6.4 below).

The importance of the subject heading cannot be overemphasized. It is the first step to more efficient note taking. By telling you at a glance what each note is about, it will greatly simplify the task of organizing your notes when you start to compose the speech. Once you start using subject headings, you'll see how helpful they can be.

Make a Separate Entry for Each Note

Many students try to record all the information from one source on a single note. This is not an effective procedure because it makes your notes almost impossible to review and organize. A better approach is to make a separate note for *each* quotation or piece of information you record. Although you may end up with several notes from the same document, you will find that this approach allows you to keep better track of your research.

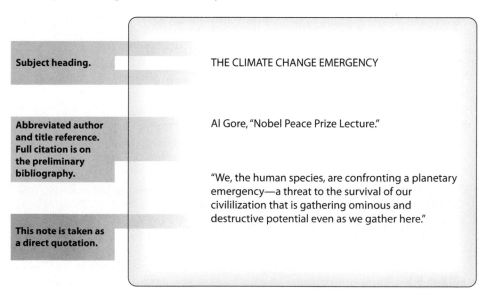

• FIGURE 6.4

Sample Research Note.

To take research notes efficiently, record them in a consistent format; make a separate entry for each note; and distinguish among direct quotations, paraphrases, and your own ideas.

Distinguish Among Direct Quotations, Paraphrases, and Your Own Ideas

As we saw in Chapter 2, it's easy to plagiarize accidentally by not taking careful research notes. As you do research for your speeches, be sure to use quotation marks whenever you copy the exact words of a source. If you paraphrase, rather than quote verbatim, don't forget to include the source when you record the note. By keeping track of quotations and paraphrases, you will be able to separate your own words and ideas from those of other people. This will help you avoid the trap of inadvertent plagiarism when you put your speech together.

THINK ABOUT YOUR MATERIALS AS YOU RESEARCH

Students often approach research as a mechanical routine that simply involves gathering the materials to be used in a speech or paper. But when done properly, research can be extremely creative.

If you *think about* what you are finding in your research, you will see your topic just a little bit differently with each note you take. You will find new relationships, develop new questions, explore new angles. You will, in short, begin to write the speech in your head even as you do the research. As you learn more about the topic, you will formulate a central idea, begin to sketch out main points and supporting points, experiment with ways of organizing your thoughts. You may even change your point of view, as did this student:

Francesca Lopez began her speech preparation with this central idea in mind: "Wild animals make more interesting pets than dogs and cats." She went about her research conscientiously, spending many hours online and in the library. In the process, she came upon some disturbing information about the capture of wild animals. She read that young chimpanzees and other apes were literally snatched out of their mothers' arms, and that the mothers were afterward heard to cry almost like humans. Back in her room that night, Francesca couldn't get her mind off the baby chimpanzees.

The next day Francesca found some more disturbing material. One source told about the extraordinarily high death rate of wild animals during shipment to the United States.

Again, that night Francesca brooded about the young animals dying of fear and cold in the cargo holds of airplanes.

By the time she finished her research, Francesca's central idea was completely different. When she spoke, her central idea was: "The importation of wild animals for use as pets is inhumane."

This is an example of creative research—and of critical thinking. Francesca kept her mind open, read everything she could find about her topic, and thought seriously about what she found. Because of this thoughtful approach, she changed her mind.[4]

Your own speech preparation may not cause you to reverse your position, but it should give you new insights into your topic. If you approach research in this way, you may find that the time you spend researching is the most productive of all the time you devote to preparing your speech.[5]

SUMMARY

There are many resources you can use when gathering information for a speech. If you have personal experience or above-average knowledge about a topic, you can use yourself as a resource. Most of the time, however, you will need outside information, which you can get in the library, on the Internet, or by interviewing people with specialized information.

Finding what you need in the library is largely a matter of knowing how to search for information. The catalogue lists all the books, periodicals, and other resources owned by the library. Databases help you find articles in magazines, journals, and newspapers. The reference section includes encyclopedias, yearbooks, biographical aids, and books of quotations. If you have trouble finding something, don't hesitate to ask a librarian.

When looking for information online, you need a search strategy that will help you find exactly what you need. Given the lack of editorial review for most documents on the Web, it is especially important to evaluate the authorship, sponsoring organization, and recency of the research materials you find there.

You can also get information by conducting a personal interview. Before the interview, you should define its purpose, decide whom you are going to interview, and prepare the interview questions. Once the interview begins, be sure to keep it on track, listen attentively, and take accurate notes. Afterward, review and transcribe your notes as soon as possible.

No matter what sources you draw upon in gathering information, your research will be more effective if you start early and make a preliminary bibliography to keep track of all the books, articles, and Internet documents that look as if they might be helpful. By learning to take research notes effectively, you will save yourself time and energy every step of the way. And if you think about your materials as you research, you may find that gathering materials is the most creative part of your speech preparation.

KEY TERMS

catalogue *(121)*

call number *(121)*

periodical database *(121)*

abstract *(122)*

reference work *(123)*

general encyclopedia *(123)*

special encyclopedia *(124)*

yearbook *(124)*

biographical aid *(124)*

virtual library *(126)*

sponsoring organization *(129)*

research interview *(130)*

preliminary bibliography *(134)*

REVIEW QUESTIONS

After reading this chapter, you should be able to answer the following questions:

1. Why is it important to draw on your own knowledge and experience in gathering materials for your speeches?

2. What are five resources for finding what you need in the library?

3. What are three criteria for evaluating the soundness of research materials that you find on the Internet?

4. What are the three stages of interviewing? What should you do in each stage to help ensure a successful interview?

5. Why is it important to start your speech research early?

6. What is a preliminary bibliography? Why is it helpful to you in researching a speech?

7. What four things should you do to take research notes efficiently?

connectlucas.com
For further review, go to the Study Questions in the online Study Aids for this chapter.

EXERCISES FOR CRITICAL THINKING

1. Using one of the periodical databases discussed on pages 121–122, find three magazine or journal articles on the topic of your next speech. Prepare a preliminary bibliography entry for each article. Read the full text of the articles and assess their value for your speech.

2. Using one of the specialized Internet resources discussed on pages 126–127, find three documents on the topic of your next speech. Prepare a preliminary bibliography entry for each article. Read the full text of the documents and assess them in light of the criteria discussed on pages 127–130 for evaluating Internet documents.

3. Plan to conduct an interview for one of your classroom speeches. Be sure to follow the guidelines presented in this chapter for effective interviewing. Afterward, evaluate the interview. Did you prepare for it adequately? Did you get the information you needed? What would you do differently if you could conduct the interview again?

Applying *the* **Power** *of* **Public Speaking**

As the new owner of a fast-food franchise, you anticipate hiring several high-school students, some of whom might be as young as 14 or 15. Before you can hire them, you need to understand employment restrictions on young workers. Among the questions to which you need answers are the following: (1) How many hours can 14- and 15-year-olds work on school days? (2) Are these hours restricted to certain times of day? If so, what times? (3) If there are conflicts between state and federal child labor regulations, which laws hold sway?

Knowing that the Internet is an excellent source of information for government agencies, you decide to check the U.S. Department of Labor Web site. What answers do you find?

Supporting Your Ideas

A confirmed believer in holistic medicine, Danielle Ashman decided to give her first classroom speech on the uses and benefits of aromatherapy. Part of her speech ran like this:

"All of us suffer from things like colds, headaches, nausea, and stress. How would you like to cure these problems without expensive pills or visits to the doctor? Well, you can with aromatherapy. Aromatherapy has been proven to treat many common ailments, and it works great for me. More than any pill you can buy, aromatherapy just works. You should try it!"

After the speech, Danielle's classmates were polite but skeptical. As one remarked, "Danielle made some interesting points, but she's no doctor. I'd be more convinced if she had some medical evidence to back up her opinion."

Good speeches are not composed of hot air and generalizations. They need strong supporting materials to bolster the speaker's point of view. In Danielle's case, there is evidence that aromatherapy may help in treating some ailments, but most of the claims about its health benefits have yet to be verified by research. So Danielle's listeners were right to be skeptical about her vague, unsupported generalizations.

The problem with generalizations is that they don't answer the three questions listeners always ask of a speaker: "What do you mean?" "Why should I believe you?" "So what?" Consider, for example, the following statements:

General	Less General	Specific
Childhood obesity is a serious problem in the United States.	The incidence of childhood obesity is now so high as to endanger the health of a whole generation of Americans.	At least 15 percent of American children are obese—more than twice the percentage only 25 years ago. The Department of Health and Social Services estimates that in the coming decades obesity will decrease life expectancy in the U.S. by two to five years.

supporting materials
The materials used to support a speaker's ideas. The three major kinds of supporting materials are examples, statistics, and testimony.

Which statement do you find most interesting? Most convincing? Chances are you prefer that in the right-hand column. It is sharp and specific, clear and credible—just what a speech needs to come alive.

The skillful use of supporting materials often makes the difference between a poor speech and a good one. In Chapters 14 and 16, we will look at special uses of supporting materials in informative and persuasive speeches. In this chapter, we focus on the basic kinds of supporting materials—examples, statistics, and testimony—and on general principles for using them effectively and responsibly.

Examples

The attack came after daybreak. The *Delta Ranger*, a cargo ship carrying bauxite, was steaming through the ink-blue Indian Ocean about 200 miles off Somalia's coast. A crewman on the bridge spied two speedboats zooming straight at the port side of his vessel.

Moments later, bullets tore into the bridge, and vapor trails from rocket-propelled grenades streaked across the bow—pirates.

These lines are from the opening of an article in *Smithsonian* magazine about modern-day pirates that prey on international shipping. It illustrates a device well known to magazine writers—and public speakers: Get the audience involved.

See how skillfully this example accomplishes the goal. It gives us a specific incident to focus on (the attack on the *Delta Ranger*). It sets the stage with details of time, place, color, and action. We can almost see ourselves on the bridge of the *Delta Ranger*, watching the pirates' speedboats and hearing their bullets tear into the ship. We would not be nearly as involved if the article had merely said, "Pirates are a growing menace to international shipping."

Research has shown that vivid, concrete examples have strong impact on listeners' beliefs and actions.[1] Without examples, ideas often seem vague, impersonal, and lifeless. With examples, ideas become specific, personal, and lively. This is nowhere better illustrated than in the Bible and the Koran, both of which use all manner of stories, parables, and anecdotes to make abstract principles clear and compelling. There are several kinds of examples you may want to try in your speeches.

BRIEF EXAMPLES

Brief examples—also called specific instances—may be referred to in passing to illustrate a point. The following excerpt uses a brief example to illustrate the miraculous nature of recent advances in creating artificial limbs for accident victims:

> Changes in technology have made it possible for doctors to work wonders that once seemed impossible. *Roger Charter, for example, lost both his feet when they were crushed in a truck accident. Now he has new feet—made of a springy plastic alloy that duplicates a normal arch. Not only can Roger walk normally, but he can run and play sports again!*

Another way to use brief examples is to pile them one upon the other until you create the desired impression. Here is how the technique might be used to reinforce the point that Mexican Americans have made many valuable contributions to U.S. life and culture:

> Many of us are familiar with prominent Mexican Americans such as actress Eva Longoria, boxer Oscar De La Hoya, and guitarist Carlos Santana. But you may be less familiar with other Americans of Mexican origin who have made important contributions to U.S. society. Nancy Lopez played a crucial role in popularizing women's professional golf and won 48 tour championships. Dr. Ellen Ochoa is an astronaut who has logged more than 480 hours in space and has invented several optical methods that aid space exploration. Dr. Mario Molina won the 1995 Nobel Prize in Chemistry for his research on the formation and decomposition of the ozone layer.

EXTENDED EXAMPLES

Extended examples are often called narratives, illustrations, or anecdotes. By telling a story vividly and dramatically, they pull listeners into the speech. Here is such an example, from a speech by Sun Yan, a student at Fudan University in Shanghai, China. Participating in China's national English-language speech competition, Sun Yan used an extended example to illustrate the spirit of the Olympic Games:

example
A specific case used to illustrate or to represent a group of people, ideas, conditions, experiences, or the like.

brief example
A specific case referred to in passing to illustrate a point.

extended example
A story, narrative, or anecdote developed at some length to illustrate a point.

In the history of the Olympic Games, there have been many shining stars. Among them was a European girl. With the lapse of time, her name has faded from memory, yet her unbending spirit shall never perish. It was she who highlighted the Olympic Creed.

In the lead though she had been, she stumbled near the terminus and her leg was injured. Competitors passed her from behind in succession until finally only her weak and lonely figure remained on the track. Doctors came and offered to take her away. Yet she refused. With the only strength left in her, she managed to get up and shuffled feebly to the endpoint with drops of blood along her trail.

But cheers broke out. Though she failed in the race, the girl won applause from people all over the world. It was she who elucidated the Olympic creed of participation. It was she who instilled perseverance in our minds.[2]

This long example captures vividly the courage of the Olympic runner and her personification of the Olympic spirit. The speaker could merely have said, "Olympic athletes often display great fortitude," but the story makes the point far more vividly.

HYPOTHETICAL EXAMPLES

connectlucas.com
View this excerpt from "The Olympic Spirit" in the online Media Library for this chapter (Video Clip 7.1).

hypothetical example
An example that describes an imaginary or fictitious situation.

All the examples presented up to now have been factual; the incidents they refer to really happened. Sometimes, however, speakers will use a hypothetical example—one that describes an imaginary situation. Usually such examples are brief stories that relate a general principle.

Here is how one student used a hypothetical example to illustrate the use of honor codes to reduce cheating:

Imagine this: You're taking your psychology exam when you notice the student sitting next to you is staring at your answers. You also see his open notebook under his desk. You feel your cheeks redden as you become angry that he may get a high score by cheating while you've worked hard to earn your grade. And you feel helpless because you think telling the professor will do nothing.

But now imagine that you attend a school with an honors system. At the beginning of each exam, you sign a statement that says you will not cheat and that you accept the responsibility to report cheating. After the professor hands out the exam, she leaves the room. In this case, you have the power and the duty to report cheaters rather than feel robbed by them.

Such a system has worked elsewhere and it can work at our school. Professor Donald McCabe, president of the Center for Academic Integrity, has surveyed more than 20,000 students at 70 colleges throughout the country, and his research shows that the level of cheating is significantly lower at schools with honor codes than at schools without them.

This hypothetical example is especially effective. The speaker creates a realistic scenario, relates it directly to her listeners, and gets them involved in the speech. In addition, she uses figures from the president of the Center for Academic Integrity to show that honor codes do help reduce the incidence of cheating on college campuses. Whenever you use a hypothetical example, it is a good idea to follow it with statistics or testimony to show that the example is not far-fetched.

connectlucas.com
View this excerpt from "College Cheating: A National Epidemic" in the online Media Library for this chapter (Video Clip 7.2).

TIPS FOR USING EXAMPLES

Use Examples to Clarify Your Ideas

You probably use clarifying examples all the time in everyday conversation. If you were explaining to a friend about different body types, you might say, "Look at Professor Shankar. He's a typical ectomorph—tall, thin, and bony."

Examples are an excellent way to clarify unfamiliar or complex ideas. They put abstract ideas into concrete terms that listeners can easily understand.

This principle works exceptionally well in speeches. Suppose you are talking about suspension bridges. You could give a technical description:

The suspension bridge has a roadway suspended by vertical cables attached to two or more main cables. The main cables are hung on two towers and have their ends anchored in concrete or bedrock.

If your audience were made up of people familiar with structural systems, they might be able to visualize what a suspension bridge looks like. But for listeners lacking this background, you might want to add a simple example:

Two well-known suspension bridges are the Golden Gate Bridge in San Francisco and the Brooklyn Bridge in New York.

Because almost everyone has at least seen a picture of the Golden Gate Bridge or the Brooklyn Bridge, using them as examples clarifies your meaning quickly and effectively.

No matter what the occasion, personal examples are an excellent way to clarify ideas and to build audience interest. To be most effective, they should be delivered sincerely and with strong eye contact.

Use Examples to Reinforce Your Ideas

In a speech titled "Coming Home: The Other Side of War," one student focused on the incidence of post-traumatic stress disorder among soldiers returning from Iraq. He cited figures from the Department of Veterans Affairs noting that 18 percent of American soldiers in Iraq experience post-traumatic stress disorder. He also explained their most common symptoms, including flashbacks, nightmares, depression, anxiety, alcohol or drug abuse, and a sense of social isolation.

To reinforce his ideas, the speaker cited the example of Robert E. Brown, a Marine from Peru, Indiana, who was part of the first wave of troops deployed to Iraq. He talked of how Brown lost his wife and began drinking heavily after returning home. How he recoiled from loud noises and shunned even his friends and family. How his dreams were filled "with ghastly memories that left him a shadow of the strong, confident man he had once been."

This example was especially effective. It put the medical facts about post-traumatic stress disorder in vivid, human terms that everyone could understand. When you use such an example, make sure it is representative—that it does not deal with rare or exceptional cases. Your listeners are likely to feel betrayed if they suspect you have chosen an atypical example to prove a general point.

connectlucas.com
View this portion of "Coming Home: The Other Side of War" in the online Media Library for this chapter (Video Clip 7.3).

Use Examples to Personalize Your Ideas

People are interested in people. As social psychologist Elliot Aronson explains, "Most people are more deeply influenced by one clear, vivid, personal example than by an abundance of statistical data."[3] Whenever you talk to a general audience (such as your speech class), you can include examples that will add human interest to your speech. So far in this section we have seen a number of such examples—the heroic Olympic runner, accident victim Roger Charter, and so on. The abstract becomes more meaningful when applied to a person. Which of the following would you be more likely to respond to?

There are many hungry families in our community who could benefit from food donations.

Or:

Let me tell you about Arturo. Arturo is four years old. He has big brown eyes and a mop of black hair and an empty belly. In all his four years on this earth, Arturo has never once enjoyed three square meals in a single day.

Try using examples with human interest in your speeches. You will soon discover why accomplished speakers consider them "the very life of the speech."[4]

Make Your Examples Vivid and Richly Textured

The richly textured example supplies everyday details that bring the example to life. Recall the example on page 144 of the Olympic runner. The speaker provided us with many details about the runner's bravery in the face of adverse conditions. The runner stumbles and injures her leg near the end of the race. She is passed by other competitors until she alone is left on the track. Doctors offer to help, but she refuses their assistance and shuffles to the finish line with drops of blood along her trail.

How much less compelling the example would have been if the speaker had merely said:

One Olympic runner courageously completed her race despite being injured and exhausted.

Instead, the details let us *see* the runner as she battles through her pain and misfortune. She is much more likely to stay in our minds than a "brave runner who completed her race." The more vivid your examples, the more impact they are likely to have on your audience.

Practice Delivery to Enhance Your Extended Examples

An extended example is just like a story or narrative. Its impact depends as much on delivery as on content. Many students have discovered this the hard way. After spending much time and energy developing a splendid example, they have seen it fall flat because they did not make it vivid and gripping for listeners.

Look again at the speaker in Video Clip 7.1. Notice how she uses her voice to increase the impact of her story about the Olympic runner. Like that speaker, you should think of yourself as a storyteller. Don't rush through your examples as though you were reading the newspaper. Use your voice to get listeners involved. Speak faster here to create a sense of action, slower there to build suspense. Raise your voice in some places; lower it in others. Pause occasionally for dramatic effect.

Most important, maintain eye contact with your audience. The easiest way to ruin a fine example is to read it dully from your notes. As you practice the speech, "talk through" your extended examples without relying on your notes.

Using Examples Checklist

	YES	NO
1. Do I use examples to clarify my ideas?	☐	☐
2. Do I use examples to reinforce my ideas?	☐	☐
3. Do I use examples to personalize my ideas?	☐	☐
4. Are my examples representative of what they are supposed to illustrate or prove?	☐	☐
5. Do I reinforce my examples with statistics or testimony?	☐	☐
6. Are my extended examples vivid and richly textured?	☐	☐
7. Have I practiced the delivery of my extended examples to give them dramatic effect?	☐	☐

connectlucas.com
This checklist is also available in the online Study Tools for this chapter.

By the day of your speech, you should be able to deliver your extended examples as naturally as if you were telling a story to a group of friends.

Statistics

We live in an age of statistics. Day in and day out we are bombarded with a staggering array of numbers: U2 has sold more than 170 million albums; 25 percent of U.S. teenage girls have some form of sexually transmitted disease; Colombia produces 190 million barrels of oil annually; China uses 45 billion pairs of disposable chopsticks each year.

What do all these numbers mean? Most of us would be hard-pressed to say. Yet we feel more secure in our knowledge when we can express it numerically. According to Lord Kelvin, the 19th-century physicist, "When you can measure what you are speaking about, and express it in numbers, you know something about it. But when you cannot measure it, when you cannot express it in numbers, your knowledge is . . . meager and unsatisfactory." It is this widely shared belief that makes statistics, when used properly, such an effective way to clarify and support ideas.[5]

Like brief examples, statistics are often cited in passing to clarify or strengthen a speaker's points. The following examples show how two students used statistics in their speeches:

> To document the role of community colleges in the U.S. educational system: "According to the *Chronicle of Higher Education,* 45 percent of all undergraduates in America study at a community college."

> To illustrate the growing popularity of organic foods: "According to MSNBC News, sales of organic crops now exceed $20 billion a year and are increasing 23 percent annually."

Statistics can also be used in combination to show the magnitude or seriousness of an issue. We find a good instance of this technique in a student presentation on the economic benefits of opening casinos on Native American tribal land. To demonstrate his point that these businesses provide economic

statistics
Numerical data.

benefits to Native Americans and to the surrounding communities, the speaker cited the following figures:

> Across the nation, Native American casinos have created more than 100,000 jobs. Four years after a casino opens, employment in the local area has typically increased by 26 percent, and the percentage of working adults who work but are poor has declined by 14 percent. Among some tribes, the decrease in unemployment is truly startling: Among the Ojibwa of Wisconsin, unemployment plummeted from 70 percent to less than 5 percent. Many other tribes have reported similar results.

This is a well-supported argument. But what if the speaker had merely said:

> Casinos increase employment among Native Americans.

connectlucas.com
View this excerpt from "The Economics of Native-American Casinos" in the online Media Library for this chapter (Video Clip 7.4).

This statement is neither as clear nor as convincing as the one containing statistics. Of course, the audience didn't remember all the numbers, but the purpose of presenting a series of figures is to create an *overall* impact on listeners. What the audience did recall is that an impressive array of statistics supported the speaker's position.

UNDERSTANDING STATISTICS

In his classic book *How to Lie with Statistics,* Darrell Huff exploded the notion that numbers don't lie. Strictly speaking, they don't. But they can be easily manipulated and distorted. For example, which of the following statements is true?

a. Enriched white bread is more nutritious than whole-wheat bread because it contains as much or more protein, calcium, niacin, thiamine, and riboflavin.

b. Whole-wheat bread is more nutritious than white bread because it contains seven times the amount of fiber, plus more iron, phosphorus, and potassium.

As you might expect, *both* statements are true. And you might hear either one of them—depending on who is trying to sell you the bread.

One can play with statistics in all kinds of areas. Which of these statements is true?

a. The cheetah, clocked at 70 miles per hour, is the fastest animal in the world.

b. The pronghorn antelope, clocked at 61 miles per hour, is the fastest animal in the world.

The cheetah, right? Not necessarily. The cheetah can go faster, but only for short sprints. The antelope can maintain its high speed over a much greater distance. So which is faster? It depends on what you're measuring. Put in terms of human races, the cheetah would win the hundred-yard dash, but the antelope would win the marathon.

When you are dealing with money, statistics become even trickier. Consider the following facts:

a. In 1942 President Franklin D. Roosevelt earned a salary of $75,000.

b. In 1972 President Richard Nixon earned a salary of $200,000.

c. In 2002 President George W. Bush earned a salary of $400,000.

A speech that is supported by statistics is usually more persuasive than an undocumented presentation. Here John Chambers, CEO of Cisco Systems, uses economic data when addressing the Boston Chamber of Commerce.

Which President was paid the most money? In purely mathematical terms, Bush is the highest earner. But a dollar today does not buy as much as it did in 1942, when Franklin Roosevelt was President. One measure of the inflation rate is the Consumer Price Index, which allows us to gauge the value of the dollar in any given year against its purchasing power in 1972. If we apply the Consumer Price Index to the three Presidents' salaries, we can see how much each earned in 1972 dollars:

a   In 1942 President Franklin D. Roosevelt earned a salary of $192,000.

b   In 1972 Richard Nixon earned a salary of $200,000.

c   In 2002 George W. Bush earned a salary of $92,800.

In other words, although Bush had the highest salary, the value of his $400,000 was less than half the value of Roosevelt's $75,000.

The point is that there is usually more to statistics than meets the eye.[6] When you track down statistics for your speeches, be sure to evaluate them in light of the following questions.

Are the Statistics Representative?

Say that on your way to class you choose ten students at random and ask them whether they favor or oppose banning recreational vehicles on public lands. Say also that six approve of such a ban and four do not. Would you then be accurate in claiming that 60 percent of the students on your campus favor banning recreational vehicles from public lands?

Of course not. Ten students is not a big enough sample. But even if it were, other problems would arise. Do the ten students interviewed accurately reflect your school's proportion of freshmen, sophomores, juniors, and seniors? Do they mirror the proportion of male and female students? Are the various majors accurately represented? What about part-time and full-time students? Students of different cultural and religious backgrounds?

In short, make sure your statistics are representative of what they claim to measure.

Are Statistical Measures Used Correctly?

Here are two groups of numbers:

Group A	Group B
7,500	5,400
6,300	5,400
5,000	5,000
4,400	2,300
4,400	1,700

mean
The average value of a group of numbers.

Let us apply to each group three basic statistical measures—the mean, the median, and the mode.

The *mean*—popularly called the average—is determined by summing all the items in a group and dividing by the number of items. The mean for group A is 5,520. For group B it is 3,960.

The *median* is the middle figure in a group once the figures are put in order from highest to lowest. The median for both group A and group B is exactly the same—5,000.

median
The middle number in a group of numbers arranged from highest to lowest.

The *mode* is the number that occurs most frequently in a group of numbers. The mode for group A is 4,400. For group B it is 5,400.

Notice the results:

	Group A	Group B
Mean	5,520	3,960
Median	5,000	5,000
Mode	4,400	5,400

mode
The number that occurs most frequently in a group of numbers.

All these measures have the same goal—to indicate what is typical or characteristic of a certain group of numbers. Yet see how different the results are, depending on which measure you use.

The differences among the various measures can be striking. For instance, the *mean* salary of local TV news anchorpersons is $79,500 a year. But the mean is inflated by the huge salaries (up to $1 million a year) paid to a few star anchors in media centers such as New York, Los Angeles, and Chicago. In contrast, the *median* salary of local news anchors is $65,000—not a sum to scoff at, but still $14,500 less than the mean.[7]

How might a speaker use these different measures? The owner of a television station would probably cite the *mean* ($79,500) to show that local news anchors are handsomely compensated for their work. An organization of news anchors might emphasize the *median* ($65,000) to demonstrate that salaries are not nearly as high as the station owner makes them out to be. Both speakers would be telling the truth, but neither would be completely honest unless she or he made clear the meaning of the statistics.

Are the Statistics from a Reliable Source?

Which is the more reliable estimate of the environmental dangers of toxic waste in a landfill—one from the U.S. Environmental Protection Agency or one compiled by the company that owns the landfill? Easy—the estimate by the EPA, which does not have a vested interest in what the figures look like. What about nutritional ratings for fast foods offered by Consumers Union (a highly respected nonprofit organization) or by Burger King? That's easy too—Consumers Union.

But now things get tougher. What about the competing statistics offered by groups for and against Social Security reform? Or the conflicting numbers tossed out by a school board and the teachers striking against it? In these cases the answer is not so clear, since both sides would present the facts according to their own partisan motives.

As a speaker, you must be aware of possible bias in the use of numbers. Since statistics can be interpreted so many ways and put to so many uses, you should seek figures gathered by objective, nonpartisan sources.

TIPS FOR USING STATISTICS

Use Statistics to Quantify Your Ideas

The main value of statistics is to give your ideas numerical precision. This can be especially important when you are trying to document the existence of a problem. Examples can bring the problem alive and dramatize it in personal terms. But your listeners may still wonder how many people the problem actually affects. In such a situation, you should turn to statistics. Research has shown that the impact of examples is greatly enhanced when they are combined with statistics that show the examples to be typical.[8]

Suppose you are talking about the need for college students to avoid credit-card debt. Part of your speech deals with the large amount of such debt the typical college student faces by the time he or she graduates. You give an example, you personalize the subject, you provide many details, as follows:

> Charles Perkins left college a changed person. Not only had he earned his degree in geography, but he had racked up almost $4,000 in credit-card debt. Charles was sure he would be able to pay off his debt easily once he got a full-time job. But when he received his first paycheck, he found, to his dismay, that after paying taxes and his living expenses, he could make only the minimum monthly payment on his credit cards. Rather than getting rid of his debt, it would take him years to pay it off.

Confronted with this example, a listener might think, "Poor Charles. But I'm not going to end up in his spot because I don't plan to leave college with a lot of credit-card debt." Anticipating just such a response, a sharp speaker would include figures to quantify the extent of credit-card debt among college students in general:

> According to the latest issue of *U.S. News & World Report*, the average credit-card debt of a graduating college student is $2,900 and new graduates spend almost 25 percent of their income on debt payments. If someone makes only the minimum monthly payment on his or her credit cards—which is what most people do—they will rack up more than $3,800 in interest charges alone before paying off their original $2,900 debt. Perhaps this explains why in the past few years the number of people under 25 filing for bankruptcy has increased by over 50 percent.

Now the audience is much more likely to agree that they need to keep a closer eye on their credit-card balance.

Use Statistics Sparingly

As helpful as statistics can be, nothing puts an audience to sleep faster than a speech cluttered with numbers from beginning to end. Insert statistics only when they are needed, and then make sure they are easy to grasp. Even the most attentive listener would have trouble sorting out this barrage of figures:

> According to the *World Factbook,* life expectancy at birth in the United States ranks 18th among 25 industrialized countries. Life expectancy of women in Japan is 84.25 years compared with 80.2 years for American women, and 77.73 years for Japanese men compared with 74.5 years for American men. The United States ranks 23rd among 25 industrialized nations in infant mortality, with a rate almost twice as high as Japan's. Canada ranks 13th. Americans spend more each year on health care than any other nation—$1 trillion dollars, or 13.7 percent of gross domestic product—yet the World Health Organization ranks the U.S. health care system 37th in overall performance among member nations.

Instead of drowning your audience in a sea of statistics, use only those that are most important. For example:

> According to the *World Factbook,* people in the United States have one of the lowest life expectancies among industrialized nations. We also have one of the highest rates of infant mortality. Even though we spend more on health care than any other nation, the World Health Organization ranks 36 other nations ahead of us with regard to the overall performance of our health care system.

This second statement makes the same point as the first statement, but now the ideas are not lost in a torrent of numbers.

Identify the Sources of Your Statistics

As we have seen, figures are easy to manipulate. This is why careful listeners keep an ear out for the sources of a speaker's statistics. One student learned this by experience. In a speech titled "Tax Reform: Fact Versus Fiction," he claimed that the wealthiest 1 percent of U.S. taxpayers pay 39 percent of federal income taxes, even though they account for only 21 percent of all earned income. He also noted that the wealthiest 25 percent of Americans pay 86 percent of federal income taxes. These are startling statistics. But because the student did not say where he got them, his classmates were sure he must be wrong.

As it turned out, the figures were quite reliable. They had come from a study by the Internal Revenue Service reported in *The New York Times.* If the speaker had mentioned the source in his speech, he would have been more successful.[9]

Explain Your Statistics

Statistics don't speak for themselves. They need to be interpreted and related to your listeners. Notice how effectively one student did this in a speech about Chinese culture in the United States:

> Food is another aspect of Chinese culture that has become part of American life. According to Jennifer Lee's *The Fortune Cookie Chronicles,* published in 2008, there are

Using Statistics Checklist

	YES ✓	NO
1. Do I use statistics to quantify my ideas?	☐	☐
2. Are my statistics representative of what they purport to measure?	☐	☐
3. Are my statistics from reliable sources?	☐	☐
4. Do I cite the sources of my statistics?	☐	☐
5. Do I use statistical measures (mean, median, mode) correctly?	☐	☐
6. Do I round off complicated statistics?	☐	☐
7. Do I use visual aids to clarify statistical trends?	☐	☐
8. Do I explain my statistics and relate them to the audience?	☐	☐

connectlucas.com
This checklist is also available in the online Study Tools for this chapter.

some 43,000 Chinese restaurants in the United States. That's more than all the McDonalds, Burger Kings, and KFCs combined.

Explaining what statistics mean is particularly important when you deal with large numbers, since they are hard to visualize. How, for example, can we comprehend the $9 trillion U.S. national debt? We could explain that a trillion is a thousand billion and a billion is a thousand million. But millions and billions are almost as hard to visualize as trillions. Suppose, instead, we translate the huge numbers into terms a listener can relate to. Here is one speaker's solution:

How much money is a trillion dollars? Think of it this way. If you had $1 million and spent it at the rate of $1,000 a day, you would run out of money in less than three years. If you had $1 billion and spent it at the rate of $1,000 a day, you would not run out of money for almost 3,000 years. And if you had $1 trillion and spent it at the rate of $1,000 a day, you wouldn't run out of money for nearly 3 million years!

Whenever you use statistics in your speeches, think of how you can make them meaningful to your audience. Rather than simply reciting figures about, say, the continuing destruction of the world's rainforests, find a way to bring those figures home to your audience. You might say, as did one speaker:

According to the Rainforest Action Network, rainforest is disappearing at an alarming rate. Within the next second, we will lose an area of rainforest equal to two football fields. Within the next fifteen minutes, an area the size of this campus will be erased. By this time tomorrow, 214,000 acres, an area equivalent to the size of New York City, will be gone forever.

connectlucas.com
View this excerpt from "The Rainforests: Nature's Pharmacy" in the online Media Library for this chapter (Video Clip 7.5).

Be creative in thinking of ways to relate your statistics to your audience. This is probably the single most important step you can take to make statistics work in your speeches.

Round Off Complicated Statistics

Mount Kilimanjaro is 19,341 feet high; the official world land speed record is 763.065 miles per hour; the population of Saudi Arabia is 27,601,038 people; the moon is 238,855 miles from earth.

These are intriguing figures, but they are too complicated to be readily understood by listeners. Unless there is an important reason to give exact numbers, you should round off most statistics. You might say that Mount Kilimanjaro is 19,300 feet high; the world land speed record is 763 miles per hour; the population of Saudi Arabia is more than 28 million; and the moon is 239,000 miles from earth.

Use Visual Aids to Clarify Statistical Trends

Visual aids can save you a lot of time, as well as make your statistics easier to comprehend. Suppose you are discussing the number of major strikes by labor unions in the United States since World War II. You could start by explaining that after the war, during the early 1950s, there were a record number of strikes involving 1,000 or more workers. Then, after the start of Dwight Eisenhower's presidency in 1953, the number of strikes declined fairly steadily until 1964, when they started climbing to a peak of more than 400 in 1968. After a sharp decline in the early 1970s, they jumped again in 1975, before taking a dramatic turn downward during the 1980s and reaching a record low under President George W. Bush.

These are interesting statistics, and you could build a good speech around them. But strung together in a few sentences they are hard to digest. Figure 7.1 below shows how much more clearly the points can be made with a simple graph. We shall discuss visual aids in detail in Chapter 13. For the moment, keep in mind that they can be helpful in presenting statistical information.

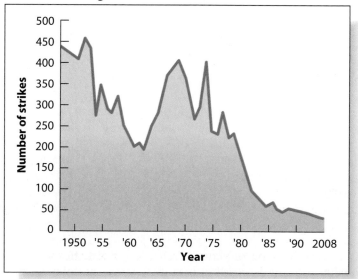

Strikes involving 1,000 workers or more

● **FIGURE 7.1**

Imagine you are talking with a friend about the classes you plan to take next term. You are not sure whether to sign up for Psychology 230 or Accounting 181. Both are requirements; both meet at the same time of day. Your friend says, "I took those classes last year. They're both good, but Professor Hassam was excellent in Psych 230. If she's teaching it next term, I'd take it for sure." You check the timetable and find that Professor Hassam is indeed slated for Psychology 230. You sign up for her course.

As this story illustrates, we are often influenced by the *testimony* of other people. Just as you are likely to be swayed by your friend's recommendation about which class to take, so audiences tend to respect the opinions of people who have special knowledge or experience on the topic at hand. By quoting or paraphrasing such people, you can give your ideas greater strength and impact. The two major kinds of testimony are expert testimony and peer testimony.

testimony
Quotations or paraphrases used to support a point.

EXPERT TESTIMONY

In most speeches you will probably rely on expert testimony—testimony from people who are acknowledged authorities in their fields. Citing the views of people who are experts is a good way to lend credibility to your speeches. It shows that you are not just mouthing your own opinions, but that your position is supported by people who are knowledgeable about the topic.[10]

Expert testimony is even more important when a topic is controversial or when the audience is skeptical about a speaker's point of view. The following story explains how one student enlisted expert testimony for a speech on household antibacterial products:

expert testimony
Testimony from people who are recognized experts in their fields.

As Rebecca Shannon investigated the topic of household antibacterial products, she became convinced that they did not produce the health benefits they claimed and, in fact, could be harmful to consumers and the environment alike. Yet Rebecca was not an expert. How could she convince her classmates to accept her ideas?

Statistics helped, and so did examples. But on such a controversial topic that was not enough. So, to reinforce her credibility, Rebecca quoted a wide range of experts who agreed with her—including the U.S. Centers for Disease Control; Eric Kupferberg, associate director of the Harvard School of Public Health; Stuart Levy, professor of microbiology at Tufts University; Elaine Larson of Columbia University's School of Nursing; Myron Genel, chair of the American Medical Association's council on scientific affairs; and Rolf Halden of the Johns Hopkins University School of Public Health. By citing the views of these experts, Rebecca made her speech much more persuasive.

connectlucas.com
View an excerpt from "Bursting the Antibacterial Bubble" in the online Media Library for this chapter (Video Clip 7.6).

PEER TESTIMONY

Another type of testimony often used in speeches is peer testimony—opinions of people like ourselves; not prominent figures, but ordinary citizens who have firsthand experience on the topic. This kind of testimony is especially valuable because it gives a more personal viewpoint on issues than can be gained from expert testimony.

For example, if you were speaking about the barriers faced by people with physical disabilities, you would surely include testimony from doctors and other medical authorities. But in this case, the expert testimony would be limited

peer testimony
Testimony from ordinary people with firsthand experience or insight on a topic.

because it cannot communicate what it really means to have a physical disability. To communicate that, you need a statement from someone who can speak with the voice of genuine experience—as in the following case:

> Itzhak Perlman, the world-renowned violinist whose legs are paralyzed, once said: "When you are in a wheelchair, people don't talk to you. Perhaps they think it is contagious, or perhaps they think crippled legs mean a crippled mind. But whatever the reason, they treat you like a thing."

There is no way expert testimony can express these ideas with the same authenticity and emotional impact.

QUOTING VERSUS PARAPHRASING

direct quotation
Testimony that is presented word for word.

The statement from Itzhak Perlman is presented as a direct quotation. Testimony can also be presented by paraphrasing. Rather than quoting someone verbatim, you present the gist of that person's ideas in your own words—as did one student in her speech about America's potential water crisis:

> Writing in *Audubon* magazine, Dr. Peter Bourne, president of Global Water, a nonpartisan educational group in Washington, D.C., said most Americans do not yet realize the extent and urgency of the water problem. At the present rate, he says, we are headed for a crisis that will change the way we live in every part of the nation.

paraphrase
To restate or summarize a source's ideas in one's own words.

When should you use a direct quotation as opposed to paraphrasing? The standard rule is that quotations are most effective when they are brief, when they convey your meaning better than you can, and when they are particularly eloquent, witty, or compelling. If you find a quotation that fits these criteria, then recite the quotation word for word.

Paraphrasing is better than direct quotation in two situations: (1) when the wording of a quotation is obscure or cumbersome, as is often the case with government documents; (2) when a quotation is longer than two or three sentences. Audiences often tune out partway through lengthy quotations, which tend to interrupt the flow of a speaker's ideas. Since the rest of the speech is in your own words, you should put longer quotations in your own words as well.

TIPS FOR USING TESTIMONY
Quote or Paraphrase Accurately

quoting out of context
Quoting a statement in such a way as to distort its meaning by removing the statement from the words and phrases surrounding it.

Accurate quotation involves three things: making sure you do not misquote someone; making sure you do not violate the meaning of statements you paraphrase; making sure you do not quote out of context. Of these, the last is the most subtle—and the most dangerous. By quoting out of context, you can twist someone's remarks so as to prove almost anything. Take movie advertisements. A critic pans a movie with these words:

> This movie is a colossal bore. From beginning to end it is a disaster. What is meant to be brilliant dialogue is about as fascinating as the stuff you clean out of your kitchen drain.

But when the movie is advertised in the newspapers, what appears in huge letters over the critic's name? "COLOSSAL! FROM BEGINNING TO END— BRILLIANT! FASCINATING!"

Citing expert testimony is an excellent way for students to lend credibility to their speeches. It shows that the speaker's views are shared by people who have special knowledge on the topic.

This is so flagrant as to be humorous. But quoting out of context can have serious consequences. Consider the following statement by a political candidate:

Creating a national sales tax would provide needed revenue for programs such as education, health care, and national defense. Several European countries have such a tax, and it could certainly work in the U.S. However, I do not support such a tax here—in fact, I don't support new taxes of any kind.

Now look what happens when the first part of that statement is quoted out of context by a competing candidate:

Americans already pay too much in taxes. Yet my opponent in this election has stated—and I quote: "Creating a national sales tax would provide needed revenue for programs such as education, health care, and national defense. Several European countries have such a tax, and it could certainly work in the U.S." Well, my opponent may think new taxes are good for Europe, but they're the last thing we need in this country.

By quoting the original statement out of context, the competing candidate has created a false impression. Such behavior is highly unethical. Be sure, when you quote or paraphrase someone, that you represent their words and ideas with complete accuracy.

Use Testimony from Qualified Sources

We have all become accustomed to the celebrity testimonial in television and magazine advertising. The professional golfer endorses a brand of clubs. The movie star praises a hair spray or shampoo. So far, so good. These are the tools of the trade for the people who endorse them.

But what happens when an Academy Award winner endorses a cell phone company? A tennis player represents a line of cameras? Do they know more about these products than you or I? Probably not.

Being a celebrity or an authority in one area does not make someone competent in other areas. Listeners will find your speeches much more credible if you use testimony from sources qualified *on the subject at hand.* As we have seen, this may include either recognized experts or ordinary citizens with special experience on the speech topic.

Use Testimony from Unbiased Sources

In a speech about the use of stun guns by police officers to subdue unruly students in public schools, a student said:

> Steve Tuttle, a spokesman for Taser International, said in a statement that "the Taser device has been shown to be medically safe when used on children" and that there is no reason to prohibit its use when necessary to maintain security in the public schools.

As you might expect, the students' classmates were not persuaded. After all, what would you expect someone at Taser International, the leading manufacturer of stun guns, to say—that its product is unsafe and should be banned?

Careful listeners are suspicious of testimony from biased or self-interested sources. Be sure to use testimony from credible, objective authorities.

Identify the People You Quote or Paraphrase

The usual way to identify your source is to name the person and sketch his or her qualifications before presenting the testimony. The following excerpt is from a speech arguing that excessive hours spent at work is harming the quality of education for many American high-school students:

> In their book, *When Children Work,* psychology professors Ellen Greenberger of the University of California and Lawrence Steinberg of Temple University note that intensive

levels of work among youth tend to produce higher truancy and lower grades. According to Greenberger and Steinberg, one study after another has found that working more than a few hours a week has a negative impact on teenagers' academic performance.

Had the speaker not identified Greenberger and Steinberg, listeners would not have had the foggiest idea who they are or why their opinion should be heeded.

As we saw in Chapter 2, identifying the source of testimony is also an important ethical responsibility. If you use another person's words or ideas without giving credit to that person, you will be guilty of plagiarism. This is true whether you paraphrase the original source or quote it verbatim.

Citing Sources Orally

We have mentioned more than once in this chapter the importance of citing the sources of your supporting materials. Careful listeners are skeptical. They keep an ear out both for a speaker's information and for the sources of that information.

The bibliography in your speech outline should state the sources you used in constructing the speech (see Chapter 10, page 211). But listeners do not have access to your outline. You have to identify your sources orally, as you are speaking.

Unlike a written bibliography, oral source citations do not follow a standard format. What you include depends on your topic, your audience, the kind of supporting material you are using, and the claim you are making. The key is to tell your audience enough that they will know where you got your information and why they should accept it as qualified and credible. In most cases, you will need to identify some combination of the following:

- The book, magazine, newspaper, or Web document you are citing.

- The author or sponsoring organization of the document.

- The author's qualifications with regard to the topic.

- The date on which the document was published, posted, or updated.

Here is an example of a speech citation that includes all the above:

connectlucas.com
This checklist is also available in the online Study Tools for this chapter.

While more students are going to college than ever before, they are paying a high price. Kimberly Palmer, financial columnist for *U.S. News & World Report,* reported in the magazine's January 28, 2008, issue that graduating students now owe an average of $15,500 in student-loan debt, up from $8,800 just ten years ago.

Because this speaker was citing statistics, she needed to show they were up-to-date and came from a credible source. In the following example, the speaker is using testimony, but notice how he also establishes the credibility of his source and the recency of his information:

Human smuggling is big business, and the U.S. government has made little headway in stopping it. Just ask Scott Hatfield, chief of the Human Smuggling division at Immigration and Customs Enforcement, who was quoted last month in *The New York Times:* "Any time we shut down a smuggling organization, there's always somebody to take their place."

On the other hand, if you were quoting Abraham Lincoln's Gettysburg Address of November 19, 1863, about "government of the people, by the people, for the people," you would not need to explain Lincoln's qualifications (because he is so well known) or the date of his statement (because it does not affect the relevance of his words).

The same principles apply if you are citing online sources. It is not enough to say, "As I found on the Web," or "As the Internet states." On the other hand, it is not necessary to recite the entire address of the Web page. If you are citing a specific person, you should identify him or her and the name of the Web site on which you found the information—as in this example:

In an article posted on CNN.com in July 2007, Joseph A. Califano Jr., President of the National Center on Alcohol and Substance Abuse at Columbia University, stated: "I wouldn't be surprised if right now at this point in time, there are more kids abusing prescription drugs than abusing marijuana."

If you are citing an organization, rather than an individual, you need to provide the name of the organization:

The Web page for the Robotics Institute at Carnegie Mellon University explains that scientists at that school have designed and built a six-ton hybrid electric vehicle that can be used by the U.S. Army for armed reconnaissance missions.

Finally, notice how skillfully the speakers quoted above blend their citations into their speeches. They do not always say, "According to . . ." or "As stated by. . . ." Nor do they use words like "quote . . . unquote." Usually you can modify your tone of voice or use brief pauses to let your listeners know when you are making a direct quotation.

In the online Speech Tools for this chapter, you will find more examples of how you can cite different kinds of sources in your speeches. Whether you are using examples, statistics, or testimony, citing your sources properly is a crucial part of being an effective—and ethical—public speaker.

connectlucas.com
For additional examples of how to cite sources in your speeches, check the Sample Oral Citations in the online Speech Tools for this chapter.

SUMMARY

Good speeches need strong supporting materials to bolster the speaker's point of view. The three basic types of supporting materials are examples, statistics, and testimony.

In the course of a speech you may use brief examples—specific instances referred to in passing—and sometimes you may want to give several brief examples in a row to create a stronger impression. Extended examples are longer and more detailed. Hypothetical examples describe imaginary situations and can be quite effective for relating ideas to the audience. All three kinds of examples help clarify ideas, reinforce ideas, or personalize ideas. To be most effective, they should be vivid and richly textured.

Statistics can be extremely helpful in conveying your message as long as you use them sparingly and make them meaningful to your audience. Above all, you should understand your statistics and use them fairly. Make sure your figures are representative of what they claim to measure, that you use statistical measures correctly, and that you take statistics only from reliable sources.

Citing the testimony of experts is a good way to make your ideas more credible. You can also use peer testimony, from ordinary people who have firsthand experience on the topic. Regardless of the kind of testimony, you can either quote someone verbatim or paraphrase his or her words. Be sure to quote or paraphrase accurately and to use qualified, unbiased sources.

When citing sources in a speech, you need to let your audience know where you got your information and why they should accept it as qualified and credible. In most cases, this means identifying the document you are citing, its date of publication or posting, the author or sponsoring organization, and the author's credentials.

KEY TERMS

supporting materials *(142)*   extended example *(143)*
example *(143)*   hypothetical example *(144)*
brief example *(143)*   statistics *(147)*

mean *(150)*   peer testimony *(155)*
median *(150)*   direct quotation *(156)*
mode *(150)*   paraphrase *(156)*
testimony *(155)*   quoting out of context *(156)*
expert testimony *(155)*

REVIEW QUESTIONS

connectlucas.com
For further review, go to the
Study Questions in the online
Study Aids for this chapter.

After reading this chapter, you should be able to answer the following questions:

1. Why do you need supporting materials in your speeches?

2. What are the three kinds of examples discussed in this chapter? How might you use each kind to support your ideas?

3. What are five tips for using examples in your speeches?

4. Why is it so easy to lie with statistics? What three questions should you ask to judge the reliability of statistics?

5. What are six tips for using statistics in your speeches?

6. What is testimony? Explain the difference between expert testimony and peer testimony.

7. What are four tips for using testimony in your speeches?

EXERCISES FOR CRITICAL THINKING

1. Each of the following statements violates at least one of the criteria for effective supporting materials discussed in this chapter. Identify the flaw (or flaws) in each statement.

   a. As Miley Cyrus stated in a recent interview, the Canadian system provides the best model for creating universal health care in the United States.

   b. According to *The New York Times Almanac,* California has the largest Native American population of any state in the union—421,346. Arizona is second with 294,118; Oklahoma is third with 287,124; and New Mexico is fourth with a total Native American population of 190,826.

   c. I don't know why insurance companies should charge higher rates for drivers under the age of 25. All my friends drive a lot and none of them have been in car accidents.

   d. In a random survey conducted last month among members of People for the Ethical Treatment of Animals, 99 percent of respondents opposed using animals for medical experiments. Clearly, then, the American people oppose such experiments.

   e. In the words of one expert, "The state education budget has been cut so much in recent years that any further cuts will do irreparable harm to our schools and the children they serve."

   f. Figures compiled by the Bureau of Labor Statistics show that the median salary for lawyers in the U.S. is $106,121. This shows that lawyers average more than $106,000 a year in salary.

g. According to a study by Verizon Wireless, there is no evidence that the use of cell phones is a significant cause of automobile accidents.

2. Analyze "Bursting the Antibacterial Bubble" in the appendix of sample speeches following Chapter 18. Identify the main points of the speech and the supporting materials used for each. Evaluate the speaker's use of supporting materials in light of the criteria discussed in this chapter.

Applying *the* **Power** *of* **Public Speaking**

After receiving your master's degree in education administration, you took a job at the state department of education. At the request of the governor, your section of the department has developed a new early childhood intervention program for children from impoverished households. Now you have been asked to help publicize the program and to build support for it. You will be speaking to church groups, teachers' associations, family advocacy groups, and others with an interest in children's welfare. You want to prepare a talk that makes good use of statistics and expert testimony to demonstrate the value of early childhood education programs, especially for poor children.

As part of your research, you decide to search the Web for supporting materials. List three reputable Web sites that provide useful statistics or testimony on the value of early childhood education. Explain why each Web site is reputable and list one statistic or expert quotation you obtain from each source.

Organizing the Body of the Speech

Organization Is Important

Main Points
  Number of Main Points
  Strategic Order of Main Points
  Tips for Preparing Main Points

Supporting Materials

Connectives
  Transitions
  Internal Previews
  Internal Summaries
  Signposts

Think about shopping in a store such as Ikea, Target, or Best Buy. Many of the items for sale are *organizers*—drawer organizers, desk organizers, closet organizers, kitchen organizers, bathroom organizers, office organizers, audio and video organizers.

Why all this quest for organization? Obviously, when the objects you possess are well organized, they serve you better. Organization allows you to see what you have and to put your hands immediately on the garment, the tool, the piece of paper, the CD you want without a frenzied search.

Much the same is true of your speeches. If they are well organized, they will serve you better. Organization allows you—and your listeners—to see what ideas you have and to put mental "hands" on the most important ones.

Organization Is Important

strategic organization

Putting a speech together in a particular way to achieve a particular result with a particular audience.

In a classic study, a college professor took a well-organized speech and scrambled it by randomly changing the order of its sentences. He then had a speaker deliver the original version to one group of listeners and the scrambled version to another group. After the speeches, he gave a test to see how well each group understood what they had heard. Not surprisingly, the group that heard the original, unscrambled speech scored much higher than the other group.[1]

A few years later, two professors repeated the same experiment at another school. But instead of testing how well the listeners comprehended each speech, they tested to see what effects the speeches had on the listeners' attitudes toward the speakers. They found that people who heard the well-organized speech believed the speaker to be much more competent and trustworthy than did those who heard the scrambled speech.[2]

These are just two of many studies that show the importance of organization in effective speechmaking.[3] Listeners demand coherence. Unlike readers, they cannot flip back to a previous page if they have trouble grasping a speaker's ideas. In this respect a speech is much like a movie. Just as a director must be sure viewers can follow the plot of a film from beginning to end, so must a speaker be sure listeners can follow the progression of ideas in a speech from beginning to end. This requires that speeches be organized *strategically*. They should be put together in particular ways to achieve particular results with particular audiences.

Speech organization is important for other reasons as well. As we saw in Chapter 1, it is closely connected to critical thinking. When you work to organize your speeches, you gain practice in the general skill of establishing clear relationships among your ideas. This skill will serve you well throughout your college days and in almost any career you may choose. In addition, using a clear, specific method of speech organization can boost your confidence as a speaker and improve your ability to deliver a message fluently.

The first step in developing a strong sense of speech organization is to gain command of the three basic parts of a speech—introduction, body, and conclusion—and the strategic role of each. In this chapter we deal with the body of the speech. The next chapter will take up the introduction and the conclusion.

There are good reasons for talking first about the body of the speech. The body is the longest and most important part. Also, you will usually prepare the body first. It is easier to create an effective introduction after you know exactly what you will say in the body.

The process of organizing the body of a speech begins when you determine the main points.

Main Points ●●

The main points are the central features of your speech. You should select them carefully, phrase them precisely, and arrange them strategically. Here are the main points of a student speech about the medical uses of hypnosis:

Specific Purpose: To inform my audience about the major uses of hypnosis.

Central Idea: The major uses of hypnosis today are to control pain in surgery, to help people stop smoking, and to help students improve their academic performance.

Main Points:
    I. Hypnosis is used in surgery as an adjunct to chemical anesthesia.
    II. Hypnosis is used to help people stop smoking.
    III. Hypnosis is used to help students improve their academic performance.

main points
The major points developed in the body of a speech. Most speeches contain from two to five main points.

These three main points form the skeleton of the body of the speech. If there are three major *uses* of hypnosis for medical purposes, then logically there can be three *main points* in the speech.

How do you choose your main points? Sometimes they will be evident from your specific purpose statement. Suppose your specific purpose is "To inform my audience about the development, technology, and benefits of hydrogen fuel cells." Obviously, your speech will have three main points. The first will deal with the development of hydrogen fuel cells, the second with the technology behind hydrogen fuel cells, the third with the benefits of hydrogen fuel cells. Written in outline form, the main points might be:

Specific Purpose: To inform my audience about the development, technology, and benefits of hydrogen fuel cells.

Central Idea: Developed as a highly efficient form of energy, hydrogen fuel cells use sophisticated technology and offer a number of economic and environmental benefits.

Main Points:
    I. Hydrogen fuel cells were developed to provide a highly efficient form of energy.
    II. Hydrogen fuel cells produce power through an electro-chemical reaction involving hydrogen gas.
    III. Hydrogen fuel cells provide an economically and environmentally superior method of powering motor vehicles.

Even if your main points are not stated expressly in your specific purpose, they may be easy to project from it. Let's say your specific purpose is "To inform my audience of the basic steps in making stained-glass windows." You know each of your main points will correspond to a step in the window-making process. They might look like this in outline form:

Specific Purpose: To inform my audience of the basic steps in making stained-glass windows.

Central Idea: There are four steps in making stained-glass windows.

Main Points: I. The first step is designing the window.
II. The second step is cutting the glass to fit the design.
III. The third step is painting the glass.
IV. The fourth step is assembling the window.

You will not always settle on your main points so easily. Often they will emerge as you research the speech and evaluate your findings. Suppose your specific purpose is "To persuade my audience that our state should not approve proposals for online voting." You know that each main point in the speech will present a *reason* why online voting should not be instituted in your state. But you aren't sure how many main points there will be or what they will be. As you research and study the topic, you decide there are two major reasons to support your view. Each of these reasons will become a main point in your speech. Written in outline form, they might be:

Specific Purpose: To persuade my audience that our state should not approve proposals for online voting.

Central Idea: Our state should not approve online voting because it will increase voter fraud and disfranchise people without Internet access.

Main Points: I. Our state should not approve online voting because it will increase voter fraud.
II. Our state should not approve online voting because it will disfranchise people without access to the Internet.

NUMBER OF MAIN POINTS

You will not have time in your classroom speeches to develop more than four or five main points, and most speeches will contain only two or three. Regardless of how long a speech might run, if you have too many main points, the audience will have trouble sorting them out.

If, when you list your main points, you find that you have too many, you may be able to condense them into categories. Here is a set of main points for a speech about yoga:

Specific Purpose: To inform my audience about the practice of yoga.

Central Idea: Yoga is an ancient practice that involves the whole body.

Main Points: I. Yoga breathing starts with deep inhalation.
II. Yoga breathing requires slow exhalation.
III. Yoga breathing includes prolonged pauses.
IV. Yoga breathing provides many benefits.
V. Yoga postures involve all parts of the body.

Research studies confirm that clear organization is vital to effective public speaking. Listeners must be able to follow the progression of ideas in a speech from beginning to end.

VI. Yoga postures increase flexibility.
VII. Yoga postures strengthen muscle tone.
VIII. Yoga postures demand precise movements.

You have eight main points—which is too many. But if you look at the list, you see that the eight points fall into two broad categories: yoga breathing and yoga postures. You might, therefore, restate your main points this way:

I. One part of practicing yoga involves proper breathing.
II. Another part of yoga involves body postures.

STRATEGIC ORDER OF MAIN POINTS

Once you establish your main points, you need to decide the order in which you will present them. The most effective order depends on three things—your topic, your purpose, and your audience. Chapters 14 and 15 will cover special aspects of organizing informative speeches and persuasive speeches. Here we look briefly at the five basic patterns of organization used most often by public speakers.

Chronological Order

Speeches arranged chronologically follow a time pattern. They may narrate a series of events in the sequence in which they happened. For example:

Specific Purpose: To inform my audience how the Great Wall of China was built.

connectlucas.com
View an excerpt from "Yoga: Uniting Mind, Body, and Spirit" in the online Media Library for this chapter (Video Clip 8.1).

chronological order
A method of speech organization in which the main points follow a time pattern.

Central Idea:	The Great Wall of China was built in three major stages.
Main Points:	I. Building of the Great Wall began during the Qin dynasty of 221–206 B.C.
	II. New sections of the Great Wall were added during the Han dynasty of 206 B.C.–220 A.D.
	III. The Great Wall was completed during the Ming dynasty of 1368–1644.

Chronological order is also used in speeches explaining a process or demonstrating how to do something. For example:

Specific Purpose:	To inform my audience of the steps in laser-assisted corrective eye surgery.
Central Idea:	There are three main steps in laser-assisted corrective eye surgery.
Main Points:	I. First, a thin layer is sliced off the surface of the eye to expose the cornea.
	II. Second, an ultraviolet laser is used to reshape the cornea.
	III. Third, the thin layer sliced off at the beginning of the surgery is reaffixed to the eye.

As this outline shows, chronological order is especially useful for informative speeches.

Spatial Order

Speeches arranged in spatial order follow a directional pattern. That is, the main points proceed from top to bottom, left to right, front to back, inside to outside, east to west, or some other route. For example:

Specific Purpose:	To inform my audience about the structure of a hurricane.
Central Idea:	A hurricane is made up of three parts going from inside to outside.
Main Points:	I. At the center of a hurricane is the calm, cloud-free eye.
	II. Surrounding the eye is the eyewall, a dense ring of clouds that produces the most intense wind and rainfall.
	III. Rotating around the eyewall are large bands of clouds and precipitation called spiral rain bands.

Or:

Specific Purpose:	To inform my audience about the three major regions in Italy.
Central Idea:	Northern, central, and southern Italy have their own identities and attractions.
	I. Northern Italy is home to Venice and its world-famous canals.

connectlucas.com
View an excerpt from "The Great Wall of China" in the online Media Library for this chapter (Video Clip 8.2).

spatial order
A method of speech organization in which the main points follow a directional pattern.

The main points of a speech should be organized to communicate the speaker's message. Chronological order would work very well for a speech on the history of the U.S. space program.

    II. Central Italy is home to Rome and its historical treasures.

   III. Southern Italy is home to Sicily and its culinary traditions.

Spatial order, like chronological order, is used most often in informative speeches.

Causal Order

Speeches arranged in causal order organize main points so as to show a cause-effect relationship. When you put your speech in causal order, you have two main points—one dealing with the causes of an event, the other dealing with its effects. Depending on your topic, you can either devote your first main point to the causes and the second to the effects, or you can deal first with the effects and then with the causes.

    Suppose your specific purpose is "To persuade my audience that a growing shortage of air-traffic controllers is a serious problem for U.S. aviation." Then you would begin with the causes of the shortage and work toward its effects:

Specific Purpose: To persuade my audience that a growing shortage of qualified air-traffic controllers is a serious problem for U.S. aviation.

Central Idea: The growing shortage of certified air-traffic controllers threatens the safety of air travel.

Main Points: I. The U.S. aviation system faces a growing shortage of qualified air-traffic controllers.

            II. If this shortage continues, it will create serious problems for airline safety.

causal order

A method of speech organization in which the main points show a cause-effect relationship.

When the effects you are discussing have already occurred, you may want to reverse the order and talk first about the effects and then about their causes—as in this speech about the Mayan civilization of Central America:

Specific Purpose: To inform my audience about the possible causes for the collapse of Mayan civilization.

Central Idea: The causes for the collapse of Mayan civilization have not yet been fully explained.

Main Points: I. Mayan civilization flourished for over a thousand years until 900 A.D., when it mysteriously began to disintegrate.
II. Scholars have advanced three major explanations for the causes of this disintegration.

Because of its versatility, causal order can be used for both persuasive speeches and informative speeches.

Problem-Solution Order

problem-solution order
A method of speech organization in which the first main point deals with the existence of a problem and the second main point presents a solution to the problem.

Speeches arranged in problem-solution order are divided into two main parts. The first shows the existence and seriousness of a problem. The second presents a workable solution to the problem. For example:

Specific Purpose: To persuade my audience that action is needed to combat the abuses of puppy mills.

Central Idea: Puppy mills are a serious problem that can be solved by a combination of legislation and individual initiative.

Main Points: I. Puppy mills are a serious problem across the United States.
II. Solving the problem requires legislation and individual initiative.

Or:

connectlucas.com
View an excerpt from "The Horrors of Puppy Mills" in the online Media Library for this chapter (Video Clip 8.3).

Specific Purpose: To persuade my audience that the electoral college should be abolished.

Central Idea: Because the electoral college does not give equal weight to the vote of each citizen, it should be replaced with direct popular election of the President.

Main Points: I. The electoral college is a serious problem in the U.S. political system because it does not give equal weight to each citizen's vote in electing the President.
II. The problem can be solved by abolishing the electoral college and electing the President by popular vote.

As these examples indicate, problem-solution order is most appropriate for persuasive speeches.

Topical Order

Topical order results when you divide the speech topic into *subtopics,* each of which becomes a main point in the speech.

topical order

A method of speech organization in which the main points divide the topic into logical and consistent subtopics.

Suppose your specific purpose is "To inform my audience of the major kinds of fireworks." This topic does not lend itself to chronological, spatial, causal, or problem-solution order. Rather, you separate the subject—kinds of fireworks—into its constituent parts, so that each main point deals with a single kind of fireworks. Your central idea and main points might look like this:

Specific Purpose: To inform my audience of the major kinds of fireworks.

Central Idea: The major kinds of fireworks are skyrockets, Roman candles, pinwheels, and lances.

Main Points:
I. Skyrockets explode high in the air, producing the most dramatic effects of all fireworks.
II. Roman candles shoot out separate groups of sparks and colored flames with a series of booming noises.
III. Pinwheels throw off sparks and flames as they whirl on the end of a stick.
IV. Lances are thin, colorful fireworks used in ground displays.

To take another example, let's say your specific purpose is "To inform my audience about the achievements of Ida Wells-Barnett." Wells-Barnett, an African American who lived at the turn of the 20th century, was an outspoken champion of social and political justice for her race. You could organize your speech chronologically—by discussing Wells-Barnett's exploits during each decade of her career. On the other hand, you could arrange the speech topically—by dividing Wells-Barnett's accomplishments into categories. Then your central idea and main points might be:

Specific Purpose: To inform my audience about the achievements of Ida Wells-Barnett.

Central Idea: Ida Wells-Barnett was a multitalented figure in the fight for racial justice.

Main Points:
I. As a teacher, Wells-Barnett spoke out against inferior school facilities for African-American children.
II. As a journalist, Wells-Barnett campaigned against lynching.
III. As a civic organizer, Wells-Barnett helped found the NAACP.

Notice how the main points subdivide the speech topic logically and consistently. Each main point isolates one aspect of Wells-Barnett's achievements. But suppose your main points look like this:

I. As a teacher, Wells-Barnett spoke out against inferior school facilities for African-American children.
II. As a journalist, Wells-Barnett campaigned against lynching.
III. In the early 20th century, Wells-Barnett expanded her activities and the scope of her influence.

Checklist   Main Points

YES ✓ **NO**

☐ ☐   1. Does the body of my speech contain two to five main points?

☐ ☐   2. Are my main points organized according to one of the following methods of organization? (Check the one that applies.)

    ☐ ☐   Chronological order

    ☐ ☐   Spatial order

    ☐ ☐   Causal order

    ☐ ☐   Topical order

    ☐ ☐   Problem-solution order

☐ ☐   3. Are my main points clearly separate from one another?

☐ ☐   4. As much as possible, have I used the same pattern of wording for all my main points?

☐ ☐   5. Have I roughly balanced the amount of time devoted to each main point?

☐ ☐   6. Is each main point backed up with strong, credible supporting materials?

☐ ☐   7. Do I use connectives to make sure my audience knows when I am moving from one main point to another?

This would *not* be a good topical order because main point III is inconsistent with the rest of the main points. It deals with a *period* in Wells-Barnett's life, whereas main points I and II deal with *kinds* of activism.

Because it is applicable to almost any subject and to any kind of speech, topical order is used more often than any other method of speech organization.

TIPS FOR PREPARING MAIN POINTS

Keep Main Points Separate

Each main point in a speech should be clearly independent of the others. Compare these two sets of main points for a speech about the process of producing a Broadway play:

Ineffective

  I. The first step is choosing the play.

 II. The second step is selecting the cast.

III. The third step is conducting rehearsals and then performing the play.

More Effective

  I. The first step is choosing the play.

 II. The second step is selecting the cast.

III. The third step is conducting the rehearsals.

IV. The fourth step is performing the play.

The problem with the left-hand list is that point III contains two main points. It should be divided, as shown in the right-hand list.

Try to Use the Same Pattern of Wording for Main Points

Consider the following main points for an informative speech about the benefits of exercise.

Ineffective

   I. Regular exercise increases your endurance.
  II. Your sleeping pattern is improved by regular exercise.
 III. It is possible to help control your weight by regular exercise.

More Effective

   I. Regular exercise increases your endurance.
  II. Regular exercise improves your sleeping pattern.
 III. Regular exercise helps control your weight.

The set of main points on the right follows a consistent pattern of wording throughout. Therefore, it is easier to understand and easier to remember than the set on the left.

You will find that it is not always possible to use this kind of parallel wording. Some speeches just don't lend themselves to such a tidy arrangement. But try to keep the wording parallel when you can, for it is a good way to make your main points stand out from the details surrounding them.

Balance the Amount of Time Devoted to Main Points

Because your main points are so important, you want to be sure they all receive enough emphasis to be clear and convincing. This means allowing sufficient time to develop each main point. Suppose you discover that the proportion of time devoted to your main points is something like this:

   I. 85 percent
  II. 10 percent
 III. 5 percent

A breakdown of this sort indicates one of two things. Either points II and III aren't really *main* points and you have only one main point, or points II and III haven't been given the attention they need. If the latter, you should revise the body of the speech to bring the main points into better balance.

This is not to say that all main points must receive exactly equal emphasis, but only that they should be roughly balanced. For example, either of the following would be fine:

   I. 30 percent   I. 20 percent
  II. 40 percent   II. 30 percent
 III. 30 percent   III. 50 percent

The amount of time spent on each main point depends on the amount and complexity of supporting materials for each point.

Supporting Materials

By themselves, main points are only assertions. As we saw in Chapter 7, listeners need supporting materials to accept what a speaker says. When the supporting materials are added, the body of a speech looks like the following in outline form:

supporting materials
The materials used to support a speaker's ideas. The three major kinds of supporting materials are examples, statistics, and testimony.

I. Hypnosis is used in surgery as an adjunct to chemical anesthesia.
   A. Hypnosis reduces both the physical and psychological aspects of pain.
      1. Hypnosis can double a person's pain threshold.
      2. It also reduces the fear that intensifies physical pain.
   B. Hypnosis is most useful in cases when the patient is known to have problems with general anesthesia.
      1. Quotation from Dr. Harold Wain of Walter Reed Army Hospital.
      2. Story of Linda Kuay.
      3. Statistics from *Psychology Today*.
II. Hypnosis is used to help people stop smoking.
   A. Many therapists utilize hypnosis to help people break their addiction to cigarettes.
      1. The U.S. Department of Health and Human Services considers hypnosis a safe and effective means of stopping smoking.
      2. Success rates are as high as 70 percent.
         a. Story of Alex Hamilton.
         b. Quotation from New York psychiatrist Dr. Herbert Spiegel.
   B. Hypnosis does not work for all smokers.
      1. A person must want to stop smoking for hypnosis to work.
      2. A person must also be responsive to hypnotic suggestion.
III. Hypnosis is used to help students improve their academic performance.
   A. Hypnosis enables people to use their minds more effectively.
      1. The conscious mind uses about 10 percent of a person's mental ability.
      2. Hypnosis allows people to tap more of their mental power.
   B. Studies show that hypnosis can help people overcome many obstacles to academic success.
      1. It improves ability to concentrate.
      2. It increases reading speed.
      3. It reduces test anxiety.

In Chapter 7 we discussed the major kinds of supporting materials and how to use them. Here, we need stress only the importance of *organizing* your supporting materials so they are directly relevant to the main points they are supposed to support. Misplaced supporting materials are confusing. Here's an example:

I. There are several reasons why people immigrate to the United States.
   A. Over the years, millions of people have immigrated to the United States.
   B. Many people immigrate in search of economic opportunity.
   C. Others immigrate to attain political freedom.
   D. Still others immigrate to escape religious persecution.

The main point deals with the reasons immigrants come to the United States, as do supporting points B, C, and D. Supporting point A ("Over the years, millions of people have immigrated to the United States") does not. It is out of place and should not be included with this main point.

If you find such a situation in your own speeches, try to reorganize your supporting points under appropriate main points, like this:

I. Over the years, millions of people have immigrated to the United States.
   A. Since the American Revolution, almost 90 million people have immigrated to the U.S.
   B. Today there are 37 million Americans who were born in other countries.
II. There are several reasons why people immigrate to the United States.
   A. Many people immigrate in search of economic opportunity.
   B. Others immigrate to attain political freedom.
   C. Still others immigrate to escape religious persecution.

Now you have two supporting points to back up your "millions of people" point and three supporting points to back up your "reasons" point.

Once you have organized your main points and supporting points, you must give attention to the third element in the body of a speech—connectives.

Connectives

Carla Maggio was speaking to her class about the need for medical malpractice reform. She had rehearsed the speech several times, had a well-defined central idea, three sharp main points, and strong evidence to support her position. But when Carla delivered the speech, she said "All right" every time she moved from one thought to the next. After a while, her classmates started counting. By the end of the speech, most were too busy waiting for the next "All right" to pay attention to Carla's message. Afterward, Carla said, "I never even thought about saying 'All right.' I guess it just popped out when I didn't know what else to say."

We all have stock phrases that we use to fill the space between thoughts. In casual conversation they are seldom troublesome. But in speechmaking they distract listeners by calling attention to themselves.

What Carla's speech lacked were strong *connectives*—words or phrases that join one thought to another and indicate the relationship between them. Without connectives, a speech is disjointed and uncoordinated—much as a person would be without ligaments and tendons to join the bones and hold the organs in place. Four types of speech connectives are transitions, internal previews, internal summaries, and signposts.

TRANSITIONS

Transitions are words or phrases that indicate when a speaker has just completed one thought and is moving on to another. Technically, the transitions state both the idea the speaker is leaving and the idea she or he is coming up to. In the following examples, the transitional phrases are underlined:

Now that we have a clear understanding of the problem, let me share the solution with you.

connective
A word or phrase that connects the ideas of a speech and indicates the relationship between them.

transition
A word or phrase that indicates when a speaker has finished one thought and is moving on to another.

I have spoken so far of bravery and patriotism, but it is the sacrifice of the Massachusetts 54th that has etched them into the pages of history.

Keeping these points in mind about sign language, let's return to the sentence I started with and see if we can learn the signs for "You are my friend."

Notice how these phrases remind the listener of the thought just completed, as well as reveal the thought about to be developed.

INTERNAL PREVIEWS

internal preview
A statement in the body of the speech that lets the audience know what the speaker is going to discuss next.

Internal previews let the audience know what the speaker will take up next, but they are more detailed than transitions. In effect, an internal preview works just like the preview statement in a speech introduction, except that it comes in the body of the speech—usually as the speaker is starting to discuss a main point. For example:

In discussing how Asian Americans have been stereotyped in the mass media, we'll look first at the origins of the problem and second at its continuing impact today.

After hearing this, the audience knows exactly what to listen for as the speaker develops the "problem" main point.

Internal previews are often combined with transitions. For example:

[*Transition*]: Now that we have seen how serious the problem of faulty credit reports is, let's look at some solutions. [*Internal Preview*]: I will focus on three solutions—instituting tighter government regulation of credit bureaus, holding credit bureaus financially responsible for their errors, and giving individuals easier access to their credit reports.

You will seldom need an internal preview for each main point in your speech, but be sure to use one whenever you think it will help listeners keep track of your ideas.

INTERNAL SUMMARIES

internal summary
A statement in the body of the speech that summarizes the speaker's preceding point or points.

Internal summaries are the reverse of internal previews. Rather than letting listeners know what is coming up next, internal summaries remind listeners of what they have just heard. Such summaries are usually used when a speaker finishes a complicated or particularly important main point or set of main points. For example:

In short, palm reading is an ancient art. Developed in China more than five thousand years ago, it was practiced in classical Greece and Rome, flourished during the Middle Ages, survived the Industrial Revolution, and remains popular today in many parts of the world.

Internal summaries are an excellent way to clarify and reinforce ideas. By combining them with transitions, you can also lead your audience smoothly into your next main point:

[*Internal Summary*]: Let's pause for a moment to summarize what we have found so far. First, we have seen that America's criminal justice system is less effective than it should be in deterring crime. Second, we have seen that prison programs to rehabilitate prisoners have been far from successful. [*Transition*]: We are now ready to explore solutions to these problems.

Experienced speakers include transitions and other connectives to help listeners keep track of their ideas. The result is a crisp presentation that moves clearly from point to point.

SIGNPOSTS

Signposts are very brief statements that indicate exactly where you are in the speech. Frequently they are just numbers. Here is how one student used simple numerical signposts to help her audience keep track of the major causes for the continuing problem of famine in Africa:

> <u>The first cause</u> of this problem is inefficient agricultural production.
>
> <u>The second cause</u> is recurrent drought in the affected countries.
>
> <u>The final cause</u> is mismanagement of available food resources by local leaders.

Another way to accomplish the same thing is to introduce your main points with a question, as did one student in his speech on mail-order fraud. His first main point showed that mail-order fraud continues to be a serious problem despite the growth of the Internet. He introduced it this way:

> So just how serious is the problem of mail-order fraud? Is it just a few isolated cases, or is it widespread enough to require serious measures to protect consumers?

His second main point dealt with ways to curb mail-order fraud. He introduced it by saying:

> So how can we solve this problem? Is there a way to protect the rights of legitimate mail-order companies while attacking the fraudulent ones?

Questions are particularly effective as signposts because they invite subliminal answers and thereby get the audience more involved with the speech.

Besides using signposts to indicate where you are in the speech, you can use them to focus attention on key ideas. You can do this with a simple phrase, as in the following example:

signpost
A very brief statement that indicates where a speaker is in the speech or that focuses attention on key ideas.

<u>The most important thing to remember</u> about abstract art is that it is always based on forms in the natural world.

The underlined words alert the audience to the fact that an especially significant point is coming up. So do phrases such as these:

Be sure to keep this in mind . . .

This is crucial to understanding the rest of the speech . . .

Above all, you need to know . . .

Depending on the needs of your speech, you may want to use two, three, or even all four kinds of connectives in combination. You needn't worry too much about what they are called—whether this one is a signpost and that a transition. The important thing is to be aware of their functions. Properly applied, connectives can make your speeches much more unified and coherent.

SUMMARY

Clear organization is vital to speechmaking. Listeners demand coherence. They get only one chance to grasp a speaker's ideas, and they have little patience for speakers who ramble aimlessly from one idea to another. A well-organized speech will enhance your credibility and make it easier for the audience to understand your message.

The process of planning the body of a speech begins when you determine the main points. You should choose them carefully, phrase them precisely, and organize them strategically. Because listeners cannot keep track of a multitude of main points, most speeches should contain no more than two to five. Each should focus on a single idea, should be worded clearly, and should receive enough emphasis to be clear and convincing.

You can organize main points in various ways, depending on your topic, purpose, and audience. Chronological order follows a time pattern, whereas spatial order follows a directional pattern. In causal order, main points are organized according to their cause-effect relationship. Topical order results when you divide your main topic into subtopics. Problem-solution order breaks the body of the speech into two main parts—the first showing a problem, the second giving a solution.

Supporting materials are the backup ideas for your main points. When organizing supporting materials, make sure they are directly relevant to the main points they are supposed to support.

Connectives help tie a speech together. They are words or phrases that join one thought to another and indicate the relationship between them. The four major types of speech connectives are transitions, internal previews, internal summaries, and signposts. Using them effectively will make your speeches more unified and coherent.

strategic organization *(166)*

main points *(167)*

chronological order *(169)*

spatial order *(170)*

causal order *(171)*

problem-solution order *(172)*

topical order *(173)*

supporting materials *(176)*

connective *(177)*

transition *(177)*

internal preview *(178)*

internal summary *(178)*

signpost *(179)*

REVIEW QUESTIONS

After reading this chapter, you should be able to answer the following questions:

1. Why is it important that speeches be organized clearly and coherently?

2. How many main points will your speeches usually contain? Why is it important to limit the number of main points in your speeches?

3. What are the five basic patterns of organizing main points in a speech? Which are appropriate for informative speeches? Which is used only in persuasive speeches? Which is used most often?

4. What are three tips for preparing your main points?

5. What is the most important thing to remember when organizing supporting materials in the body of your speech?

6. What are the four kinds of speech connectives? What role does each play in a speech?

connectlucas.com
For further review, go to the Study Questions in the online Study Aids for this chapter.

EXERCISES FOR CRITICAL THINKING

1. What organizational method (or methods) might you use to arrange main points for speeches with the following specific purpose statements?

    To inform my audience about the geographical regions of Australia.

    To inform my audience about the major kinds of symbols used in Native American art.

    To inform my audience of the causes and effects of Parkinson's disease.

    To persuade my audience that the state legislature should enact tougher laws to curb the problem of repeated drunk-driving offenders.

    To inform my audience about the educational philosophy of Jean Piaget.

    To inform my audience about the major stages of the civil rights movement from 1955 to 1970.

2. Turn to the outline of main points and supporting materials for the speech about hypnosis on page 176. Create appropriate transitions, internal previews, internal summaries, and signposts for the speech.

3. Identify the organizational method used in each of the following sets of main points.

    I. Cesar Chavez is best known for his efforts to protect the rights of Mexican-American farmworkers in California.
   II. Cesar Chavez was also a tireless advocate for Mexican-American racial and cultural pride in general.

    I. The peak of Mount Kilimanjaro has an arctic climate with snow, ice, and violent winds.
   II. The middle of Mount Kilimanjaro has a rain forest climate with lush vegetation and diverse animal species.
  III. The base of Mount Kilimanjaro has a bushland climate with grassy pastures and farming communities.

    I. Caused by an antibiotic-resistant strain of staphylococcus bacteria, MRSA has become increasingly prevalent among college students.
   II. The effects of MRSA include skin infections, damage to internal organs, pneumonia, and, in some cases, death.

    I. Fraudulent charity fund-raising is a widespread national problem.
   II. The problem can be solved by a combination of government regulation and individual awareness.

    I. Founded in 1948, NASCAR was limited primarily to the South through the 1950s and 1960s.
   II. The modern era of NASCAR began in the 1970s with the development of the points system to crown a yearly champion.
  III. Today NASCAR is second only to football as the most popular spectator sport in America.

Applying *the* Power *of* Public Speaking

You are in the purchasing department of a large clothing manufacturer. The company's design team has come up with an idea for a new shirt requiring a lightweight, stretchable fabric. The fabric cannot be provided by your company's usual suppliers, so you were sent to visit a number of textile firms in the U.S. and abroad to see what they can offer. You were asked to evaluate their products for quality, availability, and cost.

You have just returned from a 10-day trip to textile manufacturers in North Carolina, Italy, India, and China. You will present your findings and recommendations to the purchasing and design departments, but you're not sure how best to organize your speech. Your major choices are chronological order, problem-solution order, and topical order. What might be the main points of your speech with each of these methods of organization? Explain which method you think would be most effective for your presentation.

Beginning and Ending the Speech

On the night of January 26, 1988, a conductor stepped to the podium at the Majestic Theatre in New York City, tapped his baton, raised his arms, and signaled the orchestra to play. Moments later, American theatergoers first heard the dramatic opening chords of *The Phantom of the Opera*. Today, this scene has been repeated more than 8,500 times and *Phantom* has become the longest-running musical in Broadway history.

Like most classic musicals, *Phantom of the Opera* begins with an overture—an orchestral introduction that captures the audience's attention and gives them a preview of the music they are going to hear. Without such an introduction—if the characters simply walked onstage and began singing or speaking—the beginning of the play would seem too abrupt, and the audience would not be suitably "primed" for the entertainment.

Similarly, most musicals end with a finale, when the whole cast is onstage, elements of the dramatic plot are resolved, portions of the principal songs are recalled, and the music is brought to a dramatic climax. If there were no such conclusion, if the actors merely stopped and walked offstage, the audience would be left unsatisfied.

Just as musical plays need appropriate beginnings and endings, so do speeches. The beginning, or introduction, prepares listeners for what is to come. The conclusion ties up the speech and alerts listeners that the speech is going to end. Ideally, it is a satisfying conclusion.

In this chapter we explore the roles played by an introduction and a conclusion in speechmaking. We also discuss techniques aimed at fulfilling those roles. If you apply these techniques imaginatively, you will take a big step toward elevating your speeches from the ordinary to the splendid.

The Introduction

First impressions are important. A poor beginning may so distract or alienate listeners that the speaker can never fully recover. Moreover, getting off on the right foot is vital to a speaker's self-confidence. What could be more encouraging than watching your listeners' faces begin to register interest, attention, and pleasure? A good introduction, you will find, is an excellent confidence booster.

In most speech situations, the introduction has four objectives:

- Get the attention and interest of your audience.
- Reveal the topic of your speech.
- Establish your credibility and goodwill.
- Preview the body of the speech.

We'll look at each of these objectives in turn.

GET ATTENTION AND INTEREST

"Unless a speaker can interest his audience at once, his effort will be a failure." So said the great lawyer Clarence Darrow. If your topic is not one of extraordinary interest, your listeners are likely to say to themselves, "So what? Who cares?" A speaker can quickly lose an audience if she or he doesn't use the introduction to get their attention and quicken their interest.

Getting the initial attention of your audience is usually easy—even before you utter a single word. After you are introduced and step to the lectern, your audience will normally give you their attention. If they don't, wait patiently. Look directly at the audience without saying a word. In a few moments all talking and physical commotion will stop. Your listeners will be attentive. You will be ready to start speaking.

Keeping the attention of your audience once you start talking is more difficult. Here are the methods used most often. Employed individually or in combination, they will help get the audience caught up in your speech.

Relate the Topic to the Audience

People pay attention to things that affect them directly. If you can relate the topic to your listeners, they are much more likely to be interested in it.

Suppose, for example, one of your classmates begins her speech like this:

> Today I am going to talk about collecting postcards—a hobby that is both fascinating and financially rewarding. I would like to explain the basic kinds of collectible postcards, why they are so valuable, and how collectors buy and sell their cards.

This is certainly a clear introduction, but it is not one to get you hooked on the speech. Now what if your classmate were to begin her speech this way—as one student actually did.

> It's Saturday morning, and you are helping clean out your grandmother's attic. After working a while, you stumble upon a trunk, open it, and discover hundreds of old postcards. Thinking about getting to the football game on time, you start tossing the cards into the trash can. Congratulations! You have just thrown away a year's tuition.

This time the speaker has used just the right bait. Chances are you will be hooked.

Even when you use other interest-arousing lures, you should *always* relate your topic to the audience. At times this will test your ingenuity, but it pays dividends. Here is an excellent example from a student speech about dreams. The speaker began by saying:

> You're being chased by an object of unspeakable horror, yet your legs can only move in slow motion. Each step takes unbearably long, and your frantic struggle to run faster is hopeless. Your pursuer gets closer, and your desperation turns to terror. You're completely helpless—eye to eye with death.
>
> Then you wake up, gasping for air, your heart pounding, your face clammy with sweat. It takes a few minutes for your heart and breathing to slow down. You reassure yourself that it was "just a dream." Soon you drift back to sleep.

connectlucas.com
View the beginning of "In Your Dreams" in the online Media Library for this chapter (Video Clip 9.1).

By using vivid language to describe something all his classmates had experienced, the speaker made sure of an attentive audience.

State the Importance of Your Topic

Presumably, you think your speech is important. Tell your audience why they should think so too. Here is how Judith Kaye, Chief Judge of the State of New York, used this method to involve her audience in a speech to the American Bar Association Center on Children and the Law:

> We know that a child is born into poverty in the United States every 36 seconds, and we see 12.8 million children living below the poverty line. . . . We see an estimated

8.5 million children, nearly 12 percent of all U.S. children, without health insurance programs. . . . A child dies from neglect or abuse every six hours, a child is killed by gunfire almost every three hours, and the number of neglected or abused children each year would fill up the city of Detroit.[1]

These are striking statistics. By citing them in her introduction, Kaye emphasized the importance of her topic and captured the attention of her audience.

Clearly this technique is easy to use when discussing social and political issues such as child abuse, endangered species, terrorism, and stem cell research, but it is appropriate for other topics as well. Here is how one student handled it in a speech about starting a home aquarium:

It is very hard to cuddle a fish. Fish won't roll over or fetch the morning paper. You won't find them curling up on your lap, chasing a ball of string, or rescuing a child from a burning building.

Yet despite these shortcomings, 300 million tropical fish have found their way into 15 million American homes. Each year $60 million of tropical fish are sold in the United States, and they have earned a spot next to the all-American dog and the cuddly kitten in the hearts of millions of people. Today I would like to explain how you can start a home aquarium and discover the pleasures of owning tropical fish.

Whenever you discuss a topic whose importance may not be clear to the audience, you should think about ways to demonstrate its significance in the introduction.

Startle the Audience

One surefire way to arouse interest quickly is to startle your listeners with an arresting or intriguing statement. Everyone in the audience paid close attention after this speaker's introduction:

Take a moment and think of the three women closest to you. Who comes to mind? Your mother? Your sister? Your girlfriend? Your wife? Your best friend? Now guess which one will be sexually assaulted during her lifetime. It's not a pleasant thought, but according to the U.S. Department of Justice, one of every three American women will be sexually assaulted sometime during her life.

Notice the gradual buildup to the speaker's arresting statement, "Now guess which one will be sexually assaulted during her lifetime." This statement startles the audience—especially the men—and drives home at a personal level the problem of sexual assault against women. The effect would have been much less if the speaker had said, "Sexual assault against women is a serious problem."

Sometimes you may want to startle your audience in the very first sentence of your speech. Here is how one student began her speech opposing the use of Native American names for sports teams:

In tonight's games, the San Antonio Spics are playing the New Jersey Japs, while the Los Angeles Jews will take on the Minnesota Polacks.

This technique is highly effective and easy to use. Just be sure the startling introduction relates directly to the subject of your speech. If you choose a strong opening simply for its shock value and then go on to talk about something else, your audience will be confused and possibly annoyed.

A good introduction will get your speech off to a strong start. To be most effective, it should relate the topic to the audience and be delivered from a minimum of notes.

Arouse the Curiosity of the Audience

People are curious. One way to draw them into your speech is with a series of statements that progressively whet their curiosity about the subject of the speech. For example:

> It is the most common chronic disease in the United States. Controllable but incurable, it is a symptomless disease. You can have it for years and never know until it kills you. Some 73 million Americans have this disease, and 300,000 will die from it before the year is out. Odds are that five of us in this class have it.
>
> What am I talking about? Not cancer. Not AIDS. Not heart disease. I am talking about hypertension—high blood pressure.

For another example, look at this splendid opening from a student speech entitled "The Gift of Life":

> Each of you has a gift. What kind of gift is it? It's not a Christmas gift or a birthday gift. It's not some special talent or skill. It's a gift that could save a life—maybe more than one. If you decide to give it, you lose nothing.
>
> Some people bury their gift. Others burn it. All but one of you who completed my questionnaire would gladly receive the gift, but only 20 percent of you have decided to give it. This gift is the donation of your vital organs when you die.

Not only does this speaker relate the topic directly to his classmates, he gets them further involved by building suspense about the "gift" that each of us has. Notice how much less effective the introduction would have been if he had simply said, "Today I am going to talk about organ donation."

Question the Audience

Asking a *rhetorical question* is another way to get your listeners thinking about your speech. Sometimes a single question will do:

Internet Connection

www.connectlucas.com

Looking for a quotation to use in the introduction or conclusion of your speech? Visit Yahoo Quotations (**http://dir.yahoo.com/Reference/Quotations/**) for a comprehensive roster of links to collected quotations on the Web.

Are you interested in reading introductions and conclusions from famous speeches in world history? You can find them at The History Place: Great Speeches Collection (**www.historyplace.com/speeches/previous.htm**).

How would you respond if a loved one was the victim of terrorism?

What would you think if you went to the doctor because you were ill and she told you to watch *The Simpsons* as part of your treatment?

rhetorical question
A question that the audience answers mentally rather than out loud.

In other circumstances, you may want to pose a series of questions, each of which draws the audience deeper and deeper into the speech. Here is how one speaker used this method:

Have you ever spent a sleepless night studying for an exam? Can you remember rushing to finish a term paper because you waited too long to start writing it? Do you often feel overwhelmed by all the things you have to get done at school? At work? At home?

If so, you may be the victim of poor time management. Fortunately, there are proven strategies you can follow to use your time more effectively and to keep control of your life.

Like beginning with a startling statement, opening with a question works best when the question is meaningful to the audience and firmly related to the content of the speech. It also works most effectively when you pause for just a moment after each question. This adds dramatic impact and gives the question time to sink in. The audience, of course, will answer mentally—not out loud.

Begin with a Quotation

Another way to arouse the interest of your audience is to start with an attention-getting quotation. You might choose your quotation from Shakespeare or Confucius, from the Bible or Talmud, from a poem, song, or film. Here is how one student used a quotation to begin a speech about scientist Jonas Salk, who developed the first polio vaccine:

"If one is lucky, a solitary fantasy can totally transform one million realities." These words from poet and writer Maya Angelou could apply easily to the dedicated researcher Jonas Salk, who created a vaccine for polio. A half century ago this crippling disease struck indiscriminately, but today widespread use of the vaccine has virtually wiped out polio. In my talk I would like to describe how Salk persevered and triumphed in his quest despite doubts and major setbacks.

A humorous quotation can afford double impact, as in this speech about the need for political reform in the U.S. Congress:

Mark Twain once said, "It could probably be shown by facts and figures that there is no distinctly American criminal class except Congress."

As you research your speeches, keep an eye out for quotations, stories, and other materials you can use to craft an introduction that will capture the attention of your listeners.

By opening with Twain's words, the speaker not only got the audience's attention but also foreshadowed a central theme of her speech. Notice, too, that both of the quotations used here as examples are relatively short. Opening your speech with a lengthy quotation is a sure way to set your audience yawning.

Tell a Story

We all enjoy stories—especially if they are provocative, amusing, dramatic, or suspenseful. To work well as introductions, they should also be clearly relevant to the main point of the speech. Used in this way, stories are perhaps the most effective way to begin a speech.

Consider, for example, the story one student told to open his speech about America's crumbling bridges:

Gary Babineau thought he was dead. It was August 1, 2007, and he had just driven his blue Chevy truck onto the I-35 West bridge in Minneapolis when the 30-year-old structure began collapsing. "I heard a rumbling, like a jackhammer," he said later, "and then it completely gave way." His pickup plummeted 35 feet, landing upside down, the bed severed from the cab. Miraculously, Babineau, who was wearing his seat belt, survived, but others were not so lucky. Thirteen people died that day; more than a hundred were injured.

The collapse of the I-35 bridge in Minneapolis was a tragedy, but it will not be the last one. There are 79,000 bridges across the country rated as "structurally deficient" by the Federal Highway Administration. These bridges carry 300 million vehicles a day, and one can only wonder which will be the next to go.

Like many good introductions, this one does a double job—it arouses the interest of the audience and gets listeners emotionally involved in the speech.

You can also use stories based on your personal experience. Here is how one pre-med student used such a story. She began by recounting the first time she observed doctors performing surgery in the operating room:

There I stood, wearing a surgical mask, in the middle of a large, brightly lit room. In the center of the room were five figures huddled over a table. I found it difficult to see since everything was draped in blue sheets, yet I didn't dare take a step toward the table.

Then one of the figures called to me, "Angela, get over here and take a closer look." My knees buckled as I walked through the sterile environment. But eventually I was there, standing over an unconscious body in the operating room.

connectlucas.com
View the beginning of "Hoping to Heal" in the online Media Library for this chapter (Video Clip 9.2).

The effectiveness of any story—especially a personal one—hinges on the speaker's delivery as well as on the content. As you can see from the excerpt of this speech on Video Clip 9.2 in the online Media Library for this chapter, the speaker uses pauses, eye contact, and changes in her tone of voice to help draw her audience into the speech. See if you can do the same in your introduction.

The seven methods discussed above are the ones used most often by student speakers to gain attention and interest. Other methods include referring to the occasion, inviting audience participation, using audio equipment or visual aids, relating to a previous speaker, and beginning with humor. For any given speech, try to choose the method that is most suitable for the topic, the audience, and the occasion.

REVEAL THE TOPIC

In the process of gaining attention, be sure to state clearly the topic of your speech. If you do not, your listeners will be confused. And once they are confused, your chances of getting them absorbed in the speech are almost nil.

This is a basic point—so basic that it may hardly seem worth mentioning. Yet you would be surprised how many students need to be reminded of it. You may hear speeches in your own class in which the topic is not clear by the end of the introduction. So you will know what to avoid, here is such an introduction, presented in a public speaking class:

Imagine taking a leisurely boat ride along a peaceful waterway. The sun is high in the sky, reflecting brightly off the ripples around you. The banks are lush with mangrove and cypress trees. You see a stately pelican resting on a low-lying branch. You grab your camera, snap a shot, and check the result. The picture is perfect. But will it be perfect in the future? That is the question I want to explore today.

What is the topic of this speech? Nature photography? No. Birding? No. Tourism in the tropics? No. The student was talking about efforts to restore the natural beauty of the Florida Everglades. But she did not make that clear to her audience. Suppose, instead, she had begun her speech differently:

Alligators, panthers, otters, brown pelicans—these and other creatures have lost 50 percent of their habitat in south Florida over the past few decades. Now, however, there is an $8 billion program to preserve their home in the Florida Everglades. The largest restoration effort in the history of the world, it will rejuvenate one of America's most diverse ecosystems and protect it for future generations.

This opening would have provided a way to get the audience's attention, but it also would have related directly to the speech topic. If you beat around the bush in your introduction, you may lose your listeners. Even if they already know your topic, you should restate it clearly and concisely at some point in the introduction.

Telling a story is an excellent way to gain attention in a speech introduction. The story should be clearly relevant to the topic and should be delivered expressively with strong eye contact.

ESTABLISH CREDIBILITY AND GOODWILL

Besides getting attention and revealing the topic, there is a third objective you may need to accomplish in your introduction—establishing your credibility and goodwill.

Credibility is mostly a matter of being qualified to speak on a given topic—and of being *perceived* as qualified by your listeners. Here is how one student established her credibility on the subject of weight lifting without sounding like a braggart:

> What is the fastest growing sport today among American women? If you answered weight lifting, you are absolutely correct. Once seen as an exclusively male activity, weight lifting has crossed the gender barrier—and with good reason. Regardless of whether you are male or female, weight lifting can give you a sense of strength and power, enhance your self-esteem, and make you look and feel better.
>
> I started lifting weights when I was in high school, and I have kept at it for the past eight years. I have also taught weight lifting in several health clubs, and I am a certified instructor through the Aerobics and Fitness Association of America.
>
> Using some of my experience, I would like to explain the basic kinds of weights and how to use them properly.

Whether or not you lift weights, you will probably be more interested in the speech when you realize the speaker knows what she is talking about.

Your credibility need not be based on firsthand knowledge and experience. It can come from reading, from classes, from interviews, from friends—as in these cases:

> I have been interested in the history of the civil rights movement for several years, and I have read a number of books and articles about it.

> The information I am going to share with you today comes mostly from my biology class and an interview with Reyna Vasquez of the local Audubon Society.

Whatever the source of your expertise, be sure to let the audience know.

credibility
The audience's perception of whether a speaker is qualified to speak on a given topic.

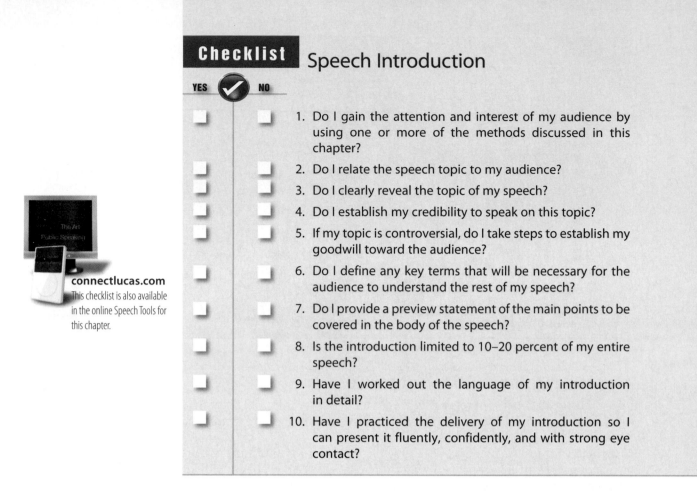

Checklist — Speech Introduction

YES ✓ NO

1. Do I gain the attention and interest of my audience by using one or more of the methods discussed in this chapter?

2. Do I relate the speech topic to my audience?

3. Do I clearly reveal the topic of my speech?

4. Do I establish my credibility to speak on this topic?

5. If my topic is controversial, do I take steps to establish my goodwill toward the audience?

6. Do I define any key terms that will be necessary for the audience to understand the rest of my speech?

7. Do I provide a preview statement of the main points to be covered in the body of the speech?

8. Is the introduction limited to 10–20 percent of my entire speech?

9. Have I worked out the language of my introduction in detail?

10. Have I practiced the delivery of my introduction so I can present it fluently, confidently, and with strong eye contact?

connectlucas.com
This checklist is also available in the online Speech Tools for this chapter.

goodwill
The audience's perception of whether the speaker has the best interests of the audience in mind.

Establishing your *goodwill* is a slightly different challenge. It is often crucial outside the classroom, where speakers have well-established reputations and may be identified with causes that arouse hostility among listeners. In such a situation, the speaker must try to defuse that hostility right at the start of the speech.

Occasionally you may have to do the same thing in your classroom speeches. Suppose you advocate a highly unpopular position. You will need to make a special effort to ensure that your classmates will consider your point of view. This is how one student tried to minimize his classmates' opposition at the start of a speech in favor of building more nuclear power plants:

The development of new nuclear power plants in the United States came to a standstill during the 1980s. Yet, as *Discover* magazine stated just last month, the time has come to look again at the benefits of nuclear power. Unlike fossil fuels, it does not contribute to global warming; it does not leave America at the mercy of foreign oil; and, with advances in technology, it is much safer than before.

That's why I'm speaking in favor of building more nuclear power plants to meet our future energy needs. I know most of you oppose nuclear power—I did, too, until I started researching this speech. Today I'd like to share with you some of the facts I have found. I know I can't persuade all of you. But I do ask you to listen with an open mind and to consider the merit of my arguments.

What reasonable listener could ignore such a sincere, forthright plea?

PREVIEW THE BODY OF THE SPEECH

As we saw in Chapter 3, most people are poor listeners. Even good listeners need all the help they can get in sorting out a speaker's ideas. One way to help your listeners is to tell them in the introduction what they should listen for in the rest of the speech. Here is an excellent example, from a speech by FBI Director Robert S. Mueller III at the Department of Justice Project Safe Childhood Conference in Washington, D.C.:

> Today I want to talk about what we in the FBI are doing to attack child exploitation on the Internet. I want to touch on what we must do to meet your needs in terms of evidence collection and prosecution. Lastly, I want to talk about the role of both parents and the private sector in addressing this scourge.[2]

preview statement
A statement in the introduction of a speech that identifies the main points to be discussed in the body.

After this introduction, there was no doubt about Mueller's topic or the main points he would cover in his speech.

In some types of persuasive speeches, you may not want to reveal your central idea until later in the speech. But even in such a situation you must be sure your audience is not left guessing about the main points they should listen for as the speech unfolds. Nearly always, you should include a *preview statement* like the following:

> Today I will share part of what I have learned by explaining what happens when you receive an acupuncture treatment, how acupuncture works, the kinds of medical conditions that can be treated with acupuncture, and the growing use of acupuncture in combination with Western medical techniques.

> I'm here to tell you that, try as we might, we cannot build a bubble between ourselves and germs with antibacterial products and that these products actually create more problems than they solve. After looking at the problems created by antibacterial products, we'll explore some solutions.

connectlucas.com
View these preview statements from students speeches in the online Media Library for this chapter (Video Clip 9.3).

Preview statements such as these serve another purpose as well. Because they usually come at the very end of the introduction, they provide a smooth lead-in to the body of the speech. They signal that the body of the speech is about to begin.

There is one other aspect you may want to cover in previewing your speech. You can use your introduction to give specialized information—definitions or background—that your listeners will need if they are to understand the rest of the speech. Often you can do this very quickly, as in the following example:

> A triathlon is a race made up of three different events completed in succession. The events are usually swimming, biking, and running, though canoeing is sometimes substituted for one of these.

In other circumstances, you may have to explain an important term in more detail. Here is how one student handled the problem in a speech about the Underground Railroad used by slaves to escape from the South before the Civil War:

> The term "Underground Railroad" was first used about 1830. But in fact, the Underground Railroad was neither underground nor a railroad. It was an informal network that provided runaway slaves food, clothing, directions, and places to hide on their escape routes to the North and to Canada.

Why was it called the Underground Railroad? Because of its secrecy and because many of the people involved used railroad terms as code words. Hiding places, for example, were called "stations," and people who helped the slaves were called "conductors." Over the years, the Underground Railroad helped thousands of slaves make their way from bondage to freedom.

SAMPLE INTRODUCTION WITH COMMENTARY

So far we have seen many excerpts showing how to fulfill the various objectives of an introduction. Now here is a complete introduction from a student speech. The side comments indicate the principles used in developing the introduction.

The Miracle of Bone Marrow Transplants

COMMENTARY	INTRODUCTION
The speaker uses a story to gain attention. This story works particularly well because it is richly detailed and is high in human interest.	Katy Hubbell was four years old when she was diagnosed with a severe case of aplastic anemia, a disease in which the bone marrow stops producing new blood cells. After several types of treatment failed, Katy underwent a bone marrow transplant. Her donor was a 40-year-old airline manager who lived thousands of miles away. His generosity saved the life of a little girl he had never met. Today Katy is an active preteen girl who loves Harry Potter books and wants to be a cheerleader.
Now the speaker reveals her topic. Calling bone marrow transplants a "medical miracle" reinforces the importance of the subject, while explaining her personal involvement shows the speaker's goodwill and helps establish her credibility.	Bone marrow transplants have been called a medical miracle because of their lifesaving capability. I first became interested in the subject when a 12-year-old member of my church was diagnosed with leukemia. I joined a committee to publicize Greg's case and to seek potential donors. Eventually a suitable donor was found and Greg is now a healthy high-school sophomore.
Here the speaker relates the topic directly to her audience and shows why they should care about it. The combination of statistics with the quotation from the Food and Drug Administration reinforces the importance of the topic.	Because of Greg's illness, I learned that anyone can get sick and need a bone marrow donation. It could be any of us in this room, a close friend, or even a family member. An estimated 15,000 bone marrow transplants are performed in the U.S. each year. According to the U.S. Food and Drug Administration, these transplants give patients "a chance to beat diseases once believed to have no cure."
By mentioning her research, the speaker further bolsters her credibility. She then ends the introduction by previewing the main points to be discussed in the body of the speech.	Through my research for this speech, I have learned much more about this remarkable procedure. Today I would like to talk with you about bone marrow donation—how simple a process it is for the donor, how absolutely vital it is for the recipient, and how donors and recipients find one another.

Establishing goodwill in the introduction is especially important for speakers who confront controversial issues—as with Canadian official John Gerretsen, speaking here on negotiations about land use.

TIPS FOR PREPARING THE INTRODUCTION

1. Keep the introduction relatively brief. Under normal circumstances it should not constitute more than 10 to 20 percent of your speech.

2. Be on the lookout for possible introductory materials as you do your research. File them with your notes so they will be handy when you are ready for them.

3. Be creative in devising your introduction. Experiment with two or three different openings and choose the one that seems most likely to get the audience interested in your speech.

4. Don't worry about the exact wording of your introduction until you have finished preparing the body of the speech. After you have determined your main points, it will be much easier to make final decisions about how to begin the speech.

5. Work out your introduction in detail. Some teachers recommend that you write it out word for word; others prefer that you outline it. Whichever method you use, practice the introduction over and over until you can deliver it smoothly from a minimum of notes and with strong eye contact. This will get your speech off to a good start and give you a big boost of confidence.

The Conclusion

"Great is the art of beginning," said Longfellow, "but greater the art is of ending." Longfellow was thinking of poetry, but his insight is equally applicable to public speaking. Many a speaker has marred an otherwise fine speech by a long-winded, silly, or antagonistic conclusion. Your closing remarks are your last chance to drive home your ideas. Moreover, your final impression will probably linger in your listeners' minds. Thus you need to craft your conclusion with as much care as your introduction.

No matter what kind of speech you are giving, the conclusion has two major functions:

- To let the audience know you are ending the speech.

- To reinforce the audience's understanding of, or commitment to, the central idea.

Let us look at each.

SIGNAL THE END OF THE SPEECH

It may seem obvious that you should let your audience know you are going to stop soon. However, you will almost certainly hear speeches in your class in which the speaker concludes so abruptly that you are taken by surprise. Too sudden an ending leaves the audience puzzled and unfulfilled.

How do you let an audience know your speech is ending? One way is through what you say. "In conclusion," "My purpose has been," "Let me end by saying"—these are all brief cues that you are getting ready to stop.

You can also let your audience know the end is in sight by your manner of delivery. The conclusion is the climax of a speech. A speaker who has carefully built to a peak of interest and involvement will not need to say anything like "in conclusion." By use of the voice—its tone, pacing, intonation, and rhythm—a speaker can build the momentum of a speech so there is no doubt when it is over.

One method of doing this has been likened to a musical crescendo. As in a symphony in which one instrument after another joins in until the entire orchestra is playing, the speech builds in force until it reaches a zenith of power and intensity.[3] (This does *not* mean simply getting louder and louder. It is a combination of many things, including vocal pitch, choice of words, dramatic content, gestures, pauses—and possibly loudness.)

A superb example of this method is the memorable conclusion to Martin Luther King's "I've Been to the Mountaintop," the speech he delivered the night before he was assassinated in April 1968. Speaking to an audience of 2,000 people in Memphis, Tennessee, he ended his speech with a stirring declaration that the civil rights movement would succeed despite the many threats on his life:

> Like anybody, I would like to live a long life. Longevity has its place, but I'm not concerned about that now. I just want to do God's will, and he's allowed me to go up to the mountain, and I've looked over and I've seen the Promised Land. I may not get there with you, but I want you to know tonight that we as a people will get to the Promised Land. So I'm happy tonight. I'm not worried about anything; I'm not fearing any man. Mine eyes have seen the glory of the coming of the Lord.

Another effective method might be compared to the dissolve ending of a concert song that evokes deep emotions: "The song seems to fade away while the light on the singer shrinks gradually to a smaller and smaller circle until it lights only the face, then the eyes. Finally, it is a pinpoint, and disappears with the last note of the song."[4] Here is a speech ending that does much the same thing. It is from General Douglas MacArthur's moving farewell to the cadets at the U.S. Military Academy:

crescendo ending
A conclusion in which the speech builds to a zenith of power and intensity.

connectlucas.com
View the ending of Martin Luther King's "I've Been to the Mountaintop" in the online Media Library for this chapter (Video Clip 9.4).

The conclusion is your last chance to drive home your ideas. Successful speakers such as South African statesman Nelson Mandela craft their endings with great care to leave a strong final impression.

In my dreams I hear again the crash of guns, the rattle of musketry, the strange, mournful mutter of the battlefield. But in the evening of my memory always I come back to West Point. Always there echoes and re-echoes: duty, honor, country.

Today marks my final roll call with you. But I want you to know that when I cross the river, my last conscious thoughts will be of the Corps, and the Corps, and the Corps.

I bid you farewell.

The final words fade like the spotlight, bringing the speech to an emotional close.

You may think that you couldn't possibly end a speech with that much pathos—and you'd be right. MacArthur was an eloquent speaker discussing a grave issue with extraordinary poignance. This combination rarely occurs. But that doesn't mean you can't use the dissolve ending effectively. One student used it with great effect in a speech about the immigrant experience in the United States. During the body of the speech, the student spoke about the numbers of immigrants and the challenges they faced. Then, in her conclusion, she created a moving dissolve ending by evoking the emotional images of her grandfather's arrival in the United States:

On a recent trip to Ellis Island, where my grandfather first stepped on American soil, I saw his name etched into the wall along with the names of tens of thousands of other immigrants. I saw the entry hall where he lined up to process his forms. I saw the room where he underwent a physical examination. I sensed the fear and the insecurity he must have felt. But I could also sense his excitement as he looked forward to life in a land of opportunity—a land he came to think of as home.

Both the crescendo and the dissolve endings must be worked out with great care. Practice until you get the words and the timing just right. The benefits will be well worth your time.

connectlucas.com
To read these speeches by King and MacArthur, log on to the Top 100 American Speeches of the 20th Century in the online Research Library.

dissolve ending
A conclusion that generates emotional appeal by fading step by step to a dramatic final statement.

REINFORCE THE CENTRAL IDEA

The second major function of a conclusion is to reinforce the audience's understanding of, or commitment to, the central idea. There are many ways to do this. Here are the ones you are most likely to use.

Summarize Your Speech

Restating the main points is the easiest way to end a speech. One student used this technique effectively in his persuasive speech about the AIDS epidemic in Africa:

connectlucas.com
View the conclusion of "AIDS in Africa: A World Crisis" in the online Media Library for this chapter (Video Clip 9.5).

> In conclusion, we have seen that the AIDS epidemic is having a devastating effect on African society. An entire adult generation is slowly being wiped out. An entirely new generation of AIDS orphans is being created. Governments in the nations most afflicted have neither the resources nor the expertise to counter the epidemic. Many African economies are being crippled by the loss of people in the workplace.
>
> Before it's too late, the United Nations and developed countries need to increase their efforts to halt the epidemic and bring it under control. The lives and well-being of tens of millions of people hang in the balance.

The value of a summary is that it explicitly restates the central idea and main points one last time. But as we shall see, there are more imaginative and compelling ways to end a speech. They can be used in combination with a summary or, at times, in place of it.

End with a Quotation

A quotation is one of the most common and effective devices to conclude a speech. Here is a fine example, from a speech on the misuse of television advertisements in political campaigns:

> We cannot ignore the evils of television commercials in which candidates for the highest offices are sold to the voters in 30-second spots. These ads cheapen the elective process and degrade our political institutions. In the words of historian Arthur Schlesinger, Jr., "You cannot merchandise candidates like soap and hope to preserve a rational democracy."

The closing quotation is particularly good because its urgency is exactly suited to the speech. When you run across a *brief* quotation that so perfectly captures your central idea, keep it in mind as a possible conclusion.

Make a Dramatic Statement

Rather than using a quotation to give your conclusion force and vitality, you may want to devise your own dramatic statement. Some speeches have become famous because of their powerful closing lines. One is Patrick Henry's legendary "Liberty or Death" oration. It takes its name from the final sentences Henry uttered on March 23, 1775, as he exhorted his audience to resist British tyranny:

> Is life so dear, or peace so sweet, as to be purchased at the price of chains and slavery? Forbid it, Almighty God! I know not what course others may take; but as for me, give me liberty, or give me death.

Although your classroom speeches are not likely to become famous, you can still rivet your listeners—as Henry did—with a dramatic concluding statement. What follows is a particularly striking example, from a speech on suicide prevention. Throughout the speech, the student referred to a friend who had tried to commit suicide the previous year. Then, in the conclusion, she said:

> My friend is back in school, participating in activities she never did before—and enjoying it. I'm happy and proud to say that she's still fighting for her life and even happier that she failed to kill herself. Otherwise, I wouldn't be here today trying to help you. You see, I am my "friend," and I'm more than glad to say I've made it.

As you can imagine, the audience was stunned. The closing lines brought the speech to a dramatic conclusion. The speaker made it even more effective by pausing just a moment before the last words and by using her voice to give them just the right inflection.

Refer to the Introduction

An excellent way to give your speech psychological unity is to conclude by referring to ideas in the introduction. Here is how one student used the method in her speech about the Special Olympics:

Introduction: In Seattle, nine young athletes assembled at the starting line for the 100-yard dash. At the gun, they all started off—not exactly in a dash, but with a desire to run the race to the finish and win. All except one little boy who stumbled on the asphalt, tumbled over a couple of times, and began to cry. The other runners heard the boy cry. They stopped; they looked back. Then they all went back to the boy's side—every single one of them. One girl with Down syndrome kissed him and said, "This will make it better." Then all nine linked arms and walked to the finish line—together.

These athletes were not competing on national television; they were not sponsored or idolized. But they were given an opportunity to flourish under the glow of their own spotlights, to feel the brush of the ribbon cross their chests as they ran through their own finish line in their own Olympics—the Special Olympics.

In the body of her speech, the student explained the Special Olympics and called on members of the audience to become volunteers. Then, in her closing words, she tied the whole speech together by returning to the story described in her introduction:

Conclusion: Remember the nine children I mentioned at the beginning of this speech. Think of their happiness and their support for one another. Think of how much they gained from running in that race. And think how you can help others experience the same benefits as they strive to fulfill the motto of the Special Olympics: "Let me win. But if I can't win, let me be brave in the attempt."

Summarizing the speech, ending with a quotation, making a dramatic statement, referring to the introduction—all these techniques can be used separately. But you have probably noticed that speakers often combine two or more in their conclusions. Actually, all four techniques can be fused into one—for example, a dramatic quotation that summarizes the central idea while referring to the introduction.

connectlucas.com
View the beginning and ending of "Making a Difference Through the Special Olympics" in the online Media Library for this chapter (Video Clip 9.6).

Checklist — Speech Conclusion

YES	NO	
☐	☐	1. Do I signal that my speech is coming to an end?
☐	☐	2. Do I reinforce my central idea by (check all that apply):
☐	☐	Summarizing the main points of my speech
☐	☐	Ending with a quotation
☐	☐	Making a dramatic statement
☐	☐	Referring to the introduction
☐	☐	3. Is the conclusion limited to 5–10 percent of my entire speech?
☐	☐	4. Have I worked out the language of my conclusion in detail?
☐	☐	5. Have I practiced the delivery of my conclusion so I can present it fluently, confidently, and with strong eye contact?

connectlucas.com
This checklist is also available in the online Speech Tools for this chapter.

One other concluding technique is making a direct appeal to your audience for action. This technique applies only to a particular type of persuasive speech, however, and will be discussed in Chapter 15. The four methods covered in this chapter are appropriate for all kinds of speeches and occasions.

SAMPLE CONCLUSION WITH COMMENTARY

How do you fit these methods together to make a conclusion? Here is an example, from the speech about bone marrow transplants whose introduction we looked at earlier (page 196).

COMMENTARY	CONCLUSION
The speaker gives an excellent summary of her speech. This is particularly important when speaking to inform because it gives you one last chance to make sure the audience remembers your main points	We have seen, then, that becoming a bone marrow donor is safe and relatively painless. We have also seen the immense benefits to the people who receive bone marrow transplants. Finally, we have seen how donors and recipients are matched up through a national network of bone marrow organizations.
By referring to Greg, whom she had mentioned in her introduction, the speaker unifies the entire speech. The quotation from Greg and the speaker's final sentence end the speech on a strong note.	It is now more than three years since Greg received his bone marrow transplant. In that time, he has changed from a very sick young boy to a busy, healthy, active young man. Greg says of his donor, "Without her, I wouldn't be here today. I owe my whole life, and everything I ever accomplish, to her." Through bone marrow donation, all of us have the opportunity to make that kind of contribution.

TIPS FOR PREPARING THE CONCLUSION

1. As with the introduction, keep an eye out for possible concluding materials as you research and develop the speech.

2. Conclude with a bang, not a whimper. Be creative in devising a conclusion that hits the hearts and minds of your audience. Work on several possible endings, and select the one that seems likely to have the greatest impact.

3. Don't be long-winded. The conclusion will normally make up no more than 5 to 10 percent of your speech.

4. Don't leave anything in your conclusion to chance. Work it out in detail, and give yourself plenty of time to practice delivering it. Many students like to write out the conclusion word for word to guarantee it is just right. If you do this, make sure you can present it smoothly, confidently, and with feeling—without relying on your notes or sounding wooden. Make your last impression as forceful and as favorable as you can.

SUMMARY

First impressions are important. So are final impressions. This is why speeches need strong introductions and conclusions.

In most speech situations you need to accomplish four objectives with your introduction—get the attention and interest of the audience, reveal the topic of your speech, establish your credibility and goodwill, and preview the body of the speech. Gaining attention and interest can be done in several ways. You can show the importance of your topic, especially as it relates to your audience. You can startle or question your audience or arouse their curiosity. You can begin with a quotation or a story.

Be sure to state the topic of your speech clearly in your introduction so the audience knows where the speech is going. Establishing credibility means that you tell the audience why you are qualified to speak on the topic at hand. Establishing goodwill may be necessary if your point of view is unpopular. Previewing the body of the speech helps the audience listen effectively and provides a smooth lead-in to the body of the speech.

The first objective of a speech conclusion is to let the audience know you are ending, which you can do by your words or by your manner of delivery. The second objective of a conclusion is to reinforce your central idea. You can accomplish this by summarizing the speech, ending with a quotation, making a dramatic statement, or referring to the introduction. Sometimes you may want to combine two or more of these techniques. Be creative in devising a vivid, forceful conclusion.

KEY TERMS

REVIEW QUESTIONS

After reading this chapter, you should be able to answer the following questions:

1. What are four objectives of a speech introduction?

2. What are seven methods you can use in the introduction to get the attention and interest of your audience?

3. Why is it important to establish your credibility at the beginning of your speech?

4. What is a preview statement? Why should you nearly always include a preview statement in the introduction of your speech?

5. What are five tips for preparing your introduction?

6. What are the major functions of a speech conclusion?

7. What are two ways you can signal the end of your speech?

8. What are four ways to reinforce the central idea when concluding your speech?

9. What are four tips for preparing your conclusion?

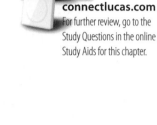

connectlucas.com
For further review, go to the Study Questions in the online Study Aids for this chapter.

EXERCISES FOR CRITICAL THINKING

1. Here are six speech topics. Explain how you might relate each to your classmates in the introduction of a speech.

Social Security	laughter
illiteracy	steroids
soap operas	blood donation

2. Think of a speech topic (preferably one for your next speech in class). Create an introduction for a speech dealing with any aspect of the topic you wish. In your introduction be sure to gain the attention of the audience, to reveal the topic and relate it to the audience, to establish your credibility, and to preview the body of the speech.

3. Using the same topic as in Exercise 2, create a speech conclusion. Be sure to let your audience know the speech is ending, to reinforce the central idea, and to make the conclusion vivid and memorable.

Applying *the* **Power** *of* **Public Speaking**

Your degree in civil engineering has served you well and you are now the chief city planner for a major metropolis. After studying the issue for more than a year, you and the planning commission have decided that the best way to relieve the city's growing traffic congestion is to build a new downtown freeway. Unfortunately, there is no way to build the freeway without knocking down a number of houses and businesses. You are not happy about this, and you know it will create difficulty for the people affected, but your research and computer simulations show that it is by far the most effective long-range option for improving the city's traffic flow.

Not surprisingly, the neighborhood association that represents the area through which you plan to build the freeway has expressed a number of concerns about the proposal. Because of your excellent public speaking skills, you have been chosen to represent the city at a meeting of the neighborhood association. Your job at the meeting will be to address the audience's concerns and provide a convincing explanation of the city's decision to build the freeway. You know that if your speech is to be persuasive, you must use the introduction to establish your credibility and goodwill so your listeners will be willing to listen receptively to what you say in the body.

Write a draft of your introduction. In it be sure to address all four functions of a speech introduction discussed in this chapter.

Outlining the Speech

The Preparation Outline
   Guidelines for the Preparation Outline
   Sample Preparation Outline with Commentary

The Speaking Outline
   Guidelines for the Speaking Outline
   Sample Speaking Outline with Commentary

Think what might happen if you tried to build a house without a floor plan or an architect's blueprint. You place the kitchen next to the driveway to make it convenient for carrying in groceries. But the dining room turns up at the other end of the house. When you cook and serve a meal, you have to run with the plates to keep the food from getting cold. You put the bathroom at the head of the stairs to make it accessible to visitors. But the door opens in such a way that the unwary guest is catapulted down the steps. You think it's a wonderful idea to have almost no interior walls. But when the first snowfall comes, your (unsupported) roof collapses.

Plans and blueprints are essential to architecture. So, too, are outlines essential to effective speeches. An outline is like a blueprint for your speech. It allows you to see the full scope and content of your speech at a glance. By outlining, you can judge whether each part of the speech is fully developed, whether you have adequate supporting materials for your main points, and whether the main points are properly balanced. An outline helps you make sure that related items are together, that ideas flow from one to another, that the structure of your speech will "stand up"—and not collapse.

Probably you will use two kinds of outlines for your speeches—one very detailed, for the planning stage, and one very brief, for the delivery of the speech.

The Preparation Outline

The preparation outline is just what its name implies—an outline that helps you prepare the speech. Writing a preparation outline means putting your speech together—deciding what you will say in the introduction, how you will organize the main points and supporting materials in the body, and what you will say in the conclusion.

GUIDELINES FOR THE PREPARATION OUTLINE

preparation outline
A detailed outline developed during the process of speech preparation that includes the title, specific purpose, central idea, introduction, main points, subpoints, connectives, conclusion, and bibliography of a speech.

Over the years, a relatively uniform system for preparation outlines has developed. It is explained below and is exemplified in the sample outline on pages 213–215. You should check with your teacher to see exactly what format you are to follow.

State the Specific Purpose of Your Speech

The specific purpose statement should be a separate unit that comes before the outline itself. Including the specific purpose makes it easier to assess how well you have constructed the speech to accomplish your purpose.

Identify the Central Idea

Some teachers prefer that the central idea be given immediately after the purpose statement. Others prefer that it be given and identified in the text of the outline. Check to see which your teacher wants.

Label the Introduction, Body, and Conclusion

If you label the parts of your speech, you will be sure that you indeed *have* an introduction and conclusion and have accomplished the essential objectives of each. Usually the names of the speech parts are placed in the middle of the page or in the far left margin. They are technical labels only and are not included in the system of symbolization used to identify main points and supporting materials.

Use a Consistent Pattern of Symbolization and Indentation

In the most common system of outlining, main points are identified by Roman numerals and are indented equally so as to be aligned down the page. Subpoints (components of the main points) are identified by capital letters and are also indented equally so as to be aligned with each other. Beyond this, there may be sub-subpoints and even sub-sub-subpoints. For example:

I. Main point
  A. Subpoint
  B. Subpoint
    1. Sub-subpoint
    2. Sub-subpoint
      a. Sub-sub-subpoint
      b. Sub-sub-subpoint
II. Main point
  A. Subpoint
    1. Sub-subpoint
    2. Sub-subpoint
  B. Subpoint
    1. Sub-subpoint
    2. Sub-subpoint

The clear *visual framework* of this outline immediately shows the relationships among the ideas of the speech. The most important ideas (main points) are farthest to the left. Less important ideas (subpoints, sub-subpoints, and so on) are progressively farther to the right. This pattern reveals the structure of your entire speech.

Once you have organized the body of your speech (see Chapter 8), you should have identified the main points. You need only flesh out your outline with subpoints and sub-subpoints, as necessary, to support the main points. But suppose, as sometimes happens, you find yourself with a list of statements and are not sure which are main points, which are subpoints, and so forth. Such a list might look like this:

There were 13 people at the Last Supper—Jesus and his 12 disciples.

One of the most common sources of superstition is numbers.

In the United States, 13 is often omitted in the floor numbering of hotels and skyscrapers.

The number 13 has meant bad luck as long as anyone can remember.

Which statement is the main point? The second statement ("One of the most common sources of superstition is numbers"), which is broader in scope than any of the other statements. This would be one of the main ideas of your speech. The fourth statement is the subpoint; it immediately supports the main point. The other two statements are sub-subpoints; they illustrate the subpoint. Rearranged properly, they look like this:

visual framework
The pattern of symbolization and indentation in a speech outline that shows the relationships among the speaker's ideas.

I. One of the most common sources of superstition is numbers.
   A. The number 13 has meant bad luck as long as anyone can remember.
      1. There were 13 people at the Last Supper—Jesus and his 12 disciples.
      2. In the United States, 13 is often omitted in the floor numbering of hotels and skyscrapers.

Above all, remember that all points at the same level should immediately support the point that is just above and one notch to the left in your outline.

State Main Points and Subpoints in Full Sentences

Below are two sets of main points and subpoints for the same speech on the life of Martin Luther King.

connectlucas.com
For help formatting your outlines, use the automated Speech Outliner in the online Speech Tools for this chapter.

Ineffective	More Effective
I. Montgomery	I. King began his civil rights career in the Montgomery bus boycott of 1955–1956.
II. 1960s	II. King's greatest triumphs came during the early 1960s.
A. Birmingham	A. In 1963 he campaigned against segregation in Birmingham, Alabama.
B. March	B. Later that year he participated in the famous march on Washington, D.C.
1. 200,000	1. More than 200,000 people took part.
2. "Dream"	2. King gave his "I Have a Dream" speech.
C. Prize	C. In 1964 he received the Nobel Peace Prize.
III. Final years	III. King faced great turmoil during his final years.
A. Criticized	A. He was criticized by more militant blacks for being nonviolent.
B. Vietnam	B. He protested against the war in Vietnam.
C. Assassination	C. He was assassinated in Memphis, Tennessee, on April 4, 1968.

The sample at left might serve as a speaking outline, but it is virtually useless as a preparation outline. It gives only vague labels rather than distinct ideas. It does not indicate clearly the content of the main points and subpoints. Nor does it reveal whether the speaker has thought out his or her ideas. But there is no concern about any of these matters with the outline on the right.

In sum, a skimpy preparation outline is of little value. Stating your main points and subpoints in full sentences will ensure that you develop your ideas fully.

Label Transitions, Internal Summaries, and Internal Previews

One way to make sure you have strong transitions, internal summaries, and internal previews is to include them in the preparation outline. Usually they are not incorporated into the system of symbolization and indentation, but are labeled separately and inserted in the outline where they will appear in the speech.

As blueprints are essential to architecture, so outlines are essential to speech-making. Developing an outline helps ensure that the structure of your speech is clear and coherent.

Attach a Bibliography

You should include with the outline a bibliography that shows all the books, magazines, newspapers, and Internet sources you consulted, as well as any interviews or field research you conducted.

The two major bibliographic formats are those developed by the Modern Language Association (MLA) and the American Psychological Association (APA). Both are widely used by communication scholars; ask your instructor which he or she prefers. No matter which format you adopt, make sure your statement of sources is clear, accurate, and consistent. For help, turn to page 135 in Chapter 6, where you will find sample citations for the kinds of sources used most frequently in classroom speeches. If you don't find what you need there, check the complete Bibliography Formats in the online Speech Tools for this chapter at www.connectlucas.com.

bibliography
A list of all the sources used in preparing a speech.

Give Your Speech a Title, If One Is Desired

In the classroom you probably do not need a title for your speech unless your teacher requires one. In some other situations, however, a speech title is necessary—as when the speech is publicized in advance or is going to be published. Whatever the reason, if you do decide to use a title, it should (1) be brief, (2) attract the attention of your audience, and (3) encapsulate the main thrust of your speech.

A good title need not have what Madison Avenue would call "sex appeal"—lots of glitter and pizzazz. By the same token, there is certainly nothing wrong with a catchy title—as long as it is germane to the speech. Here are two groups of titles. Those on the left are straightforward and descriptive. Those on the right are figurative alternatives to the ones on the left.

connectlucas.com
Use the Bibliomaker in the online Speech Tools for this chapter to automatically format your bibliography according to MLA or APA standards.

Checklist — Preparation Outline

YES ✓ NO

☐	☐	1. Does my speech have a title, if one is required?
☐	☐	2. Do I state the specific purpose before the text of the outline itself?
☐	☐	3. Do I state the central idea before the text of the outline itself?
☐	☐	4. Are the introduction, body, and conclusion clearly labeled?
☐	☐	5. Are main points and subpoints written in full sentences?
☐	☐	6. Are transitions, internal summaries, and internal previews clearly labeled?
☐	☐	7. Does the outline follow a consistent pattern of symbolization and indentation?
☐	☐	8. Does the outline provide a clear visual framework that shows the relationships among the ideas of my speech?
☐	☐	9. Does the bibliography identify all the sources I consulted in preparing the outline?
☐	☐	10. Does the bibliography follow the format required by my instructor?

Group I	Group II
Unsafe Drinking Water	Toxins on Tap
Living with Deafness	The Sounds of Silence
The Rage to Diet	The Art of Wishful Shrinking
The United States Mint	The Buck Starts Here
Gambling Addiction	Against All Odds

Which group do you prefer? There are advantages and disadvantages to both. Those in the first group clearly reveal the topic, but they are not as provocative as those in the second group. Those in the second group are sure to arouse interest, but they do not give as clear an idea of what the speeches are about.

There is one other kind of title you should consider—the question. Phrasing your title as a question can be both descriptive and provocative. Using this method, we can construct a third set of titles combining the virtues of groups I and II:

Group III

Is Your Water Safe to Drink?

Can You See What I'm Saying?

Diets: How Effective Are They?

Where Is Making Money a Way of Life?

Do You Really Think You Can Beat the Odds?

Sometimes you will choose a title for your speech very early. At other times you may not find one you like until the last minute. Either way, try to be resourceful about creating titles for your speeches. Experiment with several and choose the one that seems most appropriate.

SAMPLE PREPARATION OUTLINE WITH COMMENTARY

The following outline for a six-minute informative speech illustrates the principles just discussed. The commentary explains the procedures used in organizing the speech and writing the outline. (Check with your teacher to see if she or he wants you to include a title with your outline.)

Panic Attacks

COMMENTARY	OUTLINE
Stating your specific purpose and central idea as separate units before the text of the outline makes it easier to judge how well you have constructed the outline to achieve your purpose and to communicate your central idea.	*Specific Purpose:* To inform my audience about the nature, extent, and symptoms of panic attacks. *Central Idea:* Panic attacks are serious medical conditions whose fearful symptoms affect millions of people.
Labeling the introduction marks it as a distinct section that plays a special role in the speech.	*Introduction*

The opening story gets attention and, as it progresses, reveals the topic of the speech.	I. I can't breathe, my arms are tingling, I'm really dizzy, and it feels as if my heart is about to fly out of my chest.
	II. When this happened to me three years ago at an outdoor concert, I was really frightened.
	   A. At the time, I had no idea what was going on.
	   B. My doctor told me later that I had experienced a panic attack.

Here the speaker establishes her credibility and previews the main points to be discussed in the body of the speech.	III. I have learned a lot about my condition during the past three years, and I did additional research for this speech. IV. Today I would like to inform you about the nature of panic attacks, the people affected most often by them, and the options for treatment.
Including transitions ensures that the speaker has worked out how to connect one idea to the next. Notice that the transition is not included in the system of symbolization and indentation used for the rest of the speech.	(*Transition:* Let's start with the nature of panic attacks.)

Labeling the body marks it as a distinct part of the speech.

Main point I is phrased as a full sentence. As the outline progresses, notice that the main points are arranged in topical order.

The two subpoints of main point I are shown by the capital letters A and B and are written out in full sentences to ensure that the speaker has thought them out fully. Points below the level of subpoint are indicated by Arabic numerals and lowercase letters. Sometimes they are not written as full sentences. Check to see what your teacher prefers.

The transition shows how the speaker will move from main point I to main point II.

Like main point I, main point II is phrased as a full sentence.

The progressive indentation shows visually the relationships among main points, subpoints, and sub-subpoints.

The transition indicates that the speaker is moving to her next main point.

This main point, like the first two, is stated as a full sentence.

Notice the pattern of subordination in this section. Subpoint B notes that cognitive-behavioral therapy is one of the options for treating panic attacks. Sub-subpoint 1 identifies the kinds of techniques involved in this therapy. Because items a and b expand upon the techniques point, they are subordinated to it.

Body

I. Panic attacks are a severe medical condition with a number of physical and mental symptoms.
   A. As defined by the National Institute of Mental Health, panic attacks involve "unexpected and repeated episodes of intense fear accompanied by physical symptoms."
      1. The attacks usually come out of nowhere and strike when least expected.
      2. Their length can vary from a few minutes to several hours.
   B. There are a number of symptoms common to most panic attacks.
      1. Physical symptoms include a pounding heart, shortness of breath, lightheadedness, and numbness or tingling sensations in the arms and legs.
      2. Mental symptoms include acute fear, a sense of disaster or helplessness, and a feeling of being detached from one's own body.

(*Transition:* Now that you know something about the nature of panic attacks, let's look at how widespread they are.)

II. Panic attacks affect millions of people.
   A. According to the American Psychiatric Association, six million Americans suffer from panic attacks.
   B. Some groups have a higher incidence of panic attacks than do other groups.
      1. The National Institute of Mental Health reports that panic attacks strike women twice as often as men.
      2. Half the people who suffer from panic attacks develop symptoms before the age of 24.

(*Transition:* Given the severity of panic attacks, I'm sure you are wondering how they can be treated.)

III. There are two major options for treating panic attacks.
   A. One option is medication.
      1. Antidepressants are the most frequently prescribed medication for panic attacks.
      2. They rearrange the brain's chemical levels so as to get rid of unwanted fear responses.
   B. Another option is cognitive-behavioral therapy.
      1. This therapy involves techniques that help people with panic attacks gain control of their symptoms and feelings.
         a. Some techniques involve breathing exercises.
         b. Other techniques target thought patterns that can trigger panic attacks.

Labeling the conclusion marks it as a distinct part of the speech.

Summarizing the main points is usually standard procedure in an informative speech.

Referring back to the speaker's personal experience mentioned in the introduction gives the speech a sense of unity and provides an effective ending.

This is the final bibliography. It lists the sources actually used in writing the speech and is shorter than the preliminary bibliography compiled in the early stages of research. (See Chapter 6 for a discussion of the preliminary bibliography.)

This bibliography follows the 2008 Modern Language Association (MLA) format. Check with your instructor to see what format you should use for your bibliography.

2. According to David Barlow, author of the *Clinical Handbook of Psychological Disorders,* cognitive-behavioral therapy can be highly effective.

Conclusion

I. As we have seen, panic attacks affect millions of people.
II. Fortunately, there are treatment options to help prevent panic attacks and to deal with them when they occur.
III. In my case, the combination of medication and cognitive-behavioral therapy has been extremely helpful.
IV. I don't know if I will ever be completely free of panic attacks, but at least I understand now what they are and what I can do about them.

Bibliography

Barlow, David. *Clinical Handbook of Psychological Disorders,* 4th ed. New York: Guilford Press, 2008. Print.

Baskin, Kara. "Not Just Any Old Butterflies." *Washington Post* 9 Jan. 2007: F1. *LexisNexis.* Web. 23 Oct. 2008.

Brantley, Jeffrey. *Calming Your Anxious Mind: How Mindfulness and Compassion Can Free You from Anxiety, Fear, and Panic,* 2nd ed. Oakland, CA: New Harbinger Publications, 2007. Print.

Choy, Yujuan. "Treatment Planning for Panic Disorder." *Psychiatric Times* Feb. 2008: 40–44. Print.

United States. Dept. of Health and Human Services. National Institute of Mental Health. *Panic Disorder. National Institutes of Health* 2 Apr. 2008. Web. 23 Oct. 2008.

The Speaking Outline

"I was never so excited by public speaking before in my life," wrote one listener in 1820 after listening to Daniel Webster. "Three or four times I thought my temples would burst with the gush of blood. . . . I was beside myself, and am so still."[1]

Such reactions were not unusual among Webster's audiences. He thrilled two generations of Americans with his masterful orations. Incredible as it seems today, he did so while speaking for several hours at a time, often without using any notes! A reporter once asked how he managed this. "It is my memory," Webster said. "I can prepare a speech, revise and correct it in my memory, then deliver the corrected speech exactly as finished."[2]

Few people have Webster's remarkable powers of memory. Fortunately, it is no longer customary to speak from memory. Today most people speak extemporaneously—which means the speech is carefully prepared and practiced in advance, but much of the exact wording is selected while the speech is being delivered (see Chapter 12). Your speeches will probably be of this type. You should know, then, about the *speaking outline*—the most widely recommended form of notes for extemporaneous speeches.

speaking outline

A brief outline used to jog a speaker's memory during the presentation of a speech.

The aim of a speaking outline is to help you remember what you want to say. In some ways it is a condensed version of your preparation outline. It should contain key words or phrases to jog your memory, as well as essential statistics and quotations that you don't want to risk forgetting. But it should also include material *not* in your preparation outline—especially cues to direct and sharpen your delivery.

Most speakers develop their own variations on the speaking outline. As you acquire more experience, you, too, should feel free to experiment. But for now, your best bet is to follow the basic guidelines below and to use the sample speaking outline on pages 218–219 as your model.

GUIDELINES FOR THE SPEAKING OUTLINE

Follow the Visual Framework Used in the Preparation Outline

Your speaking outline should use the same visual framework—the same symbols and the same pattern of indentation—as your preparation outline. This will make it much easier to prepare the speaking outline. More important, it will allow you to see instantly where you are in the speech at any given moment while you are speaking. You will find this a great advantage. As you speak, you will look down at your outline periodically to make sure you are covering the right ideas in the right order.

Compare the following two versions of a partial speaking outline. They are from an informative speech about the history of the U.S. women's rights movement.

Ineffective

I. 1840–1860
A. World Anti-Slavery
    Convention
B. Seneca Falls convention
1. Lucretia Mott
2. Elizabeth Cady Stanton
3. Declaration of Sentiments
II. 1900–1920
A. National American Woman
    Suffrage Association
1. Founding
2. Objectives
B. Nineteenth Amendment
1. Campaign
2. Ratification

More Effective

I. 1840–1860
    A. World Anti-Slavery
        Convention
    B. Seneca Falls convention
        1. Lucretia Mott
        2. Elizabeth Cady Stanton
        3. Declaration of Sentiments
II. 1900–1920
    A. National American Woman
        Suffrage Association
        1. Founding
        2. Objectives
    B. Nineteenth Amendment
        1. Campaign
        2. Ratification

Many experienced speakers are more comfortable with a brief set of notes, or no notes at all, which allows them to maintain eye contact and to communicate directly with the audience.

The wording of both outlines is exactly the same. But the visual framework of the one on the right makes it easier to take in at a glance and reduces the odds of the speaker losing her or his place.

Make Sure the Outline Is Legible

Your speaking outline is all but worthless unless it is instantly readable at a distance. When you make your outline, use large lettering, leave extra space between lines, provide ample margins, and write or type on only one side of the paper.

Some speakers put their notes on index cards. Most find the 3 × 5 size too cramped and prefer the 4 × 6 or 5 × 8 size instead. Other people write their speaking outlines on regular paper. Either practice is fine, as long as your notes are immediately legible to you while you are speaking.

Keep the Outline as Brief as Possible

If your notes are too detailed, you will have difficulty maintaining eye contact with your audience. A detailed outline will tempt you to look at it far too often, as one student discovered:

Angela Granato was speaking about the benefits of Pilates. She had prepared the speech thoroughly and practiced it until it was nearly perfect. But when she delivered the speech in class, she referred constantly to her detailed notes. As a result, her delivery was choppy and strained. After the speech, Angela's classmates remarked on how often she had looked at her notes, and she was amazed. "I didn't even know I was doing it," she said. "Most of the time I wasn't even paying attention to the outline. I knew the speech cold."

Many students have had the same experience. "As long as I have plenty of notes," they feel, "disaster will not strike." In fact, most beginning speakers use too many notes. Like Angela, they don't need all of them to remember the speech, and they find that too many notes can actually interfere with good communication.

To guard against this, keep your speaking outline as brief as possible. It should contain key words or phrases to help you remember major points, subpoints, and connectives. If you are citing statistics, you will probably want to include them in your notes. Unless you are good at memorizing quotations, write them out fully as well. Finally, there may be two, three, or four key ideas whose wording is so important that you want to state them in simple complete sentences. The best rule is that your notes should be the *minimum* you need to jog your memory and keep you on track.

Give Yourself Cues for Delivering the Speech

A good speaking outline reminds you not only of *what* you want to say but also of *how* you want to say it. As you practice the speech, you will decide that certain ideas and phrases need special emphasis—that they should be spoken more loudly, softly, slowly, or rapidly than other parts of the speech. You will also determine how you want to pace the speech—how you will control its timing, rhythm, and momentum. But no matter how you work these things out ahead of time, no matter how often you practice, it is easy to forget them once you get in front of an audience.

delivery cues
Directions in a speaking outline to help a speaker remember how she or he wants to deliver key parts of the speech.

The solution is to include in your speaking outline *delivery cues*—directions for delivering the speech. One way to do this is by underlining or otherwise highlighting key ideas that you want to be sure to emphasize. Then, when you reach them in the outline, you will be reminded to stress them. Another way is to jot down on the outline explicit cues such as "pause," "repeat," "slow down," "louder," and so forth. Both techniques are good aids for beginning speakers, but they are also used by most experienced speakers.

SAMPLE SPEAKING OUTLINE WITH COMMENTARY

Below is a sample speaking outline for a six-minute informative talk about panic attacks. By comparing it with the preparation outline for the same speech on pages 213–215, you can see how a detailed preparation outline is transformed into a concise speaking outline.

COMMENTARY	OUTLINE
These comments remind the speaker to establish eye contact and not to race through the speech.	*Eye Contact!!* *Slow Down* I. Can't breathe, arms tingling, dizzy, heart flying.
The word "pause" reminds the speaker to pause after her opening lines.	*—Pause—* II. Happened three years ago—told later I had a panic attack.
Including the main ideas of the introduction helps keep the speaker on track at the start of the speech.	III. Learned about condition and researched for speech. IV. Today—nature of panic attacks, people affected, and treatment options.

It's usually a good idea to pause briefly before launching into the first main point. This is another way of signaling that you are moving from the introduction to the body.

Most speakers find it helpful to demarcate the body of the speech in the speaking outline as well as in the preparation outline.

Quotations are usually written out in full in the speaking outline.

Notice how the body of the speech follows the same visual format as the preparation outline. This makes the outline easy to read at a glance.

Inserting transitions makes sure the speaker doesn't forget them.

Underlining reminds the speaker to stress key words or ideas.

Throughout the outline, key words are used to jog the speaker's memory. Because the final wording of an extemporaneous speech is chosen at the moment of delivery, it will not be exactly the same as that in the preparation outline.

Sources of statistics or testimony should be included in the speaking outline to make sure the speaker identifies them during the speech.

It's usually a good idea to pause before entering the conclusion.

Most speakers label the conclusion in the speaking outline as well as in the preparation outline.

Including key ideas and phrases from the conclusion jogs the speaker's memory and ensures that the speech will end as planned.

(Let's start with nature of panic attacks.)

—Pause—

Body

I. Severe condition with physical and mental symptoms.
  A. Defined by NIMH: "unexpected and repeated episodes of intense fear accompanied by physical symptoms."
    1. Come out of nowhere.
    2. Few minutes to several hours.
  B. Common symptoms.
    1. Physical—heart, breath, dizziness, numbness or tingling.
    2. Mental—fear, disaster or helplessness, detached from body.

(Now you know nature . . . look at people affected.)

II. Affect <u>millions</u> of people.
  A. American Psychiatric Assn—6 million.
  B. Groups with higher incidence.
    1. NIMH: Women <u>twice as often</u> as men
    2. Most people develop symptoms <u>before age 24.</u>

(Given severity . . . wonder how treated.)

III. Two major options for treatment.
  A. Medication.
    1. Antidepressants most prescribed.
    2. Rearrange brain's chemical levels.
  B. Cognitive-behavioral therapy.
    1. Techniques to control symptoms and feelings.
      a. Breathing.
      b. Thought patterns.
    2. Effective says *Clinical Handbook of Psychological Disorders*

—Pause—

Conclusion

I. As we have seen, panic attacks affect millions of people.
II. Fortunately, there are treatments for preventing and dealing with attacks.
III. In my case, both medication and cognitive-behavioral therapy have helped.
IV. May never be free of attacks, but now I know what they are and what I can do about them.

SUMMARY

Outlines are essential to effective speeches. By outlining, you make sure that related ideas are together, that your thoughts flow from one to another, and that the structure of your speech is coherent. You will probably use two kinds of outlines for your speeches—the detailed preparation outline and the brief speaking outline.

In the preparation outline you state your specific purpose and central idea; label the introduction, body, and conclusion; and designate transitions, internal summaries, and internal previews. You should identify main points, subpoints, and sub-subpoints by a consistent pattern of symbolization and indentation. Your teacher may require a bibliography with your preparation outline.

The speaking outline should contain key words or phrases to jog your memory, as well as essential statistics and quotations. Make sure your speaking outline is legible, follows the same visual framework as your preparation outline, and includes cues for delivering the speech.

KEY TERMS

preparation outline *(208)*

visual framework *(209)*

bibliography *(211)*

speaking outline *(216)*

delivery cues *(218)*

REVIEW QUESTIONS

connectlucas.com
For further review, go to the Study Questions in the online Study Aids for this chapter.

After reading this chapter, you should be able to answer the following questions:

1. Why is it important to outline your speeches?

2. What is a preparation outline? What are the eight guidelines discussed in the chapter for writing a preparation outline?

3. What is a speaking outline? What are four guidelines for your speaking outline?

EXERCISES FOR CRITICAL THINKING

1. In the left-hand column on page 221 is a partially blank outline from a speech about robots. In the right-hand column, arranged in random order, are the subpoints to fill in the outline. Choose the appropriate subpoint for each blank in the outline.

   To complete this exercise online, go to the interactive Outline Exercises in the Study Aids for this chapter at connectlucas.com. You will also find several additional scrambled outlines that you can use to hone your outlining skills.

Outline	Subpoints
I. Robots have captured the human imagination for centuries.	Astronauts use robots to perform maintenance on the International Space Station.
A.	In 1937, Westinghouse created a seven-foot robot that could walk, talk, blow up balloons, and smoke cigarettes.
B.	They also allow surgeons to operate on patients from thousands of miles away.
C.	Robots have become indispensable to space exploration.
II. Today robots are used in many fields, including space exploration and medicine.	In 1497, Leonardo da Vinci designed a mechanical suit of armor that could sit up and move its arms, neck, and jaw.
A.	They can navigate hospital corridors to deliver pharmaceuticals, x-rays, and bandages.
1.	In addition, NASA sends robotic spacecraft to explore distant planets.
2.	Robots are becoming more and more important in medicine.
B.	In 1773, Pierre and Henri Jaquet-Droz built dolls that could write, play music, and draw pictures.
1.	
2.	

2. From the preparation outline on robots you constructed in Exercise 1, create a speaking outline that you might use in delivering the speech. Follow the guidelines for a speaking outline discussed in this chapter.

Applying *the* Power *of* Public Speaking

● ●

As the defense attorney in a car theft case, you need to prepare your closing argument to the jury before it begins its deliberations. After reviewing evidence from the trial, you decide to stress the following points to demonstrate the innocence of your client:

a. The stolen car was found abandoned three hours after the theft with the engine still warm; at the time the car was found, your client was at the airport to meet the flight of a friend who was flying into town.
b. Lab analysis of muddy shoe prints on the floor mat of the car indicates that the prints came from a size 13 shoe; your client wears a size 10.
c. Lab analysis shows the presence of cigarette smoke in the car, but your client does not smoke.
d. The only eyewitness to the crime, who was 50 feet from the car, said the thief "looked like" your client; yet the eyewitness admitted that at the time of the theft she was not wearing her corrective lenses, which had been prescribed for improving distance vision.
e. The car was stolen at about 1 P.M.; your client testified that he was in a small town 175 miles away at 11 A.M.
f. In a statement to police, the eyewitness described the thief as blond; your client has red hair.

As you work on the outline of your speech, you see that these points can be organized into three main points, each with two supporting points. Compose an outline that organizes the points in this manner.

Using Language

Contrary to popular belief, language does not mirror reality. It does not simply describe the world as it is. Instead, language helps create our sense of reality by giving meaning to events. The words we use to label an event determine to a great extent how we respond to it.

For example, if you see the medical use of stem cells as "immoral," as "scientifically irresponsible," and as a "violation of human life," you will likely oppose it. But if you see the medical use of stem cells as "moral," as "scientifically responsible," and as a way to "alleviate pain and suffering," you will likely support it.

What separates these two viewpoints? Not the capabilities of modern medicine; not the conditions of people with genetic disorders; not the medical procedures of using stem cells. All those are the same for both sides. The difference is in the *meaning* given to them by the words that label them.

Words are the tools of a speaker's craft. They have special uses, just like the tools of any other profession. Have you ever watched a carpenter at work? The job that would take you or me a couple of hours is done by the carpenter in 10 minutes—with the right tools. You can't drive a nail with a screwdriver or turn a screw with a hammer. It is the same with public speaking. You must choose the right words for the job you want to do.

Good speakers are aware of the meaning of words—both their obvious and their subtle meanings. They also know how to use language accurately, clearly, vividly, appropriately, and inclusively. This chapter will explore each of these areas.

Meanings of Words

denotative meaning
The literal or dictionary meaning of a word or phrase.

Words have two kinds of meanings—denotative and connotative. *Denotative* meaning is precise, literal, and objective. It describes the object, person, place, idea, or event to which the word refers. One way to think of a word's denotative meaning is as its dictionary definition. For example, denotatively, the noun "school" means "a place, institution, or building where instruction is given."

Connotative meaning is more variable, figurative, and subjective. The connotative meaning of a word is what the word suggests or implies. For instance, the connotative meaning of the word "school" includes all the feelings, associations, and emotions that the word touches off in different people. For some people, "school" might connote personal growth, childhood friends, and a special teacher. For others, it might connote frustration, discipline, and boring homework assignments.

connotative meaning
The meaning suggested by the associations or emotions triggered by a word or phrase.

Connotative meaning gives words their intensity and emotional power. It arouses in listeners feelings of anger, pity, love, fear, friendship, nostalgia, greed, guilt, and the like. Speakers, like poets, often use connotation to enrich their meaning. For example:

Terrorists neither listen to reason nor engage in reasoning with others. Their aim is to generate fear—to frighten people into submission. They measure success by the magnitude of the fear they generate through brutal, savage acts of violence. Terrorists are prepared to kill to further whatever cause they claim to be pursuing. And the heinousness of these murders is accentuated by the fact that terrorists murder without passion. They murder with cool deliberation and deliberate planning. They are utterly amoral.

The underlined words in this passage have powerful connotations that are almost certain to produce a strong emotional revulsion to terrorism.

Words are the tools of the speaker's craft. Good speakers use them accurately and correctly. They also use language that will be clear, vivid, and appropriate for their listeners.

Here, in contrast, is another version of the same statement—this time using words with a different set of connotations:

Terrorists do not seek to negotiate with their opponents. They seek victory by using political and psychological pressure, including acts of violence that may endanger the lives of some people. To the terrorist, ultimate objectives are more important than the means used to achieve them.

With the exception of "terrorist," the words in this statement are less likely to evoke an intensely negative response than those in the first statement.

Which statement is preferable? That depends on the audience, the occasion, and the speaker's purpose. Do you want to stir up your listeners' emotions, rally them to some cause? Then select words with more intense connotative meanings. Or are you addressing a controversial issue and trying to seem completely impartial? Then stick with words that touch off less intense reactions. Choosing words skillfully for their denotative and connotative meanings is a crucial part of the speaker's craft.

Using Language Accurately

Using language accurately is as vital to a speaker as using numbers accurately is to an accountant. One student found this out the hard way. In a speech about America's criminal justice system, he referred several times to "criminal *persecution.*" What he meant, of course, was "criminal *prosecution.*" This one error virtually ruined his speech. As one of his classmates said, "How can I believe what you say about our courts when you don't even know the difference between prosecution and persecution?"

Fortunately, such outright blunders are relatively rare among college students. However, we all commit more subtle errors—especially using one word

Internet Connection
www.connectlucas.com

Looking for just the right word to express your ideas? There's a good chance you will find it at Merriam-Webster Online (**www.merriam-webster.com**). In addition to providing a dictionary and thesaurus, this site contains links to a number of language-related items from Merriam-Webster.

Are you a non-native speaker of English? If so, you will find many helpful resources on the Web. One of the best is Ohio University's Resources for ESL Learners (**www.ohiou.edu/linguistics/esl/**), which provides dozens of links on subjects such as grammar, vocabulary, reading, writing, and speaking.

thesaurus
A book of synonyms.

when another will capture our ideas more precisely. Every word has shades of meaning that distinguish it from every other word. As Mark Twain said, "The difference between the right word and the almost right word is the difference between lightning and the lightning bug."

If you look in a thesaurus, you'll find the following words given as synonyms:

victory   accomplishment   success

All mean roughly the same thing—a favorable outcome. But all these words have different shades of meaning. See if you can fill in the best word to complete each of the sentences below:

1. My most important _____ this year was getting an A in calculus.

2. Priya's business _____ results from a combination of hard work and street smarts.

3. Paul's _____ on the parallel bars gave him confidence to pursue the gold medal for best all-around gymnast.

The best answers for the four statements are

1. accomplishment   2. success   3. victory

Each of the words means something a little different from the others, and each says something special to listeners.

As you prepare your speeches, ask yourself constantly, "What do I *really* want to say? What do I *really* mean?" When in doubt, consult a dictionary or thesaurus to make sure you have the best words to express your ideas.

Using Language Clearly

People are different. What makes perfect sense to some may be gobbledygook to others. You cannot assume that what is clear to you is clear to your audience. Listeners, unlike readers, cannot turn to a dictionary or reread an author's words to discover their meaning. A speaker's meaning must be *immediately* comprehensible; it must be so clear that there is no chance of misunderstanding. You can ensure this by using familiar words, by choosing concrete words over abstract words, and by eliminating verbal clutter.

USE FAMILIAR WORDS

One of the biggest barriers to clear speech is using big, bloated words where short, sharp ones will do the job better.[1] This is especially true when it comes to technical language that may be familiar to the speaker but not to the audience. Yet, if you work at it, you will almost always be able to translate even the most specialized topic into clear, familiar language.

Here, for instance, are three passages explaining the devastating effects of a pregnant woman's drinking on her unborn child. The first passage is in medical jargon, and it defies comprehension by ordinary listeners:

Alcohol consumption by the pregnant woman seriously influences the intrauterine milieu and therefore contributes to the morbidity and mortality of children born to these mothers. In regard to the pathophysiology of this syndrome, genetic polymorphism of enzymes for ethanol metabolism may alter fetal susceptibility. There may also be poor microsomal or mitochondrial function or decreased ATP activity.

Even an educated person without a medical background would have trouble with "pathophysiology" and "polymorphism" and "mitochondrial," much less be able to put them all together.

The second passage represents an attempt to adapt to a nonmedical audience. It is in more familiar language but retains enough obscure words to be difficult:

The deleterious effects of alcohol on the unborn child are very serious. When a pregnant mother consumes alcohol, the ethanol in the bloodstream easily crosses the placenta from mother to child and invades the amniotic fluid. This can produce a number of abnormal birth syndromes, including central-nervous-system dysfunctions, growth deficiencies, a cluster of facial aberrations, and variable major and minor malformations.

Well-informed listeners could probably figure out "deleterious effects," "central-nervous-system dysfunctions," and "facial aberrations." But these terms don't create a sharp mental image of what the speaker is trying to say. We still need to go one step further away from medical jargon toward ordinary language.

So we come to the third passage, which is utterly clear. It shows what can be done with work, imagination, and a healthy respect for everyday words:

When the expectant mother drinks, alcohol is absorbed into her bloodstream and distributed throughout her entire body. After a few beers or a couple of martinis, she begins to feel tipsy and decides to sober up. She grabs a cup of coffee, two aspirin, and takes a little nap. After a while she'll be fine.

But while she sleeps, the fetus is surrounded by the same alcoholic content as its mother had. After being drowned in alcohol, the fetus begins to feel the effect. But it can't sober up. It can't grab a cup of coffee. It can't grab a couple of aspirin. For the fetus's liver, the key organ in removing alcohol from the blood, is just not developed. The fetus is literally pickled in alcohol.[2]

This kind of plain talk is what listeners want. You cannot go wrong by following the advice of Winston Churchill to speak in "short, homely words of common usage." If you think big words (or a lot of words) are needed to impress listeners, bear in mind that the Gettysburg Address—considered the finest speech in the English language—contains 271 words, of which 251 have only one or two syllables.

CHOOSE CONCRETE WORDS

concrete words
Words that refer to tangible objects.

abstract words
Words that refer to ideas or concepts.

Concrete words refer to tangible objects—people, places, and things. They differ from abstract words, which refer to general concepts, qualities, or attributes. "Carrot," "pencil," "nose," and "door" are concrete words. "Humility," "science," "progress," and "philosophy" are abstract words.

Of course, few words are completely abstract or concrete. "Apple pie" is concrete, but in the United States, the phrase also has abstract values of patriotism and conventional morals. Usually, the more specific a word, the more concrete it is. Let us say you are talking about golf. Here are several words and phrases you might use:

physical activity	abstract/general
sports	
golf	
professional golf	
Tiger Woods	concrete/specific

As you move down the list, the words become less abstract and more concrete. You begin with a general concept (physical activity), descend to one type of activity (sports), to a particular sport (golf), to a division of that sport (professional golf), to one specific professional golfer (Tiger Woods).

Although abstract words are necessary to express certain kinds of ideas, they are much easier to misinterpret than are concrete words. Also, concrete words are much more likely to claim your listeners' attention. Suppose you make a speech about fire ants, which have long plagued the South and are now attacking western states. Here are two ways you could approach the subject—one featuring abstract words, the other concrete words:

Abstract Words

Fire ants have been a problem ever since they arrived in the United States. They have spread across the South and now threaten various parts of the West as well. This is a serious problem because fire ants are highly aggressive. There have even been human casualties from fire ant stings.

Concrete Words

Since fire ants came here from South America sometime before World War II, they have spread like a biblical plague across 11 states from Florida to Texas. Now they are invading New Mexico, Arizona, and California. Fire ants attack in swarms and they will climb any foot that is left in the wrong spot for a few seconds. They have even turned up indoors, in clothes hampers, beds, and closets. Fortunately, fewer than 1 percent of people who are stung have to see a doctor, but toddlers who have fallen on fire ant mounds have sometimes died from stings, as have highly allergic adults.[3]

Notice how much more persuasive the second version is. A speech dominated by concrete words will almost always be clearer, more interesting, and easier to recall than one dominated by abstract words.

Even when discussing technical subjects, effective speakers such as biologist Francis Collins look for ways to communicate their ideas in clear, familiar language.

ELIMINATE CLUTTER

Cluttered speech has become a national epidemic. Whatever happened to such simple words as "before," "if," and "now"? When last seen they were being routed by their cluttered counterparts: "prior to," "in the eventuality of," and "at this point in time." By the same token, why can't weather forecasters say, "It's raining," instead of saying, "It appears as if we are currently experiencing precipitation activity"? And why can't politicians say, "We have a crisis," instead of saying, "We are facing a difficult crisis situation that will be troublesome to successfully resolve"?

This type of clutter forces listeners to hack through a tangle of words to discover the meaning. When you make a speech, keep your language lean and lively. Beware of using several words where one or two will do. Avoid flabby phrases. Let your ideas emerge sharply and firmly. Above all, watch out for redundant adjectives and adverbs. Inexperienced speakers (and writers) tend to string together two or three synonymous adjectives, such as "a learned and educated person" or "a hot, steamy, torrid day."

Here is part of a student speech that has been revised to eliminate clutter:

clutter
Discourse that takes many more words than are necessary to express an idea.

Sitting Bull was one of the most important ~~and significant of all~~ Native American

leaders. He was born in ~~the year of~~ 1831 near Grand River, in ~~an area that is now part of~~

present-day

~~the state of~~ South Dakota. A fearless ~~and courageous~~ warrior, he ~~ended up being~~ elected

was

chief of the Hunkpapa Sioux in 1867. In the following years, he also attracted a large ~~and~~

~~numerous~~ following among the ~~tribes of the~~ Cheyenne and Arapaho. He is best known

today   *defeating*

~~to people in this day and age~~ for his ~~instrumental~~ role in ~~helping to lead the defeat of~~

Using Language Clearly **229**

General Custer at the Battle of Little Big Horn in 1876. Although eventually ~~required against~~ *forced*

~~his will~~ to live ~~his life~~ on the Standing Rock Reservation in South Dakota, he never surrendered

~~to anyone~~ his dignity or his ~~personal~~ devotion to the Sioux way of life.

Notice how much cleaner and easier to follow the revised version is. No longer are the speaker's ideas hidden in a thicket of wasted words.

This kind of pruning is easy once you get the knack of it. The hardest part—and it is often very hard—is recognizing clutter and forcing yourself to throw away the unnecessary words. Watch for clutter when you write your speech outlines. Be prepared to revise the outline until your ideas emerge clearly and crisply.

You can also help eliminate clutter by practicing your speeches with a digital recorder. As you play the speech back, keep an ear out not just for flabby phrases but for verbal fillers such as "you know," "like," and "really." Practice delivering the speech again, this time making a special effort to trim it of wasted or distracting words. This will not only make you a better public speaker, but it will help you present ideas more effectively in meetings, conversations, and group discussions.

Using Language Vividly

Just as you can be accurate without being clear, so you can be both accurate and clear without being interesting. Here, for example, is how Martin Luther King *might have* phrased part of his great "I Have a Dream" speech:

Turning back is something we cannot do. We must continue to work against police brutality, segregated housing, disfranchisement, and alienation. Only when these problems are solved will we be satisfied.

Here is what King *actually* said:

We cannot turn back. There are those who ask the devotees of civil rights, "When will you be satisfied?" We can never be satisfied as long as the Negro is the victim of the unspeakable horrors of police brutality. We can never be satisfied as long as our bodies, heavy with the fatigue of travel, cannot gain lodging in the motels of the highways and the hotels of the cities. . . . We cannot be satisfied as long as a Negro in Mississippi cannot vote and a Negro in New York believes he has nothing for which to vote. No, no, we are not satisfied, and we will not be satisfied until justice rolls down like waters and righteousness like a mighty stream.

Much more stirring, isn't it? If you want to move people with your speeches, use vivid, animated language. Although there are several ways to do this, two of the most important are imagery and rhythm.

IMAGERY

One sign of a good novelist is the ability to create word pictures that let you "see" the haunted house, or "hear" the birds chirping on a warm spring morning, or "taste" the hot enchiladas at a Mexican restaurant.

Speakers can use imagery in much the same way to make their ideas come alive. Three ways to generate imagery are by using concrete words, simile, and metaphor.

Concrete Words

As we saw earlier in this chapter, choosing concrete words over abstract words is one way to enhance the clarity of your speeches. Concrete words are also the key to effective imagery. Consider the following excerpt from Ronald Reagan's famous address commemorating the 40th anniversary of D-Day. Speaking at the scene of the battle, Reagan dramatically recounted the heroism of the U.S. Rangers who scaled the cliffs at Pointe du Hoc to help free Europe from Hitler's stranglehold:

Clear, vivid, uncluttered language is a hallmark of Thomas Friedman's speeches. The Pulitzer-Prize-winning journalist gives a great deal of thought to finding just the right words to express his ideas.

We stand on a lonely, windswept point on the northern shore of France. The air is soft, but 40 years ago at this moment, the air was dense with smoke and the cries of men, and the air was filled with the crack of rifle fire and the roar of cannon.

At dawn, on the morning of the 6th of June, 1944, 225 Rangers jumped off the British landing craft and ran to the bottom of these cliffs . . . The Rangers looked up and saw the enemy soldiers—at the edge of the cliffs shooting down at them with machine guns and throwing grenades. And the American Rangers began to climb. They shot rope ladders over the face of these cliffs and began to pull themselves up.

When one Ranger fell, another would take his place. When one rope was cut, a Ranger would grab another and begin his climb again. They climbed, shot back, and held their footing. Soon, one by one, the Rangers pulled themselves over the top, and in seizing the firm land at the top of these cliffs, they began to seize back the continent of Europe.

Concrete words call up mental impressions of sights, sounds, touch, smell, and taste. In Reagan's speech, we do not merely learn that the U.S. Rangers helped win the battle of D-Day. We visualize the Rangers landing at the foot of the cliffs. We see them fighting their way up the cliffs in the face of enemy grenades and machine guns. We hear the crack of rifle fire and the cries of the soldiers. The concrete words create images that pull us irresistibly into the speech.

Simile

Another way to create imagery is through the use of simile. Simile is an explicit comparison between things that are essentially different yet have something in

imagery
The use of vivid language to create mental images of objects, actions, or ideas.

connectlucas.com
View this excerpt from Ronald Reagan's speech at Pointe du Hoc in the online Media Library for this chapter (Video Clip 11.1).

common. It always contains the words "like" or "as." Here are some examples from student speeches:

> Walking into my grandparents' home when I was a child was like being wrapped in a giant security blanket.

> Air pollution is eating away at the monuments in Washington, D.C., like a giant Alka-Seltzer tablet.

simile
An explicit comparison, introduced with the word "like" or "as," between things that are essentially different yet have something in common.

These are bright, fresh similes that clarify and vitalize ideas. Some similes, however, have become stale through overuse. Here are a few:

fresh as a daisy	hungry as a bear
fit as a fiddle	busy as a bee
strong as an ox	big as a mountain
stubborn as a mule	happy as a lark

cliché
A trite or overused expression.

Such *clichés* are fine in everyday conversation, but you should avoid them in speechmaking. Otherwise, you are likely to be "dull as dishwater" and to find your audience "sleeping like a log"!

Metaphor

metaphor
An implicit comparison, not introduced with the word "like" or "as," between two things that are essentially different yet have something in common.

You can also use metaphor to create imagery in your speeches. Metaphor is an implicit comparison between things that are essentially different yet have something in common. Unlike simile, metaphor does not contain the words "like" or "as." For example:

> America's cities are the windows through which the world looks at American society. (Henry Cisneros)

> With globalization, the same sea washes all of humankind. We are all in the same boat. There are no safe islands. (Kofi Annan)

These are both brief metaphors. Sometimes, however, a speaker will develop a longer metaphor. Here is an excellent example, from Al Gore's speech accepting the 2007 Nobel Peace Prize for his efforts to help the world deal with climate change:

> The earth has a fever. And the fever is rising. The experts have told us it is not a passing affliction that will heal by itself. We asked for a second opinion. And a third. And a fourth. And the consistent conclusion, restated with increasing alarm, is that something basic is wrong.

When used effectively, metaphor—like simile—is an excellent way to bring color to a speech, to make abstract ideas concrete, to clarify the unknown, and to express feelings and emotions.

RHYTHM

Language has a rhythm created by the choice and arrangement of words. Speakers, like poets, sometimes seek to exploit the rhythm of language to enhance the impact of their words. Winston Churchill was a master at this. Here is a passage from one of his famous speeches during World War II. To emphasize its cadence, the passage has been printed as if it were poetry rather than prose:

> We cannot tell what the course
>   of this fell war will be
> as it spreads remorseless
>   through ever-wider regions.
> We cannot predict or measure
>   its episodes or its tribulations . . . .
> We cannot yet see
>   how deliverance will come,
> or when it will come.
>   But nothing is more certain
> than that every trace of Hitler's footsteps,
>   every stain of his infected and corroding fingers,
> will be sponged and purged
>   and, if need be,
> blasted from the surface of the earth.

connectlucas.com
View this excerpt from Winston Churchill's speech of June 12, 1941, in the online Media Library for this chapter (Video Clip 11.2).

The impact of the passage was heightened by Churchill's superb delivery; but even by themselves the words take on an emphatic rhythm that reinforces the message. You can see why one observer said that Churchill "mobilized the English language and sent it into battle."[4]

A speech, however, is not a poem. You should never emphasize sound and rhythm at the expense of meaning. The aim is to think about ways you can use the rhythm and flow of language to enhance your meaning. Although you may never have paid much conscious attention to this subject, you can develop an ear for vocal rhythms by study and practice. What's more, you can easily begin now to use four basic stylistic devices employed by Churchill and other fine speakers to improve the rhythm of their prose.

rhythm
The pattern of sound in a speech created by the choice and arrangement of words

Parallelism

The first device is parallelism—the similar arrangement of a pair or series of related words, phrases, or sentences. For example:

> *Rich and poor, intelligent and ignorant, wise and foolish, virtuous and vicious, man and woman*—it is ever the same, each soul must depend wholly on itself. (Elizabeth Cady Stanton)

parallelism
The similar arrangement of a pair or series of related words, phrases, or sentences.

The effects of parallelism are perhaps best illustrated by seeing what happens when it is absent. For instance, compare this statement:

> I speak as a Republican. I speak as a woman. I speak as a United States Senator. I speak as an American. (Margaret Chase Smith)

with this one:

> I speak as a Republican. I speak as a woman. I speak as a United States Senator. And I am also addressing you as an American.

The first statement is clear, consistent, and compelling. The second is not. By violating the principle of parallel structure, its final sentence ("And I am also addressing you as an American") destroys the progression begun by the preceding three sentences. It turns a strong, lucid, harmonious statement into one that is fuzzy and jarring.

Repetition

repetition

Reiteration of the same word or set of words at the beginning or end of successive clauses or sentences.

Repetition means reiterating the same word or set of words at the beginning or end of successive clauses or sentences. For example:

> *If not* now, when? *If not* us, who? *If not* together, how? (Gordon Brown)

> *This was the moment when we* began to provide care for the sick and good jobs to the jobless; *this was the moment when* the rise of the oceans began to slow and our planet began to heal; *this was the moment when* we ended a war and secured our nation. (Barack Obama)

As you can see, repetition usually results in parallelism. In addition to building a strong cadence, it also unifies a sequence of ideas, emphasizes an idea by stating it more than once, and helps create a strong emotional effect.

Alliteration

alliteration

Repetition of the initial consonant sound of close or adjoining words.

The third device you can use to enhance the rhythm of your speeches is alliteration. The most common method of alliteration is repeating the initial consonant sound of close or adjoining words. For example:

> *P*eace is essential for *p*rogress, but *p*rogress is no less essential for *p*eace. (Liaquat Ali Khan)

> Our *c*olleges, our *c*ommunities, our *c*ountry should challenge hatred wherever we find it. (Hillary Clinton)

By highlighting the sounds of words, alliteration catches the attention of listeners and can make ideas easier to remember. Used sparingly, it is a marvelous way to spruce up your speeches. Used to excess, however, it can be laughable and draw too much attention, so that listeners get more involved in listening for the next alliteration than in absorbing the content of the speech.

Antithesis

antithesis

The juxtaposition of contrasting ideas, usually in parallel structure.

Finally, you might try using antithesis—the juxtaposition of contrasting ideas, usually in parallel structure. For example:

> Ask not what your country can do for you; ask what you can do for your country. (John F. Kennedy)

> Your success as a family, our success as a society, depends not on what happens at the White House, but on what happens inside your house. (Barbara Bush)

Antithesis has long been a favorite device of accomplished speakers. Because it nearly always produces a neatly turned phrase, it is a fine way to give your speeches a special touch of class.

You may be thinking that imagery and rhythm are too fancy for ordinary speeches like yours. This is not true. Take a look at the following excerpt from one student's speech about the Massachusetts 54th, the regiment of African-American soldiers during the Civil War featured in the movie *Glory:*

> To join an army that didn't believe in you. To fight with an army who didn't like you. To die for an army that didn't respect you. This was the Massachusetts 54th. Today they lay where they died, on the beaches of South Carolina. Colonel Shaw and his men were piled together in a mass grave, which has since been covered by the shifting tides of the Atlantic. A small statue stands in Boston—a reminder of their sacrifice.
>
> Bravery, patriotism, and sacrifice. These are qualities of the Massachusetts 54th. With the help of their efforts, along with all the other black regiments that followed them, slavery did eventually come to an end.

connectlucas.com
View this excerpt from "The Massachusetts 54th" in the online Media Library for this chapter (Video Clip 11.3).

This is vivid, moving language. The imagery is sharp and poignant, the rhythm strong and insistent. Think of how you can do similar things in your own speeches.

Using Language Appropriately

Here is part of a famous oration given by John Hancock in 1774, during the American Revolution. Speaking of the British soldiers who killed five Americans in the Boston Massacre, Hancock exclaimed:

> Ye dark designing knaves, ye murderers, parricides! How dare you tread upon the earth, which has drank in the blood of slaughtered innocents shed by your wicked hands? How dare you breathe that air which wafted to the ear of heaven the groans of those who fell a sacrifice to your accursed ambition? . . . Tell me, ye bloody butchers, ye villains high and low, ye wretches . . . do you not feel the goads and stings of conscious guilt pierce through your savage bosoms?

This is certainly vivid language—and Hancock's audience loved it. But can you imagine speaking the same way today? In addition to being accurate, clear, and vivid, language should be appropriate—to the occasion, to the audience, to the topic, and to the speaker.

APPROPRIATENESS TO THE OCCASION

Language that is appropriate for some occasions may not be appropriate for others. "There is a time for dialect, a place for slang, an occasion for literary form. What is correct on the sports page is out of place on the op-ed page; what is with-it on the street may well be without it in the classroom."[5] As a simple example, a coach might address the football team as "you guys" (or worse!), whereas the speaker in a more formal situation would begin with "distinguished guests." Try reversing these two situations, and see how ridiculous it becomes. It's only common sense to adjust your language to different occasions.

APPROPRIATENESS TO THE AUDIENCE

Appropriateness also depends on the audience. If you keep this in mind, it will help you greatly when dealing with technical topics. When addressing an audience of physicians, you might use the word "parotitis" to refer to a viral disease marked by the swelling of the parotid glands. Your audience would know just what you meant. But when talking to a nonmedical audience, such as your classmates, the appropriate word would be "mumps."

You should be especially careful to avoid language that might offend your audience. Off-color humor or profanity might be appropriate in a comedy routine, but most listeners would find it offensive in a formal public speech. Remember, speakers are expected to elevate and polish their language when addressing an audience.

Of course, you cannot always be sure of how listeners will respond to what you say. When it comes to appropriateness, you will seldom go wrong by erring on the side of caution. (Put simply, "erring on the side of caution" means "when in doubt—don't.")

APPROPRIATENESS TO THE TOPIC

Language should also be appropriate to the topic. You would not use metaphor, antithesis, and alliteration when explaining how to change a bicycle tire. But you might use all three in a speech honoring U.S. soldiers who have died in defense of their country. The first topic calls for straightforward description and explanation. The second calls for special language skills to evoke emotion, admiration, and appreciation.

APPROPRIATENESS TO THE SPEAKER

No matter what the occasion, audience, or topic, language should also be appropriate to the speaker. Imagine the effect if John McCain tried to adopt the religious imagery and rhythmical cadence of Al Sharpton. The results would be comical. Every public speaker develops his or her own language style.

"Terrific," you may be thinking. "I have my own style too. I feel more comfortable using abstract words, slang, and technical jargon. That's just me. It's *my* way of speaking." But to say that language should be appropriate to the speaker does not justify ignoring the other needs for appropriateness. There is a difference between one's everyday style and one's *developed* style as a public speaker. Accomplished speakers have developed their speaking styles over many years of trial, error, and practice. They have *worked* at using language effectively.

You can do the same if you become language-conscious. One way to develop this consciousness is to read and listen to effective speakers. Study their techniques for achieving accuracy, clarity, and vividness, and try to adapt those techniques to your own speeches. But do not try to "become" someone else when you speak. Learn from other speakers, blend what you learn into your own language style, and seek to become the best possible you.

A Note on Inclusive Language

As the United States has become more diverse, our language has evolved to reflect that diversity. Regardless of the situation, audiences expect public speakers to use inclusive language that is respectful of the different groups that make

Language needs to be appropriate to a speaker's topic, as well as to the audience. A speech on beach volleyball would use more action-oriented words than a speech about theories of psychology.

up American society. Today a number of principles for inclusive language have become so widespread that no aspiring speaker (or writer) can afford to ignore them. Here are a few of the most important.

Avoid the Generic "He"

Ineffective: Each time a surgeon walks into the operating room, *he* risks being sued for malpractice.

More Effective: Each time a surgeon walks into the operating room, *she or he* risks being sued for malpractice.

Often, a more graceful alternative is to pluralize. For example:

More Effective: Whenever surgeons walk into the operating room, *they* risk being sued for malpractice.

Avoid the Use of "Man" When Referring to Both Men and Women

Ineffective: If a large comet struck the Earth, it could destroy all of mankind.

More Effective: If a large comet struck the Earth, it could destroy all human life.

Avoid Stereotyping Jobs and Social Roles by Gender

Ineffective: Being a small businessman in the current economic climate is not easy.

More Effective: Being a small businessperson in the current economic climate is not easy.

Sometimes you can solve this problem with a simple twist in sentence construction. For example:

More Effective: Owning a small business is not easy in the current economic climate.

Use Names That Groups Use to Identify Themselves

One of the most fundamental ways of showing respect for others is to refer to them by the names they use to identify themselves and to avoid names they consider offensive.

Ineffective: Despite progress in recent years, homosexuals still face many forms of discrimination.

More Effective: Despite progress in recent years, lesbians and gay men still face many forms of discrimination.

Ineffective: The Paralympics show what handicapped people can accomplish in the athletic arena.

More Effective: The Paralympics show what people with disabilities can accomplish in the athletic arena.

The terms preferred by various groups continue to evolve. There is currently a trend away from broad words such as "Asian" and "Hispanic" to more precise terms that do not lump people of distinct nationalities and cultures under one label. For example:

Less Effective: Kristi Yamaguchi is one of many Asians who have had a major impact on U.S. life.

More Effective: Kristi Yamaguchi is one of many Japanese Americans who have had a major impact on U.S. life.

Less Effective: Antonio Villaraigosa was the first Hispanic elected mayor of Los Angeles since 1872.

More Effective: Antonio Villaraigosa was the first Mexican American elected mayor of Los Angeles since 1872.

More Effective: Antonio Villaraigosa was the first Latino elected mayor of Los Angeles since 1872.

When using words such as "Latino" or "Chicano," keep in mind that they refer to males. The correct term for females is "Latina" or "Chicana."

Like many other aspects of American life, issues of inclusive language can sometimes be confusing. Language is alive and constantly evolving, so what is considered inclusive today may shift down the road. If you have questions in any particular case, check the Internet for the most up-to-date information. Using inclusive and respectful language is not a matter of political correctness, but it is a matter of P.C.—personal courtesy.[6]

Good speakers have respect for language and how it works. As a speaker, you should be aware of the meanings of words and know how to use language accurately, clearly, vividly, and appropriately.

Words have two kinds of meanings—denotative and connotative. Denotative meaning is precise, literal, and objective. Connotative meaning is more variable, figurative, and subjective. It includes all the feelings, associations, and emotions that a word touches off in different people.

Using language accurately is vital to a speaker. Never use a word unless you are sure of its meaning. If you are not sure, look up the word in a dictionary. As you prepare your speeches, ask yourself constantly, "What do I *really* want to say? What do I *really* mean?" Choose words that are precise and accurate.

Using language clearly allows listeners to grasp your meaning immediately. You can ensure this by using words that are known to the average person and require no specialized background, by choosing concrete words in preference to more abstract ones, and by eliminating verbal clutter.

Using language vividly helps bring your speech to life. One way to make your language more vivid is through imagery, which you can develop by using concrete language, simile, and metaphor. Another way to make your speeches vivid is by exploiting the rhythm of language with parallelism, repetition, alliteration, and antithesis.

Using language appropriately means adapting to the particular occasion, audience, and topic at hand. It also means developing your own language style instead of trying to copy someone else's.

The subject of inclusive language can be complex, but a number of inclusive usages have become so widely accepted that no aspiring speaker can afford to ignore them. They include avoiding the generic "he," dropping the use of "man" when referring to both men and women, refraining from stereotyping jobs and social roles by gender, and using names that groups use to identify themselves.

KEY TERMS

denotative meaning *(224)*

connotative meaning *(224)*

thesaurus *(226)*

concrete words *(228)*

abstract words *(228)*

clutter *(229)*

imagery *(231)*

simile *(231)*

cliché *(232)*

metaphor *(232)*

rhythm *(232)*

parallelism *(233)*

repetition *(234)*

alliteration *(234)*

antithesis *(234)*

inclusive language *(237)*

generic "he" *(237)*

REVIEW QUESTIONS

After reading this chapter, you should be able to answer the following questions:

1. How does language help create our sense of reality?

2. What is the difference between denotative and connotative meaning? How might you use each to convey your message most effectively?

connectlucas.com
For further review, go to the Study Questions in the online Study Aids for this chapter.

3. What are four criteria for using language effectively in your speeches?

4. What are three things you should do to use language clearly in your speeches?

5. What are two ways to bring your speeches to life with vivid, animated language?

6. What does it mean to say you should use language appropriately in your speeches?

7. Why is it important for a public speaker to use inclusive language? What four usages of inclusive language have become so widely accepted that no speaker can afford to ignore them?

EXERCISES FOR CRITICAL THINKING

1. Arrange each of the sequences below in order, from the most abstract word to the most concrete word.

   a. housing complex, building, dining room, structure, apartment

   b. *Mona Lisa,* art, painting, creative activity, portrait

   c. automobile, vehicle, Ferrari, transportation, sports car

2. Rewrite each of the following sentences using clear, familiar words.

   a. My employment objective is to attain a position of maximum financial reward.

   b. All professors at this school are expected to achieve high standards of excellence in their instructional duties.

   c. In the eventuality of a fire, it is imperative that all persons evacuate the building without undue delay.

3. Each of the statements below uses one or more of the following stylistic devices: metaphor, simile, parallelism, repetition, alliteration, antithesis. Identify the device (or devices) used in each statement.

   a. "We are a people in a quandary about the present. We are a people in search of our future. We are a people in search of a national community." (Barbara Jordan)

   b. "The vice presidency is the sand trap of American politics. It's near the prize, and designed to be limiting." (Howard Fineman)

   c. "People the world over have always been more impressed by the power of our example than by the example of our power." (Bill Clinton)

   d. "America is not like a blanket—one piece of unbroken cloth, the same color, the same texture, the same size. America is more like a quilt—many patches, many sizes, and woven and held together by a common thread." (Jesse Jackson)

4. Analyze Martin Luther King's "I Have a Dream" in the appendix of sample speeches that follows Chapter 18. Identify the methods King uses to make his language clear, vivid, and appropriate. Look particularly at King's use of familiar words, concrete words, imagery, and rhythm.

Since graduating from college, you have developed a successful business that is located near the campus. As part of its plan to involve more alumni and community members in college affairs, the school has asked you to speak with new students during registration week for the fall term. In the opening section of your speech, you want the audience to feel what you felt the first few days you were on campus as a new student. The best strategy, you decide, is to present two or three similes that complete the sentence "Beginning college is like . . . ." Write your similes.

Delivery

If you were to record one of Conan O'Brien's comedy routines, memorize it word for word, and stand up before your friends to recite it, would you get the same response O'Brien does? Not very likely. And why not? Because you would not *deliver* the jokes as O'Brien does. Of course, the jokes are basically funny. But Conan O'Brien brings something extra to the jokes—his manner of presentation, his vocal inflections, his perfectly timed pauses, his facial expressions, his gestures. All these are part of an expert delivery. It would take you years of practice—as it took O'Brien—to duplicate his results.

No one expects your speech class to transform you into a multimillion-dollar talk show host. Still, this example demonstrates how important delivery can be to any public speaking situation. Even a mediocre speech will be more effective if it is presented well, whereas a wonderfully written speech can be ruined by poor delivery.

This does not mean dazzling delivery will turn a mindless string of nonsense into a triumphant oration. You cannot make a good speech without having something to say. But having something to say is not enough. You must also know *how* to say it.

nonverbal communication
Communication based on a person's use of voice and body, rather than on the use of words.

Speech delivery is a matter of *nonverbal communication*. It is based on how you use your voice and body to convey the message expressed by your words. There is a great deal of research showing that the impact of a speaker's words is powerfully influenced by his or her nonverbal communication. In this chapter, we will explain how you can use nonverbal communication to deliver your speeches effectively and to increase the impact of your verbal message.

What Is Good Delivery?

Wendell Phillips was a leader in the movement to abolish slavery in the United States during the 1800s. Some people considered him the greatest speaker of his time. The following story suggests one reason why:

> Shortly before the Civil War an Andover student, learning that Phillips was to lecture in Boston, made a 22-mile pilgrimage on foot to hear him. At first the trip seemed hardly worthwhile, for the student discovered that Phillips was not an orator in the grand manner, but spoke in an almost conversational style. He stood on the platform, one hand lightly resting on a table, talked for what seemed to be about 20 minutes, concluded, and sat down. When the student looked at his watch, he found to his astonishment that he had been listening for an hour and a half![1]

Good delivery does not call attention to itself. It conveys the speaker's ideas clearly, interestingly, and without distracting the audience. Most audiences prefer delivery that combines a certain degree of formality with the best attributes of good conversation—directness, spontaneity, animation, vocal and facial expressiveness, and a lively sense of communication.

Speech delivery is an art, not a science. What works for one speaker may fail for another. And what succeeds with today's audience may not with tomorrow's. You cannot become a skilled speaker just by following a set of rules in a textbook. In the long run, there is no substitute for experience. But take heart! A textbook *can* give you basic pointers to get you started in the right direction.

When you plan your first speech (or your second or third), you should concentrate on such basics as speaking intelligibly, avoiding distracting mannerisms, and establishing eye contact with your listeners. Once you get these elements under control and begin to feel fairly comfortable in front of an audience, you can work on polishing your delivery to enhance the impact of your ideas. Eventually, you may find yourself able to control the timing, rhythm, and momentum of a speech as skillfully as a conductor controls an orchestra.

Methods of Delivery

There are four basic methods of delivering a speech: (1) reading verbatim from a manuscript; (2) reciting a memorized text; (3) speaking impromptu; and (4) speaking extemporaneously. Let us look at each.

READING FROM A MANUSCRIPT

Certain speeches *must* be delivered word for word, according to a meticulously prepared manuscript. Examples include a Pope's religious proclamation, an engineer's report to a professional meeting, or a President's message to Congress. In such situations, absolute accuracy is essential. Every word of the speech will be analyzed by the press, by colleagues, perhaps by enemies. In the case of the President, a misstated phrase could cause an international incident.

manuscript speech
A speech that is written out word for word and read to the audience.

Although it looks easy, delivering a speech from manuscript requires great skill. Some people do it well. Their words "come alive as if coined on the spot."[2] Others ruin it every time. Instead of sounding vibrant and conversational, they come across as wooden and artificial. They falter over words, pause in the wrong places, read too quickly or too slowly, speak in a monotone, and march through the speech without even glancing at their audience. In short, they come across as *reading to* their listeners, rather than *talking with* them.

If you are in a situation where you must speak from a manuscript, practice aloud to make sure the speech sounds natural. Work on establishing eye contact with your listeners. Be certain the final manuscript is legible at a glance. Above all, reach out to your audience with the same directness and sincerity that you would if you were speaking extemporaneously.

RECITING FROM MEMORY

Among the feats of the legendary orators, none leaves us more in awe than their practice of presenting even the longest and most complex speeches entirely from memory. Nowadays it is no longer customary to memorize any but the shortest of speeches—toasts, congratulatory remarks, acceptance speeches, introductions, and the like.

If you are giving a speech of this kind and want to memorize it, by all means do so. However, be sure to memorize it so thoroughly that you will be able to concentrate on communicating with the audience, not on trying to remember the words. Speakers who gaze at the ceiling or stare out the window trying to recall what they have memorized are no better off than those who read dully from a manuscript.

SPEAKING IMPROMPTU

An impromptu speech is delivered with little or no immediate preparation. Few people choose to speak impromptu, but sometimes it cannot be avoided. In fact, many of the speeches you give in life will be impromptu. You might be called on suddenly to "say a few words" or, in the course of a class discussion, business meeting, or committee report, want to respond to a previous speaker.

When such situations arise, don't panic. No one expects you to deliver a perfect speech on the spur of the moment. If you are in a meeting or discussion, pay close attention to what the other speakers say. Take notes of major points with which you agree or disagree. In the process, you will automatically begin to formulate what you will say when it is your turn to speak.

Whenever you are responding to a previous speaker, try to present your speech in four simple steps: First, state the point you are answering. Second, state the point you wish to make. Third, support your point with appropriate statistics, examples, or testimony. Fourth, summarize your point. This four-step method will help you organize your thoughts quickly and clearly.

If time allows, sketch a quick outline of your remarks on a piece of paper before you rise to speak. Use the same method of jotting down key words and phrases followed in a more formal speaking outline (see Chapter 10). This will help you remember what you want to say and will keep you from rambling.

In many cases, you will be able to speak informally without rising from your chair. But if the situation calls for you to speak from a lectern, walk to it calmly, take a deep breath or two (not a visible gasp), establish eye contact with your audience, and begin speaking. No matter how nervous you are inside, do your best to look calm and assured on the outside.

Once you begin speaking, maintain strong eye contact with the audience. If you are prone to talking rapidly when you are nervous, concentrate on speaking at a slower pace. Help the audience keep track of your ideas with signposts such as "My first point is . . . ; second, we can see that . . . ; in conclusion, I would like to say . . . ." If you have had time to prepare notes, stick to what you have written. By stating your points clearly and concisely, you will come across as organized and confident.

Whether you realize it or not, you have given thousands of impromptu "speeches" in daily conversation—as when you informed a new student how to register for classes, explained to your boss why you were late for work, or answered questions in a job interview. There is no reason to fall apart when you are asked to speak impromptu in a more formal situation. If you keep cool, organize your thoughts, and limit yourself to a few remarks, you should do just fine.

As with other kinds of public speaking, the best way to become a better impromptu speaker is to practice. If you are assigned an impromptu speech in class, do your best to follow the guidelines discussed here. You can also practice impromptu speaking on your own. Simply choose a topic on which you are already well informed, and give a one- or two-minute impromptu talk on some aspect of that topic. Any topic will do, no matter how serious or frivolous it may be. Nor do you need an audience—you can speak to an empty room. Better yet, you can speak to a digital recorder and play the speech back to hear how you sound. The purpose is to gain experience in pulling your ideas together quickly and stating them succinctly.

Extemporaneous speeches are prepared ahead of time, but the exact words are chosen at the moment of presentation. This allows for more direct delivery than does reading from a manuscript.

SPEAKING EXTEMPORANEOUSLY

In popular usage, "extemporaneous" means the same as "impromptu." But technically the two are different. Unlike an impromptu speech, which is delivered off-the-cuff, an extemporaneous speech is carefully prepared and practiced in advance. In presenting the speech, the extemporaneous speaker uses only a set of brief notes or a speaking outline to jog the memory (see Chapter 10). The exact wording is chosen at the moment of delivery.

This is not as hard as it sounds. Once you have your outline (or notes) and know what topics you are going to cover and in what order, you can begin to practice the speech. Every time you run through it, the wording will be slightly different. As you practice the speech over and over, the best way to present each part will emerge and stick in your mind.

The extemporaneous method has several advantages. It gives more precise control over thought and language than does impromptu speaking; it offers greater spontaneity and directness than does speaking from memory or from a full manuscript; and it is adaptable to a wide range of situations. It also encourages the conversational quality audiences look for in speech delivery. "Conversational quality" means that no matter how many times a speech has been rehearsed, it still *sounds* spontaneous. When you speak extemporaneously—and have prepared properly—you have full control over your ideas, yet you are not tied to a manuscript. You are free to establish strong eye contact, to gesture naturally, and to concentrate on talking *with* the audience rather than declaiming *to* them.

For an example of extemporaneous delivery, look at Video Clip 12.1 in the online Media Library for this chapter. The student is demonstrating how to breathe when practicing yoga. She clearly has practiced a great deal, and she knows what she wants to say, but she has not memorized the speech. She has a brief set of speaking notes in case she needs them, but she is not tied to the

extemporaneous speech
A carefully prepared and rehearsed speech that is presented from a brief set of notes.

connectlucas.com
View an excerpt from "Yoga: Uniting Mind, Body, and Spirit" in the online Media Library for this chapter (Video Clip 12.1).

notes. Rather, she selects her words as she goes along, maintains strong eye contact with the audience, and has excellent conversational quality.

Like thousands of previous students, you can become adept at speaking extemporaneously by the end of the term. As one student commented in looking back at his class: "At the start, I never thought I'd be able to give my speeches without a ton of notes, but I'm amazed at how much progress I've made. It's one of the most valuable things I learned in the entire class."

Most experienced speakers prefer the extemporaneous method, and most teachers emphasize it. Later in this chapter (pages 258–259), we'll look at a step-by-step program for practicing your extemporaneous delivery.

conversational quality
Presenting a speech so it sounds spontaneous no matter how many times it has been rehearsed.

The Speaker's Voice

What kind of voice do you have? Is it rich and resonant like James Earl Jones's? Thin and nasal like Willie Nelson's? Deep and raspy like Al Sharpton's? Soft and alluring like Catherine Zeta Jones's? Loud and irritating like Dick Vitale's?

Whatever the characteristics of your voice, you can be sure it is unique. Because no two people are exactly the same physically, no two people have identical voices. The human voice is produced by a complex series of steps that starts with the exhalation of air from the lungs. (Try talking intelligibly while inhaling and see what happens.) As air is exhaled, it passes through the larynx (or voice box), where it is vibrated to generate sound. This sound is then amplified and modified as it resonates through the throat, mouth, and nasal passages. Finally, the resonated sound is shaped into specific vowel and consonant sounds by the movement of the tongue, lips, teeth, and roof of the mouth.

The voice produced by this physical process will greatly affect the success of your speeches. A golden voice is certainly an asset, but some of the most famous speakers in history had undistinguished voices. Abraham Lincoln had a harsh and penetrating voice; Winston Churchill suffered from a slight lisp and an awkward stammer. Like them, you can overcome natural disadvantages and use your voice to the best effect. Lincoln and Churchill learned to *control* their voices. You can do the same thing.

The aspects of voice you should work to control are volume, pitch, rate, pauses, variety, pronunciation, articulation, and dialect.

VOLUME

volume
The loudness or softness of the speaker's voice.

At one time a powerful voice was essential for an orator. Today, electronic amplification allows even a soft-spoken person to be heard in any setting. But in the classroom you will speak without a microphone. When you do, be sure to adjust your voice to the acoustics of the room, the size of the audience, and the level of background noise. If you speak too loudly, your listeners will think you boorish. If you speak too softly, they will not understand you. Remember that your own voice always sounds louder to you than to a listener. Soon after beginning your speech, glance at the people farthest away from you. If they look puzzled, are leaning forward in their seats, or are otherwise straining to hear, you need to talk louder.

PITCH

Pitch is the highness or lowness of the speaker's voice. The faster sound waves vibrate, the higher their pitch; the slower they vibrate, the lower their pitch. Pitch distinguishes the sound produced by the keys at one end of a piano from that produced by the keys at the other end.

In speech, pitch can affect the meaning of words or sounds. Pitch is what makes the difference between the "Aha!" triumphantly exclaimed by Sherlock Holmes upon discovering a seemingly decisive clue and the "Aha" he mutters when he learns the clue is not decisive after all. If you were to read the preceding sentence aloud, your voice would probably go up in pitch on the first "Aha" and down in pitch on the second.

Changes in pitch are known as *inflections*. They give your voice luster, warmth, and vitality. Inflection reveals whether you are asking a question or making a statement; whether you are being sincere or sarcastic. Your inflections can also make you sound happy or sad, angry or pleased, dynamic or listless, tense or relaxed, interested or bored.

In ordinary conversation we instinctively use inflections to convey meaning and emotion. People who do not are said to speak in a *monotone,* a trait whose only known benefit is to cure insomnia in one's listeners. Few people speak in an absolute monotone, with no variation whatever in pitch, but many fall into repetitious pitch patterns that are just as hypnotic. You can guard against this by recording your speeches as you practice them. If all your sentences end on the same inflection—either upward or downward—work on varying your pitch patterns to fit the meaning of your words. As with breaking any other habit, this may seem awkward at first, but it is guaranteed to make you a better speaker.

RATE

Rate refers to the speed at which a person speaks. People in the U.S. usually speak at a rate between 120 and 150 words per minute, but there is no uniform rate for effective speechmaking. Franklin Roosevelt spoke at 110 words per minute, John Kennedy at 180. Martin Luther King opened his "I Have a Dream" speech at 92 words per minute and finished it at 145. The best rate of speech depends on several things—the vocal attributes of the speaker, the mood she or he is trying to create, the composition of the audience, and the nature of the occasion.

For example, if you wanted to convey the excitement of the Daytona 500 car race, you would probably speak rather quickly, but a slower rate would be more appropriate to describe the serenity of the Alaskan wilderness. A fast rate helps create feelings of happiness, fear, anger, and surprise, whereas a slow rate is better for expressing sadness or disgust. A slower tempo is called for when you explain complex information, a faster tempo when the information is already familiar to the audience.

Two obvious faults to avoid are speaking so slowly that your listeners become bored or so quickly that they lose track of your ideas. Novice speakers are particularly prone to racing through their speeches at a frantic rate. Fortunately, this is usually an easy habit to break, as is the less common one of crawling through one's speech at a snail's pace.

The key in both cases is becoming aware of the problem and concentrating on solving it. Use a digital recorder to check how fast you speak. Pay special attention to rate when practicing your speech. Finally, be sure to include

pitch
The highness or lowness of the speaker's voice.

inflections
Changes in the pitch or tone of a speaker's voice.

monotone
A constant pitch or tone of voice.

rate
The speed at which a person speaks.

reminders about delivery on your speaking outline so you won't forget to make the adjustments when you give your speech in class.

PAUSES

pause
A momentary break in the vocal delivery of a speech.

Learning how and when to pause is a major challenge for most beginning speakers. Even a moment of silence can seem like an eternity. As you gain more poise and confidence, however, you will discover how useful the pause can be. It can signal the end of a thought unit, give an idea time to sink in, and lend dramatic impact to a statement. "The right word may be effective," said Mark Twain, "but no word was ever as effective as a rightly timed pause."

Developing a keen sense of timing is partly a matter of common sense, partly a matter of experience. You will not always get your pauses just right at first, but keep trying. Listen to accomplished speakers to see how they use pauses to modulate the rate and rhythm of their messages. Work on pauses when you practice your speeches.

vocalized pause
A pause that occurs when a speaker fills the silence between words with vocalizations such as "uh," "er," and "um."

Make sure you pause at the end of thought units and not in the middle. Otherwise, you may distract listeners from your ideas. Most important, do not fill the silence with "uh," "er," or "um." These *vocalized pauses* can create negative perceptions about a speaker's intelligence and often make a speaker appear deceptive.[3]

VOCAL VARIETY

Just as variety is the spice of life, so is it the spice of public speaking. A flat, listless, unchanging voice is just as deadly to speechmaking as a flat, listless, unchanging routine is to daily life.

Try reading this limerick aloud:

I sat next to the Duchess at tea.
It was just as I feared it would be:
    Her rumblings abdominal
    Were simply abominable
And everyone thought it was me!

Now recite this passage from James Joyce's "All Day I Hear the Noise of Waters":

The gray winds, the cold winds are blowing
    Where I go.
I hear the noise of many waters
    Far below.
All day, all night, I hear them flowing
    To and fro.[4]

vocal variety
Changes in a speaker's rate, pitch, and volume that give the voice variety and expressiveness.

Certainly you did not utter both passages the same way. You instinctively varied the rate, pitch, volume, and pauses to distinguish the light-hearted limerick from Joyce's melancholic poem. When giving a speech, you should modulate your voice in just this way to communicate your ideas and feelings.

For an excellent example of vocal variety, look at Video Clip 12.2 in the online Media Library for this chapter. The speaker, Sajjid Zahir Chinoy, was

The best rate of speech depends partly on the mood a speaker wants to create. To communicate the serenity of a mountain lake, you would probably speak at a slower-than-normal rate.

born and raised in Bombay, India, before coming to the United States to attend college at the University of Richmond. At the end of his senior year, Chinoy was selected as the student commencement speaker in a campuswide competition. He spoke of the warm reception he received at Richmond and of how cultural differences can be overcome by attempting to understand other people.

At the end of his speech, Chinoy received thunderous applause—partly because of what he said, but also because of how he said it. Addressing the audience of 3,000 people without notes, he spoke extemporaneously with strong eye contact and excellent vocal variety. The speech was so inspiring that the main speaker, Harvard psychiatrist Robert Coles, began his presentation by paying tribute to Chinoy. "I've been to a number of commencements," said Coles, "but I've never heard a speech quite like that!"

How can you develop a lively, expressive voice? Above all, by approaching every speech as Chinoy approached his—as an opportunity to share with your listeners ideas that are important to you. Your sense of conviction and your desire to communicate will give your voice the same spark it has in spontaneous conversation.

Diagnose your present speaking voice to decide which aspects need improvement. Record your speeches to hear how they sound. Try them out on members of your family, a friend, or a roommate. Check with your teacher for suggestions. Practice the vocal variety exercise at the end of this chapter. Vocal variety is a natural feature of ordinary conversation. There is no reason it should not be as natural a feature of your speeches.

PRONUNCIATION

We all mispronounce words now and again. Here, for example, are six words with which you are probably familiar. Say each one aloud.

genuine	arctic	theater
err	nuclear	February

connectlucas.com
View an excerpt from "Questions of Culture" in the online Media Library for this chapter (Video Clip 12.2).

pronunciation
The accepted standard of sound and rhythm for words in a given language.

Very likely you made a mistake on at least one, for they are among the most frequently mispronounced words in the English language. Let's see:

Word	Common Error	Correct Pronunciation
genuine	gen-u-wine	gen-u-win
arctic	ar-tic	arc-tic
theater	thee-até-er	theé-a-ter
err	air	ur
nuclear	nu-cu-lar	nu-cle-ar
February	Feb-u-ary	Feb-ru-ary

Every word leads a triple life: it is read, written, and spoken. Most people recognize and understand many more words in reading than they use in ordinary writing, and about three times as many as occur in spontaneous speech.[5] This is why we occasionally stumble when speaking words that are part of our reading or writing vocabularies. In other cases, we may mispronounce the most commonplace words out of habit.

The problem is that we usually don't *know* when we are mispronouncing a word. If we are lucky, we learn the right pronunciation by hearing someone else say the word properly or by having someone gently correct us in private. If we are unlucky, we mispronounce the word in front of a roomful of people, who may raise their eyebrows, groan, or laugh.

All of this argues for practicing your speech in front of as many trusted friends and relatives as you can corner. If you have any doubts about the proper pronunciation of certain words, be sure to check a dictionary.

ARTICULATION

articulation

The physical production of particular speech sounds.

Articulation and pronunciation are not identical. Sloppy articulation is the failure to form particular speech sounds crisply and distinctly. It is one of several causes of mispronunciation, but you can articulate a word sharply and still mispronounce it. For example, if you say the "s" in "Illinois" or the "p" in "pneumonia," you are making a mistake in pronunciation, regardless of how precisely you articulate the sounds.

Most of the time poor articulation is caused by laziness—by failing to manipulate the lips, tongue, jaw, and soft palate so as to produce speech sounds clearly and precisely. People in the United States seem particularly prone to chopping, slurring, and mumbling words, rather than articulating them plainly.

Among college students, poor articulation is more common than ignorance of correct pronunciation. We know that "let me" is not "lemme," that "going to" is not "gonna," that "did you" is not "didja," yet we persist in articulating these words improperly. Here are some other common errors in articulation you should work to avoid:

Word	Misarticulation
ought to	otta
didn't	dint
for	fur
don't know	dunno
have to	hafta
them	em
want to	wanna
will you	wilya

If you have sloppy articulation, work on identifying and eliminating your most common errors. Like other bad habits, careless articulation can be broken only by persistent effort—but the results are well worth it. Not only will your speeches be more intelligible, but employers will be more likely to hire you, to place you in positions of responsibility, and to promote you. As Shakespeare advised, "Mend your speech a little, lest you may mar your fortunes."

DIALECT

Most languages have dialects, each with a distinctive accent, grammar, and vocabulary. Dialects are usually based on regional or ethnic speech patterns. The United States has four major regional dialects—Eastern, New England, Southern, and General American. In Boston people may get "idears" about "dee-ah" friends. In Alabama parents tell their children to stop "squinching" their eyes while watching television and to go clean up their rooms "rat" now. In Utah people praise the "lard" and put the "lord" in the refrigerator.

There are also several well-established ethnic dialects in the United States, including Black English, Jewish English, Hispanic English, and Cajun English. In recent years we have also seen the emergence of newer dialects such as Haitian English and Cuban English. As the United States has become more diverse culturally, it has also become more diverse linguistically.

Linguists have concluded that no dialect is inherently better or worse than another. There is no such thing as a right or wrong dialect. Dialects are not linguistic badges of superiority or inferiority. They are usually shaped by our regional or ethnic background, and every dialect is "right" for the community of people who use it.

When is a given dialect appropriate in public speaking? The answer depends above all on the composition of your audience. Heavy use of any dialect—regional or ethnic—can be troublesome when the audience does not share that

dialect
A variety of a language distinguished by variations of accent, grammar, or vocabulary.

dialect. In such a situation, the dialect may cause listeners to make negative judgments about the speaker's personality, intelligence, and competence. This is why professional speakers have been known to invest large amounts of time (and money) to master the General American dialect used by most television news broadcasters.

Does this mean you must talk like a television news broadcaster if you want to be successful in your speeches? Not at all. Regional or ethnic dialects do not pose a problem as long as the audience is familiar with them and finds them appropriate. When speaking in the North, for example, a southern politician will probably avoid heavy use of regional dialect. But when addressing audiences in the South, the same politician may intentionally include regional dialect as a way of creating common ground with his or her listeners.

Although not strictly speaking a matter of dialect, the proficiency of non-native speakers of English often arises in the speech classroom. Fortunately, teachers and students alike usually go out of their way to be helpful and encouraging to international students and others for whom English is not the primary language. Over the years many non-native speakers of English have found speech class a supportive environment in which to improve their proficiency in spoken English.[7]

The Speaker's Body

Imagine you are at a party. During the evening you form impressions about the people around you. Jonte seems relaxed and even-tempered, Nicole tense and irritable. Kyndra seems open and straightforward, Bekah hostile and evasive. Amin seems happy to see you; Seth definitely is not.

How do you reach these conclusions? To a surprising extent, you reach them not on the basis of what people say with words, but because of what they say with their posture, gestures, eyes, and facial expressions. Suppose you are sitting next to Amin, and he says, "This is a great party. I'm really glad to be here with you." However, his body is turned slightly away from you, and he keeps looking at someone across the room. Despite what he says, you know he is *not* glad to be there with you.

Much the same thing happens in speechmaking. Here is the story of one student's first two classroom speeches and the effect created by his physical actions on each occasion:

Sean O'Connor's first speech did not go very well. Even though he had chosen an interesting topic, researched the speech with care, and practiced it faithfully, he did not take into account the importance of using his body effectively. When the time came for him to speak, a stricken look crossed his face. He got up from his chair and plodded to the lectern as though going to the guillotine. His vocal delivery was good enough, but all the while his hands were living a life of their own. They fidgeted with his notes, played with the buttons of his shirt, and drummed on the lectern. Throughout the speech Sean kept his head down, and he looked at his watch repeatedly. Regardless of what his *words* were saying, his *body* was saying, "I don't want to be here!"

Finally it was over. Sean rushed to his seat and collapsed into it, looking enormously relieved. Needless to say, his speech was not a great success.

Good speakers such as Nobel Peace Prize Laureate Muhammad Yunus use a lively voice to bring their ideas to life. They also use gestures, eye contact, and facial expressions to create a bond with their audience.

Fortunately, when Sean's problem was pointed out to him, he worked hard to correct it. His next speech was quite a different story. This time he got up from his chair and strode to the lectern confidently. He kept his hands under control and concentrated on making eye contact with his listeners. This was truly an achievement, because Sean was just as nervous as the first time. However, he found that the more he made himself *look* confident, the more confident he *became*. After the speech his classmates were enthusiastic. "Great speech," they said. "You really seemed to care about the subject, and you brought this caring to the audience."

In fact, the wording of Sean's second speech wasn't much better than that of the first. It was his physical actions that made all the difference. From the time he left his seat until he returned, his body said, "I am confident and in control of the situation. I have something worthwhile to say, and I want you to think so too."

Posture, facial expression, gestures, eye contact—all affect the way listeners respond to a speaker. How we use these and other body motions to communicate is the subject of a fascinating area of study called kinesics. One of its founders, Ray Birdwhistell, estimated that more than 700,000 physical signals can be sent through bodily movement. Studies have shown that these signals have a significant impact on the meaning communicated by speakers. Research has also confirmed what the Greek historian Herodotus observed more than 2,400 years ago: "People trust their ears less than their eyes." When a speaker's body language is inconsistent with his or her words, listeners often believe the body language rather than the words.[8]

Here are the major aspects of physical action that will affect the outcome of your speeches.

kinesics
The study of body motions as a systematic mode of communication.

PERSONAL APPEARANCE

If you were Paris Hilton, you could show up to make an MTV Music Video Award presentation speech wearing a bizarre creation that left little to the imagination. If you were Albert Einstein, you could show up to address an international science conference wearing wrinkled trousers, a sweater, and tennis shoes. While the members of your audience would certainly comment on your attire, your reputation would not be harmed. In fact, it might be enhanced. You would be one of the few, the very few, who live outside the rules, who are expected to be unusual.

Now imagine what would happen if the president of a corporation showed up to address a stockholders' meeting attired like Paris Hilton, or if the President of the United States spoke on national television wearing wrinkled clothes and tennis shoes. Both presidents would soon be looking for work. Barring the occasional eccentric, every speaker is expected by her or his audience to exhibit a personal appearance in keeping with the occasion of the speech.

A number of studies have confirmed that personal appearance plays an important role in speechmaking.[9] Listeners always see you before they hear you. Just as you adapt your language to the audience and the occasion, so should you dress and groom appropriately. Although the force of your speech can sometimes overcome a poor impression created by personal appearance, the odds are against it. Regardless of the speaking situation, you should try to evoke a favorable first impression.

MOVEMENT

Novice speakers are often unsure about what to do with their body while giving a speech. Some pace nonstop back and forth across the podium, fearing that if they stop, they will forget everything. Others constantly shift their weight from one foot to the other, fidget with their notes, or jingle coins in their pockets. Still others turn into statues, standing rigid and expressionless from beginning to end.

Such quirks usually stem from nervousness. If you are prone to distracting mannerisms, your teacher will identify them so you can work on controlling them. With a little concentration, these mannerisms should disappear as you become more comfortable speaking in front of an audience.

As important as how you act during the speech is what you do just *before* you begin and *after* you finish. As you rise to speak, try to appear calm, poised, and confident, despite the butterflies in your stomach. When you reach the lectern, don't lean on it, and don't rush into your speech. Give yourself time to get set. Arrange your notes just the way you want them. Stand quietly as you wait to make sure the audience is paying attention. Establish eye contact with your listeners. Then—and only then—should you start to talk.

When you reach the end of your speech, maintain eye contact for a few moments after you stop talking. This will give your closing line time to sink in. Unless you are staying at the lectern to answer questions, collect your notes and return to your seat. As you do so, maintain your cool, collected demeanor. Whatever you do, don't start to gather your notes before you have finished talking; and don't cap off your speech with a huge sigh of relief or some remark like, "Whew! Am I glad that's over!"

All this advice is common sense, yet you would be surprised how many people need it. When practicing your speeches, spend a little time rehearsing how you will behave at the beginning and at the end. It is one of the easiest—and one of the most effective—things you can do to improve your image with an audience.

GESTURES

Few aspects of delivery cause students more anguish than deciding what to do with their hands. "Should I clasp them behind my back? Let them hang at my sides? Rest them on the lectern? And what about gesturing? When should I do that—and how?" Even people who use their hands expressively in everyday conversation seem to regard them as awkward appendages when speaking before an audience.

Over the years, more nonsense has been written about gesturing than about any other aspect of speech delivery. Adroit gestures *can* add to the impact of a speech; but effective speakers do not need a vast repertoire of gestures. Some accomplished speakers gesture frequently, others hardly at all. The primary rule is this: Whatever gestures you make should not distract from your message. They should *appear* natural and spontaneous, help clarify or reinforce your ideas, and be suited to the audience and occasion.

Gesturing tends to work itself out as you acquire experience and confidence. For now, make sure your hands do not upstage your ideas. Avoid flailing them about, wringing them together, or toying with your rings. Once you have eliminated these distractions, forget about your hands. Think about communicating with your listeners, and your gestures will take care of themselves—just as they do in conversation.

gestures
Motions of a speaker's hands or arms during a speech.

EYE CONTACT

The eyeball itself expresses no emotion. Yet by manipulating the eyeball and the areas of the face around it—especially the upper eyelids and the eyebrows—we convey an intricate array of nonverbal messages. So revealing are these messages that we think of the eyes as "the windows of the soul." We look to them to help gauge a speaker's truthfulness, intelligence, attitudes, and feelings.

Like many aspects of communication, eye contact is influenced by cultural background. When engaged in conversation, Arabs, Latin Americans, and Southern Europeans tend to look directly at the person with whom they are talking. People from Asian countries and parts of Africa tend to engage in less eye contact.

When it comes to public speaking, there is wide agreement across cultures on the importance of some degree of eye contact. In most circumstances, one of the quickest ways to establish a communicative bond with your listeners is to look at them personally and pleasantly. Avoiding their gaze is one of the surest ways to lose them. Speakers in the United States who refuse to establish eye contact are perceived as tentative or ill at ease and may be seen as insincere or dishonest. It is no wonder, then, that teachers urge students to look at the audience 80 to 90 percent of the time they are talking.

eye contact
Direct visual contact with the eyes of another person.

You may find this disconcerting at first. But after one or two speeches, you should be able to meet the gaze of your audience fairly comfortably. As you look at your listeners, be alert for their reactions. Can they hear you? Do they understand you? Are they awake? Your eyes will help you answer these questions.

It isn't enough just to look at your listeners; *how* you look at them also counts. A blank stare is almost as bad as no eye contact at all. So is a fierce, hostile glower or a series of frightened, bewildered glances. Also beware of the tendency to gaze intently at one part of the audience while ignoring the rest. In speech class some students look only at the section of the room where the teacher is sitting. Others avoid looking anywhere near the teacher and focus on one or two sympathetic friends. You should try to establish eye contact with your whole audience.

When addressing a small audience such as your class, you can usually look briefly from one person to another. For a larger group, you will probably scan the audience rather than try to engage the eyes of each person individually. No matter what the size of your audience, you want your eyes to convey confidence, sincerity, and conviction. They should say, "I am pleased to be able to talk with you. I believe deeply in what I am saying, and I want you to believe in it too."

Look at Video Clip 12.3 in the online Media Library for this chapter to see a fine example of eye contact. The speaker is telling her classmates how they can become volunteers for the Special Olympics. Notice how she uses her eyes to connect with her listeners at a personal level. This is the kind of strong communication you should try to develop in your speeches.

connectlucas.com
View an excerpt from "Making a Difference Through the Special Olympics" in the online Media Library for this chapter (Video Clip 12.3).

Practicing Delivery

Popular wisdom promises that practice makes perfect. This is true, but only if we practice properly. You will do little to improve your speech delivery unless you practice the right things in the right ways. Here is a five-step method that has worked well for many students:

1. Go through your preparation outline *aloud* to check how what you have written translates into spoken discourse. Is it too long? Too short? Are the main points clear when you speak them? Are the supporting materials distinct, convincing, interesting? Do the introduction and conclusion come across well? As you answer these questions, revise the speech as needed.

2. Prepare your speaking outline. In doing so, be sure to follow the guidelines in Chapter 10. Use the same visual framework as in the preparation outline. Make sure the speaking outline is easy to read at a glance. Give yourself cues on the outline for delivering the speech.

3. Practice the speech aloud several times using only the speaking outline. Be sure to "talk through" all examples and to recite in full all quotations and statistics. If your speech includes visual aids, use them as you practice. The first couple of times you will probably forget something or make a mistake,

but don't worry. Keep going and complete the speech as well as you can. Concentrate on gaining control of the *ideas;* don't try to learn the speech word for word. After a few tries you should be able to get through the speech extemporaneously with surprising ease.

4. Now begin to polish and refine your delivery. Practice the speech in front of a mirror to check for eye contact and distracting mannerisms. Record the speech to gauge volume, pitch, rate, pauses, and vocal variety. Most important, try it out on friends, roommates, family members—anyone who will listen and give you an honest appraisal. Since your speech is designed for people rather than for mirrors or recorders, you need to find out ahead of time how it goes over with people.

5. Finally, give your speech a dress rehearsal under conditions as close as possible to those you will face in class. Some students like to try the speech a couple of times in an empty classroom the day before the speech is due. No matter where you hold your last practice session, you should leave it feeling confident and looking forward to speaking in your class.

As experienced speakers know, you need to practice a speech thoroughly before delivering it. If possible, try to rehearse under conditions as close as possible to those you will face during the speech itself.

If this or any practice method is to work, you must start early. Don't wait until the night before your speech to begin working on delivery. A single practice session—no matter how long—is rarely enough. Allow yourself *at least* a couple of days, preferably more, to gain command of the speech and its presentation.

Answering Audience Questions

If you have ever watched a press conference or heard a speaker answer questions after a talk, you know the question-and-answer session can make or break a presentation. A speaker who handles questions well can strengthen the impact of his or her speech. On the other hand, a speaker who evades questions or shows annoyance will almost certainly create the opposite effect.

The question-and-answer session is a common part of public speaking, whether the occasion is a press conference, business presentation, public hearing, or classroom assignment. An answer to a question is often the final word an audience hears and is likely to leave a lasting impression.

PREPARING FOR THE QUESTION-AND-ANSWER SESSION

The first step to doing well in a question-and-answer session is to take it as seriously as the speech itself. The two major steps in preparing are working out answers to possible questions and practicing the delivery of those answers.

Formulate Answers to Possible Questions

Once you know your presentation will include questions from the audience, you should be thinking about possible questions even as you are writing your speech. If you practice your speech in front of friends, family, or coworkers, ask them to jot down questions. Keep track of all the questions and formulate answers. Write your answers in full to make sure you have thought them through completely.

If you are giving a persuasive speech, be sure to work out answers to objections the audience may have to your proposal. No matter how careful you are to deal with those objections in your speech, you can be sure they will come up in the question-and-answer session.

If you are speaking on a topic with technical aspects, be ready to answer specialized inquiries about them, as well as questions that seek clarification in nontechnical terms. You might even prepare a handout that you can distribute afterward for people who want more information.

Practice the Delivery of Your Answers

You would not present a speech to a room full of people without rehearsing. Neither should you go into a question-and-answer session without practicing the delivery of your answers.

One possibility is to have a friend or colleague listen to your presentation, ask questions, and critique your answers. This method is used by political candidates and business leaders before debates or press conferences. Another possibility is to record your answers to anticipated questions, play them back, and revise them until they are just right.

As you rehearse, work on making your answers brief and to the point. Many simple questions can be answered in 30 seconds, and even complex ones should be answered in a minute or two. If you practice answering questions beforehand, you will find it much easier to keep to these time limits.

Of course, there is no way to predict every question you will receive. But if you go into the question-and-answer period fully prepared, you will find it much easier to adapt to whatever occurs.

MANAGING THE QUESTION-AND-ANSWER SESSION

If you have ever watched a skillful speaker field questions from the audience, you know there is an art to managing a question-and-answer session. Entire books have been written on this subject, but the following suggestions will help get you started on the right foot.

Approach Questions with a Positive Attitude

A positive attitude will help you answer questions graciously and respectfully. Try to view questions from the audience as signs of genuine interest and a desire to learn more about your subject. If someone asks about a point that seems clear to you, don't respond by saying, "I discussed that at the beginning of my talk," or "The answer seems obvious." Instead, use moments like these to reiterate or expand upon your ideas.

Many speeches are followed by a question-and-answer session. Here Modesto, California, police chief Ray Wasden responds to questions from the press after making prepared remarks on a crime investigation.

A speaker who adopts a sharp or defensive tone while answering questions will alienate many people in the audience. Even if you are asked a hostile question, keep your cool. Avoid the temptation to answer defensively, sarcastically, or argumentatively. Most people in the audience will respect you for trying to avoid a quarrel.

Listen Carefully

It's hard to answer a question well if you don't listen carefully to it. Give the questioner your full attention. When faced with an unclear or unwieldy question, try to rephrase it by saying something like, "If I understand your question, it seems to me that you are asking . . . ." Another option is simply to ask the audience member to repeat the question. Most people will restate it more succinctly and clearly.

Direct Answers to the Entire Audience

When you are being asked a question, look at the questioner. Direct your answer, however, to the entire audience. Make occasional eye contact with the questioner as you answer, but speak primarily to the audience as a whole. If you speak just to the questioner, the rest of your audience may drift off.

When speaking to a large audience, repeat or paraphrase each question after it is asked. This involves the entire audience and ensures that they know the question. In addition, repeating or paraphrasing the question gives you a moment to frame an answer before you respond.

Be Honest and Straightforward

If you don't know the answer to a question, say so. Don't apologize, don't evade, and most important, don't try to bluff. Do, however, let the questioner know that you take the question seriously. Offer to check into the answer as soon as possible after the speech. If a more knowledgeable person is at hand, ask if she or he knows the answer.

Stay on Track

It's easy to get diverted or lose control of time in a lively question-and-answer session. Unless there is a moderator, the speaker is responsible for keeping things on track. Allow one follow-up question from each person, and don't let yourself be dragged into a personal debate with any questioner. If someone attempts to ask more than two questions, respond graciously yet firmly by saying, "This is an interesting line of questioning, but we need to give other people a chance to ask questions."

Sometimes, a listener will launch into an extended monologue instead of posing a question. When this happens, you can retain control of the situation by saying something like, "Those are very interesting ideas, but do you have a specific question I can answer?" If the person persists, offer to talk individually with him or her after the session.

On some occasions, the length of the question-and-answer session is predetermined. On other occasions, it's up to the speaker. Make sure you allow enough time to get through issues of major importance, but don't let things drag on after the momentum of the session has started winding down. As the end approaches, offer to respond to another question or two. Then wrap things up by thanking the audience for its time and attention.[10]

SUMMARY

Speech delivery is a matter of nonverbal communication. It is based on how you use your voice and body to convey the message expressed by your words. Rather than calling attention to itself, effective delivery conveys the speaker's ideas clearly, engagingly, and without distracting the audience.

There are four basic methods of delivering a speech: reading verbatim from a manuscript, reciting a memorized text, speaking impromptu, and speaking extemporaneously. When speaking extemporaneously, you will have a brief set of notes or a speaking outline and will choose the exact wording of your speech at the moment of delivery.

To use your voice effectively you should work on controlling your volume, pitch, rate, pauses, vocal variety, pronunciation, articulation, and dialect. Volume is the relative loudness of your voice, and pitch is the relative highness or lowness. Rate refers to the speed at which you talk. Pauses, when carefully timed, can add great impact to your speech, but you should avoid vocalized pauses ("er," "um," and the like). Vocal variety refers to changes in volume, pitch, rate, and pauses, and is crucial to making your voice lively and animated. For public speaking you should be sure to pronounce words correctly and to articulate them distinctly. You should also avoid heavy use of dialect in situations where the audience does not share the dialect or will find it inappropriate.

Posture, personal appearance, facial expression, gestures, and eye contact also affect the way listeners respond to speakers. Dress and groom appropriately, use gestures and bodily movement to enhance your message, and make eye contact with your listeners.

You should practice all these aspects of delivery along with the words of your speech. Start your practice sessions early so you will have plenty of time to gain command of the speech and its presentation.

If your speech includes a question-and-answer session, anticipate the most likely questions, prepare answers to them, and practice delivering those answers. During the question-and-answer period, listen carefully to the questions, approach them positively, and respond to them briefly, graciously, and straightforwardly. Direct your answers to the full audience, rather than to the questioner alone, and make sure to end the session in a timely fashion.

KEY TERMS

nonverbal communication (244)

manuscript speech (245)

impromptu speech (246)

extemporaneous speech (247)

conversational quality (247)

volume (248)

pitch (249)

inflections (249)

monotone (249)

rate (249)

pause (250)

vocalized pause (250)

vocal variety (250)

pronunciation (251)

articulation (252)

dialect (253)

kinesics (255)

gestures (257)

eye contact (257)

REVIEW QUESTIONS

After reading this chapter, you should be able to answer the following questions:

1. What is nonverbal communication? Why is it important to effective public speaking?

2. What are the elements of good speech delivery?

3. What are the four methods of speech delivery?

4. What are the eight aspects of voice usage you should concentrate on in your speeches?

connectlucas.com
For further review, go to the Study Questions in the online Study Aids for this chapter.

5. What are four aspects of bodily action you should concentrate on in your speeches?

6. What are the five steps you should follow when practicing your speech delivery?

7. What steps should you take when preparing for a question-and-answer session? What should you concentrate on when responding to questions during the session?

EXERCISES FOR CRITICAL THINKING

1. An excellent way to improve your vocal variety is to read aloud selections from poetry that require emphasis and feeling. Choose one of your favorite poems that falls into this category, or find one by leafing through a poetry anthology. Practice reading the selection aloud. As you read, use your voice to make the poem come alive. Vary your volume, rate, and pitch. Find the appropriate places for pauses. Underline the key words or phrases you think should be stressed. Modulate your tone of voice; use inflections for emphasis and meaning.

   For this to work, you must overcome your fear of sounding affected or "dramatic." Most beginning speakers do better if they exaggerate changes in volume, rate, pitch, and expression. This will make you more aware of the many ways you can use your voice to express a wide range of moods and meanings. Besides, what sounds overly "dramatic" to you usually does not sound that way to an audience. By adding luster, warmth, and enthusiasm to your voice, you will go a long way toward capturing and keeping the interest of your listeners.

   If possible, practice reading the selection into a digital recorder. Listen to the playback. If you are not satisfied with what you hear, practice the selection some more and record it again.

2. Watch a 10-minute segment of a television drama with the sound turned off. What do the characters say with their dress, gestures, facial expressions, and the like? Do the same with a television comedy. How do the nonverbal messages in the two shows differ? Be prepared to report your observations in class.

3. Attend a speech on campus. You may choose either a presentation by a guest speaker from outside the college or a class session by a professor who has a reputation as a good lecturer. Prepare a brief report on the speaker's vocal and nonverbal communication.

   In your report, first analyze the speaker's volume, pitch, rate, pauses, vocal variety, pronunciation, and articulation. Then evaluate the speaker's personal appearance, bodily action, gestures, and eye contact. Explain how the speaker's delivery added to or detracted from what the speaker said. Finally, note at least two techniques of delivery used by the speaker that you might want to try in your next speech.

Utilizing your business degree and computer savvy, you have made a success of the online marketing company you started after graduating from college. Now in its third year, the company has prepared a proposal to design the e-commerce site for a major sporting goods retailer. In your 30-minute presentation to the retailer's management team, you will review the homepage designs, site maps, and security protocols.

You notice on the agenda that another 30 minutes has been allotted after your presentation for questions and answers. Knowing from your previous experience with clients how important the Q&A session can be, you want to be sure you are ready for it. What steps will you take to prepare?

Using Visual Aids

Kinds of Visual Aids
  Objects
  Models
  Photographs
  Drawings
  Graphs
  Charts
  Transparencies
  Video
  Multimedia Presentations
  The Speaker

Guidelines for Preparing Visual Aids
  Prepare Visual Aids in Advance
  Keep Visual Aids Simple
  Make Sure Visual Aids Are Large Enough
  Use Fonts That Are Easy to Read
  Use a Limited Number of Fonts
  Use Color Effectively

Guidelines for Presenting Visual Aids
  Avoid Using the Chalkboard
  Display Visual Aids Where Listeners Can See Them
  Avoid Passing Visual Aids Among the Audience
  Display Visual Aids Only While Discussing Them
  Talk to Your Audience, Not to Your Visual Aid
  Explain Visual Aids Clearly and Concisely
  Practice with Your Visual Aids

Diagnosed with high blood pressure when he was in high school, Devin Marshall decided to give his persuasive speech on the excessive amount of salt in the American diet. On the day of his speech, he brought to class a large box, which he set on the table next to him. This immediately aroused the curiosity of his audience. Devin took from the box a container of Morton Salt, a measuring cup, and two plates. Then he began his speech.

First, he explained the monthly salt consumption recommended by the American Medical Association. To illustrate, he measured a cup of salt onto one plate and showed it to the audience. Next, he gave statistics about how much salt the average American consumes in a month. Again, as he spoke, he measured. When he was finished measuring, the second plate had three cups, almost two pounds of salt.

Finally, Devin said, "Now let's multiply that amount by 12 and see how much salt we eat over the course of a year." And he began taking out of the box one container of Morton Salt after another, until he had piled up a pyramid of 14 containers, or nearly 24 pounds of salt!

As the old saying tells us, one picture is worth a thousand words. Can you picture 2 pounds of salt? Or 24 pounds of salt? You could if you had watched Devin measure out the salt and stack up the Morton containers. This dramatic visual evidence brought home Devin's point more forcefully than would have been possible with words alone.

People find a speaker's message more interesting, grasp it more easily, and retain it longer when it is presented visually as well as verbally.[1] In fact, when used properly, visual aids can enhance almost *every* aspect of a speech. One study showed that an average speaker who uses visual aids will come across as better prepared, more credible, and more professional than a dynamic speaker who does not use visual aids. According to the same study, visual aids can increase the persuasiveness of a speech by more than 40 percent.[2] Visual aids can even help you combat stage fright. They heighten audience interest, shift attention away from the speaker, and give the speaker greater confidence in the presentation as a whole.

For all these reasons, you will find visual aids of great value in your speeches. In this chapter, we will concentrate primarily on visual aids suitable for classroom speeches, but the same principles apply in all circumstances. For speeches outside the classroom—in business or community situations, for instance—you should have no difficulty if you follow the suggestions given here.

Let us look first at the kinds of visual aids you are most likely to use, then at guidelines for preparing visual aids, and finally at guidelines for using visual aids. Because PowerPoint is such an important way of presenting visual aids today, we focus on that subject in the appendix that follows this chapter (pages 285–297).

Kinds of Visual Aids

OBJECTS

Bringing the object of your speech to class can be an excellent way to clarify your ideas and give them dramatic impact. If your specific purpose is "To inform my audience how to choose the right ski equipment," why not bring the equipment to class to show your listeners? Or suppose you want to inform

Photographs make excellent visual aids if they are large enough to be seen easily. Check Video Clip 13.2 in the online Media Library for this chapter to see how one speaker used this photograph of the famous Incan ruins at Machu Picchu.

your classmates about the Peruvian art of doll making. You could bring several dolls to class and explain how they were made.

Some objects, however, cannot be used effectively in classroom speeches. Some are too big. Others are too small to be seen clearly. Still others may not be available to you. If you were speaking about a rare suit of armor in a local museum, you could, theoretically, transport it to class, but it is most unlikely that the museum would let you borrow it. You would have to look for another kind of visual aid.

MODELS

If the item you want to discuss is too large, too small, or unavailable, you may be able to work with a model. One student, a criminal science major, used a model of a human skull to show how forensic scientists use bone fragments to reconstruct crime injuries. Another used a scaled-down model of a hang glider to illustrate the equipment and techniques of hang gliding.

model
An object, usually built to scale, that represents another object in detail.

No matter what kind of model (or object) you use, make sure the audience can see it and that you explain it clearly. For an example, check Video Clip 13.1 in the online Media Library for this chapter. The speaker is talking about CPR, which he demonstrates on a training dummy he borrowed from the local Red Cross.

PHOTOGRAPHS

In the absence of an object or a model, you may be able to use photographs. They will not work effectively, however, unless they are large enough for the audience to view without straining. Normal-size photos are too small to be seen clearly without being passed around—which only diverts the audience from what you are saying. The same is true of photographs in books.

How can you get large-scale photos for a speech? One student used art posters to illustrate her points about the painter Frida Kahlo. Another speaker

connectlucas.com
View an excerpt from "CPR" in the online Media Library for this chapter (Video Clip 13.1).

used 18 × 24 enlargements from a color copier to show the markings of various species of saltwater tropical fish. Another option is to take your photographs to a copy service and have them converted to transparencies that can be shown with an overhead projector. The cost is minimal, and the results can be dramatic.

Finally, PowerPoint and other multimedia programs are excellent vehicles for incorporating photographs into a speech. You can use your own photographs or ones you have downloaded from the Web, and you can easily adjust the size and placement of the photos for maximum clarity and impact. Notice, for example, the way the speaker in Video Clip 13.2 in the online Media Library for this chapter used PowerPoint to present a photograph of the famous Incan ruins at Machu Picchu. No other method of showing the photograph would have worked as well.

connectlucas.com

View an excerpt from "Machu Picchu: City of the Gods" in the online Media Library for this chapter (Video Clip 13.2).

DRAWINGS

Diagrams, sketches, and other kinds of drawings are inexpensive to make and can be designed to illustrate your points exactly. This more than compensates for what they may lack in realism.

For example, Figure 13.1 (page 271) is a drawing used by a student in a speech about Navajo sandpainting. The student wanted to show his audience what sandpainting looks like and to explain its symbolism and religious significance.

Figure 13.2 (page 271) shows a drawing used in a speech about the kinds of problems faced by people who have dyslexia. It allowed the speaker to translate complex ideas into visual terms the audience could grasp immediately.

GRAPHS

graph

A visual aid used to show statistical trends and patterns.

Audiences often have trouble grasping a complex series of numbers. You can ease their difficulty by using graphs to show statistical trends and patterns.

The most common type is the *line graph*. Figure 13.3 (page 272) shows such a graph, used in a speech about the American movie industry. If you look at Video Clip 13.3 in the online Media Library for this chapter, you can see how the speaker explained the graph. He said:

As you can see from this graph based on figures in *Newsweek* magazine, the video revolution has had a profound impact on the American movie industry. From 1980 to

• FIGURE 13.1

2005, the percent of movie revenues generated by box office receipts fell dramatically—from 61 percent to 21 percent. At the same time, the percent of movie industry revenues generated by DVD, VHS, and television more than doubled—from 39 percent in 1981 to 79 percent in 2005.

The *pie graph* is best suited for illustrating simple distribution patterns. Figure 13.4 (page 272) shows how one speaker used a pie graph to help listeners visualize changes in marital status among working women in the past century. The graph on the left shows the percentages of working women who were single, married, and widowed or divorced in 1900. The graph on the right shows percentages for the same groups in 2008.

Because a pie graph is used to dramatize relationships among the parts of a whole, you should keep the number of different segments in the graph as small as possible. A pie graph should ideally have from two to five segments; under no circumstances should it have more than eight.

connectlucas.com
View the presentation of this graph in "American Movies: From the Studio System to the Video Age" in the online Media Library for this chapter (Video Clip 13.3).

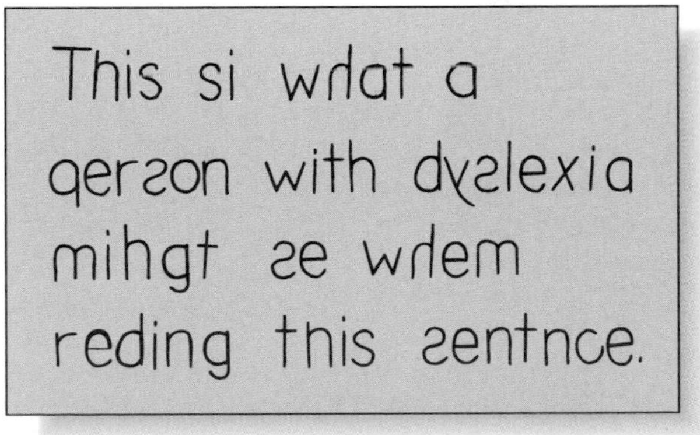

This si wﾍat a qerƧon with dyƧlexia mihgt Ƨe wﾍem reding this Ƨentnce.

• FIGURE 13.2

Movie industry revenues

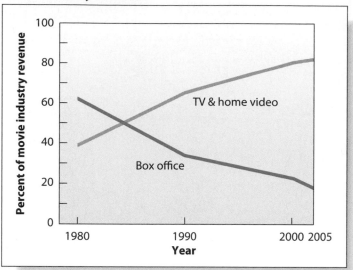

line graph
A graph that uses one or more lines to show changes in statistics over time or space.

• **FIGURE 13.3**

The *bar graph* is a particularly good way to show comparisons among two or more items. It also has the advantage of being easy to understand, even by people who have no background in reading graphs. Figure 13.5 (page 273) is an example of a bar graph from a speech titled "The Politics of Race in America." It shows visually the relative standing of whites and blacks with respect to median household income, infant mortality, unemployment, and college education. By using a bar graph, the speaker made her points much more vividly than if she had just cited the numbers orally.[3]

CHARTS

Charts are particularly useful for summarizing large blocks of information. One student, in a speech titled "The United States: A Nation of Immigrants," used a chart to show the leading regions of the world for U.S. immigrants (Figure 13.6,

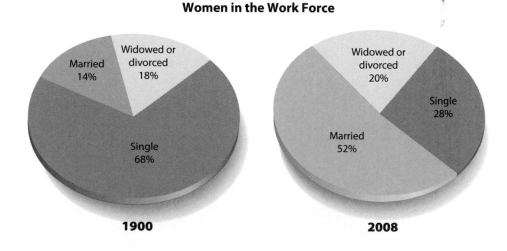

pie graph
A graph that highlights segments of a circle to show simple distribution patterns.

• **FIGURE 13.4**

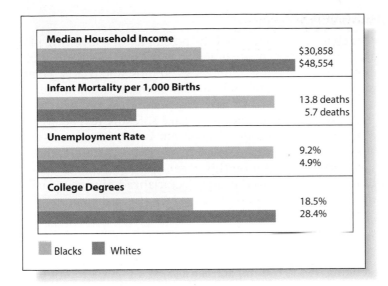

Median Household Income
$30,858
$48,554

Infant Mortality per 1,000 Births
13.8 deaths
5.7 deaths

Unemployment Rate
9.2%
4.9%

College Degrees
18.5%
28.4%

■ Blacks ■ Whites

bar graph
A graph that uses vertical or horizontal bars to show comparisons among two or more items.

• FIGURE 13.5

page 273). These are too many categories to be conveyed in a pie graph. By listing them on a chart, the speaker made it easier for listeners to keep the information straight. Look at Video Clip 13.4 in the online Media Library for this chapter to see how the student presented the chart during her speech.

Charts are also valuable for showing the steps of a process. One speaker used several charts in a speech about survival techniques in the wilderness, including one outlining the steps in emergency treatment of snakebites. Another speaker used charts to help her listeners keep track of the steps involved in making cappuccino and other specialty coffee drinks.

The biggest mistake made by beginning speakers when using a chart is to include too much information. As we will discuss later, visual aids should be clear, simple, and uncluttered. Lists on a chart should rarely exceed seven or eight items, with generous spacing between items. If you cannot fit everything on a single chart, make a second one.

Region of Birth	Percent of U.S. Immigrants
Asia	36 percent
Mexico	14 percent
Europe	11 percent
Caribbean	11 percent
South America	10 percent
Africa	9 percent
Central America	5 percent
Other	4 percent

chart
A visual aid that summarizes a large block of information, usually in list form.

• FIGURE 13.6

TRANSPARENCIES

Earlier in this chapter we mentioned the possibility of converting photographs to transparencies, which can be shown with an overhead projector. You can also use transparencies to present drawings, graphs, and charts. Transparencies are inexpensive, easy to create, and produce a strong visual image.

transparency
A visual aid drawn, written, or printed on a sheet of clear acetate and shown with an overhead projector.

If you use transparencies, don't try to write or draw on them while you are speaking. Prepare them in advance and make sure any text is large enough to be seen from the back of the room. A good rule is that all numbers and letters—whether typed or handwritten—should be at least one-third inch high (about four times as large as the print on this page).

In addition, check the overhead projector ahead of time to make sure it's working and that you know how to operate it. If possible, arrange to practice with a projector when you rehearse the speech.

VIDEO

If you are talking about the impact caused by a low-speed automobile accident, what could be more effective than showing slow-motion video of crash tests? Or suppose you are explaining the different kinds of roller coasters found in amusement parks. Your best visual aid would be a video showing those coasters in action. The detail, immediacy, and vividness of video are hard to match. Now that it is readily available in digital formats—on DVDs, peer-to-peer networks, and Web sites like YouTube—it's easier than ever to incorporate into a speech.

Despite its advantages, however, adding video to a speech can cause more harm than good if it is not done carefully and expertly. First, make sure the clip is not too long. While a 30-second video can illustrate your ideas in a memorable way, anything much longer will distract attention from the speech itself. Second, make sure the video is cued to start exactly where you want it. Third, if necessary, edit the video to the precise length you need so it will blend smoothly into your speech. Fourth, beware of low-resolution video. This is particularly important in the case of YouTube clips, which may look fine on a computer but are blurry and distorted when projected on a large screen or monitor.

MULTIMEDIA PRESENTATIONS

multimedia presentation
A speech that combines several kinds of visual and/or audio aids in the same talk.

Multimedia presentations allow you to integrate a variety of visual aids—including charts, graphs, photographs, and video—in the same talk. Depending on the technological resources at your school, you may be able to give multimedia presentations in your speech class. If so, it will provide training for speeches outside the classroom—especially in business settings, where multimedia presentations are made every day.

Microsoft PowerPoint is far and away the most widely used program for multimedia presentations. In the appendix that follows this chapter, you will find a discussion of how to use PowerPoint to best effect in your speeches. If you go to the online Speech Tools for this chapter at connectlucas.com, you will also find detailed, how-to guides for PowerPoint 2003 and PowerPoint 2007.

THE SPEAKER

Sometimes you can use your own body as a visual aid—by illustrating how a conductor directs an orchestra, by revealing the secrets behind magic tricks, by showing how to perform sign language, and so forth. In addition to clarifying

Sometimes a speaker can use her or his body as a visual aid, as in this speech demonstrating yoga postures. Such a speech requires careful practice to coordinate the speaker's actions and words while maintaining eye contact with the audience.

a speaker's ideas, doing some kind of demonstration helps keep the audience involved. It also can reduce a speaker's nervousness by providing an outlet for extra adrenaline.

Doing a demonstration well requires special practice to coordinate your actions with your words and to control the timing of your speech. You can see an excellent example on Video Clip 13.5 in the online Media Library for this chapter. The subject is yoga. After talking about the role of proper breathing in yoga, the speaker demonstrates three yoga poses. Notice how clearly she explains each pose, communicates directly with the audience, and maintains eye contact throughout her demonstration.

Special care is required if you are demonstrating a process that takes longer to complete than the time allotted for your speech. If you plan to show a long process, you might borrow the techniques of television personalities such as Ming Tsai and Martha Stewart. They work through most of the steps in making a perfect marinated chicken or holiday decoration, but they have a second, finished chicken or decoration ready to show you at the last minute.

connectlucas.com
View an excerpt from "Yoga, Uniting Body, Mind, and Spirit" in the online Media Library for this chapter (Video Clip 13.5).

Guidelines for Preparing Visual Aids

Whether you are creating visual aids by hand or designing them on a computer, there are six basic guidelines you should follow to make your aids clear and visually appealing. These guidelines apply whether you are speaking in or out of the classroom, at a business meeting or a political forum, to an audience of 20 or of 200.

Checklist · Preparing Visual Aids

YES ✓ NO

1. Have I prepared my visual aids well in advance?
2. Are my visual aids clear and easy to comprehend?
3. Does each visual aid contain only the information needed to make my point?
4. Are my visual aids large enough to be seen clearly by the entire audience?
5. Do the colors on my visual aids work well together?
6. Is there a clear contrast between the lettering and background on my charts, graphs, and drawings?
7. Do I use line graphs, pie graphs, and bar graphs correctly to show statistical trends and patterns?
8. Do I limit charts to no more than eight items?
9. Do I use fonts that are easy to read?
10. Do I use a limited number of fonts?

connectlucas.com
This checklist is also available in the online Study Tools for this chapter.

PREPARE VISUAL AIDS IN ADVANCE

No matter what visual aids you plan to use, prepare them well before your speech is due. This has two advantages. First, it means you will have the time and resources to devise creative, attractive aids. Second, it means you can use them while practicing your speech. Visual aids are effective only when they are integrated smoothly with the rest of the speech. If you lose your place, drop your aids, or otherwise stumble around when presenting them, you will distract your audience and shatter your concentration. You can avoid such disasters by preparing your visual aids well in advance.

KEEP VISUAL AIDS SIMPLE

Visual aids should be simple, clear, and to the point. Limit each aid to a manageable amount of information, and beware of the tendency to go overboard when using programs such as PowerPoint. It is possible to create a graphic that displays two charts, a photograph, and ten lines of text in five different typefaces with 250 colors. But who would be able to read it?

The basic rule is to include in your visual aid only what you need to make your point. If you look back at the aids presented earlier in this chapter, you will see that all of them are clear and uncluttered. They contain enough information to communicate the speaker's point, but not so much as to confuse or distract the audience.[4]

MAKE SURE VISUAL AIDS ARE LARGE ENOUGH

A visual aid is useless if no one can see it. Keep in mind the size of the room in which you will be speaking and make sure your aid is big enough to be seen easily by everyone. As you prepare the aid, check its visibility by moving to a point as far away from it as your most distant listener will be sitting. If you have trouble making out the words or drawings, your audience will too. By making sure your visual aid is large enough, you will avoid having to introduce it with the comment "I know some of you can't see this, but . . ."

If you are creating your visual aid by computer, remember that regular-size type (such as that in this book) is much too small for a visual aid—even for one that is enlarged with PowerPoint or an overhead projector. Most experts recommend printing all words and numbers in bold and using at least 36-point type for titles, 24-point type for subtitles, and 18-point type for other text.

What about using all capital letters? That might seem a great way to ensure that your print is large enough to be read easily. But research has shown that a long string of words in ALL CAPS is actually harder to read than is normal text. Reserve ALL CAPS for titles or for individual words that require special emphasis.

USE FONTS THAT ARE EASY TO READ

Not all fonts are suitable for visual aids. For the most part, you should avoid decorative fonts such as those on the left in Figure 13.7, below. They are hard to read and can easily distract the attention of listeners. In contrast, the fonts on the right in Figure 13.7 are less exciting, but they are clear and easy to read. If you use fonts such as these, your visual aids will be audience-friendly.

USE A LIMITED NUMBER OF FONTS

Some variety of fonts in a visual aid is appealing, but too much can be distracting—as in the aid on the left in Figure 13.8 (page 278), which uses a different font for each line. Most experts recommend using no more than two fonts in a single visual aid—one for the title or major headings, another for subtitles or other text. Standard procedure is to use a block typeface for the title and a rounder typeface for subtitles and text—as in the aid on the right in Figure 13.8.

font
A complete set of type of the same design.

Ineffective	More Effective
Airfoil Script	**AHD Symbol**
Bauble	**Arial**
Black Tie Engraved	**Antique Olive**
Corruga	Courier
Marker Board	Times New Roman
Twinkie	Univers
TWOSIE	**Swiss 721**

• **FIGURE 13.7**

Ineffective	More Effective
MAJOR CLASSES OF WINE	**MAJOR CLASSES OF WINE**
appetizer wines	Appetizer Wines
Table Wines	Table Wines
Dessert Wines	Dessert Wines
Sparkling Wines	Sparkling Wines

• FIGURE 13.8

USE COLOR EFFECTIVELY

Color adds clout to a visual aid. When used effectively, it increases recognition by 78 percent and comprehension by 73 percent.[5] The key words, of course, are "when used effectively." Some colors do not work well together. Red and green are a tough combination for anyone to read, and they look the same to people who are color-blind. Many shades of blue and green are too close to each other to be easily differentiated—as are orange and red, blue and purple.

It is also possible to have too many colors on a visual aid. In most circumstances, charts and graphs should be limited to a few colors that are used consistently and solely for functional reasons. You can use either dark print on a light background or light print on a dark background, but in either case make sure there is enough contrast between the background and the text so listeners can see everything clearly.

You can also use color to highlight key points in a visual aid. One student, in a speech about noise pollution, used a chart to summarize the sound levels of everyday noise and to indicate their potential danger for hearing loss (Figure 13.9, below). Notice how he put sounds that are definitely harmful to hearing in red, sounds that may cause hearing loss in blue, and sounds that are loud but safe in green. These colors reinforced the speaker's ideas and made his chart easier to read.

IMPACT ON HEARING	DECIBEL LEVEL	TYPE OF NOISE
Harmful	140	Firecracker
to	130	Jackhammer
hearing	120	Jet engine
Risk	110	Rock concert
hearing	100	Chain saw
loss	90	Motorcycle
Loud	80	Alarm clock
but	70	Busy traffic
safe	60	Air conditioner

• FIGURE 13.9

No matter how well designed your visual aids may be, they will be of little value unless you display them properly, discuss them clearly, and integrate them effectively with the rest of your presentation. Here are seven guidelines that will help you get the maximum impact out of your visual aids.

AVOID USING THE CHALKBOARD

At first thought, using the chalkboard or whiteboard in your classroom to present visual aids seems like a splendid idea. Usually, however, it is not. You have too much to do during a speech to worry about drawing or writing legibly on the board. Even if your visual aid is put on the board ahead of time, it will not be as vivid or as neat as one composed on poster board, a transparency, or a PowerPoint slide.

DISPLAY VISUAL AIDS WHERE LISTENERS CAN SEE THEM

Check the speech room ahead of time to decide exactly where you will display your visual aids. If you are using poster board, make sure it is sturdy enough to be displayed without curling up or falling over. Another choice is foamcore, a thin sheet of styrofoam with graphics-quality paper on both sides.

If you are displaying an object or a model, be sure to place it where it can be seen easily by everyone in the room. If necessary, hold up the object or model while you are discussing it.

Once you have set the aid in the best location, don't undo all your preparation by standing where you block the audience's view of the aid. Stand to one side of the aid, and point with the arm nearest it. If possible, use a pencil, a ruler, or some other pointer. This will allow you to stand farther away from the visual aid, thereby reducing the likelihood that you will obstruct the view.

AVOID PASSING VISUAL AIDS AMONG THE AUDIENCE

Once visual aids get into the hands of your listeners, you are in trouble. At least three people will be paying more attention to the aid than to you—the person who has just had it, the person who has it now, and the person waiting to get it next. By the time the visual aid moves on, all three may have lost track of what you are saying.

Nor do you solve this problem by preparing a handout for every member of the audience. They are likely to spend a good part of the speech looking over the handout at their own pace, rather than listening to you. Although handouts can be valuable, they usually just create competition for beginning speakers.

Every once in a while, of course, you will want listeners to have copies of some material to take home. When such a situation arises, keep the copies until after you've finished talking and distribute them at the end. Keeping control of your visual aids is essential to keeping control of your speech.

DISPLAY VISUAL AIDS ONLY WHILE DISCUSSING THEM

Just as circulating visual aids distracts attention, so does displaying them throughout a speech. If you are using an object or a model, keep it out of sight until you are ready to discuss it. When you finish your discussion, place the object or model back out of sight.

Checklist — Presenting Visual Aids

YES ✓ NO

1. Can I present my visual aids without writing or drawing on the chalkboard?

2. Have I checked the speech room to decide where I can display my visual aids most effectively?

3. Have I practiced presenting my visual aids so they will be clearly visible to everyone in the audience?

4. Have I practiced setting up and taking down my visual aids so I can do both smoothly during the speech?

5. Have I practiced keeping eye contact with my audience while presenting my visual aids?

6. Have I practiced explaining my visual aids clearly and concisely in terms my audience will understand?

7. If I am using handouts, have I planned to distribute them after the speech rather than during it?

8. Have I double checked all equipment to make sure it works properly?

9. Have I rehearsed my speech with the equipment I will use during the final presentation?

connectlucas.com
This checklist is also available in the online Study Tools for this chapter.

The same is true of charts, graphs, drawings, or photographs prepared on poster board. If you are using an easel, put a blank sheet of poster board in front of the sheet with the visual aid. When the time comes, remove the blank sheet to show the aid. When you are finished with the aid, remove it from the easel or cover it again.

If you are using a multimedia program, you can achieve the same effect by projecting a blank slide when you are not discussing a visual aid. Regardless of the kind of aid employed or the technology used to present it, the principle remains the same: Display the aid *only* while you are discussing it.

TALK TO YOUR AUDIENCE, NOT TO YOUR VISUAL AID

When explaining a visual aid, it is easy to break eye contact with your audience and speak to the aid. Of course, your listeners are looking primarily at the aid, and you will need to glance at it periodically as you talk. But if you keep your eyes fixed on the visual aid, you may lose your audience. By keeping eye contact with your listeners, you will also pick up feedback about how the visual aid and your explanation of it are coming across.

EXPLAIN VISUAL AIDS CLEARLY AND CONCISELY

Visual aids don't explain themselves. Like statistics, they need to be translated and related to the audience. For example, Figure 13.10 (page 281) is an excellent visual aid, but do you know what it represents? You may if you suffer from migraine headaches, since it shows the different regions of pain experienced

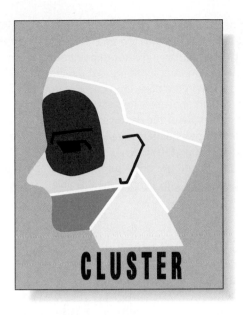

CLUSTER

• **FIGURE 13.10**

during a cluster migraine attack. But even then, the full meaning of the drawing may not be clear until it is explained to you.

A visual aid can be of enormous benefit—but only if the viewer knows what to look for and why. Unfortunately, beginning speakers often rush over their visual aids without explaining them clearly and concisely. Be sure to adapt your visual aids to the audience. Don't just say, "As you can see . . ." and then pass quickly over the aid. Tell listeners what the aid means. Describe its major features. Spell out the meaning of charts and graphs. Interpret statistics and percentages. Remember, a visual aid is only as useful as the explanation that goes with it.

As you can see from Video Clip 13.6 in the online Media Library for this chapter, the speaker who used the diagram of the migraine headache discussed above did an excellent job explaining how each color on the drawing corresponds with an area of intense pain suffered during a cluster migraine. Having used the drawing during her practice sessions, she was able to integrate it into the speech smoothly and skillfully—and to maintain eye contact with her listeners throughout her discussion of it. You should strive to do the same when you present visual aids in your speeches.

connectlucas.com
View an excerpt from "The Agony of Migraines" in the online Media Library for this chapter (Video Clip 13.6).

PRACTICE WITH YOUR VISUAL AIDS

This chapter has mentioned several times the need to practice with visual aids, but the point bears repeating. You do not want to suffer through an experience like the one that follows:

Several years ago, a young engineer came up with a cutting-edge design for a new machine. He then needed to explain the machine to his supervisors and convince them it was a worthwhile investment. He was told to plan his speech carefully, to prepare slides and other visual aids, and to practice in the conference room, using its complex lectern and projection system.

Unfortunately, although he had done a brilliant job designing the machine, the engineer failed to plan his presentation with similar care. His worst mistake was not practicing with the equipment he now needed to operate. When he dimmed the lights, he couldn't read his text.

When the first slide came on, it wasn't his but belonged to a previous speaker. When he reached the first correct slide, the type was too small for anyone past the first row to see.

Unable to turn on the light-arrow indicator to point out the line he was talking about, he walked away from the lectern to point things out directly on the screen. But he left the microphone behind, so people in the back rows could neither see nor hear.

When a slide of his design appeared, he was too close to see the critical parts. Since he couldn't check his text because of the darkness, he lost track of what he was supposed to say. Reaching for a steel-tipped pointer because he couldn't operate the optical one, he managed to punch a hole through the screen.

In desperation, he abandoned his slides, turned up the lights, and raced through the rest of his speech so fast that he was almost unintelligible. Finally, in embarrassment for both himself and the audience, he sat down.[6]

This sounds like a routine from *Saturday Night Live,* but it is a true story. You can avoid such a series of mishaps if you practice with the visual aids you have chosen. Rehearse with your equipment to be sure you can present your aids with a minimum of fuss. Run through the entire speech several times, practicing how you will show the aids, the gestures you will make, and the timing of each move. In using visual aids, as in other aspects of speechmaking, there is no substitute for preparation.[7]

SUMMARY

There are many kinds of visual aids. Most obvious is the object about which you are speaking, or a model of it. Diagrams, sketches, and other kinds of drawings are valuable because you can design them to illustrate your points exactly. Graphs are an excellent way to illustrate any subject dealing with numbers, while charts are used to summarize large blocks of information. Although video can be useful as a visual aid, it needs to be carefully edited and integrated into the speech. Photographs should be large enough to be seen clearly by all your listeners. If you have access to the right equipment, you may be able to use a multimedia presentation. Finally, you can act as your own visual aid by performing actions that demonstrate processes or ideas.

No matter what kind of visual aid you use, you need to prepare it carefully. You will be most successful if you prepare your aids in advance, keep them simple, make sure they are large enough to be seen clearly, and use color effectively for emphasis and visual appeal. If you are creating visual aids on a computer, use a limited number of fonts and make sure the ones you select will be easy to read.

In addition to being designed with care, visual aids need to be presented skillfully. Avoid writing or drawing visual aids on the chalkboard or passing them among the audience. Instead, display each aid only while you are talking about it, and be sure to place it where everyone can see it without straining. When presenting a visual aid, maintain eye contact with your listeners and explain the aid clearly and concisely. Above all, practice with your visual aids so they fit into your speech smoothly and expertly.

KEY TERMS

model *(269)*

graph *(270)*

line graph *(270)*

pie graph *(271)*

bar graph *(272)*

chart *(272)*

transparency *(274)*

multimedia presentation *(274)*

font *(277)*

REVIEW QUESTIONS

After reading this chapter, you should be able to answer the following questions:

1. What are the major advantages of using visual aids in your speeches?

2. What kinds of visual aids might you use in a speech?

3. What guidelines are given in the chapter for preparing visual aids?

4. What guidelines are given in the chapter for presenting visual aids?

connectlucas.com
For further review, go to the
Study Questions in the online
Study Aids for this chapter.

EXERCISES FOR CRITICAL THINKING

1. Watch a how-to television program (a cooking or gardening show, for example) or the weather portion of a local newscast. Notice how the speaker uses visual aids to help communicate the message. What kinds of visual aids are used? How do they enhance the clarity, interest, and retainability of the speaker's message? What would the speaker have to do to communicate the message effectively without visual aids?

2. Consider how you might use visual aids to explain each of the following:

   a. How to perform the Heimlich maneuver to help a choking victim.

   b. The proportion of the electorate that votes in major national elections in the United States, France, Germany, England, and Japan, respectively.

   c. Where to obtain information about student loans.

   d. The wing patterns of various species of butterflies.

   e. The increase in the amount of money spent by Americans on health care since 1985.

   f. How to change a bicycle tire.

   g. The basic equipment and techniques of rock climbing.

3. Plan to use visual aids in at least one of your classroom speeches. Be creative in devising your aids, and be sure to follow the guidelines discussed in the chapter for using them. After the speech, analyze how effectively you employed your visual aids, what you learned about the use of visual aids from your experience, and what changes you would make in using visual aids if you were to deliver the speech again.

As a veterinarian and owner of a small-animal practice, you work closely with your local humane society to help control a growing population of unwanted dogs and cats. You and your staff devote many hours annually in free and reduced-cost medical services to animals adopted from the society. Now you have been asked to speak to the city council in support of legislation proposed by the society for stronger enforcement of animal licensing and leash laws.

In your speech, you plan to include statistics that (1) compare estimates of the city's dog population with the number of licenses issued during the past five years and (2) show the small number of citations given by local law enforcement for unleashed pets during the same period of time. Knowing from your college public speaking class how valuable visual aids can be in presenting statistics, you decide to illustrate one set of statistics with a chart and the other with a graph.

For which set of statistics will a chart be more appropriate? For which set will a graph be more appropriate? Of the three kinds of graphs discussed in this chapter (bar, line, pie), which will work best for your statistics and why?

Using
PowerPoint

W hat do a business meeting, a courtroom presentation, a military briefing, and a college lecture have in common? In all four situations there is a good chance you will encounter a speaker using PowerPoint to help communicate her or his ideas. A survey of 300 professional speakers showed that 94 percent use PowerPoint during at least part of their talks, and Microsoft estimates that 30 million PowerPoint presentations are given every day.[1] Depending on the technology at your school, you may have an opportunity to use PowerPoint in one or more of your classroom speeches.

In Chapter 13, we discussed general principles for effective multimedia presentations. Here we focus specifically on PowerPoint. As with any method of presenting visual or audio aids, PowerPoint has its pluses and minuses. We'll begin by looking at both, as well as at the major factors to consider when planning to use PowerPoint in a speech.

Pluses and Minuses of PowerPoint

When used well, PowerPoint is a great boon to communication. It allows you to employ all kinds of visual aids without having to juggle poster board and overhead transparencies while also trying to operate a DVD player and slide projector. Instead, you can use PowerPoint to incorporate text, photographs, charts, graphs, sound, even video into your speech.

Unfortunately, PowerPoint is not always used well. Too often speakers allow it to dominate their presentations, wowing the audience with their technical proficiency while losing the message in a flurry of sounds and images. As technology expert Herb Lovelace states, it sometimes seems that "the fancier the PowerPoint presentation, the less valuable the ideas being presented."[2]

At the other extreme are speakers who throw their presentations together carelessly, assuming that using PowerPoint will magically produce a superb speech. Plodding through one poorly designed slide after another with little or no eye contact with an audience seated in a darkened room, these speakers would be better off if they had never heard of PowerPoint.

Another problem is that some speakers use PowerPoint to illustrate every point of their talk, so the speaker is virtually reading the speech to the audience as the words appear on screen. This is no more effective than reading dully from a manuscript, and it seldom produces genuine communication.

Planning to Use PowerPoint

If you are going to employ PowerPoint effectively, you need a clear idea of exactly why, how, and when to use it in your speech. Rather than putting everything you say on screen for the audience to read, you need to choose which aspects of your speech to illustrate. This requires careful planning.

One of the most surprising aspects of PowerPoint to people who have not used it before is how much time and effort are required to put together a first-rate presentation. Not only are you responsible for all the other activities involved in speechmaking, but you face the additional tasks of deciding where to use PowerPoint, of gathering images and/or sounds, of designing first-rate slides, and of mastering the equipment and PowerPoint commands needed to deliver your speech smoothly and expertly.

The first step is deciding where you can use PowerPoint to greatest advantage. After you have finished developing the speech, think about where you might employ PowerPoint to clarify or strengthen your ideas. Rather than using PowerPoint to illustrate every thought, look for spots where it will genuinely enhance your message.

For example, in a speech about skyscrapers one student included information about the world's five tallest buildings. He created a PowerPoint slide that showed the progression of buildings from shortest to tallest, accompanied by a photograph of each. By using PowerPoint's animation feature, he was able to control the display of each building, so it came on screen just as he was discussing it. As you can see in Video Clip A2.1 in the online Media Library for this appendix, there is no way he could have achieved the same result with a traditional visual aid.

connectlucas.com
View this excerpt from "The Ups and Downs of Skyscrapers" in the online Media Library for this appendix (Video Clip A2.1).

For another example, look at Video Clip A2.2, in which the speaker discusses Georges Seurat's famous painting *Sunday Afternoon on the Island of la Grand Jatte*. The speaker uses a series of PowerPoint slides to show details of the painting that could not have been seen otherwise. He also does an excellent job of explaining each slide as he goes along.

As you plan your speeches, think how you can use PowerPoint in a similar manner to enhance your ideas. At the same time, remember that too many visuals—or poor visuals—can do more harm than good. Be creative and resourceful without allowing PowerPoint to overwhelm your entire speech.

connectlucas.com
View this excerpt from "Georges Seurat and the Art of Pointillism" in the online Media Library for this appendix (Video Clip A2.2).

Formatting PowerPoint Slides

If you have questions about the basic features of PowerPoint, check the tutorials in the online Speech Tools for this appendix at connectlucas.com. You can select from PowerPoint 2003 or PowerPoint 2007, depending on which version is on your computer. The tutorials will lead you step by step through the entire process of creating and formatting slides. Here we focus less on technical information than on principles for the use of color, text, fonts, images, space, and animation.

COLOR

PowerPoint offers a wide selection of colors, and you may be tempted to try all of them. But to produce effective slides, you need to stick to a limited number of colors and use them consistently. Use one color for background, one color for titles, and one color for other text throughout all your slides. This consistency will unify the slides and give your speech a professional appearance.

connectlucas.com
For step-by-step guides to creating PowerPoint slides, check the tutorials in the online Speech Tools for this appendix.

When PowerPoint was first developed, most experts recommended using light text on a dark background. Today, dark text on a light background is used just as often. In most cases, either is fine as long as there is enough contrast between the colors to make the slides easy to read.

TEXT

Most PowerPoint slides contain some kind of text. It might be no more than a title indicating the subject of the slide, or it might include several lines in the body of the slide. Text can be used by itself or in conjunction with photographs, charts, drawings, and other images.

Whatever kind of text you include, it should be brief. One of the biggest mistakes people make when using PowerPoint is putting too much text on a single slide. A general rule for slides that contain only text is to include no more than a half-dozen lines of type. If you are combining text with images, you may need to limit yourself to fewer lines to keep the text from getting too small. If you have a number of important points to cover, spread them out over multiple slides.

For example, Figure A.1 below shows a slide from a speech about Easter Island, famous for its mysterious statues of unknown origin. Notice that the slide is not bogged down with information, presenting only an image of the statues, as well as a title and text identifying the location of Easter Island and the date it was discovered by Europeans. Because the slide is simple and clear, the speaker was able to present it succinctly and move to her next point.

FONTS

serif font
A typeface with rounded edges on the letters.

PowerPoint has dozens of fonts to choose from, but they all fall into one or another of two basic categories—serif or sans-serif. Serif fonts have little tails on each letter, like the type you are reading right now. Sans-serif fonts do not have tails, like the type used for the heading Fonts at the start of this section. For examples, see Figure A.2 (page 289).

sans-serif font
A typeface with straight edges on the letters.

Serif fonts are easier to read in large patches of text, while sans-serif fonts are better for headings and short bursts of text. Most multimedia experts recommend sans-serif fonts for titles and headings on PowerPoint slides—and some say sans-serif should be used for *all* text in PowerPoint.

• FIGURE A.1

Sample PowerPoint Slide

Serif Fonts	Sans-Serif Fonts
Times New Roman	Arial
Bookman Old Style	Antique Olive
MS Reference Serif	MS Reference Sans Serif
Book Antiqua	Tahoma
Palatino Linotype	Verdana

• FIGURE A.2

When choosing fonts, keep the following guidelines in mind:

- Choose fonts that are clear and easy to read. (For examples, see Chapter 13, pages 277–278).

- Avoid using ALL CAPS because they are difficult to read.

- Don't use more than two fonts on a single slide—one for the title or major heading and another for subtitles or other text.

- Use the same fonts on all your slides.

- Put titles and major headings in 44- to 36-point type; make subheads and other text 32- to 24-point.

IMAGES

One of the benefits of PowerPoint is the ease with which it allows you to include photographs, charts, graphs, and other images, including video. Unfortunately, some speakers are prone to adding images simply because it is easy, rather than because it is essential for communicating their message. You should *never* add images of any sort to a PowerPoint slide unless they are truly needed. There is a great deal of research showing that extraneous images distract listeners and reduce comprehension of the speaker's point.[3]

In addition to keeping your slides free of extraneous images, keep these guidelines in mind:

- Make sure images are large enough to be seen clearly.

- Choose high-resolution images that will project without blurring.

- Keep graphs and charts clear and simple.

- In most cases, include a title above charts and graphs so the audience knows what they are viewing.

- Edit video so it is integrated seamlessly into your slides.

- Include copyright information when applicable. (See page 295.)

SPACE

No matter what elements you include on your slides, you should strive for a pleasing sense of visual balance. Consider, for example, Figure A.3 (page 290), which shows a slide from a speech about Eleanor Roosevelt. Notice how the

title is displayed in a single line at the top of the slide, the photograph fills most of the left side, and the text occupies enough space on the right to compensate for the size of the photograph.

Compare this slide with the one in Figure A.4 (below). The second slide contains the same elements as the first, but they are not arranged effectively. The title is located over the photograph, where it takes up two lines rather than one. To compensate, the photograph of Roosevelt has been reduced in size, so it has less visual impact. The photograph is also too close to the bottom of the slide, thereby separating it from the title. Finally, the text on the right is too close to the photograph and is placed too high to provide a good sense of visual balance.

If you stick with PowerPoint's default layouts, you should have little trouble creating slides that are visually balanced. Be sure, though, to leave a little extra room at the edges of your slides because what is projected on the viewing screen is sometimes smaller than what you see on your computer.

ANIMATION

When you read the word "animation," you might think of cartoon characters and Walt Disney movies. In PowerPoint, however, animation refers to the way objects enter or exit a slide. Without animation, all the items on a slide appear at the same time when the slide is displayed. With animation, you can control when words, pictures, even parts of graphs show up on screen. When used properly, it's a terrific way to spruce up your slides.

Look, for example, at the speech on the Great Wall of China that is reprinted at the end of this appendix. For the most part, the speaker avoids special animation effects because they are not necessary to communicate his ideas. However, when explaining the architectural changes made to the Wall during the Ming dynasty, he uses animation to make sure the appropriate text appears on screen just as he begins to discuss each point. By doing so, he focuses the audience's attention and reinforces his ideas at the same time.

When working on your speeches, think about ways you can use animation to help communicate your message. Be wary, however, of animation effects that might distract the attention of listeners. Stick with a limited number of animation effects and use them consistently from slide to slide.

animation
The way objects enter or exit a PowerPoint slide.

connectlucas.com
View this excerpt from "The Great Wall of China" in the online Media Library for this appendix (Video Clip A2.3).

Delivering Your Speech with PowerPoint

Once you have created your slides, it's time to work on the delivery of your speech. As with other aspects of PowerPoint, this requires careful planning. Even the most professional-looking slides will do little good if you can't get the computer and projector to work properly, if the slides can't be seen clearly because of poor lighting, or if you forget to display them at the right moment.

The guidelines presented in Chapter 13 for delivering speeches with other types of visual aids also apply to speeches with PowerPoint. Here we focus on aspects of delivery that are especially important for speakers who employ PowerPoint.

RECHECK YOUR SLIDES

Before rehearsing your speech, take time to double-check your slides to see if anything is missing, misplaced, or misspelled. You can review all your slides at a glance in Slide Sorter view (see Figure A.5, p. 292). It's also a good idea to run through your slides in Slide Show view, which displays the slides as they will appear on screen during your speech. Be sure to save any corrections and changes as you go along.

KNOW SLIDE SHOW COMMANDS

When delivering your speech, you should be able to move effortlessly from slide to slide, as well as among animation effects on individual slides. To do so,

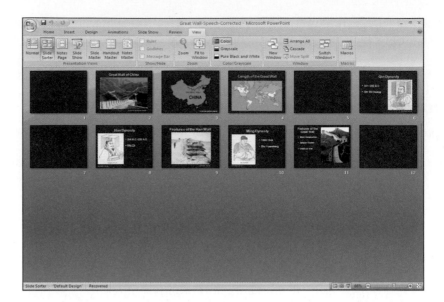

• **FIGURE A.5**

Slide Sorter View in
PowerPoint 2007

you have to know the computer commands for these operations. Figure A.6, below shows some of the most-used commands.

As you can see, there are multiple options for most commands. If you have not used PowerPoint before, practice with the various options and decide which you want to use. Then stick with them throughout your presentation.

As you gain more experience with PowerPoint, its commands will become second nature. However, just in case you forget something during your speech, you may want to follow the lead of experienced speakers and write the most important commands on a sheet of paper that you can refer to if necessary.

PowerPoint 2007 Slide Show Commands

Display slides (enter Slide Show view)	Click the Slide Show tab at the top of the screen and select From Beginning from the ribbon; or click the View tab and select Slide Show from the ribbon.
Show the next slide	Click the mouse; press Enter; press the right arrow button; or press the "N" key.
Show the previous slide	Press Backspace; press the left arrow button; or press the "P" key.
Show a specific slide	Type the number of the slide and press Enter.
End the show	Press Esc.

• **FIGURE A.6**

PRACTICE YOUR SPEECH WITH POWERPOINT

As we saw in Chapter 13, you should always practice a speech with your visual aids. This is especially important when using PowerPoint. When you practice, don't just click the mouse casually or rush quickly over your words. Go through every part of the speech and make sure you know exactly when you want each slide to appear and disappear, and what you will say while each is on screen. Mark your speaking notes with cues that will remind you when to display each slide or animation and when to remove it.

It's usually best to project a slide when you first start discussing the point it illustrates. For a good example, look at the timing of the slides in Video Clip A2.4 in the online Media Library for this appendix. The speaker is explaining the importance of using a secure connection when transmitting sensitive data over the Internet. He presents each slide at just the right moment and makes sure it is on screen only while he is discussing it.

In addition to coordinating your slides with your words, pay attention when you practice to making eye contact with the audience. This is especially challenging when you use PowerPoint because of all the equipment you are operating during the speech. Rehearse with the mouse and keyboard until you can use both without looking down for more than an instant when advancing your slides.

Also concentrate on presenting the speech without looking back at the screen to see what is being projected on it. You can check what is on screen by glancing at the computer each time you advance a slide. There is nothing wrong with looking at the screen now and again as you explain your slides, but remember to address your remarks to the audience, not to the screen.

Given all the things you have to work on when practicing a speech with PowerPoint, you need to allow extra time for rehearsal. So get an early start and give yourself plenty of time to ensure that your delivery is as impressive as your slides.

connectlucas.com
View this excerpt from "Securing Yourself Online" in the online Media Library for this appendix (Video Clip A2.4).

DISPLAY SLIDES ONLY WHILE DISCUSSING THEM

As with other types of visual aids, you want your PowerPoint slides to be visible only when you are discussing them. You can achieve this goal by adding blank slides as needed. Notice, for example, how the speaker in the Great Wall presentation uses blank slides at various parts of the speech. By doing so, he keeps his listeners focused on what he is saying at the moment, rather than having their attention diverted by the previous slide.

It's also a good idea to add a blank slide at the end of your presentation, so your last content slide will not continue to be exposed after you have finished discussing it.

CHECK THE ROOM AND EQUIPMENT

In ideal circumstances, you will be able to rehearse at least once in the room where you will present your speech, with the same computer, mouse, and projector you will use on the day of your speech. If this is not possible, try to stop by the room several days beforehand and work with the equipment. If you can't get to the room before the day of the speech, arrive an hour or so ahead of time to familiarize yourself with the equipment and to make sure it's working properly.

PowerPoint is most effective when it is used selectively, when slides are skillfully integrated with the rest of the speech, and when the speaker communicates directly with the audience.

There is wide variation among computers and projectors, as well as among rooms equipped with multimedia connections, so even if you have used PowerPoint on previous occasions, you need to check the setup in the room where you will be speaking. Most experienced speakers arrange ahead of time to have a technician present when they arrive, so she or he can take care of any problems.

Pay attention to the lighting as well. Check whether the projector is bright enough to overpower the room lights and create a sharp image. If it isn't, see if you can dim the lights near the screen.

This may all seem like a lot of fuss and bother, but anyone who has given speeches with PowerPoint will tell you it's absolutely essential.

DEVELOP A BACKUP PLAN

Despite all your preparation and practice, it's possible that technology will fail you. More than one speaker has arrived with PowerPoint in tow only to discover that the computer is acting up, the projector will not work, or the room's power connections are not compatible with the speaker's computer.

What do you do if this happens? You can't just cancel the speech. This is why you always need a backup plan—especially for speeches outside the classroom.

One option is to copy your slides to a flash drive so you can project them on another computer if something happens to yours. Many experienced speakers also e-mail themselves their slides as an extra precaution.

Another option is to print a hard copy of your slides to carry with you. Depending on the size of your audience, you may be able to distribute copies as an alternative to projecting the slides—though there may be circumstances in which even that is impossible. The important thing is to think through potential complications in advance and have a backup plan ready just in case you need it.

Copyright and Fair Use

We have mentioned several times the ease with which photographs, charts, graphs, audio, and video can be downloaded from the Internet for use with PowerPoint. It's important, when using such materials, to be aware of and to observe copyright laws.

Under copyright law, someone who wishes to use the original work of another person must obtain permission from that person (or whoever owns the material) and often must pay a usage fee. Despite these restrictions, the "fair use" provision of the law permits students and educators to employ portions of copyrighted materials—including images and sounds downloaded legally from the Internet—for educational purposes. The law is complex and often ambiguous, but in general it allows you to use copyrighted material in classroom speeches according to these guidelines:[4]

- You *may* use copyrighted materials for a PowerPoint presentation that you create for a specific class. If you include the presentation in an employment portfolio, you may continue to use copyrighted materials in it.

- You may *not* use materials you obtained illegally (e.g., copyrighted material from a file-sharing network).

- You may *not* post copyright materials back to the Web without written permission from the copyright owner.

- You *must* credit your sources and display the copyright symbol—©—when using copyrighted material. Make sure to mention the author/creator, title, and date of publication. The usual practice is to type the credit line in 10-point font and to place it below the item for which credit is being given.

Keep these guidelines in mind when you search for images, video, and audio on the Internet as well as in books, magazines, and other print sources. Remember to write down credit and copyright information as you go along; otherwise, you may have to spend extra time looking for it later.

fair use
A provision of copyright law that permits students and teachers to use portions of copyrighted materials for educational purposes.

Sample Speech with Commentary

On pages 296–297 is the text of an informative speech on the Great Wall of China that employs PowerPoint. As you read, notice how it fulfills the criteria for effective speeches discussed elsewhere in the book—sharp focus, clear organization, plentiful connectives, strong supporting materials, and the like. To see how the speaker uses PowerPoint, view the speech in the online Media Library for this appendix at connectlucas.com. Pay special attention to the quality of the speaker's slides, to the skill with which he integrates them into his discussion, and to the way he maintains eye contact with his audience while discussing his slides.

connectlucas.com
View "The Great Wall of China" in the online Media Library for this chapter (Video Clip A2.5).

The Great Wall of China

COMMENTARY	SPEECH
The speaker begins with a quotation to gain attention and interest. He also establishes his credibility by noting that he visited the Great Wall while he was in China.	In China there's a saying, "You won't be considered a great person until you've been to the Great Wall." I visited the wall last year while I was in China. I don't know if it made me a great person, but I do know that the wall is indeed great.
The speaker's first slide is a striking photograph of the Great Wall that shows how it snakes across the tops of the mountains. He then moves to a slide that illustrates the expanse of the wall as it stretches across China. He ends this paragraph by explaining how the Great Wall would stretch from New York City to Berlin, Germany. An animated slide provides visual reinforcement and helps dramatize the extraordinary length of the wall.	As you can see from this photograph, the wall is great in beauty, with its long arms resting on rolling hills and its towers peering across the valleys. The wall stretches across more than half of China, from the sea in the east, past Beijing, to Gansu province in the west. At a total length of 4,000 miles, it is the longest human-made construction in the world. If the Great Wall were transported to the United States and stretched out in a straight line, it would run from New York City completely across the Atlantic Ocean—past Spain, England, and France, all the way to Berlin, Germany.
A clear preview statement specifies the three main points to be covered in the body of the speech. As you watch the speech, notice how the speaker displays a blank slide during this paragraph so as not to distract the audience's attention.	Today I would like to share with you some of the wonders of the Great Wall. I will focus on the three major stages of its construction, moving from the first phase during the Qin Dynasty, to the second phase during the Han Dynasty, and concluding with the third phase during the Ming Dynasty. Let's start more than 2,000 years ago, when the first parts of the wall were built.
The speaker moves into his first main point. As he does so, he projects a slide showing a drawing of Emperor Qin Shi Huang and the dates of the Qin Dynasty. When he finishes this paragraph, he again projects a blank slide so the audience will be focused on his verbal message in the next paragraph.	The beginning of the Great Wall as we know it dates to 221 B.C., when Emperor Qin Shi Huang ordered his top general to lead 300,000 soldiers in rebuilding and connecting separate old walls that had been built by princes of warring states. In just 12 years, Qin had a 3,000-mile wall using primarily wood frames filled with stones and compacted earth.
This paragraph provides interesting details about the building of the wall during the Qin Dynasty. Notice how the speaker identifies the source of his quotation about the human cost of the wall's construction.	While the wall proved effective in keeping out the tribes who threatened to invade China from the north, it created dissent within China. According to Arthur Waldron's *The Great Wall of China: From History to Myth,* "ditches on the roadside were filled with corpses of men who had been forced into construction of the Great Wall." Compelled into hard labor and burdened by heavy taxes to finance the project, the people grew unhappy, and a year after Qin's death, the peasants revolted. While the wall stood, the empire collapsed.
A signpost at the start of this paragraph alerts the audience that the speaker is moving into his second main point. After	The second major period of construction for the Great Wall occurred during the Han Dynasty, which lasted from 206 B.C. to 220 A.D. Emperor Wu Di ordered expansion of the existing wall

showing a slide with the dates of the Han Dynasty and a drawing of Emperor Wu Di, he projects a photograph to demonstrate how different the Han wall was from the Great Wall as it exists today.

As the speaker starts his third main point, he moves immediately from his slide showing the ruins of the Han wall to a slide with a drawing of Emperor Zhu Yuanzhang and the dates of the Ming Dynasty. Because it is parallel in design to the slides used to introduce the first two main points, this slide reinforces the unity and organizational structure of the speech as a whole.

The speaker begins this paragraph by projecting a slide with a photograph showing the architectural features of the Great Wall. As he discusses each feature, he uses animation to make the appropriate text appear on his slide. This combination of visual and verbal elements makes this paragraph especially effective and provides an excellent illustration of how to use Power-Point to maximum advantage.

After signaling that he is moving into his conclusion, the speaker summarizes his main points and ends by reinforcing his central idea. To make sure the audience does not continue to focus on the architectural features of the Great Wall discussed in the previous paragraph, he displays a blank slide that shifts attention back to him during the conclusion.

to protect land won when his armies defeated the northern tribes. Workers added 300 miles to the existing wall. They built wooden frames, which they filled with willow reeds and a mixture of fine gravel and water. As you can see from this picture of ruins of the Han wall, it was very different in construction and appearance from the Great Wall as it exists today.

The third major building period of the Great Wall occurred 1,100 years later during the Ming Dynasty. In 1368, during the first year of the Ming Dynasty, Emperor Zhu Yuanzhang ordered more expansion of the wall. Subsequent Ming emperors strengthened and extended the wall until it reached its current length. Builders of the Ming wall made three important architectural advancements which resulted in the distinctive features of the wall as it exists today.

You can see those features especially well in this photograph. First, rather than using earth and stone, they used kiln-fired bricks to create a stronger wall. Second, they erected more than 3,000 beacon towers to watch the mountain passes for potential invaders. These towers rise from the wall like mighty outposts and are one of the most striking aspects of the wall when you see them in person. Third, the Ming builders made the wall so large that it would be almost impossible to break through. In fact, the wall is so wide that soldiers could ride several horses abreast along the top of the wall.

In conclusion, the Great Wall of China enjoys a rich history. Built over the course of more than 2,500 years during the Qin, Han, and Ming Dynasties, it is a magnificent feat of human engineering. While the wall no longer continues to defend China from invaders, it does continue to play a central role in Chinese culture and international identity. Now that you know a little more about the wall, I hope you have a fuller appreciation of why it's regarded as great, not just in China, but throughout the world.

KEY TERMS

serif font *(288)*

sans-serif font *(288)*

animation *(291)*

fair use *(295)*

Speaking to Inform

Natalya Petrovich is the advertising manager for a company that sells computer equipment such as routers, network cards, and wireless extensions. She began that particular workday by meeting with her staff to discuss the company's new line of network cards. She pointed out the special features of each piece of equipment, explained what other equipment was compatible with each, and answered questions about them.

Later that morning, Natalya had a long talk with the head of the company's technical division. "Can you show me," she asked, "how to use the new router we're developing? I need to double-check the ad copy my staff has drafted." Natalya then took notes as the head of the technical division went through the uses of the new router. Natalya also asked questions along the way to make sure she understood exactly how the router worked.

In the afternoon, Natalya met with the company's president and sales director to go over the current year's budget for her department, as well as her projections for the new fiscal year. She reviewed advertising campaigns and sales data, assessed the performance of each member of her staff, and presented her projections of staffing requirements for the next eighteen months. Afterward, the president complimented Natalya for giving such a clear presentation. "Anyone who can communicate that well," the president said, "is going to go a long way in this company."

Natalya doesn't consider herself a "public speaker," but much of her job involves absorbing and communicating information clearly and effectively. Although Natalya is just a single person, her experience is not unusual. In one survey, graduates from five U.S. colleges were asked to rank the speech skills most important to their jobs. They rated informative speaking number one. In another survey, 62 percent of the respondents said they used informative speaking "almost constantly."[1]

Public speaking to inform occurs in a wide range of everyday situations. The business manager explains next year's budget. The architect reviews plans for a new building. The union leader informs members about a new contract. The church worker outlines plans for a fund drive. There are endless situations in which people need to inform others. Competence in this form of communication will prove valuable to you throughout your life.

informative speech
A speech designed to convey knowledge and understanding.

One of your first classroom assignments probably will be to deliver an informative speech in which you will act as a lecturer or teacher. You may describe an object, show how something works, report on an event, explain a concept. Your aim will be to convey knowledge and understanding—not to advocate a cause. Your speech will be judged in light of three general criteria:

Is the information communicated accurately?

Is the information communicated clearly?

Is the information made meaningful and interesting to the audience?

In this chapter, we will look at four types of informative speeches and the basic principles of informative speaking. Along the way, we will apply various general principles discussed in previous chapters.

Types of Informative Speeches: Analysis and Organization

There are many ways to classify informative speeches. Here we focus on the kinds you are most likely to give in your speech class: (1) speeches about objects, (2) speeches about processes, (3) speeches about events, and (4) speeches about concepts.

SPEECHES ABOUT OBJECTS

As the word is used here, "objects" include anything that is visible, tangible, and stable in form. Objects may have moving parts or be alive; they may include places, structures, animals, even people. Here are examples of subjects for speeches about objects:

object
Anything that is visible, tangible, and stable in form.

Grand Canyon	stock market
the human eye	Elizabeth Cady Stanton
seaweed	GPS navigation devices
comic strips	U.S. Army

You will not have time to tell your classmates everything about any of these subjects. Instead, you will choose a specific purpose that focuses on one aspect of your subject. Working from the topics presented above, the following are examples of good specific purpose statements for informative speeches about objects:

To inform my audience about the geological features of the Grand Canyon.

To inform my audience about the role of Elizabeth Cady Stanton in the U.S. women's rights movement.

To inform my audience what to look for when buying a GPS navigation device.

Notice how precise these statements are. As we saw in Chapter 4, you should select a specific purpose that is not too broad to achieve in the allotted time. "To inform my audience about Pablo Picasso" is far too general for a classroom speech. "To inform my audience about the major contributions of Pablo Picasso to modern art" is more precise and is a purpose you could reasonably hope to achieve in a brief talk.

If your specific purpose is to explain the history or evolution of your subject, you will put your speech in *chronological* order. For example:

Specific Purpose: To inform my audience about the major achievements of Frederick Douglass.

Central Idea: Although born in slavery, Frederick Douglass became one of the greatest figures in American history.

Main Points:
   I. Douglass spent the first 20 years of his life as a slave in Maryland.
  II. After escaping to the North, Douglass became a leader in the abolitionist movement to end slavery.
 III. During the Civil War, Douglass helped establish black regiments in the Union Army.

IV. After the war, Douglass was a tireless champion of equal rights for his race.

If your specific purpose is to describe the main features of your subject, you may organize your speech in *spatial* order:

Specific Purpose: To inform my audience about the design of the St. Louis Arch.

Central Idea: The St. Louis Arch is divided into three sections, each with its own attractions.

Main Points:
   I. The base of the St. Louis Arch houses a visitor's center with a museum, two movie theaters, and retail outlets.
  II. The middle of the St. Louis Arch contains a high-speed tram that carries visitors from the base to the top.
 III. The top of the St. Louis Arch has an observation deck 630 feet above the ground.

As often as not, you will find that speeches about objects fall into *topical* order. For example:

Specific Purpose: To inform my audience about the four major elements of a Japanese garden.

Central Idea: The four major elements of a Japanese garden are stones, sand, water, and plants.

Main Points:
   I. The first element of a Japanese garden is stones, which symbolize mountains and islands.
  II. The second element of a Japanese garden is sand, which symbolizes the sea or other vast areas.
 III. The third element of a Japanese garden is water, which symbolizes purity and life.
 IV. The fourth element of a Japanese garden is plants, which symbolize life and the changing seasons.

No matter which of these organizational methods you use—chronological, spatial, or topical—be sure to follow the guidelines discussed in Chapter 8: (1) limit your speech to between two and five main points; (2) keep main points separate; (3) try to use the same pattern of wording for all main points; (4) balance the amount of time devoted to each main point.

SPEECHES ABOUT PROCESSES

process
A systematic series of actions that leads to a specific result or product.

A process is a systematic series of actions that leads to a specific result or product. Speeches about processes explain how something is made, how something is done, or how something works. Here are examples of good specific purpose statements for speeches about processes:

To inform my audience how hurricanes develop.

To inform my audience how to write an effective job resumé.

To inform my audience how to choose a study-abroad program.

To inform my audience how U.S. currency is made.

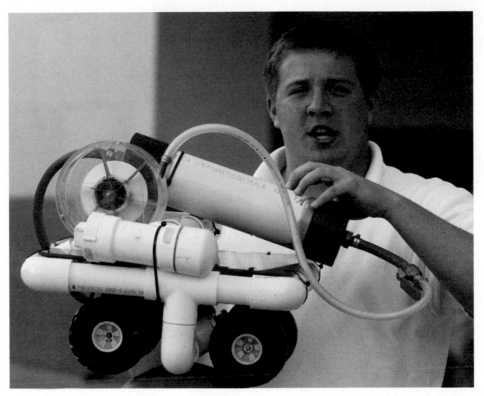

Informative speeches about objects often call for visual aids. Here Ryan McLendon, a chemical engineering major from West Virginia University, explains a model car that runs on baking soda and vinegar. The car was entered in a contest sponsored by the American Institute of Chemical Engineers.

As these examples suggest, there are two kinds of informative speeches about processes. One kind explains a process so that that listeners will *understand* it better. Your goal is to have your audience know the steps of the process and how they relate to one another. If your specific purpose is "To inform my audience how underwater robots work," you will explain the basic tasks and mechanisms of underwater robots. You will not instruct your listeners on how they can *operate* an underwater robot.

A second kind of speech explains a process so listeners will be better able to *perform* the process themselves. Your goal in this kind of speech is to have the audience learn a skill. Suppose your specific purpose is "To inform my audience how to take pictures like a professional photographer." You will present photographic techniques and show your listeners how they can utilize them. You want the audience to be able to *use* the techniques as a result of your speech.

Both kinds of speeches about processes may require visual aids. At the very least, you should prepare a chart outlining the steps or techniques of your process. In some cases you will need to demonstrate the steps or techniques by performing them in front of your audience. One student did sleight-of-hand magic tricks to show the techniques behind them. Another executed elementary tai chi maneuvers. In each case, the demonstration not only clarified the speaker's process, but captivated the audience as well. (If you are using visual aids of any kind, be sure to review Chapter 13.)

When informing about a process, you will usually arrange your speech in *chronological* order, explaining the process step by step from beginning to end. For example:

Specific Purpose: To inform my audience about the major rituals of a traditional Bengali wedding in India.

Central Idea:	A traditional Bengali wedding consists of a series of rituals that take place before, during, and after the wedding ceremony.
Main Points:	I. Pre-wedding rituals include giving gifts to the bride and groom and dressing the bride in traditional fashion.
	II. Rituals during the wedding ceremony include an exchange of garlands between the bride and groom, the chanting of mantras, and the giving away of the bride by her uncle.
	III. Post-wedding rituals include a celebration at the home of the bride's family, a reception at the home of the groom's family, and the formal exit of the bride and groom.

Sometimes, rather than moving through a process step by step, you will focus on the major principles or techniques involved in performing the process. Then you will organize your speech in *topical* order. Each main point will deal with a separate principle or technique. For example:

Specific Purpose:	To inform my audience of the common methods used by stage magicians to perform their tricks.
Central Idea:	Stage magicians use two common methods to perform their tricks—mechanical devices and sleight of hand.
Main Points:	I. Many magic tricks rely on mechanical devices that may require little skill by the magician.
	II. Other magic tricks depend on the magician's skill in fooling people by sleight-of-hand manipulation.

Concise organization is especially important in speeches about processes. You must make sure each step is clear and easy to follow. If your process has more than four or five steps, group the steps into units to limit the number of main points. For example, in a speech explaining how to set up a home aquarium, a student presented the following main points:

    I. First you must choose the size of your tank.
   II. Then you must determine the shape of your tank.
  III. You must also decide how much you can afford to pay for a tank.
  IV. Once you have the tank, you need a filter system.
   V. A heater is also absolutely necessary.
  VI. You must also get an air pump.
 VII. Once this is done, you need to choose gravel for the tank.
VIII. You will also need plants.
  IX. Other decorations will round out the effects of your aquarium.
   X. Now you are ready to add the fish.
  XI. Freshwater fish are the most common.
 XII. Saltwater fish are more expensive and require special care.

Not surprisingly, this was too much for the audience to follow. The speaker should have organized the points something like this:

I. The first step in establishing a home aquarium is choosing a tank.
   A. The size of the tank is important.
   B. The shape of the tank is important.
   C. The cost of the tank is important.

II. The second step in establishing a home aquarium is equipping the tank.
   A. You will need a filter system.
   B. You will need a heater.
   C. You will need an air pump.
   D. You will need gravel.
   E. You will need plants.
   F. You may also want other decorations.
III. The third step in establishing a home aquarium is adding the fish.
   A. Freshwater fish are the most common for home aquariums.
   B. Saltwater fish are more expensive and require special care.

The subpoints cover the same territory as the original twelve points, but three main points are much easier to understand and remember.

SPEECHES ABOUT EVENTS

The *Random House Dictionary* defines an event as "anything that happens or is regarded as happening." By this definition, the following are examples of suitable subjects for informative speeches about events:

event
Anything that happens or is regarded as happening.

Holocaust	mountain climbing
civil rights movement	job interviews
Cinco de Mayo	tsunamis
attention deficit disorder	Battle of Little Big Horn

As usual, you will need to narrow your focus and pick a specific purpose you can accomplish in a short speech. Here are examples of good specific purpose statements for informative speeches about events:

To inform my audience of the festivities at Mexico's Cinco de Mayo celebration.

To inform my audience about what happened at the Battle of Little Big Horn.

To inform my audience about the major types of therapeutic massage.

There are many ways to discuss events. If your specific purpose is to recount the history of an event, you will organize your speech in *chronological* order, relating the incidents one after another in the order they occurred. For example:

Specific Purpose: To inform my audience about the history of the Paralympics.

Central Idea: Olympic-style games for athletes with physical disabilities have made great strides since the first competition more than 60 years ago.

Main Points:
   I. What would eventually become the Paralympics began in 1948 with a sports competition in Great Britain involving World War II veterans with spinal cord injuries.
   II. In 1952 the event expanded when athletes from the Netherlands took part.
   III. The first official Paralympic Games for international athletes took place in Rome in 1960.

IV. In 2001 an agreement was signed officially holding the Paralympic Games alongside the summer and winter Olympic Games.

You can approach an event from almost any angle or combination of angles—features, origins, implications, benefits, future developments, and so forth. In such cases, you will put your speech together in *topical* order. And you should make sure your main points subdivide the subject logically and consistently. For instance:

Specific Purpose: To inform my audience about three aspects of the Mardi Gras celebration in New Orleans.

Central Idea: The Mardi Gras celebration in New Orleans is renowned for its parades, costumes, and food.

Main Points: I. The parades are lavish events that take place over the course of several weeks.
II. The costumes include disguises, medallions, and the official Mardi Gras colors of purple, green, and gold.
III. The food features Cajun and Creole dishes common to southern Louisiana.

SPEECHES ABOUT CONCEPTS

Concepts include beliefs, theories, ideas, principles, and the like. They are more abstract than objects, processes, or events. The following are examples of subjects for speeches about concepts:

Confucianism	string theory
philosophies of education	principles of feminism
original-intent doctrine	existentialism
numerology	human rights

Informative speeches take place in a wide range of situations. Here Chinese scientist Xu Xing speaks to an international audience in Beijing about the discovery of the world's largest birdlike dinosaur.

Taking a few of these general subjects, here are some specific purpose statements for speeches about concepts:

concept
A belief, theory, idea, notion, principle, or the like.

> To inform my audience about the basic principles of Confucianism.
>
> To inform my audience about the doctrine of original intent in constitutional interpretation.
>
> To inform my audience about the different philosophies of education in Europe and the United States.

Speeches about concepts are usually organized in *topical* order and focus on the main features or aspects of your concept. For example:

Specific Purpose: To inform my audience about the basic principles of nonviolent resistance.

Central Idea: The basic principles of nonviolent resistance stress using moral means to achieve social change, refusing to inflict violence on one's enemies, and using suffering as a social force.

Main Points:
    I. The first major principle of nonviolent resistance is that social change must be achieved by moral means.
    II. The second major principle of nonviolent resistance is that one should not inflict violence on one's enemies.
    III. The third major principle of nonviolent resistance is that suffering can be a powerful social force.

Another approach is to define the concept you are dealing with, identify its major elements, and illustrate it with specific examples. An excellent instance of this came in a student speech about Islam:

Specific Purpose: To inform my audience of the basic principles of Islam.

Central Idea: The beliefs of Islam can be traced to the prophet Muhammad, are written in the Koran, and have produced a number of sects.

Main Points:
    I. Islam was founded by the prophet Muhammad in the early 600s.
    II. The teachings of Islam are written in the Koran, the holy book of Islam.
    III. Today Islam is divided into a number of sects, the largest of which are the Sunnis and the Shiites.

Speeches about concepts are often more complex than other kinds of informative speeches. When dealing with concepts, pay special attention to avoiding technical language, to defining terms clearly, and to using examples and comparisons to illustrate the concepts.

Look, for example, at Video Clip 14.1 in the online Media Library for this chapter, which presents an excerpt from a student speech about the Chinese philosophy of Confucianism. Notice how the student defines Confucianism and then explains its unifying principle of *jen.* If you give an informative speech about a concept, give special thought to how you can make that concept clear and comprehensible to your listeners.

connectlucas.com
View an excerpt from "Confucianism" in the online Media Library for this chapter (Video Clip 14.1).

The lines dividing speeches about objects, processes, events, and concepts are not absolute. Some subjects could fit into more than one category, depending on how you develop the speech. For example, a speech about the destruction of ancient Pompeii by the eruption of Mount Vesuvius would probably deal with its subject as an event, but a speech on what causes volcanoes to erupt would most likely treat its subject as a process. The important step is to decide whether you will handle your subject as an object, a process, an event, or a concept. Once you do that, you can develop the speech accordingly.

Regardless of how you approach your topic, be sure to give listeners plenty of help in sorting out facts and ideas. One way is by using enough transitions, internal previews, internal summaries, and signposts (see Chapter 8). Another way is to follow the old maxim "Tell 'em what you're going to say; say it; then tell 'em what you've said." In other words, preview the main points of your speech in the introduction and summarize them in the conclusion. This will make your speech easier to understand and easier to remember.

Guidelines for Informative Speaking

All the previous chapters of this book relate to the principles of informative speaking. Selecting a topic and specific purpose, analyzing the audience, gathering materials, choosing supporting details, organizing the speech, using words to communicate meaning, delivering the speech—all must be done effectively if an informative speech is to be a success. Here we emphasize five additional points that will help make yours a success.

DON'T OVERESTIMATE WHAT THE AUDIENCE KNOWS

In a speech about meteorology, a student said, "If modern methods of weather forecasting had existed in 1900, the Galveston hurricane disaster would never have taken place." Then he was off to other matters, leaving his listeners to puzzle over what the Galveston hurricane was, when it happened, and what kind of destruction it wreaked.

The speaker assumed his audience already knew these things. But they were not experts on meteorology or on American history. Even those who had heard of the hurricane had only a fuzzy notion of it. Only the speaker knew that the hurricane, which killed more than 6,000 people when it unexpectedly struck on September 8, 1900, is still the deadliest natural disaster in American history.

As many speakers have discovered, it is easy to overestimate the audience's stock of information. In most informative speeches, your listeners will be only vaguely knowledgeable (at best) about the details of your topic. You cannot *assume* they will know what you mean. Rather, you must be *sure* to explain everything so thoroughly that they cannot help but understand. As you work on your speech, always consider whether it will be clear to someone who is hearing about the topic for the first time.

Suppose you are talking about Roth IRAs, a type of individual retirement account approved by Congress in 1998. Although some of your classmates might have heard of Roth IRAs, they probably do not have a firm grasp of the subject. So you should start by telling them what a Roth IRA is. How will you tell them? Here's one way:

Introduced in 1998, a Roth IRA is a type of individual retirement account in which annual contributions are made with after-tax dollars but in which earnings and distributions are tax-free once the holder of the account is 59.5 years of age or older.

To someone who knows a lot about economics this is perfectly clear. But someone who does not will likely get lost along the way. The tone of the statement is that of a speaker reviewing information already familiar to the audience—not of a speaker introducing new information.

Here, in contrast, is another explanation of Roth IRAs:

What is a Roth Individual Retirement Account, or IRA? Let me explain with an example.

Imagine yourself a few years down the road as a recent college graduate. Your job pays a good salary, but you're still concerned with your finances and your future. After all, everyone keeps telling you to start planning for retirement early.

In addition to Social Security, you have a number of retirement-planning options. One is the Roth IRA. Suppose you place $4,000 into a Roth IRA every year. Suppose also that your money grows at an average rate of 8 percent a year.

If you start putting money in at age 25 and withdraw it at age 65, you will have an account worth more than $1.2 million. Moreover, unlike other retirement accounts, you won't have to pay taxes on your $1.2 million, even if you take it out all at once.

So you can see why Roth IRAs are so popular. You win both ways—your money grows tax-free and it is free of taxes when you withdraw it.

This explanation is clear and simple. Its tone is that of a teacher unraveling a new subject.

Is it too simple? Not at all. The test of a good speaker is to communicate even the most complex ideas clearly and simply. Anyone can go to a book and find a learned-sounding definition of a Roth IRA. But to say in plain English what a Roth IRA is—that takes hard work and creative thinking.

Also, remember that readers can study a printed passage again and again until they extract its meaning, but listeners don't have that luxury. They must understand what you say in the time it takes you to say it. The more you assume they know about the topic, the greater your chances of being misunderstood.

RELATE THE SUBJECT DIRECTLY TO THE AUDIENCE

The British dramatist Oscar Wilde arrived at his club after the disastrous opening-night performance of his new play.

"Oscar, how did your play go?" asked a friend.

"Oh," Wilde quipped, "the play was a great success, but the audience was a failure."

Speakers have been known to give much the same answer in saving face after a dismal informative speech. "Oh," they say, "the speech was fine, but the audience just wasn't interested." And they are at least partly right—the audience *wasn't* interested. But there is no such thing as a fine speech that puts people to sleep. It is the speaker's job to get listeners interested—and to keep them interested.

Informative speakers have one big hurdle to overcome. They must recognize that what is fascinating to them may not be fascinating to everybody. Once you have chosen a topic that could possibly be interesting to your listeners, you should take special steps to relate it to them. You should tie it in with their interests and concerns.

Start in the introduction. Instead of saying,

I want to talk with you about chili peppers,

you could say:

connectlucas.com
View this excerpt from "The Hidden World of Chili Peppers" in the online Media Library for this chapter (Video Clip 14.2).

Imagine your mouth burning like wildfire, your eyes squirting out uncontrollable tears, and your face red and sweating profusely. Are you sick? No. You just took a bite of a screaming hot chili pepper. Congratulations. You're partaking in a worldwide tradition that has been spicing up lives and diets for thousands of years.

But don't stop with the introduction. Whenever you can, put your listeners into the body of the speech. After all, nothing interests people more than themselves. Find ways to talk about your topic in terms of your listeners. Bring your material home to them. Get it as close to them as possible.

Here's an example. Let's say you are explaining how people can discover whether they are "secret southpaws"—that is, people who are naturally left-handed but who have grown up using their right hand. You have plenty of facts and could recite them like this:

According to *Science* magazine, half of all people who are naturally left-handed assume they are right-handed because that is the hand they use to eat, to write, and to

Informative speakers work on communicating their ideas in clear, nontechnical language, as illustrated here by paramedic Cheryl Bishop explaining the Heimlich maneuver to a group of middle-school students.

play sports. But how can it be determined whether one is a natural southpaw? According to Abram Blau, author of *The Master Hand,* there are a number of simple tests. For one thing, most natural left-handers can write spontaneously backward or upside down with the left hand. For another, when left-handers clasp their hands in front of themselves, they usually place the left thumb on top. In contrast, when left-handers grab a broom, they normally place their left hand below the right. Finally, when using the right hand, natural left-handers will draw a circle clockwise, while natural right-handers will draw it counterclockwise. People who give a left-handed response on three or more of these tests may well be secret southpaws.

This is fascinating information, but it is not made fascinating to the audience. Let's try again:

Just because *you* use *your* right hand to eat, to write, and to play sports, *you* may assume that *you're* naturally right-handed. But, says *Science* magazine, half of all people who are naturally left-handed grow up using their right hands.

How can *you* tell if *you're* a natural lefty? Dr. Abram Blau, author of *The Master Hand,* gives some tests *you* can try.

First, on a sheet of paper see if *you* can write backward or upside down with *your* left hand. If *you* are left-handed, *you* can probably do this spontaneously, without practice or training.

Second, clasp *your* hands together in front of *you.* Whichever thumb *you* place on top is usually *your* dominant hand.

Third, grab hold of a broomstick. Odds are *you'll* place *your* dominant hand on the bottom.

Finally, draw a circle on a piece of paper with *your* right hand. If *you* draw it counter-clockwise, *you're* probably a natural right-hander. But if *you* draw it clockwise, *you're* probably a natural lefty.

If *you* test left-handed on three of these tests, there is a good chance *you* are a secret southpaw.

connectlucas.com
View this excerpt from "Secret Southpaws" in the online Media Library for this chapter (Video Clip 14.3).

Look at the frequent use of "you" and "your." The facts are the same, but now they are pointed directly at the audience. Research shows that using personal terms such as "you" and "your" in an informative speech significantly increases audience understanding of the speaker's ideas.[2]

DON'T BE TOO TECHNICAL

What does it mean to say that an informative speech is too technical? It may mean the subject matter is too specialized for the audience. Any subject can be popularized—but only up to a point. The important thing for a speaker to know is what can be explained to an ordinary audience and what cannot.

Say your subject is electronic amplifiers. It's no trick to demonstrate how to operate an amplifier (how to turn it on and off, adjust the volume, set the tone and balance controls). It's also relatively easy to explain what an amplifier does (it boosts the sound received from a radio, CD player, or live performance). But to give a full scientific account of how an amplifier works cannot be done in any reasonable time unless the audience knows the principles of audio technology. The material is just too technical to be understood by a general audience.

Even when the subject matter is not technical, the language used to explain it may be. Every activity has its jargon, whether it be golf (bogey, wedge, match play); chemistry (colloid, glycogen, heavy water); or financial analysis (covered call, reverse bid, toehold acquisition). If you are talking to a group of specialists, you can use technical words and be understood. But you must do all you can to avoid technical words when informing a general audience such as your speech class.

Here, for instance, are two statements explaining stem cells and the roles they can play in the human body. The first is heavily laden with specialized language that would have little impact on ordinary listeners:

Most multicellular organisms contain stem cells that reinvigorate themselves through the process of mitotic cellular division. Stem cells in early embryos represent basic units of life in higher organisms, while adult stem cells in somatic tissues represent cellular stores capable of regenerating tissue and maintaining organ functions. Both are characterized by unique properties that permit accurate in vivo cell copying.

The second statement is perfectly understandable and shows how technical information can be made clear to the average person:

According to the National Institutes of Health, stem cells are general cells that have the potential to develop into any of the more than 200 different kinds of cells in the human body. Basically, they turn into a cell that has a specific job to do.

For example, stem cells might become muscle cells that help rebuild damaged tissue. They might become red blood cells that help deliver oxygen to different tissues. Or they might become brain cells that help the nervous system function. No matter what type of cells need assistance, stem cells can come to the rescue and replenish the cells our bodies need.

The Genetics Learning Center at the University of Utah explains it like this: Stem cells are like actors waiting for a casting call. Just as an actor waits to find out his or her next role, stem cells wait for signals from the body that tell them what to become. Once they get those signals, they begin to change into specific cells with specific jobs to do.

Much clearer, isn't it? The only specialized words in the whole passage are "stem cells." The rest of the language is straightforward, the ideas easy to grasp. This is what you should strive for in your informative speeches.

connectlucas.com
View this excerpt from "The Promise of Stem Cells" in the online Media Library for this chapter (Video Clip 14.4).

AVOID ABSTRACTIONS

"My task," said the novelist Joseph Conrad, "is, before all, to make you see." And make the reader see is just what Conrad did. Witness this passage, in which Conrad describes the aftermath of an explosion aboard a ship:

> The first person I saw was Mahon, with eyes like saucers, his mouth open, and the long white hair standing straight on end round his head like a silver halo. He was just about to go down when the sight of the main deck stirring, heaving up, and changing into splinters before his eyes, petrified him on the top step. I stared at him in unbelief, and he stared at me with a queer kind of shocked curiosity. I did not know that I had no hair, no eyebrows, no eyelashes, that my young mustache was burnt off, that my face was black, one cheek laid open, my nose cut, and my chin bleeding.[3]

A speech is not a novel. Still, many informative speeches would be vastly improved by the novelist's bent for color, specificity, and detail.

One way to avoid abstractions is through *description*. When we think of description, we usually think of external events such as the explosion described by Conrad. But description is also used to communicate internal feelings. Here is how one student tried to convey to his audience the sensations he experienced when he first began sky diving:

description
A statement that depicts a person, event, idea, or the like with clarity and vividness.

> As we wait for the plane to climb to the jump altitude of 12,000 feet, my mind races with a frenzied jumble of thoughts: "OK, this is the moment you've been waiting for. It's going to be great. Am I really going to jump out of an airplane from 12,000 feet? What if something goes wrong? Can I still back out? Come on now, don't worry. It'll be fine."

Even if we have not been sky diving, we have all had the same kinds of emotions on similar occasions. So what happened next?

> Now it is time to jump. My palms are sweating and my heart is pounding so hard I think it may burst. "Get ready," yells the instructor. As I jump into the blue, I wonder, "What am I doing here?"

Yes—and then what?

> The blast of air resistance blows me backward like a leaf at the mercy of an autumn wind. In about 10 seconds my body levels out and accelerates to a speed of 120 miles an hour. The air supports my body like an invisible flying carpet. There is no sound except for the wind rushing around my face. The earth appears soft and green, rivers look like strips of silver, and in every direction the scenery forms a panoramic landscape. Any fears or doubts I had are gone in the exhilaration of free flight. Every nerve in my body is alive with sensation; yet I am overcome by a peaceful feeling and the sense that I am at one with the sky.

As we listen to the speaker we share his thoughts, feel his heart pound, and join his exhilaration as he floats effortlessly through the sky. The vivid description lends reality to the speech and draws us further in.

Another way to escape abstractions is with *comparisons* that put your subject in concrete, familiar terms. Do you want to convey what would happen if a comet or large asteroid struck the earth? You could say this:

> If a comet or large asteroid struck the earth, the impact would be devastating.

True, but the statement is vague and abstract. It does not communicate your meaning clearly and concretely. Now suppose you add this:

> To give you an idea how devastating the impact would be, it would be like all the nuclear bombs in the world going off at one spot.

Now you have made the abstract specific and given us a sharp new slant on things.

comparison
A statement of the similarities among two or more people, events, ideas, etc.

Like comparison, *contrast* can put an idea into concrete terms. Suppose you want to make the point that a person's chances of winning a state lottery are extremely low. You could say, "The odds, for example, of winning a state lottery are an astronomical 14 million to 1." The word "astronomical" suggests that you consider 14 million to 1 long odds, but long in comparison to what? One speaker offered this contrast:

contrast
A statement of the differences among two or more people, events, ideas, etc.

> The odds of picking the correct six-digit sequence in a typical state lottery are 14 million to 1. In contrast, the odds of getting hit by lightning are only 700,000 to 1. The odds of dying in a car accident are 6,000 to 1. In other words, the odds are much stronger that you will get hit by lightning or be killed in a car crash than that you will win the jackpot in a state lottery.

This puts an abstract fact into meaningful perspective.

PERSONALIZE YOUR IDEAS

personalize
To present one's ideas in human terms that relate in some fashion to the experience of the audience.

Listeners want to be entertained as they are being enlightened.[4] Nothing takes the edge off an informative speech more than an unbroken string of facts and figures. And nothing enlivens a speech more than personal illustrations. Whenever possible, you should try to *personalize* your ideas and dramatize them in human terms.

Let's say you are talking about autism, the developmental disability marked by impaired communication and interaction skills. You would surely note that the condition affects 1 in every 500 children, occurs four times more frequently in males than in females, and is most prevalent among Caucasians. You would also note that the symptoms of autism include abnormal introversion, severely limited use of language, repetitive behaviors, avoidance of eye contact, loss of emotional control, and passive responses to affection.

But these are dry facts and figures. If you really want to get your audience involved, you will weave in some examples of children who suffer from autism. One speaker began by telling about Sam, her autistic nephew:

> My nephew Sam was the delight of our family when he was born, the first grandchild of my parents. He cooed and babbled, smiled at his mom and dad, grasped for the playthings around his crib. At family dinners on Sunday, we took turns holding him in our arms, feeding him, and singing him to sleep. He seemed like any normal infant in a secure and loving home.
>
> Then shortly before his second birthday we began to notice unusual behaviors. Sam avoided looking us in the eye, did not seem interested in learning words, played endlessly with the same toy, rocked back and forth in his chair for hours at a time, and was easily frustrated. My sister took him to a specialist, who gave the dreaded diagnosis: Sam was autistic.

Regardless of the situation, informative speakers work to organize their ideas effectively and to explain them in clear, nontechnical language that is appropriate for their listeners' knowledge and interests.

During the body of the speech, the speaker mentioned Sam twice more to illustrate different aspects of autism. Then, at the end of the speech, she brought Sam's story to a hopeful conclusion:

> We have seen that autism is a very serious disorder whose causes are not well understood and whose effects on families and the lives of the children themselves can be devastating. But we have also seen that early diagnosis and early intervention can help to modify and even turn around the symptoms of autism.
>
> I am happy to say that Sam has benefited from such intervention. From the time he was two, he has been taught "normal" behavior patterns through aggressive therapy. Now he is able to participate in his class at the local school. He is also more responsive and affectionate at home. Sam continues to be our delight.

connectlucas.com
View this excerpt from "Autism: Heartbreak and Hope" in the online Media Library for this chapter (Video Clip 14.5).

It was a powerful ending. By putting a human face on a familiar topic, the speaker took autism out of the realm of statistics and medical jargon and brought it home in personal terms.

Sample Speech with Commentary

The following classroom speech provides an excellent example of how to apply the guidelines for informative speaking discussed in this chapter. Notice how the speaker takes what could be a dry, technical topic and makes it interesting. Pay special attention to how crisply the speech is organized, to how the speaker uses well-chosen supporting materials to develop her ideas, and to how she clarifies her ideas with concrete language and personal examples. You can view the speech in the online Media Library for this chapter.

connectlucas.com
View "Acupuncture: New Uses for an Ancient Remedy" in the online Media Library for this chapter (Video Clip 14.6).

Acupuncture: New Uses for an Ancient Remedy

COMMENTARY	SPEECH
The speaker starts with an extended example that captures attention and interest. In this case, the example works particularly well because it is personally related to the speaker and is richly detailed and vividly drawn.	Six months ago, my 78-year-old grandmother was quickly losing her independence. Severe arthritis in both knees hampered her ability to take care of herself. Shopping, getting around the neighborhood, even walking down her front steps was becoming almost impossible. Pain medications helped somewhat, but the side effects created their own problems.
As the speaker continues her opening example, she introduces the subject of her speech by talking about her grandmother's positive experience with acupuncture.	Then her doctor suggested acupuncture. My grandmother was skeptical at first, but she was willing to try just about anything. She did, and the results were miraculous. After six weeks, her pain and stiffness were significantly reduced, she was able to take care of her apartment again, she could get out on her own to go shopping, to visit friends and family, and to do the other things her arthritis had prevented in the past. Acupuncture restored her quality of life and her independence.
Mentioning her own experience with acupuncture helps establish the speaker's credibility.	My grandmother's story is not unique. Performed for well over 2,000 years in China and other parts of Asia, acupuncture is becoming more and more popular in the U.S. and other Western countries for one simple reason—it works. Impressed by my grandmother's experience, I began acupuncture treatments for my migraine headaches, and now my headaches are completely gone.
Here the speaker reinforces her credibility and previews the main points to be discussed in the body of the speech. An explicit preview statement at the end of the introduction is especially important when speaking to inform.	Not surprisingly, I wanted to learn more about this treatment that produced such miraculous results for both my grandmother and myself. Today I will share part of what I have learned by explaining what happens when you receive an acupuncture treatment, how acupuncture works, the kinds of medical conditions that can be treated by acupuncture, and the growing use of acupuncture in combination with Western medical techniques. Let's start by looking at a typical acupuncture treatment.
Now the speaker moves into her first main point. The information in this and the following paragraph answers the audience's questions about what happens during an acupuncture treatment.	Acupuncture is the insertion of needles into the skin to achieve a balanced flow of energy, which in turn restores and preserves health. To prevent any chance of contamination from one person to another, acupuncturists in the U.S. use sterilized needles that are individually packaged and are disposed of after a single use.

Knowing that many people are squeamish about being poked with needles, the speaker makes sure to explain that the needles used in acupuncture are small and essentially painless. Notice that the speaker did not pass the needles around during her speech. As mentioned in Chapter 13, putting visual aids in the hands of the audience during a speech is an almost certain recipe for disaster because listeners will end up paying more attention to the visual aids than to the speaker's words.

This paragraph begins with a transition into the speaker's second main point. As in the previous paragraph, she relates the topic directly to her audience by speaking in terms of "you."

As you can see from the video of this speech in the online Media Library for this chapter, the speaker uses a visual aid to clarify her explanation of the acupuncture meridians.

The speaker's explanation throughout this main point provides a good example of how to communicate technical information in everyday language. The quotation at the end of the paragraph nicely sums up this section of the speech.

A signpost of the beginning of this paragraph helps signal that the speaker is moving to her third main point, in which she explains some of the medical conditions that can be treated with acupuncture. As in the rest of the speech, she relies on highly credible sources and identifies them clearly. This is crucial if the audience is to accept the accuracy of the speaker's information—especially since she is not an expert on acupuncture.

I realize that the notion of having needles stuck into you may seem frightening, but the needles are so thin that the process is painless. Acupuncture needles are much smaller than the needles used for drawing blood or getting shots. Here are some needles that I received from my acupuncturist. After my speech I'll pass them around so you can see how incredibly light and small they are. They are so thin—about the thickness of a human hair—that you can hardly tell when they're inserted. And there's usually no sensation other than pain relief once they have been inserted. After being left in for 20 or 30 minutes while you lie in a darkened room, the needles are removed and the treatment is over.

Now that you know what happens when you're treated by an acupuncturist, you're probably wondering how acupuncture works. The process is explained by Dr. Felix Mann, President of the Medical Acupuncture Society, in his book *Acupuncture: The Ancient Chinese Art of Healing and How It Works Scientifically.* According to traditional Chinese medicine, every life process is based on the flow of vital energy through the body. This energy is known in Chinese as *qi* and flows along channels or pathways called meridians.

The meridians are shown in this visual aid. As you can see, they cover the entire body, running from the top of the head to the bottom of the feet and down both arms. When the free flow of energy through these meridians is blocked, the result is pain, illness, disease, or other physical problems.

The aim of acupuncture is to restore the open flow of energy through these meridians. This is done by placing needles at specific points on the meridians. Altogether there are more than 1,000 acupuncture points on the meridians. These points have been mapped out over the centuries with scientific precision. In China there is a saying: "There is no pain if there is free flow; if there is pain, there is no free flow."

Although acupuncture is based on a different view of the body from that held by Western doctors, the evidence is clear that it works in treating a wide range of medical conditions. The World Health Organization lists more than 40 conditions that can be effectively treated with acupuncture, including ear, nose, and throat ailments; asthma and other respiratory problems; and nervous system and muscular disorders. A study in the *Annals of Internal Medicine* confirms that acupuncture can relieve low-back pain, while the American Cancer Society reports that acupuncture may even help smokers kick the habit.

The speaker's final main point deals with the growing integration of acupuncture with Western medical techniques. In this and the following paragraph, she uses a mix of examples, testimony, and statistics to illustrate her point. All in all, this speech provides an excellent case study in how to use supporting materials to buttress an informative presentation.

As in the rest of her speech, the speaker's quotations are brief and well-chosen. Notice how she identifies the people she is quoting and establishes their credentials before presenting their testimony.

The phrase "Today we have learned" signals that the speaker is moving into her conclusion. She then provides a concise summary of the main points developed in the body.

After reinforcing her central idea about the benefits of acupuncture, the speaker refers back to her grandmother, whom she had discussed in the introduction. This unifies the entire speech and ends it on a personal note.

People also use acupuncture to build their immune system, to control allergies, and to combat depression and anxiety. Of course, you can't use acupuncture to heal a broken arm. But people in Asia often use acupuncture during surgery instead of Western anesthesia, and it can speed recovery time after surgery.

In light of all this, it is not surprising that a number of clinics and hospitals are combining acupuncture with Western medicine in an effort to provide patients the benefits of both. For example, Massachusetts General Hospital in Boston, the third oldest hospital in the U.S., has added acupuncture to its wellness center. Positive results have also been seen at the Mattel Children's Hospital at UCLA. Dr. Lonnie Zeltzer, director of the hospital's pediatric pain program, confirms that acupuncture "really does help. Most children accept acupuncture, and in fact, really feel good about it."

Another example of the integration of acupuncture with Western medicine is the Wasser Pain Management Center at Mount Sinai Hospital in Toronto, Canada. Neurologist Allan Gordon, Director of the Center, says that introducing acupuncture into the hospital "expands the treatment available to chronic pain sufferers" and provides "multiple options for care to our patients." The National Institutes of Health report that more than 8 million Americans have tried acupuncture, and its use throughout the rest of the Western world is growing fast.

Today we have learned what happens during an acupuncture treatment, how acupuncture works, some of the illnesses that can be treated with acupuncture, and the growing integration of acupuncture with Western approaches to medicine. I hope you now know more about this ancient medical practice and the benefits it can provide.

After years of skepticism about acupuncture, the West is finally beginning to recognize that acupuncture is a highly effective way to improve health and reduce pain and suffering. Just ask my grandmother.

Speaking to inform occurs in a wide range of everyday situations. Improving your ability to convey knowledge effectively will be valuable to you throughout your life.

Informative speeches may be grouped into four categories—speeches about objects, speeches about processes, speeches about events, and speeches about concepts.

Objects include places, structures, animals, even people. Speeches about objects usually are organized in chronological, spatial, or topical order. A process is a series of actions that work together to produce a final result. Speeches about processes explain how something is made, how something is done, or how something works. The most common types of organization for speeches about processes are chronological and topical.

An event is anything that happens or is regarded as happening. Speeches about events are usually arranged in chronological or topical order. Concepts include beliefs, theories, ideas, and principles. Speeches about concepts are often more complex than other kinds of informative speeches, and they typically follow a topical pattern of organization.

No matter what the subject of your informative speech, be careful not to overestimate what your audience knows about it. Explain everything so thoroughly that they can't help but understand. Avoid being too technical. Make sure your ideas and your language are fully comprehensible to someone who has no specialized knowledge about the topic.

Equally important, recognize that what is fascinating to you may not be fascinating to everybody. It is your job to make your informative speech interesting and meaningful to your audience. Find ways to talk about the topic in terms of your listeners. Avoid too many abstractions. Use description, comparison, and contrast to make your audience *see* what you are talking about. Finally, try to personalize your ideas and dramatize them in human terms.

KEY TERMS

informative speech *(300)*

object *(301)*

process *(302)*

event *(305)*

concept *(307)*

description *(313)*

comparison *(313)*

contrast *(314)*

personalize *(314)*

REVIEW QUESTIONS

After reading this chapter, you should be able to answer the following questions:

1. What are the four types of informative speeches discussed in the chapter? Give an example of a good specific purpose statement for each type.

2. Why must informative speakers be careful not to overestimate what the audience knows about the topic? What can you do to make sure your ideas don't pass over the heads of your listeners?

3. What should you do as an informative speaker to relate your topic directly to the audience?

4. What two things should you watch out for in making sure your speech is not overly technical?

5. What are three methods you can use to avoid abstractions in your informative speech?

6. What does it mean to say that informative speakers should personalize their ideas?

EXERCISES FOR CRITICAL THINKING

1. Below is a list of subjects for informative speeches. Your task is twofold: (a) Select four of the topics and prepare a specific purpose statement for an informative speech about each of the four. Make sure your four specific purpose statements include at least one that deals with its topic as an object, one that deals with its topic as a process, one that deals with its topic as an event, and one that deals with its topic as a concept. (b) Explain what method of organization you would most likely use in structuring a speech about each of your specific purpose statements.

hobbies	sports
animals	music
science	cultural customs
education	technology
media	health

2. Analyze "The Hidden World of Chili Peppers" in the appendix of sample speeches that follows Chapter 18. Identify the specific purpose, central idea, main points, and method of organization. Evaluate the speech in light of the guidelines for informative speaking discussed in this chapter.

Applying *the* **Power** *of* **Public Speaking**

As the manager for a local chain of coffeehouses, you have been asked to speak to a gourmet group about how to make genuine Italian cappuccino. As you write down ideas for your speech, you find that you have the following main points:

I. First you must make the espresso.
II. Grind the coffee beans so they are fine but not too fine.
III. Place the ground coffee in the filter holder of the espresso machine.
IV. Tamp the coffee once lightly to level the grind in the filter holder.
V. Lock the filter holder onto the brew head of the espresso machine.
VI. Activate the on switch to extract the espresso.
VII. In addition to making the espresso, you must prepare frothed milk for cappuccino.
VIII. Fill a steaming pitcher one-third full of very cold milk.
IX. Place the steam vent of the espresso machine just below the surface of the milk in the pitcher.
X. Fully open the steam vent.

XI. Keeping the tip of the steam vent just below the surface of the milk, move the pitcher in a circular motion.

XII. Be careful not to overheat or scald the milk, which will ruin the froth.

XIII. Once you have the desired amount and consistency of froth, turn the steam vent off and remove it from the pitcher.

XIV. Now you are ready to combine the espresso and frothed milk.

XV. The normal proportions for cappuccino are one-third espresso to two-thirds frothed milk.

XVI. Some people prefer to pour the espresso into the frothed milk in a cappuccino cup.

XVII. Other people prefer to pour or spoon the frothed milk over the espresso.

Having taken a speech class in college, you know this is too many main points for an audience to keep track of. As you look over your list again, however, you realize that it can easily be reorganized into three main points, each with several subpoints. What are those main points and subpoints?

Speaking to Persuade

The Importance of Persuasion

Ethics and Persuasion

The Psychology of Persuasion
 The Challenge of Persuasive Speaking
 How Listeners Process Persuasive Messages
 The Target Audience

Persuasive Speeches on Questions of Fact
 What Are Questions of Fact?
 Analyzing Questions of Fact
 Organizing Speeches on Questions of Fact

Persuasive Speeches on Questions of Value
 What Are Questions of Value?
 Analyzing Questions of Value
 Organizing Speeches on Questions of Value

Persuasive Speeches on Questions of Policy
 What Are Questions of Policy?
 Types of Speeches on Questions of Policy
 Analyzing Questions of Policy
 Organizing Speeches on Questions of Policy

Sample Speech with Commentary

Ramon Trujillo started that particular school day by stopping at the library to return an overdue book. "Look," he explained to the librarian, "I know this book was due last week, but I was sick with the flu and couldn't even get out of bed. Do I still have to pay the fine? I can get you a note from the doctor if you need one." The librarian hemmed and hawed. Then he said, "Okay. You don't have a record of any other fines. Just this once."

With a sigh of relief, Ramon went on to his morning classes. At noon he was dashing across campus when a friend stopped him. "How about some lunch?" she asked. "I really can't," replied Ramon. "I have to stand at the table and get signatures on the tuition petition. I'll see you later, though."

During the afternoon, Ramon went to his job at a computer sales company. He arrived just in time for the weekly staff meeting, where he presented his ideas on how to increase customer satisfaction. "One thing I've noticed," he said, "is that most people don't realize they only have 14 days to return unopened merchandise for a full refund. Most stores have a 30-day return policy, and I know we've lost some customers because ours is shorter. Changing it might be inconvenient at first, but it will definitely help business in the long run." After listening to Ramon, the sales manager said, "I've always thought 14 days was plenty of time, but you've convinced me that we ought to change. Let's give it a try."

If you asked Ramon how he spent his day, he might say, "I returned a book, I went to class, I worked the tuition-petition table, I had a staff meeting at my job." In fact, he spent a large part of his day *persuading*—persuading people to do things they were reluctant to do or that had not occurred to them.

The Importance of Persuasion

persuasion

The process of creating, reinforcing, or changing people's beliefs or actions.

Persuasion is the process of creating, reinforcing, or changing people's beliefs or actions.[1] The ability to speak (and write) persuasively will benefit you in every part of your life, from personal relations to community activities to career aspirations. When economists added up the number of people—lawyers, sales representatives, public relations specialists, counselors, administrators, and others—whose jobs depend largely on persuading people to adopt their point of view, they concluded that persuasion accounts for 26 percent of the U.S. gross domestic product![2]

Understanding the principles of persuasion is also vital to being an informed citizen and consumer. By age 20, the average American has been exposed to 1 million television commercials—an average of 150 every day. Politicians and advertisers, salespeople and interest groups, fund-raisers and community activists—all vie for your attention, votes, money, time, and support. The more you know about persuasion, the more effective you can be in using your powers of critical thinking to assess the barrage of persuasive messages you are exposed to every day.

Although persuasion has been studied for more than 2,000 years, it is still the subject of lively debate among scholars. There are a number of scientific models of the persuasive process and a wide range of respected theories about how persuasion works. In this chapter and the next, we will explore the principles of persuasion as they apply to public speaking.

When you speak to persuade, you act as an advocate. Your job is to get listeners to agree with you and, perhaps, to act on that belief. Your goal may be to defend an idea, to refute an opponent, to sell a program, or to inspire people to action. Because persuasive speakers must communicate information clearly and concisely, you will need all the skills you used in speaking to inform. But you will also need new skills that take you from giving information to affecting your listeners' attitudes, beliefs, or actions.

Ethics and Persuasion

No matter what the speaking situation, you need to make sure your goals are ethically sound and that you use ethical methods to communicate your ideas. Meeting these obligations can be especially challenging when you speak to persuade. Would you be willing to shade the truth "just a bit" if it would guarantee a successful speech? How about juggling statistics, doctoring quotations, passing off opinions as facts, or pandering to prejudice and stereotypes?

Unfortunately, there is no shortage of speakers—and other persuaders—who are willing to take ethical shortcuts to achieve their objectives. Yet, as Martin Luther King stated years ago, it is not possible to bring about a truly beneficial result by using unethical methods. Maintaining the bond of trust with listeners is also vital to a speaker's credibility. As in other kinds of public speaking, the ideal of effective persuasion is the good person speaking well.

When you work on your persuasive speech, keep in mind the guidelines for ethical speaking discussed in Chapter 2. Make sure your goals are ethically sound and that you can defend them if they are questioned or challenged. Study the topic thoroughly so you won't mislead your audience through shoddy research or muddled thinking. Learn about all sides of an issue, seek out competing viewpoints, and get your facts right.

But knowing the facts is not enough. You also need to be honest in what you say. There is no place in ethical speechmaking for deliberately false or deceptive statements. Also be on guard against more subtle forms of dishonesty such as quoting out of context, portraying a few details as the whole story, and misrepresenting the sources of facts and figures. Take care to present statistics, testimony, and other kinds of evidence fairly and accurately.

Keep in mind as well the power of language and use it responsibly. Show respect for the rights of free speech and expression, and stay away from name-calling and other forms of abusive language. Finally, check the section of Chapter 16 that discusses the role of emotional appeal (pages 370–373). Make sure that any emotional appeal you use is appropriate to the topic and that you build your speech on a firm base of facts and logic before appealing to your audience's emotions. Aim at the highest standards and construct your speech so it will be both convincing *and* ethically sound.[3]

The Psychology of Persuasion

Persuasion is a psychological process. It occurs in a situation where two or more points of view exist. The speaker supports Social Security reform, but many listeners do not. The speaker considers cloning immoral, but some in the audience think it is justified in certain circumstances. The different points of view may be completely opposed, or they may simply be different in degree. Whichever the case, there must be a disagreement, or else there would be no need for persuasion.

THE CHALLENGE OF PERSUASIVE SPEAKING

Of all the kinds of public speaking, persuasion is the most complex and the most challenging. Your objective is more ambitious than in speaking to inform, and audience analysis and adaptation become much more demanding. In some persuasive speeches you will deal with controversial topics that touch on your listeners' basic attitudes, values, and beliefs. This may increase their resistance to persuasion and make your task more difficult.

It is much easier, for example, to explain the history of capital punishment than to persuade an audience either that capital punishment should be abolished or that it should be reinstituted in every state. In the persuasive speech you must contend not only with your audience's knowledge of capital punishment but also with their attitudes toward crime and justice, their beliefs about the deterrent value of capital punishment, and their values about the taking of human life. Lines of argument that work with one part of the audience may fail with—or even upset—another part. What seems perfectly logical to some listeners may seem wildly irrational to others. No matter how expert you are on the topic, no matter how skillfully you prepare the speech, no matter how captivating your delivery—some listeners will not agree with you.

This does not mean persuasion is impossible. It does mean you should have a realistic sense of what you can accomplish. You can't expect a group of die-hard Democrats to become Republicans or a steak lover to turn vegetarian as a result of one speech.

In every persuasive speech, you will face some listeners who are strongly in favor of your position, some who are neutral, and some who are adamantly opposed. If listeners are neutral or only moderately committed one way or another, you can realistically hope your speech will move at least some of them toward your side. If listeners are strongly opposed to your viewpoint, you can consider your speech a success if it leads even a few to reexamine their views.

When thinking about the range of persuasive responses, you may find it helpful to visualize listeners on a scale such as that shown in Figure 15.1 (below). Persuasion involves any movement by a listener from left to right on the scale, no matter where the listener begins and no matter how great or small the movement.[4]

How successful you are in any particular persuasive speech will depend above all on how well you tailor your message to the values, attitudes, and

Degrees of Persuasion

Strongly Opposed	Moderately Opposed	Slightly Opposed	Neutral	Slightly in Favor	Moderately in Favor	Strongly in Favor

← Persuasion involves any movement by a listener from left to right →

• FIGURE 15.1

No matter what the situation, a persuasive speech will be more effective if the speaker has a clear goal, delivers the message sincerely, and adapts it to the target audience.

beliefs of your audience. In Chapter 5 we considered the general principles of audience analysis and adaptation. Here we emphasize two additional principles that are crucial to the psychology of persuasion. The first deals with how listeners process and respond to persuasive messages. The second pertains to the target audience for persuasive speeches.

HOW LISTENERS PROCESS PERSUASIVE MESSAGES

We often think of persuasion as something a speaker does *to* an audience. In fact, persuasion is something a speaker does *with* an audience. Listeners do not just sit passively and soak in everything the speaker has to say. Instead, they engage in a mental give-and-take with the speaker. While they listen, they assess the speaker's credibility, delivery, supporting materials, language, reasoning, and emotional appeals. They may respond positively at one point, negatively at another. At times they may argue, inside their own minds, with the speaker. This mental give-and-take is especially vigorous when listeners are highly involved with the topic and believe it has a direct bearing on their lives.[5]

In a sense, the psychological interaction between a speaker and audience during a persuasive speech is similar to what happens vocally during a conversation—as in this example:

Corey: Congress really needs to put an end to political ads funded by special-interest groups. The ads distort people's perception of the candidates and the issues.

Hannah: I agree that we shouldn't distort candidates and the issues, but I'm not sure censorship is the right approach. There's no proof that special-interest ads distort people's perceptions more than other kinds of political ads. Besides, doesn't the First Amendment guarantee free speech?

Corey:	The First Amendment is important, but special-interest groups aren't individual citizens like you and me. They're powerful organizations that corrupt government for their own purposes. Don't we have a responsibility to protect the democratic process?
Hannah:	We can't compromise on free speech. It's very dangerous to let someone in government decide what's acceptable and what's not. Once we ban special-interest ads, we might start banning other forms of political expression, too.
Corey:	Not necessarily. We already outlaw some kinds of speech because they are dangerous to the community—like threatening the life of the President or shouting "Fire" in a crowded building. Why are special-interest ads any different?

Much the same kind of interaction might occur during a persuasive speech, except that the listener would respond internally rather than out loud.

What does this mean to you as a speaker? It means you must think of your persuasive speech as a kind of *mental dialogue* with your audience. You must anticipate possible objections the audience will raise to your point of view and answer them in your speech. You cannot convert skeptical listeners unless you deal directly with the reasons for their skepticism.

As you prepare your persuasive speech, put yourself in the place of your audience and imagine how they will respond. Be as tough on your speech as your audience will be. Every place they will raise a question, answer it. Every place they will have a criticism, deal with it. Every place they will see a hole in your argument, fill it. Leave nothing to chance.[6]

mental dialogue with the audience
The mental give-and-take between speaker and listener during a persuasive speech.

THE TARGET AUDIENCE

Unfortunately, no matter how carefully you plot your speech, you will seldom be able to persuade all your listeners. Like most audiences, yours will probably contain some listeners who are hostile to your position, some who favor it, some who are undecided, and some who just don't care. You would like to make your speech equally appealing to everyone, but this is rarely possible. Most often you will have a particular *part* of the whole audience that you want to reach with your speech. That part is called the *target audience*.

Advertising gives us an effective model. Successful commercials are aimed at particular segments of the market. Mutual funds are now directing many of their advertisements at women. Why? Because more and more women are investing in the stock market. Beer commercials, on the other hand, are directed at men because they drink the most beer.

For your classroom speeches, you don't have the sophisticated research capability of a large advertising agency. But as we saw in Chapter 5, you can use questionnaires to find out where your classmates stand on your speech topic. This is your equivalent of market research. Once you know where your target audience stands, you can tailor your speech to fit their values and concerns—aim at the target, so to speak.

Here, for example, is how one student, Amy Shapiro, determined her target audience for a persuasive speech urging her classmates to pass on the gift of life by signing organ donor cards.

target audience
The portion of the whole audience that the speaker most wants to persuade.

There are 22 students in my audience. My audience-analysis questionnaires show that 3 are opposed to donating their organs under any circumstances. I can't persuade them no matter what I say. My questionnaires also show that 4 have already signed organ donor cards. I don't need to persuade them. The other 15 students could be persuaded if they knew more about the need for organ donors and about how the process works. They are my target audience.

Not only did Amy pinpoint her target audience, she also knew from her audience-analysis questionnaire the issues she would have to discuss to be convincing:

The members of my target audience break down this way: 7 give "fear of being pronounced dead prematurely" as their main reason for not signing organ cards; 5 are concerned about their body being "cut up or disfigured"; and 3 cite religious reasons for their opposition. The questionnaires also show that 8 of the 15 don't fully understand the need for organ donors.

With all this information, Amy was able to put together a first-rate speech that focused on her classmates' attitudes and beliefs about signing organ donor cards. In the speech, she showed the need for organ donations by explaining that there are thousands of people whose only hope for life is to receive a heart, liver, or kidney transplant. She also took care to answer her classmates' fears and objections. She showed that there are strict safeguards to prevent doctors from pulling the plug prematurely, that donated organs are removed as carefully as if the doctor were operating on a live patient, and that almost all religious leaders approve of organ donation to help save lives. As a result, she was able to convince several of her classmates to sign organ donor cards.

In the next chapter, we'll discuss the methods you can use to hit the target in your persuasive speeches. In the rest of this chapter, we focus on the three major kinds of persuasive speeches and how to organize them most effectively.

Persuasive Speeches on Questions of Fact

WHAT ARE QUESTIONS OF FACT?

What college basketball team has won the most games since 1990? Who was the first African American to sit on the U.S. Supreme Court? How far is it from New York to Baghdad? These questions of fact can be answered absolutely. The answers are either right or wrong.

But many questions of fact cannot be answered absolutely. There is a true answer, but we don't have enough information to know what it is. Some questions like this involve prediction: Will the economy be better or worse next year? Who will win the Super Bowl this season?

question of fact
A question about the truth or falsity of an assertion.

Other questions deal with issues on which the facts are murky or inconclusive. What will happen next in the Middle East? Is sexual orientation genetically determined? No one knows the final answers to these questions, but that doesn't stop people from speculating about them or from trying to convince other people that they have the best possible answers.

ANALYZING QUESTIONS OF FACT

In some ways, a persuasive speech on a question of fact is similar to an informative speech. But the two kinds of speeches take place in different kinds of situations and for different purposes. The situation for an informative speech is *nonpartisan*. The speaker acts as a lecturer or a teacher. The aim is to give information as impartially as possible, not to argue for a particular point of view. On the other hand, the situation for a persuasive speech on a question of fact is *partisan*. The speaker acts as an advocate. The aim is not to be impartial but to present one view of the facts as persuasively as possible. The speaker may mention competing views of the facts, but only to refute them.

For example, consider the assassination of John F. Kennedy. After more than four decades, there is still much debate about what really happened in Dallas on November 22, 1963. Did Lee Harvey Oswald act alone, or was he part of a conspiracy? How many shots were fired at President Kennedy and from what locations? If there was a conspiracy, who was involved in it? The informative speaker would recite the known facts on both sides of these questions without drawing a conclusion about which side is correct. The persuasive speaker, however, would draw a conclusion from the known facts and try to convert listeners to his or her point of view.

If there were no possibility of dispute on questions of fact, there would be no need for courtroom trials. In a criminal trial there is usually at least one known fact—a crime has been committed. But did the defendant commit the crime? The prosecuting attorney tries to persuade the jury that the defendant is guilty. The defense attorney tries to persuade the jury that the defendant is innocent. The jury must decide which view of the facts is more persuasive.[7]

ORGANIZING SPEECHES ON QUESTIONS OF FACT

Persuasive speeches on questions of fact are usually organized *topically*. Suppose, for example, you want to convince your classmates that a major earthquake of 9.0 or above on the Richter scale will hit California within the next ten years. Each main point in your speech will present a *reason* why someone should agree with you:

Specific Purpose: To persuade my audience that an earthquake of 9.0 or above on the Richter scale will hit California in the next ten years.

Central Idea: There are three good reasons to believe that an earthquake of 9.0 or above on the Richter scale will hit California in the next ten years.

Main Points:
    I. California is long overdue for a major earthquake.
    II. Many geological signs indicate that a major earthquake may happen soon.
    III. Experts agree that an earthquake of 9.0 or above could strike California any day.

To take another example, suppose you are trying to persuade your classmates that the plays attributed to William Shakespeare were not actually written by him. Your specific purpose, central idea, and main points might be:

Specific Purpose: To persuade my audience that William Shakespeare did not write the plays attributed to him.

Central Idea: There is considerable evidence that the plays attributed to William Shakespeare were actually written by Francis Bacon or Edward de Vere.

Main Points:
    I. Biographical and textual evidence suggest that William Shakespeare did not write the plays attributed to him.
    II. Historical evidence indicates that Shakespeare's plays were probably written by either Sir Francis Bacon or Edward de Vere, 17th Earl of Oxford.

Many persuasive speeches revolve around questions of value. Here Irish musician Bob Geldof speaks about the moral commitment of Western nations to help African nations deal with famine and disease.

Notice in these examples that the speaker's purpose is limited to persuading the audience to accept a particular view of the facts. Sometimes, however, the dispute that gives rise to a persuasive speech will go beyond a question of fact and will turn on a question of value.

Persuasive Speeches on Questions of Value

WHAT ARE QUESTIONS OF VALUE?

What is the best movie of all time? Is cloning morally justifiable? What are the ethical responsibilities of journalists? Such questions not only involve matters of fact, but they also demand *value judgments*—judgments based on a person's beliefs about what is right or wrong, good or bad, moral or immoral, proper or improper, fair or unfair.

Take the issue of cloning. It can be discussed at a purely factual level by asking such questions as "What are the scientific methods of cloning?" Or "What are the laws about cloning in different countries?" These are factual questions. The answers you reach are independent of your belief about the morality of cloning.

But suppose you ask, "Is it morally justifiable to clone human beings?" Or "Is it ethically acceptable to clone human cells in an effort to cure diseases such as AIDS and cancer?" Now you are dealing with questions of value. How you answer will depend not only on your factual knowledge about cloning, but also on your moral values.

question of value
A question about the worth, rightness, morality, and so forth of an idea or action.

ANALYZING QUESTIONS OF VALUE

Contrary to what many people think, questions of value are not simply matters of personal opinion or whim. If you say, "I enjoy bicycle riding," you do not have to give a reason why you enjoy it. You are making a statement about your personal taste. Even if bicycle riding were the most unpleasant activity ever invented, it could still be one of your favorites.

On the other hand, if you say, "Bicycle riding is the ideal form of land transportation," you are making a statement about a question of value. Whether bicycling is the ideal form of land transportation does not depend on your own likes and dislikes. To defend the statement, you cannot say, "Bicycle riding is the ideal form of land transportation because I like it."

Instead, you must *justify* your claim. The first step is to define what you mean by an "ideal form of land transportation." Do you mean a mode of transportation that gets people where they want to go as fast as possible? That is relatively inexpensive? That is fun? Nonpolluting? Beneficial for the user? In other words, you must establish your *standards* for an "ideal form of land transportation." Then you can show how bicycle riding measures up against those standards.

Whenever you give a speech on a question of value, be sure to give special thought to the standards for your value judgment.

ORGANIZING SPEECHES ON QUESTIONS OF VALUE

Persuasive speeches on questions of value are almost always organized *topically*. The most common approach is to devote your first main point to establishing the standards for your value judgment and your second main point to applying those standards to the subject of your speech.

Think back for a moment to the speech about bicycle riding as the ideal form of land transportation. If you organized this speech in topical order, your first main point would identify the standards for an ideal form of land transportation. Your second main point would show how biking measures up against those standards. Here is how your specific purpose, central idea, and main points might look:

Specific Purpose: To persuade my audience that bicycle riding is the ideal form of land transportation.

Central Idea: Bicycle riding is the ideal form of land transportation because it is faster than walking or running, does not exploit animals or people, is nonpolluting, and promotes the health of the rider.

Main Points: I. An ideal form of land transportation should meet four major standards.
    A. It should be faster than running or walking.
    B. It should not exploit animals or people.
    C. It should be nonpolluting.
    D. It should be beneficial for the person who uses it.
  II. Bicycle riding meets all these standards for an ideal form of land transportation.
    A. Bicycle riding is faster than walking or running.
    B. Bicycle riding does not exploit the labor of animals or of other people.
    C. Bicycle riding is not a source of air, land, water, or noise pollution.
    D. Bicycle riding is extremely beneficial for the health of the rider.

When you speak on a question of value, you must make sure to justify your judgment against some identifiable standards. In the following example, notice how the speaker devotes her first main point to judging capital punishment against moral standards and her second main point to judging it against legal standards:

Specific Purpose: To persuade my audience that capital punishment is morally and legally wrong.

Central Idea: Capital punishment violates both the Bible and the U.S. Constitution.

Main Points: I. Capital punishment violates the biblical commandment "Thou shalt not kill."

    II. Capital punishment violates the constitutional ban on "cruel and unusual punishment."

As you can see, speeches on questions of value may have strong implications for our actions. A person who is persuaded that capital punishment is morally and legally wrong is more likely to support legislation abolishing the death penalty. But speeches on questions of value do not argue directly for or against particular courses of action. Once you go beyond arguing right or wrong to arguing that something should or should not be done, you move from a question of value to a question of policy.

Persuasive Speeches on Questions of Policy

WHAT ARE QUESTIONS OF POLICY?

Questions of policy arise daily in almost everything we do. At home we debate what to do during spring vacation, whether to buy a new television, which movie to see on the weekend. At work we discuss whether to go on strike, what strategy to use in selling a product, how to improve communication between management and employees. As citizens we ponder whether to vote for or against a political candidate, what to do about airport security, how to maintain economic growth and protect the environment.

question of policy
A question about whether a specific course of action should or should not be taken.

All these are questions of policy because they deal with specific courses of action. Questions of policy inevitably involve questions of fact. (How can we decide whether to vote for a candidate unless we know the facts of her or his stand on the issues?) They may also involve questions of value. (The policy you favor on abortion will be affected by whether you think abortion is moral or immoral.) But questions of policy *always* go beyond questions of fact or value to decide whether something should or should not be done.

When put formally, questions of policy usually include the word "should," as in these examples:

What measures should be taken to protect the United States against terrorist attacks?

Should the electoral college be abolished?

What steps should be taken to ensure that all people in the United States receive adequate health care?

TYPES OF SPEECHES ON QUESTIONS OF POLICY

When you speak on a question of policy, your goal may be either to gain passive agreement or to motivate immediate action from your listeners. Deciding which goal you want to achieve will affect almost every aspect of your speech.

Speeches to Gain Passive Agreement

speech to gain passive agreement
A persuasive speech in which the speaker's goal is to convince the audience that a given policy is desirable without encouraging the audience to take action in support of the policy.

If your goal is passive agreement, you will try to get your audience to agree with you that a certain policy is desirable, but you will not necessarily encourage the audience to do anything to enact the policy. For example, suppose you want to persuade people that the United States should abolish the electoral college and elect the President by direct popular vote. If you seek passive agreement, you will try to get your audience to concur, but you will not urge them to take any action right now to help change presidential election procedures.

Here are some specific purpose statements for policy speeches that seek passive agreement:

To persuade my audience that there should be stricter safety standards on amusement-park rides.

To persuade my audience that the age for full driving privileges should be raised to 18.

To persuade my audience that the United States should put greater emphasis on nuclear power to meet the country's energy needs.

In each case, the speaker's aim is to convince listeners that the speaker's policy is necessary and practical. The speaker is not trying to get listeners to take action in support of the policy.

Speeches to Gain Immediate Action

speech to gain immediate action
A persuasive speech in which the speaker's goal is to convince the audience to take action in support of a given policy.

When your goal is immediate action, you want to do more than get your listeners to nod their heads in agreement. You want to motivate them to action—to sign a petition for abolishing the electoral college, to campaign for lower tuition, to purchase organic foods, to contribute to a fund drive, and so forth.

Here are some examples of specific purpose statements for policy speeches that seek immediate action:

To persuade my audience to give blood through the Red Cross.

To persuade my audience to vote in the next student election.

To persuade my audience to become literacy tutors.

Some experts say you should seek action from your audience whenever possible. Although it is much easier to evoke passive agreement than to elicit action, the listener is not making much of a commitment by thinking, "Sure, I agree with you." Within a day or two that same listener may forget entirely about your speech—and about her or his agreement with it.

Action, however, reinforces belief. A great deal of research shows that if you can persuade a listener to take some kind of action—even if it is no more than signing a petition, putting a bumper sticker on a car, or attending a meeting—you have gained a more serious commitment. Once a listener acts on behalf of a speaker's position, she or he is more likely to remain committed to it.[8]

Persuasive speeches on questions of policy are given whenever people debate specific courses of action. Such speeches can seek either passive agreement or immediate action.

When you call for action in a persuasive speech, you should make your recommendations as specific as possible. Don't just urge listeners to "do something." Tell them exactly what to do and how to do it. For an excellent example, look at Video Clip 15.1 in the online Media Library for this chapter. The speaker's aim was to convince her classmates to donate time to the Special Olympics. After talking about the mission of Special Olympics, the need for volunteers, and the rewarding feelings experienced by volunteers, she explained how students can get involved for whatever amount of time they are able to commit at the moment. She also brought along brochures with additional information to pass out after her speech. When you construct your persuasive speech, remember that the more specific your instructions, the more likely your call to action will succeed.[9]

connectlucas.com
View this excerpt from "Making a Difference Through the Special Olympics" in the online Media Library for this chapter (Video Clip 15.1).

ANALYZING QUESTIONS OF POLICY

Regardless of whether your aim is to elicit passive agreement or to gain immediate action, you will face three basic issues whenever you discuss a question of policy—need, plan, and practicality.

Need

There is no point in arguing for a policy unless you can show a need for it:

Is there a need for more student parking on campus?

Is there a need for the school district to institute same-sex classrooms?

Is there a need for a national ID card in the United States?

Your first step is to convince listeners that there is a serious problem with things as they are. People are not inclined to adopt a new policy unless they are convinced the old one is not working. This is why the *burden of proof* always rests with the speaker who advocates change. (Of course, you may be defending

need
The first basic issue in analyzing a question of policy: Is there a serious problem or need that requires a change from current policy?

burden of proof
The obligation facing a persuasive speaker to prove that a change from current policy is necessary.

present policy, in which case you will argue that there is *no* need to change—that things are already working as well as can be expected.)

Plan

plan
The second basic issue in analyzing a question of policy: If there is a problem with current policy, does the speaker have a plan to solve the problem?

The second basic issue of policy speeches is plan. Once you have shown that a problem exists, you must explain your plan for solving it.

What can we do to get more student parking on campus?

What topics should be taught in same-sex classrooms? Are same-sex classrooms appropriate for all grade levels?

What information should be included on a national ID card? Who will be responsible for collecting the information and creating the cards?

Answering such questions is especially important if you call for a new policy. It's easy to complain about problems; the real challenge is developing solutions.

In most classroom speeches, you will not have time to describe your plan in detail, but you should at least identify its major features. Look, for example, at the plan section in the speech on puppy mills in the online Media Library for this chapter. First, the speaker proposes legal measures to punish dog breeders that do not take proper care of their animals. Second, he presents four steps that individual listeners can take when buying a dog to make sure they are not supporting puppy mills. The speech would have been much less persuasive if the speaker had not spelled out the major features of his plan.

connectlucas.com
View this excerpt from "The Horrors of Puppy Mills" in the online Media Library for this chapter (Video Clip 15.2).

Practicality

practicality
The third basic issue in analyzing a question of policy: Will the speaker's plan solve the problem? Will it create new and more serious problems?

The third basic issue of policy speeches is practicality. Once you have presented a plan, you must show that it will work. Will it solve the problem? Or will it create new and more serious problems?

Building a multilevel parking garage on campus would provide more student parking, but the cost would require a sharp increase in tuition.

Creating same-sex classrooms would be academically beneficial for some students, but it could reinforce gender stereotypes and return education to a separate-but-equal status.

A national ID card might be an easy way for people to verify their identity for security purposes, but it could also infringe on civil liberties and give the government too much personal information about individuals.

connectlucas.com
View this excerpt from "Paid Parental Leave: Good for Families, Good for Business" in the online Media Library for this chapter (Video Clip 15.3).

These are significant concerns. Whenever you advocate a new policy, you must be prepared to show that it is workable. No matter how serious a problem may be, listeners usually want some assurance that a speaker's plan will actually solve the problem.[10] One way to provide this assurance is to show that a plan similar to yours has been successfully implemented elsewhere. For example, Video Clip 15.3 in the online Media Library for this chapter shows an excerpt from a student speech calling for paid parental leave in the speaker's state. As you view the clip, notice how the speaker points to the success of a similar plan in California as evidence that it will work in her state.

If you oppose a shift in policy, one of your major arguments will be that the change is impractical—that it will create more problems than it can solve. For example, critics of creating a national health care system in the United States similar to the one in Canada say it would produce longer waits for treatment and lower quality of care. Other opponents say the Canadian system impedes medical innovations and reduces incentives for doctors to improve their services. If listeners accept these arguments, they will probably decide that the U.S. should not use Canada as a model for a national health care system.

How much of your speech should you devote to need, to plan, and to practicality? The answer depends on your topic and your audience. If your audience is not aware of the health and environmental problems caused by the use of antibacterial chemicals in household products, you will have to give much of your time to need before covering plan and practicality. On the other hand, if your listeners already know about the problems caused by antibacterial household products, you can quickly remind them of need and then devote most of your speech to plan and practicality.

Or suppose you advocate increasing the tax on cigarettes to $4.00 a pack in order to reduce smoking among teenagers. Most people agree that teen smoking is a serious health problem, but many would question whether increasing the price of cigarettes will do much to solve the problem. Therefore, you should devote a fair part of your speech to practicality—to showing that in countries which have drastically raised their cigarette taxes, the smoking rate among teenagers has dropped by as much as 60 percent.

ORGANIZING SPEECHES ON QUESTIONS OF POLICY

Effective organization is crucial when you seek to persuade listeners on a question of policy. Although any of the basic patterns of organization explained in Chapter 8 can be used, four special patterns are especially valuable for policy speeches. They are problem-solution order, problem-cause-solution order, comparative advantages order, and Monroe's motivated sequence.

Problem-Solution Order

If you advocate a change in policy, your main points often will fall naturally into problem-solution order. In the first main point you demonstrate the need for a new policy by showing the extent and seriousness of the problem. In the second main point you explain your plan for solving the problem and show its practicality, for example:

problem-solution order
A method of organizing persuasive speeches in which the first main point deals with the existence of a problem and the second main point presents a solution to the problem.

Specific Purpose:	To persuade my audience that the use of antibacterial chemicals in household products is creating health and environmental problems.
Central Idea:	The use of antibacterial chemicals in household products is a serious problem that requires action by government and consumers alike.
Main Points:	I. The use of antibacterial chemicals in household products is a serious problem.
	A. Rather than making us more healthy, antibacterial chemicals in household products are contributing to long-term health problems.

B. The antibacterial chemicals in household products are also creating environmental problems because they eventually end up in the U.S. water supply.

II. Solving these problems requires a combination of government and consumer action.
    A. The Food and Drug Administration should institute regulations controlling the use of antibacterial chemicals in household products.
    B. Consumers should avoid purchasing household products that contain antibacterial chemicals.

connectlucas.com
View an excerpt from "Bursting the Antibacterial Bubble" in the online Media Library for this chapter (Video Clip 15.4).

You can use the problem-solution format just as easily to organize a speech opposing a change in policy. In such a speech your job is to defend the current system and to attack your opponents' proposed policy. Thus in the first main point you might argue that there is *not* a need for change. In the second main point you might show that even if there were a serious problem, the suggested new policy would *not* solve it and would create serious problems of its own. For example:

Specific Purpose: To persuade my audience that the city council should not pass legislation merging the police and fire departments.

Central Idea: Merging the police and fire departments is neither necessary nor practical.

Main Points: I. Merging the police and fire departments is not necessary.
    A. Under the current system, the police department has developed a reputation for excellence that has made it a model for departments in other cities,
    B. The fire department is equally well-respected for doing its job quickly and efficiently.
II. Besides being unnecessary, merging the police and fire departments is highly impractical.
    A. Rather than saving the city money, merging the departments would increase costs.
    B. Merging the departments would also harm morale and reduce the high level of performance we expect from our police force and firefighters.

Problem-Cause-Solution Order

problem-cause-solution order

A method of organizing persuasive speeches in which the first main point identifies a problem, the second main point analyzes the causes of the problem, and the third main point presents a solution to the problem.

For a variation on problem-solution order, you might arrange your speech in problem-cause-solution order. This produces a speech with three main points—the first identifying a problem, the second analyzing the causes of the problem, and the third presenting a solution to the problem. For example:

Specific Purpose: To persuade my audience that the age for full motor-vehicle driving privileges should be raised to 18.

Central Idea: The number of accidents and deaths involving teenage drivers is a serious problem that can be controlled by raising the age for full driving privileges to 18.

Main Points: I. The number of accidents and deaths involving teenage drivers is a serious national problem.

Regardless of how you organize your persuasive speech, you will need strong supporting materials. The better your research, the more convincing your arguments are likely to be.

    A. Each year more than 8,000 people are killed in accidents involving teenage drivers.

    B. The risks of being involved in a fatal accident are highest for 16- and 17-year-old drivers.

II. There are four main causes of the problem.

    A. Younger drivers haven't had enough experience to develop their driving skills.

    B. Younger drivers are more prone to risk-taking and dangerous driving behaviors.

    C. Younger drivers are more likely to have accidents when driving after dark.

    D. Younger drivers are easily distracted by the presence of other teenagers in the car.

III. We can help solve these problems by raising the age for full driving privileges.

    A. Although 16- and 17-year-olds should have limited driving privileges, they should not receive an unrestricted license until age 18.

    B. This will allow younger drivers time to gain maturity and experience before receiving unlimited driving privileges.

connectlucas.com
View an excerpt from "Putting the Brakes on Teenage Driving" in the online Media Library for this chapter (Video Clip 15.5).

Some teachers prefer this method of organization because it requires a speaker to identify the causes of the problem. This in turn makes it easier to check whether the proposed solution will get at the causes of the problem.

Comparative Advantages Order

When your audience already agrees that a problem exists, you can devote your speech to comparing the advantages and disadvantages of competing solutions. In such a situation, you might put your speech in comparative advantages order, devoting each main point to explaining why your solution is preferable to other proposed solutions.

comparative
advantages order

A method of organizing
persuasive speeches in which
each main point explains why a
speaker's solution to a problem
is preferable to other proposed
solutions.

Suppose you want to convince your audience that automakers should put greater emphasis on developing hydrogen fuel-cell cars than gas-electric hybrid cars. Using comparative advantages order, you would compare hydrogen cars with gas-electric hybrid cars and show why the former are a better choice. Your specific purpose, central idea, and main points might look like this:

Specific Purpose: To persuade my audience that automakers should put greater emphasis on developing hydrogen fuel-cell cars than gas-electric cars.

Central Idea: Unlike gas-electric cars, hydrogen cars run entirely without gasoline and do not emit air-polluting exhaust.

Main Points: I. Unlike hybrid cars, hydrogen cars run entirely without gasoline.
II. Unlike hybrid cars, hydrogen cars do not emit any air-polluting exhaust.

Monroe's Motivated Sequence

Monroe's motivated
sequence

A method of organizing
persuasive speeches that seek
immediate action. The five
steps of the motivated sequence
are attention, need, satisfaction,
visualization, and action.

Developed in the 1930s by Alan Monroe, a professor of speech at Purdue University, the motivated sequence is tailor-made for policy speeches that seek immediate action. The sequence has five steps that follow the psychology of persuasion:

1. *Attention.* First you gain the attention of your audience by using one or more of the methods described in Chapter 9: relating to the audience, showing the importance of the topic, making a startling statement, arousing curiosity or suspense, posing a question, telling a dramatic story, or using visual aids.

2. *Need.* Next, you make the audience feel a need for change. You show there is a serious problem with the existing situation. It is important to state the need clearly and to illustrate it with strong supporting materials. By the end of this step, listeners should be so concerned about the problem that they are psychologically primed to hear your solution.

3. *Satisfaction.* Having aroused a sense of need, you satisfy it by providing a solution to the problem. You present your plan and show how it will work. Be sure to offer enough details about the plan to give listeners a clear understanding of it.

4. *Visualization.* Having given your plan, you intensify desire for it by visualizing its benefits. The key to this step is using vivid imagery to show your listeners how *they* will profit from your policy. Make them *see* how much better conditions will be once your plan is adopted.

5. *Action.* Once the audience is convinced your policy is beneficial, you are ready to call for action. Say exactly what you want the audience to do—and how to do it. Then conclude with a final stirring appeal that reinforces their commitment to act.

Many students prefer the motivated sequence because it is more detailed than problem-solution order. It follows the process of human thinking and leads the listener step by step to the desired action. One indication of its effectiveness is that it is widely used by people who make their living by persuasion—especially advertisers. The next time you watch television, pay close attention to the commercials. You will find that many of them follow the motivated sequence, as in this example:

As a persuasive speaker, you must understand both sides of an issue so you can answer the objections of listeners who do not support your point of view. You can use the Internet to help by visiting the Web sites of organizations that take opposing views. For example, if your topic is stem cell research, visit both the Bedford Stem Cell Research Foundation (www.bedfordresearch.org/) and Do No Harm: The Coalition of Americans for Research Ethics (www.stemcellresearch.org/). Or, if you are speaking on gun control, access the National Rifle Association (www.nra.org) and the Coalition to Stop Gun Violence (www.csgv.org/).

If you want your listeners to take action by writing their U.S. Senator or Representative, encourage them to use e-mail. You can find e-mail addresses for Senators at www.senate.gov. For assistance in contacting members of the House, log on to www.house.gov.

Attention: It's a sunny spring day. Flowers are in bloom and the wind is blowing. The camera focuses on two women, both in their late twenties or early thirties, jogging through a city park. Suddenly one of the women stops, bends over, and rests her hands on her hips. Her eyes are watering and she is breathing heavily. A tightly framed close-up heightens the sense that something is wrong.

Need: "Are you all right?" asks her friend. "It's my allergies," the woman replies. "Every spring it's the same thing. I feel great and then my hay fever ruins everything. You'd better go on without me."

Satisfaction: "I used to have the same problem," says the woman's friend. "Then I tried AllArrest. It knocked out my hay fever completely. Now I can do everything I want in the spring. You should try it." The announcer, in voice-over, tells us: "AllArrest provides the most effective hay fever relief available—and without causing drowsiness."

Visualization: We see the same two women jogging a week or so later. Both are running briskly and breathing easily. "That AllArrest really does work," says the woman who had to stop running in the opening scene. "I feel like a new person since I started taking it. Thanks to AllArrest, I can enjoy spring again!"

Action: The audience is urged to use AllArrest whenever they suffer from allergies.

Try using the motivated sequence when you want to spur listeners to action. You should find it easy and effective, as did one student who used it in a speech urging classmates to work for passage of a local tenants' rights bill. Here are the highlights of his speech:

Attention: Have you ever had cockroaches running through the cupboards in your apartment? Have you sweltered in the heat because the air conditioning didn't work? Or shivered in the cold because the furnace was broken? Or waited months for the

	security deposit you never got back even though you left your apartment as clean as when you moved in?
Need:	Throughout this city students and other tenants are being victimized by unresponsive and unethical landlords. Just last year more than 200 complaints were filed with the city housing department, but no action has been taken against the landlords.
Satisfaction:	These problems could be solved by passing a strong tenants' rights bill that defines the rights of tenants, specifies the obligations of landlords, and imposes strict penalties for violators.
Visualization:	Such bills have worked in a number of college communities across the nation. If one were passed here, you would no longer have to worry about substandard sanitary or safety conditions in your apartment. Your landlord could not violate the terms of your lease or steal your security deposit.
Action:	A tenants' rights bill has been proposed to the city council. You can help get it passed by signing the petition I will pass around after my speech. I also urge you to help by circulating petitions among your friends and by turning out to support the bill when it is debated in the city council next week. If we all work together, we can get this bill through the council.

Monroe's motivated sequence is perfectly compatible with the standard method of outlining discussed in Chapter 10. The following outline shows how one speaker incorporated the sequence into a speech urging her classmates to donate blood:

Specific Purpose:	To persuade my audience to become regular blood donors.
Central Idea:	By becoming regular blood donors, college students can help save lives and replenish the U.S. blood supply.

connectlucas.com
View an excerpt from "The Ultimate Gift" in the online Media Library for this chapter (Video Clip 15.6).

Introduction

Attention:	I. Are you at least 17 years old? Do you weigh more than 110 pounds? Do you consider yourself fairly healthy? II. If you answered yes to these questions, you should be donating blood every two months. III. As a regular blood donor, I would like to show why donors are in such desperate need and encourage you to become a donor.

Body

Need:	I. The lack of participation by eligible blood donors poses a threat to the lives of many Americans. A. Someone in the U.S. undergoes a blood transfusion every three seconds. B. This amounts to 3,000 gallons of blood every hour of every day. C. Current donation levels are too low to meet this need.
Satisfaction:	II. You can help by becoming a regular blood donor. A. You can donate at your local Red Cross. B. The process is simple, easy, and painless.

Monroe's motivated sequence is especially useful for persuasive speakers who seek immediate action from their listeners, as is the case with actor and activist Danny Glover in this address to garment workers.

Visualization: III. Every unit of blood you donate can help save three lives.
  A. The blood is divided into red blood cells, white blood cells, and platelets, each of which can help a different person.
  B. If you donate 6 times a year, you can help 18 people.
  C. If you donate for 10 years, you can help save the lives of 180 people.

Conclusion

Action: I. So I encourage each of you to become a regular blood donor.
  II. Give the ultimate gift—the gift of life.

Try using the motivated sequence when you seek immediate action from your listeners. Over the years it has worked for countless speakers—and it can work for you as well.

Sample Speech with Commentary

The following persuasive speech deals with a question of policy and provides an excellent example of problem-cause-solution structure. As you read the speech, notice how the speaker deals with the issues of need, plan, and practicality. Notice also how she uses strong, well-chosen supporting materials to back up her point of view on what she knew would be an unpopular issue among her classmates. Finally, observe how clear and uncluttered the speech is. There are few wasted words and the ideas progress cleanly and crisply.

connectlucas.com
View "Putting the Brakes on Teenage Driving" in the online Media Library for this chapter (Video Clip 15.7).

Putting the Brakes on Teenage Driving

COMMENTARY	SPEECH
The speaker begins with a vivid, richly detailed story that gains attention and draws the audience into the speech.	On a chilly November night two years ago, a Ford Explorer was charging down a California highway. The 16-year-old driver and three of his friends were returning from a concert in Los Angeles. These young people were good students, gifted athletes, talented artists and musicians. And none were drunk or impaired by drugs.
As the speaker completes her opening story, she reveals that one of the students injured in the accident was her nephew. This personal involvement helps establish her credibility and goodwill, both of which are vital when one is speaking on a controversial subject.	They were, however, driving too fast, and the driver lost control of the car. The car went into a ditch and hit a tree. The driver and one passenger were killed. The other two passengers escaped with severe injuries. One of these passengers was my nephew. Today he is finishing high school in a wheelchair, a wheelchair he will occupy for the rest of his life.
The speaker strengthens her credibility and reveals the central idea of her speech.	Unfortunately, tragic auto accidents involving teenage drivers are much too common in all parts of the United States. After researching the subject for my speech, I have come to the same conclusion as the experts—that the best way to prevent such accidents is to raise the age for full driving privileges to 18 or older.
The speaker uses her audience-analysis survey both to acknowledge her classmates' opposition to raising the driving age and to stress their recognition that there are reasons to consider instituting such a policy. After asking them to listen with an open mind, she previews the main points she will discuss in the body of the speech.	I know from my audience-analysis questionnaire that most of you oppose such a plan. But I also know from my questionnaires that most of you recognize that 16- and 17-year-old drivers are less skilled and less responsible than older drivers. So I ask you to listen with an open mind while we discuss some of the problems associated with teenage driving, the major causes of the problems, and a plan that will go a long way toward solving the problems.
This speech is organized in problem-cause-solution order. Here the speaker starts the body by identifying the problem—the large number of accidents, deaths, and injuries involving teenage drivers. She supports her claim with statistics from the National Highway Traffic Safety Administration. As you can see from the video of the speech in the online Media Library for this chapter, she uses PowerPoint to present her statistics and to heighten their impact as she moves from figure to figure.	No matter how one looks at the evidence, it all leads to one fact: There are too many motor vehicle accidents, deaths, and injuries involving teenage drivers. According to the National Highway Traffic Safety Administration, while teenagers make up 7 percent of the nation's licensed drivers, they represent 14 percent of all motor vehicle fatalities. The NHTSA reports that last year 3,657 drivers aged 16 to 20 were killed in automobile accidents. In addition to killing the drivers, these same accidents took the lives of 2,384 teenage passengers. But these accidents didn't affect teenagers alone. They also took the lives of 2,625 people aged 21 or older. So the total number of people killed last year in automobile accidents involving teenage drivers was 8,666—almost exactly the number of full-time students at this campus.

As in the previous paragraph, the statistics here come from credible, clearly identified sources. Although most listeners did not favor the speaker's position at the start of her speech, the strength of her evidence eventually led some to concede that her position needed to be taken seriously.

A transition moves the speaker into her second main point, in which she explores four major causes of the problem. Notice how she uses a signpost to introduce each cause.

The evidence in this paragraph connects the tendency of younger drivers to take dangerous risks with the state of brain development among 16-year-olds. In addition to coming from respected sources, the evidence provides a scientific foundation for what the speaker's audience knew from their own experience about the propensity for risk-taking among teenagers.

Now the speaker discusses the third cause of the problem—night driving. Knowing that night driving is more dangerous for all age groups, she takes care to note that it is particularly perilous for teenagers because of their risk-taking and their inexperience behind the wheel.

This paragraph is especially effective. If you watch the speech in the online Media Library for this chapter, you can see how the speaker uses her voice, gestures, and facial expressions to enhance the impact of her ideas and to establish a strong bond with the audience

Evidence also shows that the younger the driver, the greater the risk. According to the Insurance Institute for Highway Safety, 16-year-olds have "the highest percentage of crashes involving speeding, the highest percentage of single-vehicle crashes, and the highest percentage of crashes involving driver error." Moreover, as *USA Today* reports, 16-year-olds are three times more likely to be involved in fatal crashes than are older drivers.

Now that we've seen the extent of the problem, we can explore its causes. One of the causes is inexperience. New drivers just haven't had enough time on the road to develop their driving skills. But inexperience is far from the only cause of the problem. After all, there will always be inexperienced drivers—even if the driving age is raised to 21 or even to 25.

A second cause is revealed by brain research. Findings from the National Institute of Mental Health show that the brain of an average 16-year-old has not developed to the point where he or she is able to effectively judge the risk of a given situation. Dr. Jay Giedd, who led the research team that conducted the study, states: "When a smart, talented, and very mature teen does something that a parent might call 'stupid,' it's this underdeveloped part of the brain that has most likely failed." Steven Lowenstein, a medical professor at the University of Colorado, has just finished a five-year study comparing the traffic records of 16-year-old drivers to drivers aged 25 to 49. His conclusion? "Deliberate risk-taking and dangerous and aggressive driving behaviors predominated" among the 16-year-olds.

A third cause of motor vehicle fatalities among teenage drivers is night driving. According to *The Washington Post,* when 16-year-olds get behind the wheel of a car after dark, the likelihood of having an accident increases several times over. Of course, nighttime driving is less safe for everyone, but it becomes particularly dangerous when combined with a young driver's inexperience and reduced ability to gauge risk.

Finally, there is the presence of teenage passengers in the car. We all know what it's like to drive with our friends—the stereo is up loud, cell phones are ringing, everybody's laughing and having a good time. The problem is that all these factors create distractions, distractions that too often result in accidents, injury, and death. Allan Williams, chief scientist at the Insurance Institute for Highway Safety, reports that one teenage passenger doubles the risk of a fatal crash. With two or more passengers, the risk is five times greater. Remember my nephew's accident I mentioned at the start of my speech? There were three passengers in the car.

A transition signals that the speaker is moving into her third main point. As in her second main point, she uses a signpost to introduce each of the subpoints.

As this section of the speech proceeds, notice how the speaker's plan addresses all four causes of the problem discussed in main point two—inexperience, brain development, night driving, and the number of teenage passengers in a car.

Because the speaker is not an authority on highway safety, she uses expert testimony to prove that her plan will reduce teenage driving fatalities. Notice how much less effective the speech would be if the speaker had merely stated the steps of her plan without providing evidence of its effectiveness.

Here the speaker deals with the objection that her plan would be harsh and inconvenient. The quotation from a father who lost his teenage son in a car accident puts the harshness issue in perspective and forces listeners to think about the trade-off between saving lives and instituting tougher driving-age requirements.

The conclusion builds on the emotional appeal generated by the quotation at the end of the previous paragraph. The final sentence, in which the speaker notes that her nephew would gladly accept the inconvenience caused by her policy for the chance to walk again, is compelling and ends the speech on a powerful note.

So the extent of the problem is clear. So, too, are its causes. What steps can we take to help bring about a solution? First, we need a national policy that no one can receive a learner's permit until age 16, and no one can receive full driving privileges until age 18. This will allow 16-year-olds time to gain driving experience before having an unrestricted license and to reach a stage of brain development where they are better able to handle the risk and responsibility of driving.

Second, we need to restrict nighttime driving so as to keep younger drivers off the road when conditions are riskiest. Some states have tried to address this problem by banning teenagers from driving after midnight or 1 A.M., but as the Insurance Institute for Highway Safety reports, these laws don't go far enough. According to the Institute, we need a 9:00 P.M. or 10:00 P.M. limit until drivers reach the age of 18.

Third, we need to restrict the number of teenage passengers in cars driven by younger drivers. In fact, says Kevin Quinlan from the National Transportation Safety Board, "passenger restriction is the first and foremost measure you can take" to reduce teenage driving fatalities. According to Quinlan, the optimal policy would be to bar drivers age 17 or younger from having any passengers in the car unless the riders are adults or family members. Drivers from the age of 17 to 18 should not be allowed to carry more than one teenage passenger.

Now I know all of this might sound harsh and perhaps inconvenient, but the evidence is clear that it would save a significant number of lives. "If you want to discuss harsh," said one father whose 17-year-old son died in an accident three years ago, "I can talk to you about harsh. It's being awakened at 2:30 in the morning by the State Patrol telling you that your son has just been killed."

Everyone in this room has lived to college age. But this year alone, thousands of teenage drivers will not live that long. And they won't live that long due to factors that we can prevent. There's no way to solve all the problems we encounter on the road, but we can do something to help save the lives of younger drivers and make the road safer for all of us. As I said earlier, this might sound harsh or inconvenient, but I know my nephew would gladly trade both for the chance to walk again.

Persuasion is the process of creating, reinforcing, or changing people's beliefs or actions. When you speak to persuade, you act as an advocate. The ability to speak persuasively will benefit you in every part of your life, from personal relations to community activities to career aspirations.

How successful you are in any persuasive speech depends on how well you tailor your message to your listeners' values, attitudes, and beliefs. You should think of your speech as a mental dialogue with your audience. Identify your target audience, anticipate objections they may raise to your point of view, and answer those objections in your speech.

Persuasive speeches may center on questions of fact, value, or policy. When giving a persuasive speech about a question of fact, your role is akin to that of a lawyer in a courtroom trial. You will try to get your listeners to accept your view of the facts.

Questions of value involve a person's beliefs about what is right or wrong, good or bad, moral or immoral, ethical or unethical. When speaking about a question of value, you must justify your opinion by establishing standards for your value judgment. Speeches on questions of value do not argue directly for or against particular courses of action.

Once you go beyond arguing right or wrong to urging that something should or should not be done, you move to a question of policy. When you speak on a question of policy, your goal may be to evoke passive agreement or to spark immediate action. In either case, you will face three basic issues—need, plan, and practicality. How much of your speech you devote to each issue will depend on your topic and your audience.

There are several options for organizing speeches on questions of policy. If you advocate a change in policy, your main points will often fall naturally into problem-solution order or into problem-cause-solution order. If your audience already agrees that a problem exists, you may be able to use comparative advantages order. Whenever you seek immediate action from listeners, you should consider a more specialized organizational pattern known as Monroe's motivated sequence.

Regardless of your topic or method of organization, you need to make sure your goals are ethically sound and that you use ethical methods to persuade your audience.

KEY TERMS

persuasion *(324)*

mental dialogue with the audience *(328)*

target audience *(328)*

question of fact *(329)*

question of value *(331)*

question of policy *(333)*

speech to gain passive agreement *(334)*

speech to gain immediate action *(334)*

need *(335)*

burden of proof *(335)*

plan *(336)*

practicality *(336)*

problem-solution order *(337)*

problem-cause-solution order *(338)*

comparative advantages order *(339)*

Monroe's motivated sequence *(340)*

REVIEW QUESTIONS

After reading this chapter, you should be able to answer the following questions:

1. What is the difference between an informative speech and a persuasive speech? Why is speaking to persuade more challenging than speaking to inform?

2. What does it mean to say that audiences engage in a mental dialogue with the speaker as they listen to a speech? What implications does this mental give-and-take hold for effective persuasive speaking?

3. What is the target audience for a persuasive speech?

4. What are questions of fact? How does a persuasive speech on a question of fact differ from an informative speech? Give an example of a specific purpose statement for a persuasive speech on a question of fact.

5. What are questions of value? Give an example of a specific purpose statement for a persuasive speech on a question of value.

6. What are questions of policy? Give an example of a specific purpose statement for a persuasive speech on a question of policy.

7. Explain the difference between passive agreement and immediate action as goals for persuasive speeches on questions of policy.

8. What are the three basic issues you must deal with when discussing a question of policy? What will determine the amount of attention you give to each of these issues in any particular speech?

9. What four methods of organization are used most often in persuasive speeches on questions of policy?

10. What are the five steps of Monroe's motivated sequence? Why is the motivated sequence especially useful in speeches that seek immediate action from listeners?

connectlucas.com
For further review, go to the Study Questions in the online Study Aids for this chapter.

EXERCISES FOR CRITICAL THINKING

1. Look back at the story of Ramon Trujillo at the beginning of this chapter (page 324). Like Ramon, most people do a certain amount of persuading every day in normal conversation. Keep a journal of your communication activities for an entire day, making special note of all instances in which you tried to persuade someone else to your point of view. Choose one of those instances and prepare a brief analysis of it.

   In your analysis, answer the following questions: (1) Who was the audience for your persuasive effort? (2) What were the "specific purpose" and the "central idea" of your persuasive message? (3) Did you rehearse your persuasive message ahead of time, or did it arise spontaneously from the situation? (4) Were you successful in achieving your specific purpose? (5) If you faced the same situation again, what strategic changes would you make in your persuasive effort?

2. Below are four specific purposes for persuasive speeches. In each case explain whether the speech associated with it concerns a question of fact, a question of value, or a question of policy. Then rewrite the specific purpose statement to make it appropriate for a speech about one of the other two kinds of questions. For instance, if the original purpose statement is about a question of policy, write a new specific purpose statement that deals with the same topic as either a question of fact or a question of value.

Example

Original statement: To persuade my audience that it is unfair for judges to favor natural parents over adoptive parents in child custody disputes. (question of value)

Rewritten statement: To persuade my audience that the courts should establish clear guidelines for settling disputes between adoptive parents and natural parents in child custody cases. (question of policy)

a. To persuade my audience to donate time as a community volunteer.

b. To persuade my audience that violence in video games is a major cause of violent behavior among teenagers.

c. To persuade my audience that a national sales tax should be adopted to help pay off the national debt.

d. To persuade my audience that it is unethical for businesses to use genetic testing in screening potential employees.

3. Choose a topic for a persuasive speech on a question of policy. Create two specific purpose statements about that topic—one for a speech to gain passive agreement, another for a speech to motivate immediate action. Once you have the specific purpose statements, explain how the speech seeking immediate action would differ in structure and persuasive appeals from the speech seeking passive agreement. Be specific.

4. Analyze the sample speech with commentary at the end of this chapter ("Putting the Brakes on Teenage Driving," pages 344–346). Pay special attention to how the speaker supports her ideas as she moves through the problem, cause, and solution sections. Does she present a convincing case that a serious problem exists? What does she identify as the major causes of the problem? Does her plan address all of those causes?

5. Select a television commercial that is organized according to Monroe's motivated sequence. Prepare a brief analysis in which you (a) identify the target audience for the commercial and (b) describe each step in the motivated sequence as it appears in the commercial.

6. Analyze "The Ultimate Gift," in the appendix of sample speeches that follows Chapter 18 (pp. A14–A16). Because this speech is organized in Monroe's motivated sequence, pay special attention to how the speaker develops each step in the sequence—attention, need, satisfaction, visualization, action. Identify where each step of the sequence occurs in the speech and explain how the persuasive appeal of the speech builds from step to step.

Applying *the* **Power** *of* **Public Speaking** ••

As a local union leader, it is your job to present a contract offer made by management to your striking membership. Though the proposed offer falls short of meeting all your union's demands, you believe it is a good offer, and in your speech, you will recommend that the union members vote to accept it.

The contract issues have been hotly debated, so you have an idea how some of your 42 members will cast their ballots. One issue is that management has guaranteed to maintain full benefits for current workers but wants to reduce benefits for new workers. Though the proposed offer limits these reductions, you know of 12 members who will vote against any proposal that limits the benefits of future workers. Already with you, however, are the 8 members who voted not to strike and who will vote to accept any reasonable offer. Among the undecided voters are those who think that since the strike is only in its second week, a better contract may be offered if this proposal is rejected.

Who is the target audience for your speech? How will you persuade them to vote yes on the contract offer? Which of the following methods of organization will you use for your speech, and why: problem-solution, comparative advantages, Monroe's motivated sequence?

16 Methods of Persuasion

Persuasion is big business. Thousands of authors and consultants promise to teach you the one key secret to persuading people to do what you want. Dan Lok claims to reveal "forbidden psychological tactics" that will "give you an unfair advantage in dealing with people." Scott Moldenhauer will help you unlock "the science of persuasion" to get the business results you crave. Kurt Mortensen promises to make you "a master of persuasion" so you can "get what you want when you want it." Kevin Hogan draws on "the science of influence" to give you persuasion techniques "the experts don't want you to know." These people all charge thousands of dollars for their seminars, hundreds for videos and motivational books. Companies and individuals flock—and pay—to read and hear what they have to say.

It sounds good, but can any of these people really have the "one key secret" to persuasion? Probably not. Persuasion is too complicated for that. Yet, as the number of books, seminars, and videos on the subject shows, there is a perpetual fascination with the strategies and tactics of effective persuasion.

What makes a speaker persuasive? Why do listeners accept one speaker's views and reject those of another? How can a speaker motivate listeners to act in support of a cause, a campaign, or a candidate? People have been trying to answer these questions for thousands of years—from the ancient Greek philosopher Aristotle to modern-day communication researchers. Although many answers have been given, we can say that listeners will be persuaded by a speaker for one or more of four reasons:

Because they perceive the speaker as having high *credibility*.

Because they are won over by the speaker's *evidence*.

Because they are convinced by the speaker's *reasoning*.

Because their *emotions* are touched by the speaker's ideas or language.

In this chapter we will look at each of these. We will not discover any magical secrets that will make you an irresistible persuasive speaker. But if you learn the principles discussed in this chapter, you will greatly increase your odds of winning the minds and hearts of your listeners.

Building Credibility

Here are two sets of imaginary statements. Which one of each pair would you be more likely to believe?

We can expect to see more female candidates for President in the foreseeable future. (Hillary Clinton)

We will not have more female candidates for President in the foreseeable future. (Peyton Manning)

Changes in professional football are producing a faster, more pass-oriented game. (Peyton Manning)

Changes in professional football are producing a slower, more run-oriented game. (Hillary Clinton)

Most likely you chose the first in each pair of statements. If so, you were probably influenced by your perception of the speaker. You are more likely to respect the judgment of Clinton, who almost captured the 2008 Democratic presidential nomination, when she speaks about female candidates for President, and to respect the judgment of Manning, two-time NFL Player of the Year, when he speaks about trends in professional football. Some teachers call this factor *source credibility*. Others refer to it as *ethos*, the name given by Aristotle.

FACTORS OF CREDIBILITY

Many things affect a speaker's credibility, including sociability, dynamism, physical attractiveness, and perceived similarity between speaker and audience. Above all, though, credibility is affected by two factors:

- *Competence*—how an audience regards a speaker's intelligence, expertise, and knowledge of the subject.

- *Character*—how an audience regards a speaker's sincerity, trustworthiness, and concern for the well-being of the audience.

The more favorably listeners view a speaker's competence and character, the more likely they are to accept what the speaker says. No doubt you are familiar with this from your own experience. Suppose you take a course in economics. The course is taught by a distinguished professor who has published widely in prestigious journals, who sits on a major international commission, and who has won several awards for outstanding research. In class, you hang on this professor's every word. One day the professor is absent; a colleague from the Economics Department—fully qualified but not as well known—comes to lecture instead. Possibly the fill-in instructor gives the same lecture the distinguished professor would have given, but you do not pay nearly as close attention. The other instructor does not have as high credibility as the professor.

It is important to remember that credibility is an attitude. It exists not in the speaker, but in the mind of the audience. A speaker may have high credibility for one audience and low credibility for another. A speaker may also have high credibility on one topic and low credibility on another. Looking back to our imaginary statements, most people would more readily believe Peyton Manning speaking about professional football than Peyton Manning speaking about the future of female presidential candidates.

TYPES OF CREDIBILITY

Not only can a speaker's credibility vary from audience to audience and topic to topic, but it can also change during the course of a speech—so much so that we can identify three types of credibility:

- *Initial credibility*—the credibility of the speaker before she or he starts to speak.

- *Derived credibility*—the credibility of the speaker produced by everything she or he says and does during the speech itself.

- *Terminal credibility*—the credibility of the speaker at the end of the speech.[1]

ethos
The name used by Aristotle for what modern students of communication refer to as credibility.

credibility
The audience's perception of whether a speaker is qualified to speak on a given topic. The two major factors influencing a speaker's credibility are competence and character.

initial credibility
The credibility of a speaker before she or he starts to speak.

derived credibility
The credibility of a speaker produced by everything she or he says and does during the speech.

terminal credibility
The credibility of a speaker at the end of the speech.

All three are dynamic. High initial credibility is a great advantage for any speaker, but it can be destroyed during a speech, resulting in low terminal credibility. The reverse can also occur, as in the following example:

> Barry Devins is the information technology manager for a major nonprofit research foundation. Soon after taking the job, he purchased an upgrade for the foundation's e-mail program. He assumed there would be some glitches, but they far exceeded anything he had imagined. It took six months to get the upgrade working properly, and even then people continued to grumble about messages they had lost during the phase-in period.
>
> A year later, the foundation was awarded a large contract, and the president decided to purchase a data synchronization system for the entire organization. She asked Barry to take charge of buying the system and training the staff in its use.
>
> When Barry outlined his plans at a weekly staff meeting, he had low initial credibility. Everyone remembered the e-mail program, and they were reluctant to go through the same problems again. But Barry realized this and was prepared.
>
> He began by reminding everyone that the president had authorized him to purchase a state-of-the-art system that would make their lives easier and improve office communications. He then acknowledged that he had told them the same thing about the e-mail upgrade—an admission that drew a laugh and helped everyone relax. Finally, he explained that he had checked with several other organizations that had installed the same data synchronization system he was purchasing, and they all had told him it worked flawlessly.
>
> Throughout his presentation, Barry's approach was "I know the e-mail upgrade was a disaster, and I've worked hard to make sure it doesn't happen again." By the time he finished, most staff members were eager to have the data synchronization system up and running. Barry had achieved high terminal credibility.

In every speech you give you will have some degree of initial credibility, which will be strengthened or weakened by your message and how you deliver it. And your terminal credibility from one speech will affect your initial credibility for the next one. If your audience sees you as sincere and competent, they will be much more receptive to your ideas.

ENHANCING YOUR CREDIBILITY

How can you build your credibility in your speeches? At one level, the answer is frustratingly general. Since everything you say and do in a speech will affect your credibility, you should say and do *everything* in a way that will make you appear capable and trustworthy. In other words—give a brilliant speech and you will achieve high credibility!

The advice is sound, but not all that helpful. There are, however, some specific ways you can boost your credibility while speaking. They include explaining your competence, establishing common ground with the audience, and speaking with genuine conviction.

Explain Your Competence

One way to enhance your credibility is to advertise your expertise on the speech topic. Did you investigate the topic thoroughly? Then say so. Do you have experience that gives you special knowledge or insight? Again, say so.

Here is how two students revealed their qualifications. The first stressed her study and research:

A speaker's credibility has a powerful impact on how her or his speech is received. One way to boost your credibility is to deliver your speeches expressively and with strong eye contact.

Before I studied antibacterial products in my public health class, I always used antibacterial soaps and antibacterial all-surface cleaner for my apartment. I also know from my class survey that 70 percent of you use antibacterial soaps, cleaners, or other products. But after learning about the subject in class and reading research studies for this speech, I'm here to tell you that, try as we might, we cannot build a bubble between ourselves and germs with antibacterial products and that those products actually create more problems than they solve.

The second student emphasized her background and personal experience:

Most of us have no idea what it means to be poor and hungry. But before returning to school last year, I spent three years working at local assistance centers. I worked in every part of the city and with every kind of person. I can't begin to tell you what I have seen—how poverty destroys people's souls and how hunger drives them to desperation. But on the basis of what I can tell you, I hope you will agree with me that government help for the poor and the needy must be increased.

Both speakers greatly increased their persuasiveness by establishing their credibility.

Establish Common Ground with Your Audience

Another way to bolster your credibility is to establish common ground with your audience. You do not persuade listeners by assaulting their values and rejecting their opinions. As the old saying goes, "You catch more flies with honey than with vinegar." The same is true of persuasion. Show respect for

connectlucas.com
View these excerpts from "Bursting the Antibacterial Bubble" and "Keeping the Safety Net for Those Who Need It" in the online Media Library for this chapter (Video Clip 16.1).

your listeners. You can make your speech more appealing by identifying your ideas with those of your audience—by showing how your point of view is consistent with what they believe.[2]

creating common ground
A technique in which a speaker connects himself or herself with the values, attitudes, or experiences of the audience.

Creating common ground is especially important at the start of a persuasive speech. Begin by identifying with your listeners. Show that you share their values, attitudes, and experiences. Get them nodding their heads in agreement, and they will be much more receptive to your ultimate proposal. Here is how a businesswoman from Massachusetts, hoping to sell her product to an audience of people in Colorado, began her persuasive speech:

> I have never been in Colorado before, but I really looked forward to making this trip. A lot of my ancestors left Massachusetts and came to Colorado nearly 150 years ago. Sometimes I have wondered why they did it. They came in covered wagons, carrying all their possessions, and many of them died on the journey. The ones who got through raised their houses and raised their families. Now that I've seen Colorado, I understand why they tried so hard!

The audience laughed and applauded, and the speaker was off to a good start.

Now look at a different approach, used in a classroom speech favoring a tuition increase at the speaker's school—an unpopular point of view with his classmates. He began by saying:

> As we all know, there are many differences among the people in this class. But regardless of age, major, background, or goals, we all share one thing in common—we are all concerned with the quality of education at this school. And that quality is clearly in danger. Because of budget reductions, faculty salaries have fallen below those at comparable schools, library hours have been cut back, and more and more students are being crowded out of classes they need to take.
>
> Whether we like it or not, we have a problem—a problem that affects each of us. This morning I would like to discuss this problem and whether it can be solved by an increase in tuition.

connectlucas.com
View this excerpt from "Let's Protect the Quality of Our Education" in the online Media Library for this chapter (Video Clip 16.2).

By stressing common perceptions of the problem, the student hoped to get off on the right foot with his audience. Once that was done, he moved gradually to his more controversial ideas.

Deliver Your Speeches Fluently, Expressively, and with Conviction

There is a great deal of research to show that a speaker's credibility is strongly affected by his or her delivery. Moderately fast speakers, for example, are usually seen as more intelligent and confident than slower speakers. So too are speakers who use vocal variety to communicate their ideas in a lively, animated way. On the other hand, speakers who consistently lose their place, hesitate frequently, or pepper their talk with "uh," "er," and "um" are seen as less competent than speakers who are poised and dynamic.[3]

All of this argues for practicing your persuasive speech fully ahead of time so you can deliver it fluently and expressively. In addition to being better prepared, you will take a major step toward enhancing your credibility. (Review Chapter 12 if you have questions about speech delivery.)

Speaking techniques aside, the most important way to strengthen your credibility is to deliver your speeches with genuine conviction. President Harry

Truman once said that in speaking, "sincerity, honesty, and a straightforward manner are more important than special talent or polish." If you wish to convince others, you must first convince yourself. If you want others to believe and care about your ideas, you must believe and care about them yourself. Your spirit, enthusiasm, and conviction will carry over to your listeners.

Using Evidence

Evidence consists of supporting materials—examples, statistics, testimony—used to prove or disprove something. As we saw in Chapter 7, most people are skeptical. They are suspicious of unsupported generalizations. They want speakers to justify their claims. If you hope to be persuasive, you must support your views with evidence. Whenever you say something that is open to question, you should give evidence to prove you are right.

Evidence is particularly important in classroom speeches because few students are recognized as experts on their speech topics. Research has shown that speakers with very high initial credibility do not need to use as much evidence as do speakers with lower credibility. For most speakers, though, strong evidence is absolutely necessary. It can enhance your credibility, increase both the immediate and long-term persuasiveness of your message, and help "inoculate" listeners against counterpersuasion.[4]

evidence
Supporting materials used to prove or disprove something.

Evidence is also crucial whenever your target audience opposes your point of view. As we saw in Chapter 15, listeners in such a situation will mentally argue with you—asking questions, raising objections, and creating counterarguments to "answer" what you say. The success of your speech will depend partly on how well you anticipate these internal responses and give evidence to refute them.

You may want to review Chapter 7, which shows how to use supporting materials. The following case study illustrates how they work as evidence in a persuasive speech.

HOW EVIDENCE WORKS: A CASE STUDY

Let's say one of your classmates is talking about the harmful effects of repeated exposure to loud music and other noises. Instead of just telling you what she thinks, the speaker offers strong evidence to prove her point. Notice how she carries on a mental dialogue with her listeners. She imagines what they might be thinking, anticipates their questions and objections, and gives evidence to answer the questions and resolve the objections.

She begins this way:

As college students we are exposed to loud music and other noise all the time. We go to parties, clubs, and concerts where the volume is so loud we have to shout so the person next to us can hear what we are saying. We turn our iPods so high they can be heard halfway across the room. And we seldom give it a second thought. But we should, because excessive noise can have a serious impact on our health and well-being.

How do you react? If you already know about the problems caused by noise pollution, you probably nod your head in agreement. But what if you don't know? Or don't agree? If you enjoy rock concerts and listening to your iPod at high volumes, you probably don't *want* to hear about it. Certainly you will not be persuaded by a general statement about exposure to loud music. Mentally you say to the speaker, "How do you know? Can you prove it?"

Anticipating just such a response, the speaker gives evidence to support her point:

The American Medical Association reports that 31 million Americans have some degree of hearing loss, and that 15 million of those cases are caused by too much exposure to loud noise.

"That's unfortunate," you may think. "But everyone loses some hearing as they grow old. Why should I be concerned about it now?" The speaker answers:

In an alarming trend, more and more victims of noise-induced deafness are adolescents and even younger children. According to the American Academy of Audiology, 5.2 million children in the U.S. between ages 6 and 19 have some hearing damage from amplified music and other sources. Audiologist Dean Garsetcki, head of the hearing-impairment program at Northwestern University, says, "We've got 21-year-olds walking around with hearing-loss patterns of people 40 years their senior."

"These are impressive facts," you say to yourself. "Luckily, I haven't noticed any problems with my hearing. When I do, I'll just be careful until it gets better." Keeping one step ahead of you, the speaker continues:

The problem with hearing loss is that it creeps up on you. *Sierra* magazine notes that today's hard-rock fans won't notice the effects of their hearing loss for another 15 years. And then it will be too late.

"What do you mean, too late?" you ask mentally. The speaker tells you:

Unlike some physical conditions, hearing loss is irreversible. Loud noise damages the microscopic hairs in the inner ear that transmit sound to the auditory nerve. Once damaged, those hairs can never recover and can never be repaired.

"I didn't know that," you say to yourself. "Is there anything else?"

One last point. Repeated exposure to loud music and other noise does more than damage your hearing. The latest issue of *Prevention* magazine reports that excessive noise has been linked to such problems as stress, high blood pressure, chronic headaches, fatigue, learning disorders, even heart disease. It's easy to see why Jill Lipoti, chief of Rutgers University's Noise Technical Assistance Center, warns that "noise affects more people than any other pollutant."

Now are you convinced? Chances are you will at least think about the possible consequences the next time you are set to pump up the volume on your iPod. Maybe you will use earplugs at a rock concert. You may even begin to reassess your whole attitude toward noise pollution. Why? Because the speaker supported each of her claims with evidence. You should try to do the same in your persuasive speeches.

Persuasive speeches need strong evidence to convince skeptical listeners. Finding the best evidence often takes hard digging, but it is well worth the effort.

TIPS FOR USING EVIDENCE

Any of the supporting materials discussed in Chapter 7—examples, statistics, testimony—can work as evidence in a persuasive speech. As we saw in that chapter, there are guidelines for using each kind of supporting material regardless of the kind of speech you are giving. Here we look at four special tips for using evidence in a persuasive speech.

Use Specific Evidence

No matter what kind of evidence you employ—statistics, examples, or testimony—it will be more persuasive if you state it in specific rather than general terms.[5] In the speech about noise pollution, for instance, the speaker did not say, "Lots of people suffer from hearing loss." That would have left the audience wondering how many "lots" amounts to. By saying "31 million Americans have some degree of hearing loss," the speaker made her point much more effectively. She also enhanced her credibility by showing she had a firm grasp of the facts.

Use Novel Evidence

Evidence is more likely to be persuasive if it is new to the audience.[6] You will gain little by citing facts and figures that are already well known to your listeners. If they have not persuaded your listeners already, they will not do so now. You must go beyond what the audience already knows and present striking new evidence that will get them to say, "Hmmm, I didn't know *that*. Maybe I should rethink the issue." Finding such evidence usually requires hard digging and resourceful research, but the rewards are worth the effort.

Use Evidence from Credible Sources

Listeners find evidence from competent, credible sources more persuasive than evidence from less qualified sources.[7] Above all, listeners are suspicious of evidence

Checklist Evidence

YES ✓ NO	
☐ ☐	1. Are all my major claims supported by evidence?
☐ ☐	2. Do I use sufficient evidence to convince my audience of my claims?
☐ ☐	3. Is my evidence stated in specific rather than general terms?
☐ ☐	4. Do I use evidence that is new to my audience?
☐ ☐	5. Is my evidence from credible, unbiased sources?
☐ ☐	6. Do I identify the sources of my evidence?
☐ ☐	7. Is my evidence clearly linked to each point that it is meant to prove?
☐ ☐	8. Do I provide evidence to answer possible objections the audience may have to my position?

connectlucas.com
This checklist is also available in the online Study Tools for this chapter.

connectlucas.com
View this excerpt from "Putting the Brakes on Teenage Driving" in the online Media Library for this chapter (Video Clip 16.3).

logos
The name used by Aristotle for the logical appeal of a speaker. The two major elements of *logos* are evidence and reasoning.

from sources that appear to be biased or self-interested. In assessing the current state of airline safety, for example, they are more likely to be persuaded by testimony from impartial aviation experts than from the president of American Airlines. If you wish to be persuasive, rely on evidence from objective, nonpartisan sources.

Make Clear the Point of Your Evidence

When speaking to persuade, you use evidence to prove a point. Yet you would be surprised how many novice speakers present their evidence without making clear the point it is supposed to prove. A number of studies have shown that you cannot count on listeners to draw, on their own, the conclusion you want them to reach.[8] When using evidence, be sure listeners understand the point you are trying to make.

Notice, for example, how the speaker in Video Clip 16.3 in the online Media Library for this chapter drives home the point of her evidence about the number of motor vehicle fatalities involving teenage drivers:

According to the National Highway Traffic Safety Administration, while teenagers make up 7 percent of the nation's licensed drivers, they represent 14 percent of all motor vehicle fatalities. The NHTSA reports that last year 3,657 drivers aged 16 to 20 were killed in automobile accidents. In addition to killing the drivers, these same accidents took the lives of 2,384 teenage passengers. But these accidents didn't affect teenagers alone. They also took the lives of 2,625 people aged 21 or older.

So the total number of people killed last year in automobile accidents involving teenage drivers was 8,666—almost exactly the number of full-time students at this campus.

Evidence is one element of what Aristotle referred to as *logos*—the logical appeal of a speaker. The other major element of *logos* is reasoning, which works in combination with evidence to help make a speaker's claims persuasive.

The story is told about Hack Wilson, a hard-hitting outfielder for the Brooklyn Dodgers baseball team in the 1930s.[9] Wilson was a great player, but he had a fondness for the good life. His drinking exploits were legendary. He was known to spend the entire night on the town, stagger into the team's hotel at the break of dawn, grab a couple hours sleep, and get to the ballpark just in time for the afternoon game.

This greatly distressed Max Carey, Wilson's manager. At the next team meeting, Carey spent much time explaining the evils of drink. To prove his point, he stood beside a table on which he had placed two glasses and a plate of live angleworms. One glass was filled with water, the other with gin—Wilson's favorite beverage. With a flourish Carey dropped a worm into the glass of water. It wriggled happily. Next Carey plunged the same worm into the gin. It promptly stiffened and expired.

A murmur ran through the room, and some players were obviously impressed. But not Wilson. He didn't even seem interested. Carey waited a little, hoping for some delayed reaction from his wayward slugger. When none came, he prodded, "Do you follow my reasoning, Wilson?"

"Sure, skipper," answered Wilson. "It proves that if you drink gin, you'll never get worms!"

And what does this story prove? No matter how strong your evidence, you will not be persuasive unless listeners grasp your reasoning.

Reasoning is the process of drawing a conclusion based on evidence. Sometimes we reason well—as when we conclude that ice particles forming on the trees may mean the roads will be slippery. Other times we reason less effectively— as when we conclude that spilling salt will bring bad luck. Most superstitions are actually no more than instances of faulty reasoning.

Reasoning in public speaking is an extension of reasoning in other aspects of life. As a public speaker, you have two major concerns with respect to reasoning. First, you must make sure your own reasoning is sound. Second, you must try to get listeners to agree with your reasoning. Let us look, then, at four basic methods of reasoning and how to use them in your speeches.

reasoning
The process of drawing a conclusion on the basis of evidence.

INDUCTIVE

REASONING FROM SPECIFIC INSTANCES

When you reason from specific instances, you progress from a number of particular facts to a general conclusion.[10] For example:

Fact 1:   My physical education course last term was easy.

Fact 2:   My roommate's physical education course was easy.

Fact 3:   My brother's physical education course was easy.

Conclusion: Physical education courses are easy.

reasoning from specific instances
Reasoning that moves from particular facts to a general conclusion.

As this example suggests, we use reasoning from specific instances daily, although we probably don't realize it. Think for a moment of all the general conclusions that arise in conversation: Politicians are corrupt. Professors are bookish. Dorm food is awful. Where do such conclusions come from? They come from observing particular politicians, professors, dormitories, and so on.

The same thing happens in public speaking. The speaker who concludes that unethical business practices are common in the United States because several major corporations have been guilty of fraud in recent years is reasoning from specific instances. So is the speaker who argues that anti-Semitism is increasing on college campuses because there have been a number of attacks on Jewish students and symbols at schools across the nation.

Such conclusions are never foolproof. No matter how many specific instances you give (and you can give only a few in a speech), it is always possible that an exception exists. Throughout the ages people observed countless white swans in Europe without seeing any of a different color. It seemed an undeniable fact that all swans were white. Then, in the 19th century, black swans were discovered in Australia![11]

Guidelines for Reasoning from Specific Instances

When you reason from specific instances, you should follow a few basic guidelines.

hasty generalization

An error in reasoning from specific instances, in which a speaker jumps to a general conclusion on the basis of insufficient evidence.

First, avoid generalizing too hastily. Beware of the tendency to jump to conclusions on the basis of insufficient evidence. Make sure your sample of specific instances is large enough to justify your conclusion. Also make sure the instances you present are fair, unbiased, and representative. (Are three physical education courses *enough* to conclude that physical education courses in general are easy? Are the three courses *typical* of most physical education courses?)

Second, be careful with your wording. If your evidence does not justify a sweeping conclusion, qualify your argument. Suppose you are talking about the crisis in America's national park system brought on by overuse and commercial development. You document the problem by discussing some specific instances—Yosemite, Yellowstone, the Everglades. Then you draw your conclusion. You might say:

> As we have seen, America's national park system is serving more than 400 million people a year, with the result that some parks are being overcome by traffic, pollution, and garbage. We have also seen that more and more parks are being exploited for mining, logging, and other forms of commercial development. It certainly seems fair, then, to conclude that new measures are needed to ensure that the beauty, serenity, and biological diversity of America's national parks are preserved for future generations as well as for our own.

This is not as dramatic as saying, "America's national parks are on the brink of destruction," but it is more accurate and will be more persuasive to careful listeners.

Third, reinforce your argument with statistics or testimony. Since you can never give enough specific instances to make your conclusion irrefutable, you should supplement them with testimony or statistics demonstrating that the instances are representative. When talking about prescription drug abuse, you might say:

> Prescription drug overdoses have skyrocketed in recent years. Consider the most publicized cases. In early 2008, actor Heath Ledger overdosed from a lethal cocktail of six different prescription drugs. A year earlier, model Anna Nicole Smith died from a dangerous mixture of nine prescription drugs. And five months before that, Smith's son, Daniel, died from a combination of at least three prescription drugs.

These specific examples help make the conclusion persuasive, but a listener could easily dismiss them as sensational and atypical. To prevent this, you might go on to say:

The problem is not limited to the rich and famous. As reported by the Centers for Disease Control, the number of prescription drug overdoses has almost doubled over the past decade, making it the second leading cause of accidental death in the United States, right behind automobile accidents. Each year more than 20,000 people die from adverse reactions to prescription drugs. According to Leonard Paulozzi, a medical epidemiologist with the CDC: "Judged by any measure, . . . the prescription drug problem is a crisis that is steadily worsening."

With this backup material, not even a skeptical listener could reject your examples as isolated.

When you reason from specific instances, you can either state your conclusion and then give the specific instances on which it is based or give the specific instances and then draw your conclusion. Look back at the example about national parks on page 362. In that example, the speaker first gives three facts and then draws a conclusion. In the example about prescription drug overdoses, the conclusion is stated first, followed by three specific instances. It doesn't matter which order you use as long as your facts support your conclusion.

REASONING FROM PRINCIPLE

Reasoning from principle is the opposite of reasoning from specific instances. It moves from the general to the specific.[12] When you reason from principle, you progress from a general principle to a specific conclusion. We are all familiar with this kind of reasoning from statements such as the following:

reasoning from principle
Reasoning that moves from a general principle to a specific conclusion.

1. All people are mortal.

2. Socrates is a person.

3. Therefore, Socrates is mortal.

This is a classic example of reasoning from principle. You begin with a general statement ("All people are mortal"), move to a minor premise ("Socrates is a person"), and end with a specific conclusion ("Socrates is mortal").

Speakers often use reasoning from principle when trying to persuade an audience. One of the clearest examples from American history is Susan B. Anthony's famous speech "Is It a Crime for U.S. Citizens to Vote?" Delivered on numerous occasions in 1872 and 1873, at a time when women were legally barred from voting, Anthony's speech reasoned along the following lines:

1. The United States Constitution guarantees all U.S. citizens the right to vote.

2. Women are U.S. citizens.

3. Therefore, the United States Constitution guarantees women the right to vote.

This argument progresses from a general principle ("The United States Constitution guarantees all U.S. citizens the right to vote") through a minor premise

("Women are U.S. citizens") to a conclusion ("Therefore, the United States Constitution guarantees women the right to vote").

Guidelines for Reasoning from Principle

When you use reasoning from principle in a speech, pay special attention to your general principle. Will listeners accept it without evidence? If not, give evidence to support it before moving to your minor premise. You may also need to support your minor premise with evidence. When both the general principle and the minor premise are soundly based, your audience will be much more likely to accept your conclusion.

Suppose, for example, that you plan to speak about excessive sugar in the American diet. You begin by formulating a specific purpose:

Specific Purpose: To persuade my audience to limit their consumption of soft drinks, desserts, candies, sweetened dairy products, and other foods with high sugar content.

Next, you decide to use reasoning from principle to help persuade your audience. Your argument looks like this:

1. Excessive consumption of refined sugar is unhealthy.

2. Soft drinks, desserts, candies, and sweetened dairy products contain excessive amounts of sugar.

3. Therefore, excessive consumption of soft drinks, desserts, candies, and sweetened dairy products is unhealthy.

To make the argument persuasive, you have to support your general principle: "Excessive consumption of refined sugar is unhealthy." You cite medical evidence and research studies. Part of your argument might go like this:

High sugar intake has been linked with diabetes, osteoporosis, cancer, high blood pressure, and heart disease, not to mention tooth decay and obesity. Indeed, the Harvard School of Public Health has identified sugar-sweetened sodas as a major cause of the U.S. obesity epidemic and the alarming increase in Type II diabetes. According to the American Medical Association, high sugar intake is among the most serious health problems facing the United States.

Having supported your general principle, you bolster your minor premise: "Soft drinks, desserts, candies, and sweetened dairy products contain excessive amounts of sugar." Your evidence includes the following:

The World Health Organization recommends that people consume no more than 48 grams of refined sugar a day. But just one can of Pepsi, 7-Up, or Mountain Dew delivers 40 grams. A large McDonald's milk shake contains 48 grams—as does one Cinnabon or one slice of cherry pie. Add ice cream to the pie and the sugar content exceeds 60 grams. A 5-ounce candy bar has 25 grams of sugar. Even foods that are supposed to be nutritious can contain large amounts of added sugar. An 8-ounce serving of fruit yogurt has 36 grams, while a glass of whole milk contains 16 grams. No wonder we have a sugar overload!

Reasoning is an important part of persuasive speaking. In a legal trial, for example, neither the prosecution nor the defense is likely to sway the jury unless their reasoning is clear and convincing.

Now you have supported your general principle and your minor premise. You can feel confident in going on to your conclusion:

Therefore, excessive consumption of soft drinks, desserts, candies, and sweetened dairy products is unhealthy.

And you can expect your audience to take you seriously. When used properly, reasoning from principle is highly persuasive.

CAUSAL REASONING

There is a patch of ice on the sidewalk. You slip, fall, and break your arm. You reason as follows: "*Because* that patch of ice was there, I fell and broke my arm." This is an example of causal reasoning, in which someone tries to establish the relationship between causes and effects.

As with reasoning from specific instances, we use causal reasoning daily. Something happens and we ask what caused it to happen. We want to know the causes of chronic fatigue syndrome, of the football team's latest defeat, of our roommate's peculiar habits. We also wonder about effects. We speculate about the consequences of chronic fatigue syndrome on life expectancy, of the star quarterback's leg injury, of telling our roommate that a change is needed.

causal reasoning
Reasoning that seeks to establish the relationship between causes and effects.

Guidelines for Causal Reasoning

As any scientist (or detective) will tell you, causal reasoning can be tricky. The relationship between causes and effects is not always clear. There are two common errors to avoid when using causal reasoning.

The first is the fallacy of false cause. This fallacy is often known by its Latin name, *post hoc, ergo propter hoc,* which means "after this, therefore because of this." In other words, the fact that one event happens after another does not mean that the first is the cause of the second. The closeness in time of the two

false cause
An error in causal reasoning in which a speaker mistakenly assumes that because one event follows another, the first event is the cause of the second. This error is often known by its Latin name, *post hoc, ergo propter hoc,* meaning "after this, therefore because of this."

events may be entirely coincidental. If a black cat crosses your path and five minutes later you fall and break your arm, you needn't blame your accident on the poor cat.

One student in speech class argued that a rise in SAT scores for students in her state was caused by the election of a new superintendent of public instruction the previous year. Her reasoning? The superintendent had pledged in his campaign to reverse the state's recent decline in SAT scores. Within a year after he took office, SAT scores had improved. Therefore, the improvement was caused by the new superintendent. The student's classmates were not impressed. They pointed out that the timing of the two events did not prove that one *caused* the other; SAT scores would have risen regardless of who won the election.

A second pitfall to avoid when using causal reasoning is assuming that events have only one cause. In fact, most events have several causes. What causes the economy to boom or bust? Interest rates? Gas prices? Tax policy? Labor costs? Consumer confidence? World affairs? *All* these factors—and others— affect the economy. When you use causal reasoning, be wary of the temptation to attribute complex events to single causes.

You cannot escape causal reasoning. All of us use it daily, and you are almost certain to use it when speaking to persuade—especially if you deal with a question of fact or policy.

ANALOGICAL REASONING

What do these statements have in common?

analogical reasoning
Reasoning in which a speaker compares two similar cases and infers that what is true for the first case is also true for the second.

If you're good at racquetball, you'll be great at Ping-Pong.

In Great Britain the general election campaign for Prime Minister lasts less than three weeks. Surely we can do the same with the U.S. presidential election.

Both statements use reasoning from analogy. By comparing two similar cases, they infer that what is true for one must be true for the other.

Guidelines for Analogical Reasoning

The most important question in assessing analogical reasoning is whether the two cases being compared are essentially alike. If they are essentially alike, the analogy is valid. If they are not essentially alike, the analogy is invalid.

Look back to the analogies at the start of this section. Is playing racquetball the same as playing Ping-Pong? Not really. Both involve hitting a ball with a racquet or a paddle. But racquetball uses a stringed racquet and a rubber ball. Ping-Pong uses a solid paddle and a smaller, lighter, celluloid ball. Racquetball is played by hitting the ball against the walls or ceiling of an enclosed court. Ping-Pong is played by hitting the ball back and forth over a net stretched across a table. Skill at one is no guarantee of skill at the other. The analogy is not valid.

What about the second analogy? That depends on how much alike the British and American political systems are. Are the countries similar in size and diversity? Is it possible for candidates in both countries to canvass the entire land in less than three weeks? Does the party system operate the same in both countries? In other words, are the factors that allow Great Britain to conduct campaigns for Prime Minister in less than three weeks also present in the United States? If so, the analogy is valid. If not, the analogy is invalid.

invalid analogy
An analogy in which the two cases being compared are not essentially alike.

Reasoning from analogy is used most often in persuasive speeches on questions of policy. When arguing for a new policy, you should find out whether it has been tried elsewhere. You may be able to claim that your policy will work because it has worked in like circumstances. Here is how one student used reasoning from analogy to support her claim that controlling handguns will reduce violent crime in the United States:

> Will my policy work? The experience of foreign countries suggests it will. In England, guns are tightly regulated; even the police are unarmed, and the murder rate is trivial by American standards. In Japan, the ownership of weapons is severely restricted, and handguns are completely prohibited. Japan is an almost gun-free country, and its crime rate is even lower than England's. On the basis of these comparisons, we can conclude that restricting the ownership of guns will control the crime and murder rates in America.

By the same token, if you argue against a change in policy, you should check whether the proposed policy—or something like it—has been implemented elsewhere. Here, too, you may be able to support your case by reasoning from analogy—as did one student who opposed gun control:

> Advocates of gun control point to foreign countries to prove their case. They often cite England, which has strict gun control laws and little violent crime. But the key to low personal violence in England—and other foreign countries—is not gun control laws but the generally peaceful character of the people. For example, Switzerland has a militia system; 750,000 assault rifles and military pistols are sitting at this moment in Swiss homes. Yet Switzerland's murder rate is only 15 percent of ours. In other words, cultural factors are much more important than gun control when it comes to violent crime.

As these examples illustrate, argument from analogy can be used on both sides of an issue. You are more likely to persuade your audience if the analogy shows a truly parallel situation.

FALLACIES

A fallacy is an error in reasoning. As a speaker, you need to avoid fallacies in your speeches. As a listener, you need to be alert to fallacies in the speeches you hear.

fallacy
An error in reasoning.

Logicians have identified more than 125 different fallacies. Earlier in this chapter, we discussed three of the most important: hasty generalization (pages 362–363), false cause (pages 365–366), and invalid analogy (pages 366–367). Here we look at five other fallacies you should guard against.

Red Herring

The name of this fallacy comes from an old trick used by farmers in England to keep fox hunters and their hounds from galloping through the crops. By dragging a smoked herring with a strong odor along the edge of their fields, the farmers could throw the dogs off track by destroying the scent of the fox.

red herring
A fallacy that introduces an irrelevant issue to divert attention from the subject under discussion.

A speaker who uses a red herring introduces an irrelevant issue in order to divert attention from the subject under discussion. For instance:

How dare my opponents accuse me of political corruption at a time when we are working to improve the quality of life for all people in the United States.

What does the speaker's concern about the quality of life in the U.S. have to do with whether he or she is guilty of political corruption? Nothing! It is a red herring used to divert attention away from the real issue.

Ad Hominem

ad hominem
A fallacy that attacks the person rather then dealing with the real issue in dispute.

Latin for "against the man," *ad hominem* refers to the fallacy of attacking the person rather than dealing with the real issue in dispute. For instance:

The head of the commerce commission has a number of interesting economic proposals, but let's not forget that she comes from a very wealthy family.

By impugning the commissioner's family background rather than dealing with the substance of her economic proposals, the speaker is engaging in an *ad hominem* attack.

Sometimes, of course, a person's character or integrity can be a legitimate issue—as in the case of a police chief who violates the law or a corporate president who swindles stockholders. In such cases, a speaker might well raise questions about the person without being guilty of the *ad hominem* fallacy.

Either-Or

either-or
A fallacy that forces listeners to choose between two alternatives when more than two alternatives exist.

Sometimes referred to as a false dilemma, the either-or fallacy forces listeners to choose between two alternatives when more than two alternatives exist. For example:

The government must either raise taxes or reduce services for the poor.

This statement oversimplifies a complex issue by reducing it to a simple either-or choice. Is it true that the only choices are to raise taxes or to reduce services for the poor? A careful listener might ask, "What about cutting the administrative cost of government or eliminating pork-barrel projects instead?".

In addition to using evidence to support their ideas, effective speakers such as Bill Richardson take care to avoid fallacies in reasoning that may undermine their credibility and persuasiveness.

You will be more persuasive as a speaker and more perceptive as a listener if you are alert to the either-or fallacy.

Bandwagon

How often have you heard someone say, "It's a great idea—everyone agrees with it"? This is a classic example of the bandwagon fallacy, which assumes that because something is popular, it is therefore good, correct, or desirable.

Much advertising is based on the bandwagon fallacy. The fact that more people use Tylenol than Advil does not prove that Tylenol is a better pain reliever. Tylenol's popularity could be due to aggressive marketing. The question of which product does a better job reducing pain is a medical issue that has nothing to do with popularity.

The bandwagon fallacy is also evident in political speeches. Consider the following statement:

The governor must be correct in his approach to social policy; after all, the polls show that 60 percent of the people support him.

This statement is fallacious because popular opinion cannot be taken as proof that an idea is right or wrong. Remember, "everyone" used to believe that the world is flat, that space flight is impossible, and that women should not attend college with men!

bandwagon
A fallacy that assumes that because something is popular, it is therefore good, correct, or desirable.

Slippery Slope

The slippery slope fallacy takes its name from the image of a boulder rolling uncontrollably down a steep hill. Once the boulder gets started, it can't be stopped until it reaches the bottom.

A speaker who commits the slippery slope fallacy assumes that taking a first step will lead inevitably to a second step and so on down the slope to disaster—as in the following example:

slippery slope
A fallacy that assumes that taking a first step will lead to subsequent steps that cannot be prevented.

> Passing federal laws to control the amount of violence in video games is the first step in a process that will result in absolute government control of the media and total censorship over all forms of artistic expression.

If a speaker claims that taking a first step will lead inevitably to a series of disastrous later steps, he or she needs to provide evidence or reasoning to support the claim. To assume that all the later steps will occur without proving that they will is to commit the slippery slope fallacy.[13]

Appealing to Emotions

Effective persuasion often requires emotional appeal. As the Roman rhetorician Quintilian stated, "It is feeling and force of imagination that make us eloquent."[14] By adding "feeling" and the "force of imagination" to your logical arguments, you can become a more compelling persuasive speaker.

WHAT ARE EMOTIONAL APPEALS?

pathos
The name used by Aristotle for what modern students of communication refer to as emotional appeal.

Emotional appeals—what Aristotle referred to as *pathos*—are intended to make listeners feel sad, angry, guilty, afraid, happy, proud, sympathetic, reverent, or the like. These are often appropriate reactions when the question is one of value or policy. As George Campbell wrote in his *Philosophy of Rhetoric*, "When persuasion is the end, passion also must be engaged."[15]

Below is a list of some of the emotions evoked most often by public speakers. Following each emotion are a few examples of subjects that might stir that emotion:

- *Fear*—of serious illness, of natural disasters, of sexual assault, of personal rejection, of economic hardship.

- *Compassion*—for the physically disabled, for battered women, for neglected animals, for starving children, for victims of AIDS.

- *Pride*—in one's country, in one's family, in one's school, in one's ethnic heritage, in one's personal accomplishments.

- *Anger*—at terrorists and their supporters, at business leaders who act unethically, at members of Congress who abuse the public trust, at landlords who exploit student tenants, at vandals and thieves.

- *Guilt*—about not helping people less fortunate than ourselves, about not considering the rights of others, about not doing one's best.

- *Reverence*—for an admired person, for traditions and institutions, for one's deity.

There are many other emotions and many other subjects that might stir them. However, this brief sample should give you an idea of the kinds of emotional appeals you might use to enhance the message of your persuasive speech.

Emotional appeals often make a persuasive speech more compelling. Such appeals should always be used ethically and should not be substituted for facts and logic.

GENERATING EMOTIONAL APPEAL

Use Emotional Language

As we saw in Chapter 11, one way to generate emotional appeal is to use emotion-laden words. Here, for instance, is part of the conclusion from a student speech about the challenges and rewards of working as a community volunteer with young children:

> The <u>promise of America sparkles</u> in the <u>eyes of every child</u>. Their <u>dreams</u> are the <u>glittering dreams</u> of <u>America</u>. When those <u>dreams</u> are <u>dashed</u>, when <u>innocent hopes</u> are <u>betrayed</u>, so are the <u>dreams and hopes</u> of the <u>entire nation</u>. It is our <u>duty</u>—to me, it is a <u>sacred duty</u>—to give <u>all children</u> the chance to <u>learn and grow</u>, to share <u>equally</u> in the <u>American dream</u> of <u>freedom, justice, and opportunity</u>.

The underlined words and phrases have strong emotional power, and in this case they produced the desired effect. Be aware, however, that packing too many emotionally charged words into one part of a speech can call attention to the emotional language itself and undermine its impact. The emotion rests in your audience, not in your words. Even the coldest facts can touch off an emotional response if they strike the right chords in a listener.

Develop Vivid Examples

Often a better approach than relying on emotionally charged language is to let emotional appeal grow naturally out of the content of your speech. The most effective way to do this is with vivid, richly textured examples that pull listeners into the speech.

Here is how one speaker used a vivid example for emotional appeal. She was speaking to a citizens' group on behalf of CARE, a world humanitarian organization, about the malaria epidemic in Africa. Here is what she might have said, stripping the content of emotional appeal:

> Malaria is one of the biggest problems facing Africa. Many die from it every day. If the rest of the world doesn't help, the malaria epidemic will only get worse.

What she actually said went something like this:

Nathan was only five years old when the fever struck him. At first, no one knew what was wrong. No one knew that parasites inside his body had infected his red blood cells. No one knew those cells were clumping together, choking the flow of blood through his body and damaging his vital organs. No one knew his kidneys would soon fail and seizures would begin. No one knew he would wind up in a coma.

The parasites in Nathan's body came from a mosquito bite, a bite that gave him malaria. And Nathan is not alone. The World Health Organization tells us the horrible truth: In Africa, a child dies from malaria every 30 seconds.

People who listen to a speech like that will not soon forget it. They may well be moved to action—as the speaker intends. The first speech, however, is not nearly as compelling. Listeners may well nod their heads, think to themselves "good idea"—and then forget about it. The story of Nathan and his tragic fate gives the second speech emotional impact and brings it home to listeners in personal terms.

Speak with Sincerity and Conviction

Ronald Reagan was one of the most effective speakers in recent U.S. history. Even people who disagreed with his political views often found him irresistible. Why? Partly because he seemed to speak with great sincerity and conviction.

What was true for Reagan is true for you as well. The strongest source of emotional power is your conviction and sincerity. All your emotion-laden words and examples are but empty trappings unless *you* feel the emotion yourself. And if you do, your emotion will communicate itself to the audience through everything you say and do—not only through your words, but also through your tone of voice, rate of speech, gestures, and facial expressions.

ETHICS AND EMOTIONAL APPEAL

Much has been written about the ethics of emotional appeal in speechmaking. Some people have taken the extreme position that ethical speakers should avoid emotional appeal entirely. To support this view, they point to speakers who have used emotional appeal to fan the flames of hatred, bigotry, and fanaticism.

There is no question that emotional appeals can be abused by unscrupulous speakers for detestable causes. But emotional appeals can also be wielded by honorable speakers for noble causes—by Winston Churchill to rouse the world against Adolf Hitler and the forces of Nazism, by Martin Luther King to call for racial justice. Few people would question the ethics of emotional appeal in these instances.

Nor is it always possible to draw a sharp line between reason and emotional appeal. Think back to the story of Nathan, the five-year-old boy who was infected with malaria. The story certainly has strong emotional appeal. But is there anything unreasonable about it? Or is it irrational for listeners to respond to it by donating to anti-malarial causes? By the same token, is it illogical to be compassionate for victims of terrorism? Angered by corporate wrongdoing? Fearful about cutbacks in student aid? Reason and emotion often work hand in hand.

One key to using emotional appeal ethically is to make sure it is appropriate to the speech topic. If you want to move listeners to act on a question of policy, emotional appeals are not only legitimate but perhaps necessary. If you want listeners to do something as a result of your speech, you will probably need to appeal to their hearts as well as to their heads.

Emotional language and vivid examples can help generate emotional appeal, but neither are effective unless the speaker talks with genuine sincerity and conviction.

On the other hand, emotional appeals are usually inappropriate in a persuasive speech on a question of fact. Here you should deal only in specific information and logic. Suppose someone charges your state governor with illegal campaign activities. If you respond by saying, "I'm sure the charge is false because I have always admired the governor," or "I'm sure the charge is true because I have always disliked the governor," then you are guilty of applying emotional criteria to a purely factual question.

Even when trying to move listeners to action, you should never substitute emotional appeals for evidence and reasoning. You should *always* build your persuasive speech on a firm foundation of facts and logic. This is important not just for ethical reasons, but for practical ones as well. Unless you prove your case, careful listeners will not be stirred by your emotional appeals. You need to build a good case based on reason *and* kindle the emotions of your audience.[16]

When you use emotional appeal, keep in mind the guidelines for ethical speechmaking discussed in Chapter 2. Make sure your goals are ethically sound, that you are honest in what you say, and that you avoid name-calling and other forms of abusive language. In using emotional appeal, as in other respects, your classroom speeches will offer a good testing ground for questions of ethical responsibility.

Sample Speech with Commentary

The following persuasive speech deals with a question of policy and is organized according to Monroe's motivated sequence. As you read the speech, notice how the speaker utilizes the methods of persuasion discussed in this chapter as she moves through each step of the motivated sequence. The speech also provides an excellent example of how a speaker's delivery can enhance his or her credibility and emotional appeal—as you can see by watching Video Clip 16.4 in the online Media Library for this chapter.

connectlucas.com
View "Making a Difference Through the Special Olympics" in the online Media Library for this chapter (Video Clip 16.4).

Making a Difference Through the Special Olympics

COMMENTARY	SPEECH
The first step in Monroe's motivated sequence is gaining the attention of the audience, which the speaker does with an extended example. In this case, the example also has strong emotional appeal.	In Seattle, nine young athletes gathered at the starting line for the 100-yard dash. At the gun, they all started off, not exactly in a dash, but with a desire to run the race to the finish and win. All except one little boy who stumbled on the asphalt, tumbled over a couple of times, and began to cry. The other runners heard the boy cry. They stopped; they looked back. Then they all went back to the boy's side—every single one of them. One girl with Down syndrome kissed him and said, "This will make it better." Then all nine linked arms and walked to the finish line—together.
The speaker moves from her opening example to reveal the topic of her speech.	These athletes were not competing on national television. They were not sponsored or idolized. But they were given the opportunity to flourish under the glow of their own spotlight, to feel the brush of the ribbon cross their chests as they ran through their own finish line in their own Olympics—the Special Olympics.
Even though all members of her audience knew about the Special Olympics before the speech, the speaker quickly reminds them of the organization's ideals. She then relates the topic directly to her classmates at a personal level.	Founded in 1968, Special Olympics invited the world to let go of limiting views, unyielding prejudices, and ignorant misconceptions about people with cognitive disabilities and to embrace the idea that they can be respected, valued, contributing members of society. Just think, one of the kids who ran through that finish line could have fallen into your arms. Or, maybe one day, could be your own child.
The speaker establishes her credibility and provides a preview statement that leads into the body of the speech.	After working as a volunteer for the Special Olympics and doing additional research for this speech, I'd like to encourage you to become involved as a volunteer for the Special Olympics. We'll start by looking at the need for volunteers.
Now the speaker moves into the need step of Monroe's motivated sequence. Drawing from the Special Olympics Web site, she provides information about the number of participants and the continuing need for volunteers.	According to the Special Olympics Web site, more than 1.3 million people compete in Special Olympics around the world. Participants must be at least eight years old and be identified as having a cognitive or intellectual disability. There are currently 200 Special Olympics programs running in over 150 countries.
Rather than talking about the need for volunteers in general terms, the speaker relates to the audience by focusing on the situation in Wisconsin, where the speech was delivered.	As the Special Olympics continues to grow, so does the need for volunteers. Here in Wisconsin, there are 10,000 athletes and 3,500 volunteer coaches. But because of all the individual attention required by Special Olympics athletes, there's always a need for more volunteer coaches, or for loads of other volunteers as well.

This paragraph begins with a transition into the satisfaction section of the speech. Notice how the speaker explains that one does not need to be a great athlete or have prior coaching experience to volunteer as a Special Olympics coach. This kind of specificity is important whenever a speaker wants to persuade an audience to take immediate action.

The speaker provides options for her listeners by noting that one can volunteer in ways other than coaching and that one's contributions to Special Olympics can vary depending on the level of commitment a person is able to make at a particular time.

Having explained her plan, the speaker moves into the visualization section of her speech, in which she demonstrates the benefits of her plan. This is one of the most important aspects of any persuasive speech on a question of policy.

Drawing on her own experience as a volunteer boosts the speaker's credibility as she explains the personal gratification of working with the Special Olympics. As you can see from the video of the speech in the online Media Library for this chapter, the speaker's sincerity adds immensely to the impact of her ideas.

A transition signals that the speaker is moving into the action section of her speech. Notice how she ties her call for action directly to her classmates by talking in terms of "you" and "your."

Now you know the need for Special Olympics volunteers. So the question is: What can you do to help? The answer is: Become a volunteer. The most obvious way to become a volunteer is to become a coach. Now, you don't have to be a great athlete. You don't have to have any prior coaching experience. Special Olympics offers a general course on the principles of coaching, in addition to a mentoring program in which the new coaches receive guidance from the experienced coaches.

If you don't want to be a coach, there are other ways to help out as well. You can work behind the scenes by assisting with fund-raising or organizing events or any of the other countless details involved in running a huge organization such as Special Olympics. It's also very important that you know that your contribution to Special Olympics can last from a day to a year to a lifetime, depending on the level of commitment that you're ready to make.

No matter how you decide to help, I guarantee you that working with the Special Olympics will be immensely rewarding. As a coach, your instruction and support will help your athletes develop physical skills, while your interaction and friendship will help them develop socially. Ronna Vanderslice, author of the article "Special Olympics: Beneficial to All," reports that individuals who get involved in sports and recreation through Special Olympics develop larger networks of friends, are more likely to socialize with others, and receive more social support.

But it's not just the athletes who benefit from Special Olympics. In my case, working with Special Olympics is one of the most gratifying things I have ever done in my life. Not only do I have the satisfaction that comes from helping others improve the quality of their lives, but I've met so many amazing people and met so many great friends that, really, I would not trade the experience for anything.

Now you know the need for Special Olympics volunteers, some ways that you can help out, and the benefits to the volunteers and athletes alike, so now I'd like to ask you to take the step of getting involved with the Special Olympics. If you want more information, you can check out the Web site for the Special Olympics or visit the local headquarters located on Monona Drive here in Madison. I also have brochures with contact information that I'll be handing out after the speech.

The speaker again stresses that students can adjust volunteering to their personal schedules.	I know you may not have a lot of time available right now, but you can volunteer for the time that fits your schedule. The most important thing is to get involved in some capacity, for whatever amount of time you can manage.
By returning to her opening story, the speaker relates once more to the audience, unifies the entire speech, and strengthens its emotional appeal. Brief and poignant, the closing quotation provides an excellent ending.	Remember the nine children I mentioned at the beginning of this speech. Think of their happiness and their support for one another. Think of how much they gained from running in that race. And think of how you can help others experience the same benefits as they strive to fulfill the motto of the Special Olympics: "Let me win. But if I can't win, let me be brave in the attempt."

SUMMARY

Listeners accept a speaker's ideas for one or more of four reasons—because they perceive the speaker as having high credibility, because they are won over by the speaker's evidence, because they are convinced by the speaker's reasoning, or because they are moved by the speaker's emotional appeals.

Credibility is affected by many factors, but the two most important are competence and character. The more favorably listeners view a speaker's competence and character, the more likely they are to accept her or his ideas. Although credibility is partly a matter of reputation, you can enhance your credibility during a speech by establishing common ground with your listeners, by letting them know why you are qualified to speak on the topic, and by presenting your ideas fluently and expressively.

If you hope to be persuasive, you must also support your views with evidence—examples, statistics, and testimony. Regardless of what kind of evidence you use, it will be more persuasive if it is new to the audience, stated in specific rather than general terms, and from credible sources. Your evidence will also be more persuasive if you state explicitly the point it is supposed to prove.

No matter how strong your evidence, you will not be persuasive unless listeners agree with your reasoning. In reasoning from specific instances, you move from a number of particular facts to a general conclusion. Reasoning from principle is the reverse—you move from a general principle to a particular conclusion. When you use causal reasoning, you try to establish a relationship between causes and effects. In analogical reasoning, you compare two cases and infer that what is true for one is also true for the other. Whatever kind of reasoning you use, avoid fallacies such as hasty generalization, false cause, and invalid analogy. You should also be on guard against the red herring, *ad hominem*, either-or, bandwagon, and slippery slope fallacies.

Finally, you can persuade your listeners by appealing to their emotions. One way to generate emotional appeal is by using emotion-laden language. Another is to develop vivid, richly textured examples. Neither, however, will be effective unless you feel the emotion yourself and communicate it by speaking with sincerity and conviction.

As with other methods of persuasion, your use of emotional appeal should be guided by a firm ethical rudder. Although emotional appeals are usually inappropriate in speeches on questions of fact, they are legitimate—and often necessary—in speeches that seek immediate action on questions of policy. Even when trying to move listeners to action, however, you should never substitute emotional appeals for evidence and reasoning.

ethos *(353)*

credibility *(353)*

initial credibility *(353)*

derived credibility *(353)*

terminal credibility *(353)*

creating common ground *(356)*

evidence *(357)*

logos *(360)*

reasoning *(361)*

reasoning from specific instances *(361)*

hasty generalization *(362)*

reasoning from principle *(363)*

causal reasoning *(365)*

false cause *(365)*

analogical reasoning *(366)*

invalid analogy *(367)*

fallacy *(367)*

red herring *(368)*

ad hominem *(368)*

either-or *(368)*

bandwagon *(369)*

slippery slope *(370)*

pathos *(370)*

REVIEW QUESTIONS

After reading this chapter, you should be able to answer the following questions:

1. What is credibility? What two factors exert the most influence on an audience's perception of a speaker's credibility?

2. What are the differences among initial credibility, derived credibility, and terminal credibility?

3. What are three ways you can enhance your credibility during your speeches?

4. What is evidence? Why do persuasive speakers need to use evidence?

5. What are four tips for using evidence effectively in a persuasive speech?

6. What is reasoning from specific instances? What guidelines should you follow when using this method of reasoning?

7. What is reasoning from principle? How is it different from reasoning from specific instances?

8. What is causal reasoning? What two errors must you be sure to avoid when using causal reasoning?

9. What is analogical reasoning? How do you judge the validity of an analogy?

10. What are the eight logical fallacies discussed in this chapter?

11. What is the role of emotional appeal in persuasive speaking? Identify three methods you can use to generate emotional appeal in your speeches.

connectlucas.com
For further review, go to the Study Questions in the online Study Aids for this chapter.

EXERCISES FOR CRITICAL THINKING

1. Research has shown that a speaker's initial credibility can have great impact on how the speaker's ideas are received by listeners. Research has also shown that a speaker's credibility will vary from topic to topic and audience to audience. In the left-hand column below is a list of well-known public figures. In the right-hand column is a list of potential speech topics. Assume that each speaker will be addressing your speech class.

   For each speaker, identify the topic in the right-hand column on which she or he would have the highest initial credibility for your class. Then explain how the speaker's initial credibility might be affected if the speaker were discussing the topic in the right-hand column directly across from her or his name.

Speaker	**Topic**
Oprah Winfrey	The Comedy of Politics
Bill Gates	Fantasy as Literature
Al Gore	Talk Shows: Their Role in Society
Jon Stewart	The Future of Computers
J. K. Rowling	Environmental Politics

2. Identify the kind of reasoning used in each of the following statements. What weaknesses, if any, can you find in the reasoning of each?

   a. According to a study by the American Medical Association, men with bald spots have three times the risk of heart attack as men with a full head of hair. Strange as it may seem, it looks as if baldness is a cause of heart attacks.

   b. There can be no doubt that the use of cell phones by drivers is a major reason for motor vehicle accidents. In New York, five friends who had just graduated from high school died in a head-on collision with a truck when the car driver lost control while using her phone to send a text message. In Colorado, a 17-year-old was using his cell phone when he struck and killed a bicyclist. In Massachusetts, a man driving an SUV killed a 13-year-old boy playing by the road. When police caught up to the driver, he said he was distracted by his cell phone and thought he had hit a mailbox.

   c. The United States Constitution guarantees all citizens the right to bear arms. Gun control legislation infringes on the right of citizens to bear arms. Therefore, gun control legislation is contrary to the Constitution.

   d. Almost every industrialized nation in the world except for the United States has a national curriculum and national tests to help ensure that schools throughout the country are meeting high standards of education. If such a system can work elsewhere, it can work in the United States as well.

3. Over the years there has been much debate about the role of emotional appeal in public speaking. Do you believe it is ethical for public speakers to use emotional appeals when seeking to persuade an audience? Do you feel there are certain kinds of emotions to which an ethical speaker should not appeal? Why or why not? Be prepared to explain your ideas in class.

4. Analyze "The Horrors of Puppy Mills" in the appendix of sample speeches that follows Chapter 18 (pages A9–A11). Pay special attention to the speaker's credibility, evidence, reasoning, and emotional appeal. View the video of the speech in the online Media Library for this chapter at connectlucas.com so you can also assess his delivery and use of visual aids.

As the service manager for a local home improvement company, you have been pleased to see your company expand its size and scope, but you don't want that growth to come at the expense of customer service. In particular, you're worried about losing touch with one of the company's key demographics—women, who make up 55 percent of your customer base. To prevent this from happening, you have developed a plan for a range of personalized services targeted at women, including one-on-one teaching of do-it-yourself skills and free in-home consultations.

When you present your plan at a meeting of the company's management team, you listen as one executive argues in opposition. Among his points are the following: (1) If your plan is adopted, customers will expect more and more special services and eventually will demand free installation of flooring and carpeting; (2) Because a majority of the management team opposes your plan, it must not be a good idea; (3) One of your competitors tried a customer service plan specifically for women, but it did not succeed; therefore, your plan is doomed to failure.

In your response to the executive, you will point out the fallacy in each of his points. What are those fallacies?

Speaking on Special Occasions

Speeches of Introduction

Speeches of Presentation

Speeches of Acceptance

Commemorative Speeches

Special occasions are the punctuation marks of day-to-day life, the high points that stand out above ordinary routine. Christenings, weddings, funerals, graduations, award ceremonies, inaugurals, retirement dinners—all these are occasions, and they are very special to the people who take part in them. Nearly always they are occasions for speechmaking. A close friend proposes a toast to the bride and groom; the sales manager presents an award to the sales representative of the year; the president delivers an inaugural address; the basketball coach gives a speech honoring the team's most valuable player; a family member delivers a moving eulogy to the deceased. These speeches help give the occasion its "specialness." They are part of the ceremonial aura that marks the event.

Speeches for special occasions are different from the speeches we have considered so far in this book. They may convey information or persuade, but that is not their primary purpose. Rather, they aim to fit the special needs of a special occasion. In this chapter we look at the most common special occasions and the kinds of speeches appropriate for each.

Speeches of Introduction

speech of introduction
A speech that introduces the main speaker to the audience.

"Distinguished guests, the President of the United States." If you are ever in a situation in which you have to introduce the President, you will need no more than the eight words that begin this paragraph. The President is so well known that any further remarks would be inappropriate and almost foolish.

Most of the time, however, a speech of introduction will be neither this brief nor this ritualized. If you are introducing another speaker, you will need to accomplish three purposes in your introduction:

Build enthusiasm for the upcoming speaker.

Build enthusiasm for the speaker's topic.

Establish a welcoming climate that will boost the speaker's credibility.

A good speech of introduction can be a delight to hear and can ease the task of the main speaker. Usually you will say something about the speaker and about the topic—in that order. Following are some guidelines for speeches of introduction.

Be Brief

During World War I, Lord Balfour, Great Britain's foreign secretary, was to be the main speaker at a rally in the United States. But the speaker introducing him gave a 45-minute oration on the causes of the war. Then, almost as an afterthought, he said, "Now Lord Balfour will give his address." Lord Balfour rose and said, "I'm supposed to give my address in the brief time remaining. Here it is: 10 Carleton Gardens, London, England."[1]

Everyone who has ever sat through a long-winded introduction knows how dreary it can be. The purpose of a speech of introduction is to focus attention on the main speaker, not on the person making the introduction. A speech of introduction will usually be no more than two to three minutes long and may be shorter if the speaker is already well known to the audience.

Make Sure Your Remarks Are Completely Accurate

Many an introducer has embarrassed himself or herself, as well as the main speaker, by garbling basic facts. Always check with the speaker ahead of time to make sure your introduction is accurate in every respect.

Above all, get the speaker's name right. If the speaker's name is at all difficult—especially if it involves a foreign pronunciation—practice saying it in advance. However, don't practice so much that you frighten yourself about getting it wrong. This was the plight of an announcer whose gaffe is now a classic: "Ladies and gentlemen, the President of the United States—Hoobert Heever!"

Adapt Your Remarks to the Occasion

In preparing your introduction, you may be constrained by the nature of the occasion. Formal occasions require formal speeches of introduction. If you were presenting a guest speaker at an informal business meeting, you might be much more casual than at a formal banquet.

Adapt Your Remarks to the Main Speaker

No matter how well it is received by the audience, a speech of introduction that leaves the main speaker feeling uncomfortable has failed in part of its purpose. How can you make a main speaker uncomfortable? One way is to overpraise the person—especially for his or her speaking skills. Never say, "Our speaker will keep you on the edge of your seat from beginning to end!" You create a set of expectations that are almost impossible to fulfill.

Another way to create discomfort is by revealing embarrassing details of the speaker's personal life or by making remarks that are in poor taste. An introducer may think this line is funny: "Why, I've known Anita Fratello since she was 10 years old and so fat that everybody called her Blimpo!" To the speaker, however, the statement will probably not be a bit funny and may be painful.

Adapt Your Remarks to the Audience

Just as you adapt other speeches to particular audiences, so you need to adapt a speech of introduction to the audience you are facing. Your aim is to make *this* audience want to hear *this* speaker on *this* subject. If the speaker is not well known to the audience, you will need to establish her or his credibility by recounting some of the speaker's main achievements and explaining why she or he is qualified to speak on the topic at hand. But if the speaker is already personally known to the audience, it would be absurd to act as if the audience had never heard of the person.

Also, you will want to tell each audience what *it* wants to hear—to give the kind of information that is interesting and accessible to the members of that audience. If you were introducing the same speaker to two different groups, some of the information in the speeches of introduction might be the same, but it would be slanted differently. Suppose, for example, J. K. Rowling, author of the Harry Potter series, is going to address two groups—an audience of elementary school children and an audience of educators at the annual meeting

Presidential inaugural addresses are a major kind of special-occasion speech. You can access these historical documents at either the American Presidency Project (www.presidency.ucsb.edu/inaugurals.php) or the Yale Law School's Avalon Project (www.yale.edu/lawweb/avalon/presiden/inaug/inaug.htm).

J. K. Rowling's June 5, 2008, commencement speech at Harvard University is one of the most highly regarded commemorative addresses of recent years. You can read the text and watch the video at the Harvard Magazine Web site (http://harvardmagazine.com/go/jkrowling.html).

of the International Reading Association. The introduction to the schoolchildren might go something like this:

> Children, we have a very important guest today. You know her by the character she has created—Harry Potter. What you don't know is all the hard work that goes into writing the books that we all love to read. Today she is going to tell us how she came up with the idea of Harry Potter and his friends and how she goes about writing her books. Let's give a big round of applause to J. K. Rowling.

But the introduction to the International Reading Association would be along these lines:

> Ladies and gentlemen, it is my privilege to introduce to you today the world's best-selling author. We are all well acquainted with her Harry Potter series that has captured the imagination of children—and more than a few adults—around the globe.
>
> Many of us know the remarkable story of her writing life: The inspiration for Harry Potter came on a train ride from Manchester to London in 1990. Over the next few years, she compiled notes as the story took shape in her mind. The bulk of the writing took place when she was a single mother on public assistance in Edinburgh. She was teaching French to teenagers in the mid-1990s when she heard that the first Harry Potter book had been accepted for publication. The rest is literary history.
>
> She will be telling us this afternoon more about what inspired her fascinating story of wizardry, where she gets her ideas, and what kinds of books she wants to write next. Please give a warm welcome to J. K. Rowling.

Try to Create a Sense of Anticipation and Drama

You may have noticed one detail shared by the two speeches introducing J. K. Rowling: In both cases the speaker's name was saved for last. This is a convention in speeches of introduction. While there may occasionally be a good reason to break the convention, usually you will avoid mentioning the speaker's name until the final moment—even when the audience knows exactly whom you are discussing. By doing this you build a sense of drama, and the speaker's name comes as the climax of your introduction.

Often you will find yourself in the situation of introducing someone who is fairly well known to the audience—a classmate, a colleague at a business meeting, a neighbor in a community group. Then you should try to be creative and cast the speaker in a new light. Talk to the speaker beforehand and see if

Speeches for special occasions are part of the ceremonial aura that helps make certain events special, as in this commencement address by U.S. Congresswoman Linda Sanchez.

you can learn some interesting facts that are not generally known—especially facts that relate to the speaker's topic.

Above all, if you expect to be creative and dramatic, be sure to practice your speech of introduction thoroughly. You should be able to deliver it extemporaneously, with sincerity and enthusiasm.

Speeches of Presentation

Speeches of presentation are given when someone receives a gift, an award, or some other form of public recognition. Usually such speeches are brief. They may be no more than a mere announcement ("And the winner is . . .") or be up to four or five minutes in length.

The main purpose of a speech of presentation is to tell the audience why the recipient is receiving the award. Point out her or his contributions, achievements, and so forth. Do not deal with everything the person has ever done. Focus on achievements related to the award, and discuss these achievements in a way that will make them meaningful to the audience.

speech of presentation
A speech that presents someone a gift, an award, or some other form of public recognition.

Depending on the audience and the occasion, you may also need to discuss two other matters in a speech of presentation. First, if the audience is not familiar with the award, you should explain it briefly. Second, if the award was won in a public competition and the audience knows who the losers are, you might take a moment to praise the losers.

Below is a sample speech of presentation. It was delivered by President Bill Clinton in presenting the Congressional Gold Medal to former South African President Nelson Mandela at a ceremony in the Rotunda of the United States Capitol in Washington, D.C. Because the Congressional Gold Medal is a special honor bestowed by the U.S. Congress, there are no public competitors for the award. Thus Clinton did not need to say anything about the "losers." His speech focused on Mandela's battle against apartheid and his efforts to promote reconciliation among the people of South Africa.

Presenting the Congressional Gold Medal

Bill Clinton

To my friend, President Mandela, Americans as one today, across all the lines that divide us, pay tribute to your struggle, to your achievement, and to the inspiration you have given us to do better. Today we offer a man who has received the Nobel Prize the highest honor within the gift of this country. . . .

Those of us who share his vision and lift him up in honor today owe it to him to build a permanent partnership between Americans and Africans—for the education of our children, for the solution of our problems, for the resolution of our differences, for the elevation of what is best about us all. . . .

In forgiving those who imprisoned him, he reminded us of the most fundamental lesson of all—that in the end apartheid was a defeat of the heart, the mind, the spirit. It was not just a structure outside and jail houses within which people were kept; it was a division of the mind and soul against itself. We owe it to Nelson Mandela not simply to give him this award, but to live by the lesson he taught us and to tear down every last vestige of apartheid in our own hearts—everything that divides us, one from another.

For those of us who have been privileged to know this remarkable man, no medal, no award, no fortune, nothing we could give him could possibly compare to the gift he has given to us and to the world. The only gift that is true recompense is to continue his mission and to live by the power of his profound and wonderful example.

Now, as prescribed by the law, it is my privilege to present the Congressional Gold Medal to President Nelson Mandela.

Speeches of Acceptance

acceptance speech
A speech that gives thanks for a gift, an award, or some other form of public recognition.

The purpose of an acceptance speech is to give thanks for a gift or an award. When giving such a speech, you thank the people who are bestowing the award and recognize the people who helped you gain it.

The acceptance speech on the next page is the companion piece to the speech of presentation by Bill Clinton. It was delivered by Nelson Mandela in accepting the Congressional Gold Medal, and it exemplifies the major traits of a good acceptance speech—brevity, humility, and graciousness.[2]

Commemorative Speeches

Commemorative speeches are speeches of praise or celebration. Eulogies, Fourth of July speeches, and dedications are examples of commemorative speeches. Your aim in such speeches is to pay tribute to a person, a group of people, an institution, or an idea.

As in an informative speech, you probably will have to give the audience information about your subject. After all, the audience must know *why* your

connectlucas.com
View an excerpt from Nelson Mandela's acceptance speech in the online Media Library for this chatper (Video Clip 17.1).

subject is praiseworthy. As in other speeches, you may draw on examples, testimony, even statistics to illustrate the achievements of your subject.

Your fundamental purpose in a commemorative speech, however, is not to inform your listeners but to *inspire* them—to arouse and heighten their appreciation of or admiration for the person, institution, or idea you are praising. If you are paying tribute to a person, for example, you should not simply recount the details of the person's life. Rather, you should penetrate to the *essence* of your subject and generate in your audience a deep sense of respect.

When speaking to commemorate, you want to express feelings, to stir sentiments—joy and hope when a new building is dedicated, anticipation and good wishes at a commencement celebration, lament and consolation at a funeral, admiration and respect at a testimonial dinner. A commemorative speech is like an impressionist painting—"a picture with warm colors and texture capturing a mood or a moment."[3]

But while the painter works with brush and colors, the commemorative speaker works with language. Of all the kinds of speeches, none depends more on the creative and subtle use of language. Some of the most memorable speeches in history, including Abraham Lincoln's Gettysburg Address, have been commemorative. We continue to find such speeches meaningful and inspiring largely because of their eloquent use of language.

One of the most effective commemorative speakers in our recent history was President Ronald Reagan. After the explosion of the space shuttle *Challenger*

commemorative speech
A speech that pays tribute to a person, a group of people, an institution, or an idea.

in 1986, Reagan delivered a nationally televised eulogy to the astronauts killed in the blast. Below are two versions of Reagan's closing lines. The first is what he *might* have said, stripping the text of its warm emotional content and poignant language:

> Like Francis Drake, the great explorer of the oceans, the *Challenger* astronauts gave their lives for a cause to which they were fully dedicated. We are honored by them, and we will not forget them. We will always remember seeing them for the last time this morning as they prepared for their flight.

Here is what Reagan *actually* said:

> There's a coincidence today. On this day 390 years ago, the great explorer Francis Drake died aboard ship off the coast of Panama. In his lifetime the great frontiers were the oceans, and an historian later said, "He lived by the sea, died on it, was buried in it." Well, today we can say of the *Challenger* crew: Their dedication was, like Drake's, complete.
>
> The crew of the space shuttle *Challenger* honored us by the manner in which they lived their lives. We will never forget them, nor the last time we saw them, this morning, as they prepared for their journey and waved goodbye and "slipped the surly bonds of earth" to "touch the face of God."

connectlucas.com
View the ending of Ronald Reagan's eulogy to the *Challenger* astronauts in the online Media Library for this chapter (Video Clip 17.2).

The final words—"'slipped the surly bonds of earth' to 'touch the face of God'"—are especially effective. Drawn from a sonnet called "High Flight" that many pilots keep with them, they ennoble the deaths of the astronauts and end the speech on an eloquent, moving, and poetic note.

When speaking to commemorate, your success will depend on your ability to put into language the thoughts and emotions appropriate to the occasion. It is easy—too easy—to fall back on clichés and trite sentiments. Your challenge will be to use language imaginatively to invest the occasion with dignity, meaning, and honest emotion.

In doing so, you may want to utilize the special resources of language discussed in Chapter 11. Metaphor, simile, parallelism, repetition, antithesis, alliteration—all are appropriate for commemorative speeches. Some highly acclaimed commemorative speeches—including Martin Luther King's "I Have a Dream" and John Kennedy's inaugural address—are distinguished by their creative use of such devices.

Confronted with the evocative speeches of a Kennedy or a King, you may decide that the speech of commemoration is far beyond your abilities. But other students have delivered excellent commemorative speeches—not immortal, perhaps, but nonetheless dignified and moving.

Look, for example, at "My Crazy Aunt Sue" in the appendix of sample speeches that follows Chapter 18 (pages A16–A17). The speaker's aim was to pay tribute to her aunt, who for years had battled rheumatoid arthritis. Although the speaker provides basic information about aunt Sue and her physical condition, the speech does not recount all the details of her life. Instead, it focuses on her courage, her sense of humor, and her refusal to complain about her fate. The speaker provides enough details to let us see why aunt Sue is so commendable, but not so many as to slow the pace of the speech.

Whether given on the world stage or in one's local community, speeches for special occasions should seek to invest the occasion with dignity, meaning, and honest emotion.

connectlucas.com
View "My Crazy Aunt Sue" in the online Media Library for this chapter (Video Clip 17.3).

The speaker also uses vivid language, repetition, and parallel structure to give the speech the kind of formal tone appropriate for a commemorative speech. You can see this even in the opening lines:

The strongest person I know cannot peel a potato. The strongest person I know has trouble putting on her makeup. The strongest person I know needs a special key holder to turn the key in her car's ignition.

In addition to arousing curiosity about the subject of the speech, these lines have a simple elegance that comes partly from the repetition of "The strongest person I know" at the start of each sentence. Consider, in contrast, how much less effective the opening would have been if the speaker had said:

My aunt Sue can't peel a potato, has trouble putting on her makeup, and needs a special key holder to turn the key in her car's ignition.

These lines convey the same information, but not with the same effect.

For another example, consider the student commemorative speech printed on page 390. The subject is Elie Wiesel, humanitarian, Nobel Peace Prize winner, and tireless campaigner for international justice. Notice how the speaker uses the repetition of "A-7713" to capture attention at the beginning and to give the speech artistic unity at the end. Also notice how he tells us enough about Wiesel to know why he is praiseworthy without getting bogged down in biographical details.

Elie Wiesel

A-7713. His new name, the graffiti stamped on his skin. A-7713, a concentration camp tattoo. At age fifteen, A-7713 was taken from his home by the Nazis and sent to Auschwitz, one of the twentieth century's most potent symbols of evil. Here A-7713 witnessed the deaths of thousands of human beings, including his mother and younger sister. Somehow, A-7713 survived, and when World War II ended, he put his pain and grief to work making sure the world did not forget the Holocaust and making sure another Holocaust did not take place.

Today the world knows A-7713 as Elie Wiesel, noted speaker and lecturer, author of more than 40 books, and recipient of the Presidential Medal of Freedom, the Congressional Gold Medal, and the Nobel Peace Prize, among others. Elie Wiesel is an eloquent, fearless, selfless leader who took the evils of Auschwitz as motivation to improve the world.

An eloquent leader, Elie Wiesel uses the power of language to confront the problems of humanity. Through compelling prose and brutal honesty, he explains that we cannot root out evil unless we recognize it and battle it wherever it exists. In his classic book, *Night,* he says of Auschwitz: "Never shall I forget that night, the first night in camp, which turned my life into one long night, seven times cursed and seven times sealed. Never shall I forget that smoke. Never shall I forget the little faces of the children, whose bodies I saw turned into wreaths of smoke beneath a silent blue sky." Haunting words that remind us of the reality of evil.

A fearless leader no less than an eloquent one, Elie Wiesel has spent 40 years battling the evils that continue to plague our planet. To the Miskito Indians of Nicaragua, displaced from their homeland, he brought inspiring words of strength and compassion. To men and women facing apartheid in South Africa, he brought a powerful denunciation of racial segregation and violence. To Cambodian refugees suffering from starvation and disease, he brought food and the promise of a new beginning. And to those of us who follow his work, he continues to provide inspiration.

A selfless leader as much as an eloquent and fearless one, Elie Wiesel has consistently put the needs of others before his own. With every award, his modesty stands side by side with his achievements. As he stated in his Nobel Prize acceptance speech, "Neutrality helps the oppressor, never the victim. Silence encourages the tormentor, never the tormented. . . . Wherever men and women are persecuted because of their race, religion, or political views, that place must—at that moment—become the center of the universe."

Today, at 80 years of age, Elie Wiesel continues to fight against the night. Through all his trials and all his triumphs, the tattoo remains: A-7713, a constant reminder of evil, injustice, and indifference. In battling these forces, Elie Wiesel has shown the kind of moral leadership too often lacking in today's world.

There is no better way to conclude than to quote his own words: "There may be times when we are powerless to prevent injustice, but there must never be a time when we fail to protest. . . . What these victims need above all is to know that they are not alone, that we are not forgetting them, that while their freedom depends on ours, the quality of our freedom depends on theirs."

connectlucas.com
View "Elie Wiesel" in the online Media Library for this chapter (Video Clip 17.4).

In this chapter we have considered speeches of introduction, speeches of presentation, speeches of acceptance, and commemorative speeches.

Your job in a speech of introduction is to build enthusiasm for the main speaker and to establish a welcoming climate. Keep your remarks brief, make sure they are accurate, and adapt them to the audience, the occasion, and the main speaker.

Speeches of presentation are given when someone receives a gift or an award. The main theme of such a speech is to acknowledge the achievements of the recipient. The purpose of an acceptance speech is to give thanks for a gift or an award. When delivering such a speech, you should thank the people who are bestowing the award and recognize the contributions of people who helped you gain it. Be brief, humble, and gracious.

Commemorative speeches are speeches of praise or celebration. Your aim in such a speech is to pay tribute to a person, a group of people, an institution, or an idea. A commemorative speech should inspire the audience, and its success will depend largely on how well you put into language the thoughts and feelings appropriate to the occasion.

KEY TERMS

speech of introduction *(382)*

speech of presentation *(385)*

acceptance speech *(386)*

commemorative speech *(387)*

REVIEW QUESTIONS

After reading this chapter, you should be able to answer the following questions:

1. What are the three purposes of a speech of introduction? What guidelines should you follow in preparing such a speech?

2. What is the main theme of a speech of presentation? Depending on the audience and occasion, what two other themes might you include in such a speech?

3. What are the three major traits of a good acceptance speech?

4. What is the fundamental purpose of a commemorative speech? Why does a successful commemorative speech depend so much on the creative and subtle use of language?

connectlucas.com
For further review, go to the Study Questions in the online Study Aids for this chapter.

EXERCISES FOR CRITICAL THINKING

1. Attend a speech on campus. Pay special attention to the speech introducing the main speaker. How well does it fit the guidelines discussed in this chapter?

2. Observe several speeches of presentation and acceptance—at a campus awards ceremony or on a television program such as the Academy Awards, Grammy Awards, Emmy Awards, or Tony Awards. Which speeches do you find most effective? Least effective? Why?

3. Analyze "Elie Wiesel" (page 390) in light of the criteria for commemorative speaking presented in this chapter.

Speaking in Small Groups

What Is a Small Group?

Leadership in Small Groups
  Kinds of Leadership
  Functions of Leadership

Responsibilities in a Small Group
  Commit Yourself to the Goals of Your Group
  Fulfill Individual Assignments
  Avoid Interpersonal Conflicts
  Encourage Full Participation
  Keep the Discussion on Track

The Reflective-Thinking Method
  Define the Problem
  Analyze the Problem
  Establish Criteria for Solutions
  Generate Potential Solutions
  Select the Best Solution

Presenting the Recommendations of the Grou
  Oral Report
  Symposium
  Panel Discussion

The publisher of a national sports magazine asked Mike Lee, the new head of the human resources department, to organize an October retreat for the magazine's editorial staff. Mike went to work on setting a date, finding a place to stay, and creating an agenda for the retreat.

Mike was very pleased with his plan. He thought he had taken everyone's needs into account. But when he explained his plan at the magazine's next staff meeting, no one seemed happy.

"The date you set for the retreat is over Halloween," said the editorial manager. "I know you don't have children, but no one with kids is going to want to be away at that time."

The administrative assistant responded next. "Do you realize," she said, "that the hotel you booked is the same one we used for a retreat five years ago? It was a disaster! The food was awful, the meeting rooms were uncomfortable, and the tech support was nonexistent."

Next a member of the magazine's junior editorial staff said, "I see that all the sessions involve members of the senior editorial staff. Did you mean to exclude all the younger editors? Don't you think we're important to the magazine?"

Finally, the managing editor said, "I wish you had checked with me at some point. I could have warned you about the hotel, the conflict with Halloween, and the need to include junior staff."

What went wrong? Mike did not have enough time or resources on his own to create a successful retreat. If a group, instead of a single person, had been assigned to plan the retreat, the problems might have been averted. One person could have taken charge of looking into the best dates, another of finding accommodations, a third of coordinating with other staff members about who should be included in the retreat, and so forth. The plan would have taken *all* factors into account.

Of course, you may have heard the old saying that "a camel is a horse designed by a committee." If you have ever been part of a group that seemed to get nothing done, you may be inclined to say, "Oh, let one person decide and get it over with." The problem in such cases, however, is not that there is a group, but that the group is not functioning properly. A great deal of research shows that if members of a group work well together, they can almost always resolve a problem better than a single person.[1]

This chapter deals with speaking in a particular kind of group—the problem-solving small group.

What Is a Small Group?

dyad
A group of two people.

small group
A collection of three to twelve people who assemble for a specific purpose.

As its name implies, a small group has a limited number of members. The minimum number is three. (A group of two persons is called a *dyad,* and it operates quite differently from a group of three or more.) There is some difference of opinion about the maximum number of people who constitute a small group. Most experts set the maximum number at seven or eight; some go as high as twelve. The important point is that the group must be small enough to allow free discussion among all members. In small-group communication, all participants are potentially speakers *and* listeners.

Members of a small group assemble for a specific purpose. Several shoppers milling around the clothing section of a department store are not a small group, even if they speak to one another or comment about high prices and poor service. But if those same shoppers decided to meet together and prepare a formal complaint to the store manager about high prices and poor service, they would then constitute a small group.

A *problem-solving small group* is formed to solve a particular problem. Such groups exist in every area of life. Business groups consider ways of increasing sales. Church groups discuss how to raise funds and provide for the needy. Groups of parents work on improving day care facilities. You will almost surely be a member of many problem-solving small groups during your life.

problem-solving small group
A small group formed to solve a particular problem.

Although speaking in a small group is not the same as public speaking, it involves similar skills. Members of a small group influence one another through communication. As a participant in a small group, you might influence your colleagues by giving them important information, by encouraging them to speak, by convincing them to change their minds, by leading them into a new channel of communication, even by getting them to end a meeting of the group. All other members of the group have the same opportunity to influence you through effective communication.[2]

Leadership in Small Groups ••

We have said that small groups often make better decisions than do individuals. To do so, however, they need effective leadership.

KINDS OF LEADERSHIP

Sometimes there is *no specific leader.* In such a situation, members of effective groups tend to have equal influence. When a need for leadership arises, any of the members can—and one probably will—provide the necessary leadership. A typical instance might be a class project, in which you and several classmates are working together. From time to time each of you will help the group move toward its goal by suggesting when and where to meet, by outlining the strengths and weaknesses of a certain viewpoint, by resolving disagreements among other members, and so forth.

leadership
The ability to influence group members so as to help achieve the goals of the group.

A group may have an *implied leader.* For example, if a business meeting includes one vice president and several subordinates, the vice president becomes the implied leader. The same is true if one member of the group is a specialist in the topic at hand and the others are not. Members will likely defer to the person with the highest rank or greatest expertise.

implied leader
A group member to whom other members defer because of her or his rank, expertise, or other quality.

Even when a group starts out leaderless, there may be an *emergent leader.* This is a person who, by ability or by force of personality, or just by talking the most, takes a leadership role. The emergence of a leader may or may not be desirable. If the group is stalemated or has dissolved into bickering or making jokes, an emergent leader can put it back on track. There is a danger, however, that the emergent leader may not be the most effective leader but merely the most assertive personality.

emergent leader
A group member who emerges as a leader during the group's deliberations.

Finally, there may be a *designated leader*—a person elected or appointed as leader when the group is formed. A group that meets for only one session should almost always have a designated leader who takes care of the procedural tasks and serves as spokesperson. Likewise, a formal committee will usually have a designated chairperson. The chair can perform leadership functions or delegate them, but he or she remains in charge.

designated leader
A person who is elected or appointed as leader when the group is formed.

Small groups require effective leadership to accomplish their goals. Some groups have a designated leader, while others have an implied leader or an emergent leader.

A group may or may not need a specific leader, but it always needs leader-*ship*. When all members of the group are skilled communicators, they can take turns at providing leadership even if the group has a designated or implied leader. As you develop group communication skills, you should be prepared to assume a leadership role whenever necessary.[3]

FUNCTIONS OF LEADERSHIP

An effective leader helps the group reach its goals by fulfilling three overlapping sets of needs—procedural needs, task needs, and maintenance needs.

Procedural Needs

procedural needs
Routine "housekeeping" actions necessary for the efficient conduct of business in a small group.

Procedural needs can be thought of as the "housekeeping" requirements of the group. They include:

Deciding when and where the group will meet.

Reserving the room, checking the number of chairs, making sure the heat or air conditioning is turned on.

Setting the agenda of each meeting.

Starting the meeting.

Taking notes during the meeting.

Preparing and distributing any written handouts needed for the meeting.

Summarizing the group's progress at the end of the meeting.

If there is a designated leader, she or he can attend to these needs or assign one or more group members to do so. Otherwise, members of the group must split the procedural responsibilities.

Task Needs

Task needs are substantive actions necessary to help the group complete the particular task it is working on. They include:

Analyzing the issues facing the group.

Distributing the workload among the members.

Collecting information.

Soliciting the views of other members.

Keeping the group from going off on a tangent.

Playing devil's advocate for unpopular ideas.

Formulating criteria for judging the most effective solution.

Helping the group reach consensus on its final recommendations.

Most members will help the group satisfy its task needs. Leadership becomes necessary when some task needs are not being fulfilled adequately, as in this example:

> A group of students had undertaken to solve the parking problems on their campus. The group had held several meetings, and most of its task needs had been met. Members had done a good job polling students for their opinions, discussing alternative solutions with the administration, and considering the relative merits of each solution. However, one member of the group, Pilar, noticed that two items had not been given enough attention: No one had investigated potential sources of money for new parking facilities, and no one had studied the environmental impact of constructing additional parking spaces. Therefore, Pilar briefly took a leadership role to perform a task need for the group. She pointed out that these two areas had been neglected and recommended that the group explore them further.

task needs
Substantive actions necessary to help a small group complete its assigned task.

Maintenance Needs

Maintenance needs involve interpersonal relations in the group. They include such factors as:

How well members get along with one another.

How willing members are to contribute to the group.

Whether members are supportive of one another.

Whether members feel satisfied with the group's accomplishments.

Whether members feel good about their roles in the group.

If interpersonal problems dominate discussion, the group will have a difficult time working together and reaching a decision. A leader can do much to create and sustain supportive communication in the group. By helping group members handle conflict, by working out differences of opinion, by reducing interpersonal tension, by encouraging participation from all members, by being alert to personal feelings, and by promoting solidarity within the group, a leader can make a tremendous contribution toward helping the group achieve its goals.[4]

maintenance needs
Communicative actions necessary to maintain interpersonal relations in a small group.

Responsibilities in a Small Group

Every member of a small group must assume certain responsibilities, which can be divided into five major categories: (1) commit yourself to the goals of your group; (2) fulfill individual assignments; (3) avoid interpersonal conflicts; (4) encourage full participation; (5) keep the discussion on track. Some of these responsibilities involve leadership roles, but all five are so important that each participant should take them as personal obligations, regardless of the group's leadership.

COMMIT YOURSELF TO THE GOALS OF YOUR GROUP

For a group to succeed, members must align their personal goals with the group's goal. This sounds obvious, but it is not always easy. When you are working with other students on a class project, the group goal—and most likely the goal of each member—is to get a good grade. There is a strong incentive for members to cooperate and commit themselves to completing the task.

Problems arise when one or more members have personal goals that conflict with the group's goal. Here is the kind of situation that can occur:

Sherri Baines is a member of the committee to buy new equipment for the local newspaper's employee cafeteria. Because the budget is very tight, the committee's goal is to get the best equipment for the lowest price. But unknown to the other members of the group, Sherri's son-in-law is a salesman for a distributor of high-priced kitchen appliances. Privately, Sherri has reasoned that if she can sway the committee toward that company, her son-in-law will get a large commission. Sherri does not mention this fact to the group. Instead, she argues that quality—not price—should be the determining factor in the purchase. The group process breaks down because Sherri will not surrender her private goal.

This is an extreme example, but there can be more subtle kinds of private goals, as in the following case:

Carlos and Rachel are part of a group, and Carlos would like to be on closer terms with Rachel. To impress her, he may agree with everything she says, regardless of whether he really shares her views. Consequently, Carlos's expressed views are not his actual views. In short, Carlos has a *hidden agenda* in the group meeting. The group's agenda is to solve the problem, but Carlos's agenda is to get a date with Rachel.

hidden agenda

A set of unstated individual goals that may conflict with the goals of the group as a whole.

Group members may have all sorts of hidden agendas. One may be experiencing personal problems—lowered grades, a breakup with a friend, or just a bad day. Another may have a commitment to a different group whose goals conflict with those of the present group. A third may want to take charge of the group for reasons of personal power, regardless of the group's task.

Remember that what one member of a group does affects all the other members. You should not try to advance your own interests or boost your own ego at the expense of the group and its goals. Beware of hidden agendas—whether yours or someone else's—and participate with a positive spirit.

FULFILL INDIVIDUAL ASSIGNMENTS

As mentioned earlier, one of the advantages of the group process is that it divides the workload among several people. But unless every member fulfills his or her assignments, the group's entire project may fail—as in the following example:

Several years ago, one student group decided that as a class project they would bring Easter baskets to the patients in the children's ward of a local hospital. After the project had been approved, assignments were given out. Navid would coordinate with the hospital authorities. Corrine would handle fund-raising for the needed supplies. Jesse would supervise the egg-decorating team. Liu would be responsible for buying baskets and chocolate bunnies. Justin would arrange for transportation.

Everybody completed their assignments except Justin, who was busy writing a term paper. He asked a friend to pick up a bus schedule and assumed everything would be fine. On Easter morning the group assembled at the bus stop, loaded down with baskets for the children. And they waited and waited. After an hour Justin called the bus company, only to discover that the buses did not run on holidays. By the time Justin had made other arrangements to get to the hospital, visiting hours were over, and the group could not get in.

No matter what other assignments they may have, *all* members of a group have one very critical assignment—listening. First, it helps you understand what is happening in the group. And unlike a public speaking situation, you can stop the speaker and ask for clarification at any point. Second, listening helps you evaluate the merits of the speaker's position. Third, listening provides support for the speaker and helps provide a positive climate for discussion. Without effective listening, no group is going to make much progress.

AVOID INTERPERSONAL CONFLICTS

If groups were made up of robots, there would be no interpersonal conflicts. But groups are made up of people with likes and dislikes and animosities and prejudices and very different personalities. It is vital to the group process that disagreements be kept on a task level, rather than on a personal level.

Suppose you disagree with another member's idea. Disagreement on the personal level could sound like this: "That's the most stupid idea I ever heard of! Do you realize how much money it would cost to do that?" But on the task level, disagreement is aimed at the *idea*, not the person: "Potentially that's a very good solution, but I'm not sure we have enough money to accomplish it."

No matter what the group, personal antagonism leaves a bad taste in everyone's mouth and harms the performance of the group. It's essential that someone take a leadership role and bring the discussion back to the relevant issues. Let's say you are part of a committee charged with setting up a speakers' series on your campus. The discussion might go like this:

Angela: We definitely should have Representative Hightower speak on campus. He has been very active in protecting the environment.

Minh: That liberal? He could care less what we pay for a gallon of gas. And forget about economic development with him.

Angela: So you support more offshore drilling? You're willing to destroy our coastlines so the oil companies can rake in more profits?

Minh: It's people like you that have made us dependent on foreign sources of oil— which threatens our prosperity and national security by making us vulnerable to economic blackmail from abroad.

Leader: Just a minute. This might make a good subject for our speakers' series. We can ask both Representative Hightower and a spokesperson for one of the oil companies to debate each other.

Interested in learning more about leadership? Log on to the Center for Creative Leadership's research site at www.ccl.org/research/. The center works with individuals and groups around the world to help organizations of all kinds improve their managerial and leadership skills.

Small groups are a vital part of businesses and other organizations in most parts of the world. You can get a sense of their activities by checking the Team-Building Ezine Articles at http://ezinearticles.com/?cat=Business:Team-Building.

This is not to say that members of a group should never disagree. In fact, a serious problem occurs when members get along so well and are so concerned about maintaining the harmony of the group that they will not disagree with one another about anything. When this happens, there is no chance to reach the best decision by exploring an array of perspectives, opinions, and information. The aim is not for groups to avoid conflict but to keep it at the task level so it will not degenerate into personal feuding.[5]

ENCOURAGE FULL PARTICIPATION

If a group is to work effectively, all members must contribute fully and share their ideas with one another. Every member of a group should take responsibility for encouraging other members to participate. You can do this, first of all, by listening attentively. After all, how would you like to speak in a group where everybody else appears bored or distracted?

If there are one or two quiet members in the group, you can draw them into the discussion by asking their opinions and showing interest in their ideas. When a member speaks, you can say, "I never knew that; can you tell us more about it?" Conversely, try to avoid negative comments that will squelch a speaker before she or he has finished—comments like "Oh, no, that never works" or "What a terrible idea." Supportive comments create goodwill among group members and make everyone feel free to discuss their ideas without ridicule or embarrassment.

If you are shy or afraid your ideas will be taken too critically, you may be unwilling to participate at first. To overcome your diffidence, remember that your contribution is necessary to the group. At the very least, you can help provide a supportive environment for discussion by listening, reacting, and encouraging the free exchange of ideas.

KEEP THE DISCUSSION ON TRACK

In some groups the discussion proceeds like a stream-of-consciousness exercise. Here is a hypothetical example in which a town planning board is considering installing a new traffic light at a busy intersection:

Sharif: You know, we're going to have trouble getting cars to come to a full stop even if we do put in a traffic light.

Diana: Tell me about it! I came through there yesterday and hit my brakes, and the car just kept going. Maybe I need the brakes adjusted, though.

In effective small groups, all members participate fully and interact with each other. They also feel that their contributions are respected and valued by the full group.

Mike: Get ready to pay through the nose. I had a brake job on my car last week, and it was nearly twice as much as last time.

Austin: That's nothing. Have you looked at lawnmowers lately? And if you think lawnmowers are high …

Jill: Who mows lawns? I had my yard planted with ground cover and put gravel over the rest. It's …

Leader: Excuse me, folks, but weren't we talking about the *traffic light*?

Every member has a responsibility to keep the discussion on track and to intervene if the group wanders too far afield. There is nothing wrong with a little casual conversation, but it shouldn't be allowed to get out of hand. When working in a problem-solving group, make sure the group's ultimate goal is always in the forefront. Do your best to see that discussion proceeds in an orderly fashion from one point to the next and that the group does not get bogged down in side issues.

On the other hand, you need to guard against the tendency to progress to a solution too quickly, without thoroughly exploring the problem. If you feel your group is taking the easy way out and jumping at an easy solution, try to make the other members aware of your concern. By suggesting that they talk about the problem in more detail, you may bring out vital information or ideas. One group learned the perils of making a snap decision:

The board of the town library met to discuss ways to get more children to visit the library during the upcoming spring vacation. Near the beginning of the meeting one member suggested sponsoring a parade through town in which children would march to the library dressed as their favorite book character. After a joke about all the Harry Potter clones who would show up, the board members agreed that it was a terrific idea. They wrapped up their session early, congratulating themselves on having reached a solution so easily.

But what looked at first like a great idea proved to have a crucial drawback. Any parades in the town had to be approved by the town council and cleared with the police department. There was not enough time before spring vacation to apply for these permissions and get them approved. The quick solution proved to be no solution at all.

Fortunately, there are systematic ways to keep the discussion on track and to avoid hasty group decisions. Research shows that if your group follows a tested method of decision making, it will have a much better chance of reaching a satisfactory outcome.[6] We turn, therefore, to the most common decision-making technique for small groups—the reflective-thinking method.

The Reflective-Thinking Method

reflective-thinking method
A five-step method for directing discussion in a problem-solving small group.

The reflective-thinking method is derived from the writings of the American philosopher John Dewey. It offers a step-by-step process for discussion in problem-solving groups and consists of five steps: (1) defining the problem; (2) analyzing the problem; (3) establishing criteria for solving the problem; (4) generating potential solutions; (5) selecting the best solution. As we look at these steps, we'll illustrate each by following a single group through the entire reflective-thinking process.

DEFINE THE PROBLEM

Before a problem-solving group can make progress, it must know exactly what problem it is trying to solve. Defining the problem for group discussion is akin to settling on a specific purpose for a speech. Unless it is done properly, everything that follows will suffer.

The best way to define the problem is to phrase it as a question of policy. As we saw in Chapter 15, questions of policy inquire about the necessity or practicality of specific courses of action. They typically include the word "should." For example:

question of policy
A question about whether a specific course of action should or should not be taken.

What measures should our school take to improve on-campus security for students?

What steps should the federal government take to protect civil liberties without harming the war on terrorism?

What policy should the United States adopt with respect to the exploitation of child labor in other countries around the world?

When phrasing the question for discussion, your group should follow several guidelines. First, make sure the question is as clear and specific as possible. For example:

Ineffective: What should be done about fraudulent charities?

More Effective: What should the federal government do to control the activities of fraudulent charities?

Second, phrase the question to allow for a wide variety of answers. Be especially wary of questions that can be answered with a simple yes or no. For example:

Ineffective:	Should the city build a new elementary school?
More Effective:	What steps should the city take to deal with increasing enrollment in the elementary schools?

Third, avoid biased or slanted questions. For example:

Ineffective:	How can we keep the campus bookstore from ripping off students?
More Effective:	What changes, if any, should be made in the pricing policies of the campus bookstore?

Fourth, make sure you pose a single question. For example:

Ineffective:	What revisions should the college consider in its admissions requirements and in its graduation requirements?
More Effective:	What revisions should the college consider in its admissions requirements?
More Effective:	What revisions should the college consider in its graduation requirements?

To clarify this first step of the reflective-thinking method, let's see how our model problem-solving group defined the problem:

As a class project, the group set out to discuss the problem of rising costs for attending college. Following the reflective-thinking method, they began by defining the problem. After several false starts, they phrased the problem this way: "What steps should our school take to reduce student costs for attending college?"

ANALYZE THE PROBLEM

After the problem has been defined, the group begins to analyze it. Too often, groups (like individuals) start mapping out solutions before they have a firm grasp of what is wrong. This is like a doctor prescribing treatment before fully diagnosing the patient's ailment. If your group investigates the problem as thoroughly as possible, you will be in a much better position to devise a workable solution.

In analyzing the problem, pay particular attention to two questions. First, how severe is the problem? Investigate the scope of the problem. Determine how many people it affects. Assess what might happen if the problem is not resolved. Second, what are the causes of the problem? Check the history of the problem and learn what factors contributed to it.

As you might imagine, analyzing the problem requires research. Effective group decisions depend on having the best information available. You can get this information in the same way you gather materials for a speech. Sometimes you can rely on your own knowledge and experience. More often, you need to get information from other sources—by looking on the Internet, by interviewing someone with expertise on the topic, or by working in the library (see Chapter 6). When meeting with your group, make sure you have done the research assigned to you so you can offer complete and unbiased information.

Let's return now to our sample group and see how it analyzed the problem of rapidly escalating student costs for attending college:

The group talked first about the severity of the problem. Tuition had risen dramatically, as had outlays for books and incidentals. One member found statistics showing that the cost of attending college had more than doubled in the past 10 years. Another provided evidence that average annual costs were now close to $15,000 for students at in-state public colleges and universities, and roughly $35,000 for students at private schools.

To determine the causes of the problem, the group researched articles about the rise in student costs for attending college across the nation. They also interviewed an economics professor and the head of the student aid program on campus. After studying the matter thoroughly, the group identified several major causes, including administrative costs, faculty salaries, the price of textbooks, and increased living expenses.

ESTABLISH CRITERIA FOR SOLUTIONS

If you planned to buy a car, how would you proceed? You would probably not just walk into a showroom and buy whatever appealed to you on the spur of the moment. You would most likely decide ahead of time what kind of car you wanted, what options it should have, and how much money you could spend. That is, you would establish *criteria* to guide you in deciding exactly which car to buy.

You should do the same thing in group discussion. Once your group has analyzed the problem, you should not jump immediately to proposing solutions. Instead, you should establish criteria—standards—for responsible solutions. You should work out (and write down) exactly what your solutions must achieve and any factors that might limit your choice of solutions.

criteria
Standards on which a judgment or decision can be based.

To get a better idea of how this stage of the reflective-thinking method works, let's look at the cost-cutting group we have been following:

After some discussion, the group established these criteria for possible solutions: (1) The solution should significantly reduce students' costs. (2) The solution should come into force at the start of the next school year. (3) The solution should not hurt the prestige of the college. (4) The cost of the solution should be minimal and should be paid by the administration. (5) The human resources needed to implement the solution should come from administrative personnel already working on the school's staff. (6) The solution should involve only actions controlled by the college—not matters controlled by outside individuals or agencies.

GENERATE POTENTIAL SOLUTIONS

Once your group has the criteria firmly in mind, you are ready to discuss solutions. Your goal at this stage is to come up with the widest possible range of potential solutions—not to judge the solutions. One member of the group should be responsible for writing down all the solutions proposed at this time.

brainstorming
A method of generating ideas by free association of words and thoughts.

Many groups find the technique of *brainstorming* helpful in this stage. In Chapter 4 we discussed how brainstorming can work for an individual in choosing a speech topic. Here brainstorming is expanded to the whole group.

The best approach is to begin by having each member of the group write down all the possible solutions he or she can think of. One person should then consolidate the individual lists into a master list. The group should discuss the master list to make sure potential solutions have not been overlooked. At this

Working in a small group requires many of the skills involved in public speaking. Formal presentations may occur during a group's deliberations or when the group presents its report.

stage, members often "piggyback" new ideas onto ideas on the master list. For example, if one suggestion is "Establish food co-ops," a group member might say, "Yes, and we could establish clothing co-ops, too." One member should write down these new ideas and add them to the master list. The brainstorming process continues until the group cannot think of any more solutions.

Brainstorming in this fashion has two advantages. First, it encourages creativity. Research shows that beginning with written lists usually produces more and higher-quality ideas than relying solely on oral discussion.[7] Second, this method of brainstorming encourages equal participation. Having each member create his or her own list makes it less likely that one or two members will dominate the process or that anyone will hold back ideas for fear of being hooted down.

Let's see how our cost-cutting group handled this stage:

By brainstorming, the group came up with the following possible solutions: (1) reduce the number of required books for each course; (2) cut some of the "fat" from the administrative staff; (3) make all professors teach more courses; (4) approach landlords about stabilizing rent and utility costs; (5) establish food and clothing co-ops; (6) increase financial aid; (7) decrease the amount of money available for faculty research; (8) boycott businesses around the campus where price markups are highest; (9) increase out-of-state tuition; (10) decrease dormitory expenses; (11) organize fund-raising programs with the student government; (12) redirect some money from construction of new buildings to student aid. This was a good yield from a brainstorming session—12 solid suggestions.

SELECT THE BEST SOLUTION

After all potential solutions have been listed, it is time to evaluate them. The best way to proceed is to discuss each solution with regard to the criteria established earlier, then move to the next solution, and so on. This orderly process ensures that all potential solutions receive equal consideration.

As each potential solution is discussed, the group should try to reach *consensus*. A consensus decision is one that all members accept, even though

Checklist — Reflective-Thinking Method

YES ✓ NO

1. Did the group clearly define the problem for discussion?

2. Did the group phrase the question for discussion as a question of policy?

3. Did the group phrase the question for discussion as clearly as possible?

4. Did the group phrase the question for discussion so as to allow for a wide variety of answers?

5. Did the group phrase the question for discussion in an unbiased manner?

6. Did the group phrase the question for discussion as a single question?

7. Did the group analyze the problem thoroughly before attempting to map out solutions?

8. Did the group establish criteria for an ideal solution to the problem before discussing specific solutions?

9. Did the group brainstorm to generate a wide range of potential solutions to the problem?

10. Did the group evaluate each potential solution in light of the criteria for an ideal solution?

11. Did the group make a determined effort to reach consensus with regard to the best solution?

12. Did the group achieve consensus?

consensus
A group decision that is acceptable to all members of the group.

the decision may not be ideal in the eyes of every member. Because it usually results in superior decisions as well as in a high degree of unity within the group, consensus is the ideal of group decision making. It comes about when members have been so cooperative that they reach a common decision through reasoning, honest exchange of ideas, and full examination of the issues.

Like most ideals, consensus can be difficult to achieve. If there are different viewpoints, members of the group will often try to find the easiest way to resolve the differences. Sometimes a member will call for a vote, which is very agreeable to those holding a majority opinion but not so pleasant for those in the minority. Resorting to a vote does resolve the immediate conflict, but it may not result in the best solution. Moreover, it weakens unity in the group by fostering factions and perhaps by creating bitterness among the members who lose the vote. A group should vote only when it has failed in every other attempt to agree on a solution.

What kind of final decision did our model cost-cutting group reach? Let's see:

The cost-cutting group had 12 possible solutions to evaluate. Three were rejected because they violated the group's criterion that an acceptable solution must involve only actions controlled directly by the college. Redirecting building money to student aid could be done only by the state legislature. Approaching landlords about stabilizing rent and boycotting campus businesses were also outside the jurisdiction of college administrators.

Three more solutions were rejected because they were economically impractical. Increasing financial aid would hurt many students because the funds would have to come from student fees. Raising out-of-state tuition would drive away too many out-of-state students. And decreasing dorm costs would make it impossible to provide minimally acceptable services.

The proposal to reduce funds for faculty research was also rejected since most research money comes from government, corporations, and foundations. Besides, research was recognized as a primary means of maintaining the college's prestige. Finally, the suggestion to reduce administrative "fat" was rejected as too costly because a group would have to be established to audit all administrative duties.

After refining the suggestions, the group finally reached consensus on a solution that included the following provisions: (1) A student should not have to spend more than $200 on required books for any single course. (2) The university should authorize the student government to organize food, book, and clothing co-ops. (3) The student government should conduct five fund-raising projects each academic year. (4) Each professor should teach one more class a year.

Once consensus has been reached, the group is ready to present its findings.[8]

Presenting the Recommendations of the Group

The work of a problem-solving group does not end with the last stage of the reflective-thinking process. Once a group has agreed on its recommendations, it usually needs to present them to somebody. A business group might report to the president of the company or to the board of directors. A presidential commission reports to the President and to the nation at large. A classroom group reports to the instructor and to the rest of the class. The purpose of such reports is to present the group's recommendations clearly and convincingly.

Sometimes a group will prepare a formal written report. Often, however, the written report is supplemented with—or replaced by—an oral report, a symposium, or a panel discussion.

ORAL REPORT

An oral report is much the same in content as a written report. If the group has a designated leader, she or he will probably deliver the report. Otherwise, the group will select one person for the job.

If you are picked to present your group's report, you should approach it as you would any other speech. Your task is to explain the group's purpose, procedures, and recommendations. Your report should have three main sections. The introduction will state the purpose of the report and preview its main points. The body will spell out the problem addressed by your group, the criteria set for a solution, and the solution being recommended. The conclusion will summarize the main points and, in some cases, urge that the group's recommendations be adopted.

As with any other speech, you should adapt your report to the audience. Use supporting materials to clarify and strengthen your ideas, and consider

oral report
A speech presenting the findings, conclusions, or decisions of a small group.

whether using visual aids will enhance your message. Make sure your language is accurate, clear, vivid, and appropriate. Rehearse the report so you can deliver it fluently and decisively. Afterward, you—and possibly other members of the group—may be called on to answer questions from the audience.

SYMPOSIUM

symposium
A public presentation in which several people present prepared speeches on different aspects of the same topic.

A symposium consists of a moderator and several speakers seated together in front of an audience. If the group presenting the symposium has a designated leader, he or she will typically be the moderator. The moderator's job is to introduce the topic and the speakers. Each speaker delivers a prepared speech on a different aspect of the topic. After the speeches, there may be a question-and-answer session.

The symposium is often used for group reports in speech classes. One way to organize it is to have each member of the group present a brief talk sketching the group's work and decisions during one stage of the reflective-thinking process. Another way is to have each speaker deal with a major issue relating to the discussion topic. A group dealing with capital punishment, for example, might have one speaker present the group's conclusion on the issue of whether capital punishment is an effective deterrent to crime, another speaker present the group's position on the morality of capital punishment, and so forth.

All the speeches should be carefully planned. They should also be coordinated with one another to make sure the symposium reports on all important aspects of the group's project.

PANEL DISCUSSION

panel discussion
A structured conversation on a given topic among several people in front of an audience.

A panel discussion is essentially a conversation in front of an audience. The panel should have a moderator, who introduces the topic and the panelists. Once the discussion is under way, the moderator may interject questions and comments as needed to focus the discussion. The panelists speak briefly, informally, and impromptu. They talk to each other, but loudly enough for the audience to hear. As with a symposium, a panel discussion may be followed by a question-and-answer session.

Because of its spontaneity, a panel discussion can be exciting for participants and audience alike. But, unfortunately, that spontaneity inhibits systematic presentation of a group's recommendations. Thus the panel discussion is seldom used by problem-solving groups, although it can work well for information-gathering groups.

If you are a participant in a panel discussion, beware of the common fallacy that no serious preparation is required. Although you will speak impromptu, you need to study the topic ahead of time, analyze the major issues, and map out the points you want to make. An effective panel discussion also requires planning by the moderator and panelists to decide what issues will be discussed and in what order. Finally, all panelists must be willing to share talking time, so the discussion is not monopolized by one or two people.

Whatever method your group uses to present its findings, you will benefit from the public speaking guidelines given throughout this book. The techniques of effective speech remain the same whether you are one person addressing an audience, part of a small group of people working to solve a problem, or a participant in a symposium or a panel discussion.[9]

A small group consists of three to twelve people assembled for a specific purpose. A problem-solving small group is formed to solve a particular problem. When such a group has effective leadership, it usually makes better decisions than do individuals by themselves. Most groups have a designated leader, an implied leader, or an emergent leader. Some groups have no specific leader, in which case all members of the group must assume leadership responsibilities. An effective leader helps a group reach its goals by fulfilling procedural needs, task needs, and maintenance needs.

Apart from leadership, all members of a group have five basic responsibilities. You should commit yourself to the goals of your group, fulfill your individual assignments, avoid interpersonal conflict within the group, encourage full participation by all members, and help keep the group on track.

Your group will also be more successful if it follows the reflective-thinking method, which offers a step-by-step process for decision making in problem-solving groups. The method consists of five steps: (1) defining the problem as clearly and specifically as possible; (2) analyzing the problem to determine its severity and causes; (3) establishing criteria for evaluating solutions; (4) generating a wide range of potential solutions; (5) selecting the best solution or solutions.

Once your group has agreed on its recommendations, it usually has to make an oral report by one member of the group, a symposium, or a panel discussion. Whichever kind of oral presentation your group gives will call for skills of effective speechmaking.

KEY TERMS

dyad *(394)*

small group *(394)*

problem-solving small group *(395)*

leadership *(395)*

implied leader *(395)*

emergent leader *(395)*

designated leader *(395)*

procedural needs *(396)*

task needs *(397)*

maintenance needs *(397)*

hidden agenda *(398)*

reflective-thinking method *(402)*

question of policy *(402)*

criteria *(404)*

brainstorming *(404)*

consensus *(405)*

oral report *(407)*

symposium *(408)*

panel discussion *(408)*

REVIEW QUESTIONS

After reading this chapter, you should be able to answer the following questions:

1. What is a small group? What is a problem-solving small group?

2. What are the four kinds of leadership that may occur in a small group? Explain the three kinds of needs fulfilled by leadership in a small group.

3. What are the five major responsibilities of every participant in a small group?

4. What are the stages of the reflective-thinking method? Explain the major tasks of a group at each stage.

5. What are the three methods for presenting orally the recommendations of a problem-solving group?

connectlucas.com
For further review, go to the Study Questions in the online Study Aids for this chapter.

EXERCISES FOR CRITICAL THINKING

1. Identify the flaw (or flaws) in each of the following questions for a problem-solving group discussion. Rewrite each question so it conforms with the criteria discussed in the chapter for effective discussion questions.

   a. What should be done to prevent the utterly ridiculous shortage of new computers for students at this school?

   b. What should be done about child abuse?

   c. What should our state government do to control taxes and to combat drunk driving?

   d. Should the federal government institute a national sales tax to help reduce the national debt?

2. If possible, arrange to observe a problem-solving small group in action. You might attend a meeting of your city council, the school board, the zoning commission, a local business, a church committee. To what extent does the discussion measure up to the criteria for effective discussion presented in this chapter? What kind of leadership does the group have, and how well does the leader (or leaders) fulfill the group's procedural needs, task needs, and maintenance needs? How do the other members meet their responsibilities? What aspects of the meeting are handled most effectively? Which are handled least effectively?

3. Identify a relatively important decision you have made in the last year or two. Try to reconstruct how you reached that decision. Now suppose you could remake the decision following the reflective-thinking method. Map out exactly what you would do at each stage of the method. Do you still reach the same decision? If not, do you believe the reflective-thinking method would have led you to a better decision in the first place?

4. Attend a symposium or panel discussion on campus. Prepare a brief analysis of the proceedings. First, study the role of the moderator. How does she or he introduce the topic and participants? What role does the moderator play thereafter? Does she or he help guide and focus the panel discussion? Does she or he summarize and conclude the proceedings at the end?

   Second, observe the participants. Are the speeches in the symposium well prepared and presented? Which speaker (or speakers) do you find most effective? Least effective? Why? Do participants in the panel discussion share talking time? Does their discussion appear well planned to cover major aspects of the topic? Which panelist (or panelists) do you find most effective? Least effective? Why?

Speeches for Analysis and Discussion

I Have a Dream

●●

Martin Luther King, Jr.

Martin Luther King's "I Have a Dream" is widely regarded as a masterpiece. It was delivered August 28, 1963, to some 200,000 people who had come to Washington, D.C., to participate in a peaceful demonstration to further the cause of equal rights for African Americans. King spoke from the steps of the Lincoln Memorial, in the "symbolic shadow" of Abraham Lincoln, and the crowd filled the vast area between the Memorial and the Washington Monument. In addition, millions of Americans watched the speech on television or listened to it on the radio.

Like most ceremonial addresses, "I Have a Dream" is relatively short. Although it took King only 16 minutes to deliver the speech, he prepared it more carefully than any other speech in his career to that time. His purpose was to set forth as succinctly and as eloquently as possible the guiding principles of the civil rights movement, and to reinforce the commitment of his listeners to those principles.

One of the most interesting features of this speech is King's use of language to make the abstract principles of liberty and equality clear and compelling. Throughout, King relies on familiar, concrete words that create sharp, vivid images. He uses many more metaphors than do most speakers, but they are appropriate to the occasion and help to dramatize King's ideas. Finally, King makes extensive use of repetition and parallelism to reinforce his message and to enhance the momentum of the speech.

If you have heard a recording of "I Have a Dream," you know its impact was heightened by King's delivery. In his rich baritone voice, marked by the fervor of the crusader and modulated by the cadences of the Southern Baptist preacher, King gained the total involvement of his audience. As William Robert Miller says, "The crowd more than listened, it participated, and before King had reached his last phrase, a torrent of applause was already welling up."

The text of this speech is transcribed from a recording and is reprinted with permission of Joan Daves. Copyright 1963 by Martin Luther King, Jr. The speech is also available on the video supplement to *The Art of Public Speaking*.

1 I am happy to join with you today in what will go down in history as the greatest demonstration for freedom in the history of our nation.

2 Five score years ago, a great American, in whose symbolic shadow we stand today, signed the Emancipation Proclamation. This momentous decree came as a great beacon light of hope to millions of Negro slaves, who had been seared in the flames of withering injustice. It came as a joyous daybreak to end the long night of their captivity.

3 But one hundred years later, the Negro still is not free. One hundred years later, the life of the Negro is still sadly crippled by the manacles of segregation and the chains of discrimination. One hundred years later, the Negro lives on a lonely island of poverty in the midst of a vast ocean of material prosperity. One hundred years later, the Negro is still languished in the corners of American society and finds himself an exile in his own land. And so we've come here today to dramatize a shameful condition.

4 In a sense we've come to our nation's Capitol to cash a check. When the architects of our republic wrote the magnificent words of the Constitution and the Declaration of Independence, they were signing a promissory note to which every American was to fall heir. This note was a promise that all men—yes, black men as well as white men—would be guaranteed the unalienable rights of life, liberty, and the pursuit of happiness.

5 It is obvious today that America has defaulted on this promissory note insofar as her citizens of color are concerned. Instead of honoring this sacred obligation, America has given the Negro people a bad check—a check which has come back marked "insufficient funds."

6 But we refuse to believe that the bank of justice is bankrupt. We refuse to believe that there are insufficient funds in the great vaults of opportunity of this nation. And so we've come to cash this check—a check that will give us upon demand the riches of freedom and the security of justice.

7 We have also come to this hallowed spot to remind America of the fierce urgency of now. This is no time to engage in the luxury of cooling off or to take the tranquilizing drug of gradualism. Now is the time to make real the promises of democracy. Now is the time to rise from the dark and desolate valley of segregation to the sunlit path of racial justice. Now is the time to lift our nation from the quicksands of racial injustice to the solid rock of brotherhood. Now is the time to make justice a reality for all of God's children.

8 It would be fatal for the nation to overlook the urgency of the moment. This sweltering summer of the Negro's legitimate discontent will not pass until there is an invigorating autumn of freedom and equality. Nineteen sixty-three is not an end, but a beginning. Those who hope that the Negro needed to blow off steam and will now be content will have a rude awakening if the nation returns to business as usual. There will be neither rest nor tranquility in America until the Negro is granted his citizenship rights. The whirlwinds of revolt will continue to shake the foundations of our nation until the bright day of justice emerges.

9 But there is something that I must say to my people, who stand on the warm threshold which leads into the palace of justice. In the process of gaining our rightful place, we must not be guilty of wrongful deeds. Let us not seek to satisfy our thirst for freedom by drinking from the cup of bitterness and hatred.

10 We must forever conduct our struggle on the high plane of dignity and discipline. We must not allow our creative protest to degenerate into physical violence. Again and again we must rise to the majestic heights of meeting physical force with soul force.

11 The marvelous new militancy which has engulfed the Negro community must not lead us to a distrust of all white people. For many of our white brothers, as evidenced by their presence here today, have come to realize that their destiny is tied up with our destiny. They have come to realize that their freedom is inextricably bound to our freedom. We cannot walk alone.

12 As we walk, we must make the pledge that we shall always march ahead. We cannot turn back. There are those who are asking the devotees of civil rights, "When will you be satisfied?" We can never be satisfied as long as the Negro is the victim of the unspeakable horrors of police brutality. We can never be satisfied as long as our bodies, heavy with the fatigue of travel, cannot gain lodging in the motels of the highways and the hotels of the cities. We cannot be satisfied as long as the Negro's basic mobility is from a smaller ghetto to a larger one. We can never be satisfied as long as our children are stripped of their selfhood and robbed of their dignity by signs stating "For Whites Only." We cannot be satisfied as long as a Negro in Mississippi cannot vote and a Negro in New York believes he has nothing for which to vote. No, no, we are not satisfied, and we will not be satisfied until justice rolls down like waters, and righteousness like a mighty stream.

13 I am not unmindful that some of you have come here out of great trials and tribulations. Some of you have come fresh from narrow jail cells. Some of you have come from areas where your quest for freedom left you battered by the storms of persecution and staggered by the winds of police brutality. You have been the veterans of creative suffering. Continue to work with the faith that unearned suffering is redemptive.

14 Go back to Mississippi, go back to Alabama, go back to South Carolina, go back to Georgia, go back to Louisiana, go back to the slums and ghettos of our Northern cities, knowing that somehow this situation can and will be changed. Let us not wallow in the valley of despair.

15 I say to you today, my friends, so even though we face the difficulties of today and tomorrow, I still have a dream. It is a dream deeply rooted in the American dream.

16 I have a dream that one day this nation will rise up and live out the true meaning of its creed, "We hold these truths to be self-evident, that all men are created equal."

17 I have a dream that one day on the red hills of Georgia the sons of former slaves and the sons of former slaveowners will be able to sit down together at the table of brotherhood.

18 I have a dream that one day even the state of Mississippi, a state sweltering with the heat of injustice, sweltering with the heat of oppression, will be transformed into an oasis of freedom and justice.

19 I have a dream that my four little children will one day live in a nation where they will not be judged by the color of their skin but by the content of their character. I have a dream today.

20 I have a dream that one day, down in Alabama, with its vicious racists, with its governor having his lips dripping with the words of interposition and nullification, one day right there in Alabama little black boys and black girls will be able to join hands with little white boys and white girls as sisters and brothers. I have a dream today.

21 I have a dream that one day every valley shall be exalted, every hill and mountain shall be made low, the rough places will be made plane and the crooked places will be made straight, and the glory of the Lord shall be revealed, and all flesh shall see it together.

22 This is our hope. This is the faith that I go back to the South with. With this faith we will be able to hew out of the mountain of despair a stone of hope. With this faith we will be able to transform the jangling discords of our nation into a beautiful symphony of brotherhood. With this faith we will be able to work together, to pray together, to struggle together, to go to jail together, to stand up for freedom together, knowing that we will be free one day.

23 This will be the day—this will be the day when all of God's children will be able to sing with new meaning, "My country 'tis of thee, sweet land of liberty, of thee I sing. Land where my fathers died, land of the pilgrim's pride, from every mountainside, let freedom ring." And if America is to be a great nation, this must become true.

24 So let freedom ring from the prodigious hilltops of New Hampshire. Let freedom ring from the mighty mountains of New York. Let freedom ring from the heightening Alleghenies of Pennsylvania!

25 Let freedom ring from the snowcapped Rockies of Colorado! Let freedom ring from the curvaceous slopes of California!

26 But not only that. Let freedom ring from Stone Mountain of Georgia!

27 Let freedom ring from Lookout Mountain of Tennessee!

28 Let freedom ring from every hill and molehill of Mississippi. From every mountainside, let freedom ring.

29 And when this happens, when we allow freedom ring—when we let it ring from every village and every hamlet, from every state and every city—we will be able to speed up that day when all of God's children, black men and white men, Jews and Gentiles, Protestants and Catholics, will be able to join hands and sing in the words of the old Negro spiritual, "Free at last! Free at last! Thank God almighty, we are free at last!"

Questions of Culture

●●

Sajjid Zahir Chinoy

Seldom does a student commencement address upstage the featured speaker—especially when that speaker is a Pulitzer Prize winner from Harvard University. Yet that is exactly what happened when Sajjid Zahir Chinoy spoke to his fellow graduates at the University of Richmond on May 12, 1996.

Born and raised near Bombay, India, Chinoy was selected to speak as the result of a campuswide competition. After describing the jumble of emotions that filled his mind as he came to the United States to attend school, he spoke movingly of the warm reception he received in Richmond and of how cultural differences can be overcome by attempting to understand other people.

Addressing his audience of 3,000 people extemporaneously and without notes, Chinoy received thunderous applause, and his remarks were widely reported in the press. His speech was so inspiring that the main speaker, Harvard psychiatrist Robert Coles, began his address by paying tribute to Chinoy. "I've been to a number of commencements," said Coles, "but I've never heard a speech quite like that."

The text of this speech has been transcribed from a video recording and is reprinted with permission from Sajjid Zahir Chinoy and the University of Richmond. A video is available in the online Media Library for this appendix at connectlucas.com.

connectlucas.com
View "Questions of Culture" in the online Media Library for this appendix (Video Clip A3.1).

1 Distinguished guests, faculty, staff, students, ladies and gentlemen, and, most of all, the Class of 1996:

2 I can visualize the scene again and again: 11:30 P.M., Saturday night, the fifteenth of August, 1992, Bombay International Airport, India. I was leaving home for the University of Richmond. And as I said that final goodbye to my parents, my family, and my friends; and as I saw hope, expectation, even a tinge of sadness, in their eyes; and as I stepped aboard the Boeing 747 in front, I knew my life had changed forever.

3 The next 36 hours on board the aircraft were a time of questions, of concerns, of tremendous uncertainty.

4 Had I made the right choice in leaving home? Had I made the right choice in leaving my parents, my family, my home? Had I made the right choice in leaving my country, my culture, my background? Had I made the right choice in choosing the University of Richmond?

5 And then, of course, there was that one nagging question, that one overriding concern: As one of only three Indian students on a Richmond campus of 3,000, would I ever fit in?

6 My country was different. My culture was different. My experiences were different. My background was different. My language was different. My accent was different. Would I ever fit in?

7 And so here I was, high above the clouds, grappling with questions of culture, of interaction, of ethnicity. What I didn't know was that 30,000 feet below, on the ground, the world was faced with these very same questions—the question of culture, the question of interaction, the question of ethnicity.

8 And so whether my aircraft took off from Bombay, where the Hindus and the Muslims lived together in a most fragile peace; or whether my aircraft was over Africa, where the Hutus and Tutsis of Rwanda and Burundi had long-standing animosity; or whether my aircraft was over Bosnia, where the Serbs, the Croats, the Muslims, and the Bosnians had broken yet another truce, the question was the same—could different cultures ever come together to reinforce one another?

9 Ladies and gentlemen, after that bumpy aircraft ride, this young Indian student had found his answer. He had been witness to the four most spectacular years of his life at the University of Richmond. The academics were great; the extracurriculars were great; his graduate plans were great.

10 But what left an indelible impact on his mind was none of this. No, instead it was those special moments, those moments of human interaction, those human relationships that can never quite be translated into words:

11 The time this young Indian student spent his first Thanksgiving dinner with his debate team coach. That Thanksgiving evening when I ate my first American turkey and saw my first American football game, not knowing the difference between a tackle and a touchdown. And yet, all of a sudden, just like that, this very different Indian student had become an inherent part of the great American tradition of giving thanks.

12 The time I spent my first Christmas Eve with my journalism professor. That Christmas evening when the relationship wasn't of a faculty member and a student anymore, but of two buddies who fought fiercely over every point in Ping-Pong.

13 The time I had a long and honest talk with an American friend on the eve of a calculus exam. I didn't learn much calculus that night, but what I did learn was that as different as we are—different countries, different cultures, different continents—inherently we are still the same.

14 The time in December 1992 when India was hit by communal riots, when violence and bloodshed were but a few hundred yards from my family and my home, and when my fantastic roommate from my freshman year sat up the entire night, giving me hope, strength, and courage at every step.

15 Yes, four years after that bumpy aircraft ride, I have found the answer to the question of culture.

16 I have found that it has taken just a little understanding, just a little sensitivity, just a little open-mindedness, just a little empathy on the part of this community—this University of Richmond community—to change my life like never before.

17 I have found that it makes no difference what culture you follow, what your background is, what your experiences are, what language you speak, what accent you have. The commonality of the human bond far transcends these superficial differences.

18 And yet look around at the world today. Look around at the very regions that were faced with the same question of culture that I was faced with four years ago.

19 Look at Bosnia, where, between 1992 and 1996, 300,000 people had been slaughtered—Bosnians, Serbs, Croats, Muslims—all because they came from a slightly different heritage or culture or history.

20 Look at Bombay, India. In one maddening week in 1992, 2,000 Indians—Hindus and Muslims—lost their lives fighting with one another. They fought over a mosque; they fought over a structure made of brick and mortar. Two thousand human beings lost their lives.

21 Look at Africa, where, between 1992 and 1996, 1 million Hutus and Tutsis lost their lives. Just comprehend that for a moment. Between the time you were a freshman and a senior, 1 million lost their lives fighting over culture, over history, over background.

22 Yes, just look at the madness. The world has fought hard to highlight its differences. We have forgotten our inherent similarities. All because what was missing was a little understanding. Just a little sensitivity. Just a little open-mindedness. Just a little empathy.

23 Two similar questions of culture in 1992. Two diametrically opposite results in 1996.

24 And so, to the Class of 1996, I say go and distinguish yourselves like never before. Go get the best of jobs, the most rewarding of careers. Go to the best of graduate programs. And make a real difference in your communities.

25 But not for one moment, not for one moment, ever forget the memory of these four years—the memory that just a little understanding, just a little sensitivity, just a little open-mindedness, just a little empathy on your part can mean the difference between complete despair for one young boy in Bosnia and remarkable hope for another young boy at Richmond.

26 Thank you.

The Hidden World of Chili Peppers

Do you know where chili peppers originated and how they eventually spread around the world? Why some peppers are so much hotter than others? How the heat of a chili pepper is measured? What to do if you eat a too-hot pepper? The many medicinal benefits of chili peppers?

These are just a few of the interesting facts presented in the following informative speech. As you read the speech, notice how the speaker blends historical and scientific materials to produce an entertaining, yet highly instructive, look at chili peppers. Notice, too, how the speaker applies the principles of effective informative speaking discussed in Chapter 14.

Video of this speech is available in the online Media Library for this appendix. If you watch the speech, you will see that the speaker uses a number of well-designed visual aids to enhance the communication of his ideas.

connectlucas.com
View "The Hidden World of Chili Peppers" in the online Media Library for this appendix (Video Clip A3.2).

1 Imagine your mouth burning like wildfire, your eyes squirting out uncontrollable tears, and your face red and sweating profusely. Are you sick? No, you just took a bite of a screaming hot chili pepper. Congratulations. You're partaking in a worldwide tradition that has been spicing up lives and diets for thousands of years.

2 My own desire for spicy meals led me to investigate why I get red in the face and salivate over the mere thought of eating a spicy chili. In the process, I've discovered there's a lot more to chili peppers than I'd ever imagined. Today I'd like to share with you what I've learned about the history of chili peppers,

why they can be so spicy, what to do if you eat a too-hot pepper, and some of the ways peppers are used other than in foods.

3 The chili pepper has a long and fascinating history. Its scientific name is *Capsicum.* This is different from the common black pepper you have on your dining room table, whose scientific name is *Piper nigrum.* Black pepper was first cultivated in Asia and was prized in the West as early as the Roman Empire. In contrast, the chili pepper originated more than 5,000 years ago in South America, near what is today Bolivia and Brazil. Over time, it spread to Mexico, Central America, and the Caribbean.

4 But it wasn't until Columbus came in the 1490s that the chili pepper became known to the rest of the world. As stated in *The Cambridge World History of Food,* within fifty years after Columbus returned to Spain with sample plants, chili peppers could be found growing in coastal areas from Africa to Asia. From there, they spread inland, until they took hold of the taste buds of people around the globe. Today they're most widely used in Mexico, Central and South America, Africa, Asia, the Balkans, and the United States. Carolyn Dille and Susan Belsinger, authors of *The Chili Pepper Book,* estimate that 25 percent of the world's adult population uses chili peppers as a part of their daily diet.

5 Now that we know a little bit about the history of chili peppers, let's see why they can put such a fire in our belly. The pleasure and pain involved in eating chili peppers comes from a chemical called capsaicin. Capsaicin is concentrated in the pepper's veins and seeds. To enjoy the flavor of a chili pepper without burning your stomach or mouth, avoid the veins and seeds when cooking or eating them.

6 P. W. Bosland tells us in the book *Spices, Herbs, and Edible Fungi* that chili pepper intensity is measured in two ways. The first was developed by Wilbur L. Scoville in 1912. This method uses trained testers to measure chili peppers in Scoville Heat Units. These range from zero to 300,000. According to Bosland, this test is subjective because it relies on the individual tester's sensitivity to capsaicin.

7 The second, more widely used test is called the High Performance Liquid Chromatography test, more commonly known as HPLC. This is also measured in Scoville Heat Units, but it's more objective. The chili pods are dried and ground, and then the chemicals responsible for the heat are analyzed and rated according to pungency.

8 The hottest pepper on record is the deceptively small and unimposing orange habanero pepper. It's been rated as high as 300,000 Scoville Heat Units, and it's so powerful that some people have an allergic reaction just by touching it, which is why I'm holding it by the stem. The mildest pepper is the standard green bell, which you see at the grocery store everyday. It's been rated at zero Scoville Heat Units.

9 If you eat an orange habanero pepper, it's important to know how to deal with the burning sensation. Whatever you do, do not rinse your mouth with water. Dave DeWitt in *The Chili Pepper Encyclopedia* tells us capsaicin is not soluble in water. And even if you drink a gallon of ice water, it's not going to help. According to the Chili Pepper Institute at New Mexico State University, the best solution is to consume a dairy product such as milk or yogurt, which contain a substance that strips away capsaicin from the interior cells of your mouth. This is why some hot foods, like Indian foods, are served with yogurt sauce.

10 If you burn your skin, the Institute recommends cleaning the area with rubbing alcohol and then soaking it with milk. Above all, remember two

things: First, always wear gloves when you cut a hot pepper such as a habanero. Second, never rub your eyes when working with hot chili peppers.

11 Although chili peppers are prized above all for the flavor they add to food, they have other benefits as well. Pepper sprays have become a standard weapon for the personal protection of individuals and law-enforcement agencies. *The New York Times* reports that sales of pepper sprays have risen steadily and show no sign of slowing.

12 Chili peppers are also valued for their medicinal properties. According to Jack Challem, author of *The Nutrition Reporter,* there have been more than 1,300 medical studies on capsaicin, the active ingredient in peppers. Moderate doses have been proved to aid digestion, reduce hypertension, improve circulation, and help dissolve blood clots. Preliminary research by Professor Kenji Okajima at Japan's Kumamato University School of Medicine suggests that a combination of chili peppers and soybeans can promote hair growth and might hold promise as a cure for baldness.

13 In closing, it's difficult to imagine our lives without the spice added by chili peppers. From their origins in South America to their current popularity around the world, peppers have been used not only to flavor our food but also to improve our health and personal safety. While it remains to be seen whether or not chili peppers can actually cure baldness, we can be sure this ancient plant will continue to find new uses in our modern age.

The Horrors of Puppy Mills

• •

Seventy-five million dogs are owned as pets in the United States, and 7 to 9 million puppies are purchased each year at a total cost of close to $1 billion. Most come from legitimate breeders who take good care of their animals. Two to four million, however, come from puppy mills, large-scale operations run solely for profit with no concern for the animals' physical or emotional welfare. After explaining the problem of puppy mills, the following persuasive speech presents a solution that combines legislative action with individual initiative.

In addition to reading the speech, you can watch it in the online Media Library for this Appendix at connectlucas.com. As you watch, notice how the speaker uses PowerPoint to present visual evidence of the conditions animals are subjected to in puppy mills. Do you think the speech would have been as effective without this kind of evidence? All in all, does the speaker convince you that puppy mills are a serious problem? Does he present a clear and workable solution? How well does he use the methods of persuasion presented in Chapter 16?

connectlucas.com
View "The Horrors of Puppy Mills" in the online Media Library for this appendix (Video Clip A3.3).

1 A cold, dark room. It smells disgusting. The creatures in front of you shake uncontrollably, packed one on top of another in tiny wire cages. To eat, they have only crumbs in front of them, and to drink, only a dirty bowl of water. Many have eye problems, ear problems, diseases, and infections. They've never been groomed. They've never been for a walk. And they've never seen the sun.

2 For too many dogs across America, this is how life begins—in a puppy mill. Puppy mills, as defined by the Humane Society of the United States, are "mass dog-breeding operations" that take place in "shockingly poor conditions." Puppy-mill breeders produce puppies for profit—only for profit—with little or no concern for the physical, social, or emotional needs of the dogs.

3 As a dog lover, I was shocked to discover the horrors of puppy mills across the country as I researched this speech. I know from my audience-analysis

questionnaires that most of you had a dog or another pet while you were growing up and that you believe they should be treated humanely. Today I'll show you that puppy mills are not treating their animals humanely and I'll suggest some ways of solving the problem.

4 Puppy mills have been around for a long time, but they've grown dramatically in recent years. The Humane Society estimates that there are more than 10,000 puppy mills currently operating in the United States. According to Stephanie Shain, the Society's Director of Outreach for Companionable Animals, of the 7 to 9 million dogs sold in this country each year, 2 to 4 million come from puppy mills. That's double the number from only a decade ago.

5 Rather than producing the healthy, happy pets that millions of families dream of, puppy mills produce dogs with canine herpes, respiratory infections, parasites, seizures, and *E. coli.* Dogs that are lucky enough to escape these diseases often have rotten teeth, missing eyes or limbs, hip disorders, skin problems, and a host of other deformities.

6 In addition to suffering from physical problems, dogs in puppy mills are often emotionally unstable. Some are dangerously violent and aggressive. Others are apathetic and lack any desire to interact with people or animals. Because of the overcrowding in puppy mills, some animals literally go crazy and chew off the ears, legs, and tails of other dogs.

7 But you can see for yourself what the dogs have to endure. Here's a picture of a puppy mill provided by the U.S. Humane Society. As you can see, the cages are stacked one on top of another and the dogs are packed into the cages like sardines into a can. The dogs are not let out to go to the bathroom, so the cages are filled with waste and become breeding grounds for the diseases I mentioned earlier in my speech.

8 You can get a better sense of how disgusting puppy mills are from this photo, taken after the dogs were removed by animal protection officials. You can see how narrow the cages are and how they're crammed one against the other. You can see the filth and debris everywhere.

9 Finally, take a look at a couple individual dogs. The first one came from a puppy mill here in Wisconsin. It was so malnourished that it couldn't stand up by itself, and it had lost the fur on almost all of its body.

10 The next dog was in even worse shape. Covered with its own filth, it had a rash of infections and diseases and had lost the sight in one eye. Like other puppy-mill dogs, it never saw a veterinarian until it was rescued.

11 It's time that we stop the horrors of puppy mills and help dogs and dog owners alike. Solving the problem requires action on two fronts—legislation and individual initiative.

12 The first step is for new laws that will put puppy mills out of business. Current laws, such as the Animal Welfare Act, are ineffective at best. This law only regulates a small number of breeders, leaving countless puppy mills to operate under the radar.

13 Here's the legislation I propose. It's based on a combination of proposals that have been presented in several states. All dog breeders who produce more than 30 puppies a year should be required to register with their state's Department of Agriculture, which would inspect dog-breeding facilities just as the health department inspects restaurants.

14 Breeders with dogs in substandard conditions would be dealt with accordingly. A first offense would result in a fine of $3,000. A second offense would result in a fine of $5,000 and 30 days in jail. A third offense would result

in a fine of $10,000 and 90 days in jail, plus permanent loss of the breeder's license in every state of the union.

15 But legislation alone won't do the job. You and I also have a part to play. We have to take the profit out of puppy mills by making sure we don't purchase dogs produced by puppy mills. We can do this by following guidelines laid out by the Humane Society.

16 First, consider adopting a dog from a trusted animal shelter instead of buying a new dog. The animal shelter will make sure the dog is free of physical and behavioral problems.

17 Second, if you decide to buy a new dog, visit the breeder's premises. If the breeder refuses to let you see the premises, or wants to meet you somewhere else, don't buy from that breeder.

18 Third, don't buy a dog from a pet store. The Humane Society has found that most dogs in pet stores actually come from puppy mills.

19 And fourth, don't be fooled by advertising. Just because an ad promises that a dog has been, quote, "family raised" or has a "health certificate," doesn't mean it's true. This is especially important when it comes to the Internet, where there is no way to verify the health of a dog or the trustworthiness of a breeder.

20 In conclusion, I'd like you to imagine your own pet—no matter what kind of animal it might be—living even one day in the conditions endured by dogs in puppy mills. Then imagine your pet living in those conditions day after day, week after week, month after month. Surely you would not want this for your own pet.

21 Yet even as we sit here, millions of dogs are suffering from the horrors of puppy mills. It's time to stop puppy-mill breeders from profiting on their cruelty. Even if, as the movie title says, all dogs go to heaven, we should not allow them to start their lives in hell.

Bursting the Antibacterial Bubble

During the past few years, the use of household antibacterial products has grown dramatically in the United States. Today Americans spend millions of dollars on everything from antibacterial soaps and hand wipes to tissues, sponges, shampoos, and even children's toys that have been treated with antibacterial chemicals.

The following persuasive speech argues that these products do not provide the benefits they claim and may, in fact, be contributing to long-term health and environmental problems. As a solution, the speaker recommends that the U.S. Food and Drug Administration institute regulations governing the use of antibacterial products and that consumers avoid using these products.

In addition to reading this speech, you can watch the video in the online Media Library for this appendix at connectlucas.com. Study how the speaker uses examples, statistics, and testimony to support her position. Does she convince you that the heavy use of antibacterial products is a serious problem? Does she present an effective solution to the problem? How could she have made the speech more convincing?

connectlucas.com
View "Bursting the Antibacterial Bubble" in the online Media Library for this appendix (Video Clip A3.4).

1 In the film *The Boy in the Plastic Bubble,* a boy born with a deficient immune system is forced to live in a germ-free environment to prevent him from contracting infections. His room is sealed against bacteria and viruses, his food is specially prepared, and his only human contact comes in the form of gloved hands.

2 Today millions of Americans are trying to build a bubble around themselves and their families to keep out germs. The bubble is not made of plastic, however, but of billions of dollars worth of antibacterial hand wipes, tissues, soaps, and sponges.

3 Before I studied antibacterial products in my public health class, I always used antibacterial hand soaps and antibacterial all-surface cleaner for my apartment. I also know from my class survey that 70 percent of you use antibacterial soaps, cleaners, and other products.

4 But after learning about the subject in class and reading research studies for this speech, I'm here to tell you that, try as we might, we cannot build a bubble between ourselves and germs with antibacterial products and that these products actually create more problems than they solve. After looking at the problems created by antibacterial products, we'll explore some solutions.

5 The place to begin is by noting that antibacterial products are popping up just about everywhere. The next time you go to the store, try to find a liquid soap that is not antibacterial. According to the Alliance for the Prudent Use of Antibiotics, 75 percent of all liquid soaps and 33 percent of all bar soaps are antibacterial.

6 In fact, there are more than 1,000 antibacterial household products on the market. In addition to all the soaps and cleaning products, there are also antibacterial cotton swabs, tons of antibacterial shampoos, and this antibacterial cutting board from Williams Sonoma. You can even get antibacterial socks, mouthwash, toothpaste, and, to protect you while away from home, this travel toothbrush with antibacterial bristles.

7 The *Boston Globe* reports that larger items such as mattresses, countertops, high chairs, and even children's toys have been coated with antibacterial chemicals. *The New York Times* calls the antibacterial craze "the biggest marketing coup since bottled water."

8 There's no doubt that antibacterial products are popular with consumers, but there is a great deal of doubt about whether they're effective in stopping the spread of germs. Elaine Larson, associate dean of the Columbia University School of Nursing, studied 238 families who used antibacterial products and found that they were just as likely to get fevers, sore throats, coughs, rashes, and stomach problems as families who used regular products. Larson's findings are echoed by Eric Kupferberg, associate director of the Harvard School for Public Health, who states: "Antimicrobial products don't significantly eliminate the number of germs you encounter on a daily basis."

9 Nor do antibacterial products prevent the transmission of diseases such as colds and flus. Why? Because these illnesses come from viruses, not from bacteria. Antibacterial products don't kill viruses. As Dr. Larson explains, "Most of the infections healthy people get are colds, flu, and diarrhea caused by viruses"—none of which can be prevented by the use of antibacterial products.

10 Not only do antibacterial products fail to deliver what they promise, but they actually increase your chances of getting sick. According to Stuart Levy, a professor of microbiology and medicine at Tufts University, excessive use of antibacterial products in the home can make children more likely to develop allergies and asthma.

11 In addition, people who use antibacterial products may become more susceptible to infections. Dr. James Chin, a research scientist in New South Wales, Australia, says: "The way we stay healthy is by low-dose exposure to bacteria and viruses. You need to exercise your immune system in the same way you need to exercise your muscles to be fit. If you don't do that, your

immune system doesn't have a chance to do battle when it engages with an infection."

12 The problems caused by antibacterial products are so serious that Dr. Myron Genel, chairman of the American Medical Association's council on scientific affairs, fears one result may be the creation of antibiotic-resistant bacteria "that are largely untreatable because they are resistant to existing drugs."

13 And that's not all. Besides being ineffective at preventing diseases and being potentially dangerous to our health, antibacterial household products also appear to harm the environment. Rolf Halden of Johns Hopkins University School of Public Health reports that each year the United States releases into the water supply more than 2 million pounds of the active chemicals in antibacterial soaps.

14 The U.S. Geological Survey reports that chemicals from antibacterial products are winding up in streams and groundwater from the Denver area to remote locations in the Rocky Mountains. These chemicals are known to pollute the water supply, disrupt fish reproduction and growth, and, because they do not decompose quickly, remain active for years and years.

15 Now that we've seen the seriousness of the problem, let's look at some solutions.

16 First, we need federal legislation regulating the use of household antibacterial products. Just as the Food and Drug Administration has regulations controlling the use of antibiotics, so, too, should it institute regulations controlling the use of antibacterial products.

17 We don't let people purchase antibiotics without a doctor's prescription, and there's no reason we should allow makers of soap, tissues, hand wipes, toothbrushes, and other products to add powerful antibacterial agents without oversight from the Food and Drug Administration. Given the problems being caused by these products, it is time for the federal government to take action.

18 Second, we all need to take action as consumers. Most obviously, we need to stop buying these products. The best way to avoid germs, says the Centers for Disease Control, is to wash your hands for 10–15 seconds with plain soap and water.

19 In fact, a study at the University of North Carolina found that washing your hands with soap and water is more effective at getting rid of germs than using antibacterial hand wipes. Emily Sickbert-Bennett, a public epidemiologist and co-author of the study, explains that when you use soap and water, the germs go down the drain, but with waterless antibacterial hand wipes, "you never rinse your hands. You are just rubbing a chemical into your hand and letting it dry."

20 In conclusion, Americans spend millions of dollars every year on products that promise to "kill germs on contact." But as we have seen today, the antibacterial craze is a marketing coup rather than a proven way of stopping either the spread of germs or the incidence of colds, flus, and other virus-borne illnesses. Worse, these products appear to contribute to health problems, and they are creating environmental problems in the U.S. water supply. The federal government should start regulating these products and we, as consumers, should stop throwing our money away on them.

21 We need to resist the false notion that we can use these products to create a bubble around ourselves to keep out germs and disease. Instead, we can burst the bubble of marketers who are selling us a false bill of goods and then we can thoroughly wash our hands of the whole mess.

The Ultimate Gift

●●

As the Red Cross states, "Blood is like a parachute. If it's not there when you need it, chances are you'll never need it again." Although Americans take it for granted that they will be able to get a transfusion whenever they need one, blood donations have dipped so low in recent years that a serious nationwide shortage could result. "When you need surgery, when you need cancer treatment, when a woman gives birth—we all assume the blood will be there," says Dr. Arthur Caplan of the University of Pennsylvania. "You can't make that assumption any more."

The following speech, given by a student at the University of Wisconsin, urges the audience to become regular blood donors. Like many speeches that seek immediate action, this one follows Monroe's motivated sequence. As you read it, study how the speaker develops each step in the motivated sequence. How does she gain the attention of her listeners? Does she present a convincing case that there is a need for blood donors? Is her plan explained in sufficient detail? How does she visualize the benefits of her plan? Does her call for action have strong persuasive appeal?

In addition to reading this speech, you can watch the video in the online Media Library for this appendix at connectlucas.com.

connectlucas.com
View "The Ultimate Gift" in the online Media Library for this appendix (Video Clip A3.5).

1 Are you at least 17 years old? Do you weigh more than 110 pounds? Do you consider yourself fairly healthy?

2 If you answered yes to all of these questions, you should be donating blood every two months. In my survey of the class, I found that only 50 percent of you have ever donated blood and that only 1 out of 13 of you donate on a regular basis. The lack of participation of eligible donors is a serious problem that requires immediate action. Through extensive research and two years of faithfully donating blood, I have come to realize the magnitude of this problem and just how easy the solution can be.

3 Today I would like to show why blood donors are in such desperate need and encourage you to take action to combat this need. Let's first take a look at the overwhelming need for blood donors.

4 The lack of participation of eligible blood donors poses a threat to the lives of many Americans. According to the American Red Cross Web pages, where I obtained an enormous amount of information, in the United States alone someone undergoes a blood transfusion once every three seconds, which amounts to 3,000 gallons of blood every hour, day and night. People who benefit from donations range from cancer patients to organ transplant patients to surgical patients; even premature infants and trauma victims benefit from donations. The need for blood never takes a vacation and neither should donors.

5 Let me tell you about Brooke, a three-year-old girl with long, curly blond hair and bright blue eyes. Brooke is a victim of cancer and had major surgery to remove a large tumor in her abdomen. She has spent approximately half of her life in the hospital receiving chemotherapy and other treatments for infections that resulted from a decrease in her white blood cell count after each session.

6 According to Texas Children's Hospital, Brooke's treatment will require blood products with a replacement value of 508 units of blood, of which only 250 units have been replaced. She still needs more than 250 units of blood to continue her treatment. If she doesn't receive this blood, she will not live to attend kindergarten, to go to the prom in high school, or to get married—luxuries we all too often take for granted.

7 Cases like Brooke's are becoming all too common these days, with only 1 in 20 eligible Americans donating blood and the donor rate dropping steadily at 2 percent annually. These facts are particularly distressing considering that nearly half of us here will receive blood sometime in our lives.

8 You can now see the magnitude of the problem with the lack of blood donations. Fortunately, it is a problem that can be easily solved. Each and every one of you can be part of the solution. All you have to do to save priceless lives is go to the nearest Red Cross and donate your blood.

9 For those of you who have never donated blood before, the process is so simple and easy. First, you fill out a donor information form that asks you questions about your sexual history and health. You will then receive a mini-physical. They will take a drop of blood from your finger to measure the percent of red cells in your blood. Then they will take your blood pressure, as well as your temperature and pulse. So not only are you saving lives by donating blood, you are also checking on your own.

10 After your physical, you will be asked from which arm you prefer to donate. Then you will be asked to lie on a donor chair. A staff member will clean your arm and insert a sterile, nonreusable needle, so there is no way to contract AIDS from donating blood. After a pint of your blood has been taken, which usually takes about 10 minutes, you will be asked to rest for 10 to 15 minutes while you enjoy juice and cookies. The process is over, and in eight weeks you can donate again.

11 Many of you may be scared at the thought of the anticipated pain and needles. I admit I was terrified the first time I gave blood, but then I realized I was scared over nothing. The extent of the pain as they insert the needle is equivalent to someone scratching your arm for a brief second, and while the needle is in your arm, you don't feel a thing. And as I stated before, it is impossible to contract AIDS from donating blood.

12 Now that you know how easy and safe the solution is to the lack of blood donations, let's take a look at just how much difference your donations can make. Every unit of blood you donate can help save up to three lives. You see, the blood you donate is divided three ways—into red blood cells, white blood cells, and platelets. Each of these are stored separately and used for different types of treatment. Red blood cells are used to treat anemia. White blood cells are used to fight infections, while platelets are important to control bleeding and are used in patients with leukemia and other forms of cancer.

13 The joy you get from helping three people can be increased many times over. You see, you can donate blood six times in a year. Those six donations could help as many as 18 people. Just think, if you donated for 10 years, you could help save the lives of nearly 180 people. Who knows—one of those lives could be that of a friend, a family member, or even your own, since you can now donate in advance of your own surgery.

14 Now that you know what a difference just one donation can make, I want to encourage you to take action. I urge you to take a stand and become a regular blood donor. Forty-five minutes out of your day is a small price to pay for the lifetime of satisfaction you receive by knowing you may have saved a life. If you have never donated blood before, pull deep inside yourself to find some courage and become a proud wearer of the "I am a first time blood donor" sticker. If you have donated before, think back to the feeling of pride you received from making your donation.

15 Finally, I ask all of you to think of a loved one you hold so dear to your heart. Imagine they need a blood transfusion and there is a shortage of

donations that day so they can't receive the treatment they so desperately need—just like Brooke, the three-year-old girl I talked about earlier. Go to the nearest Red Cross in Madison, which is on Sheboygan Avenue, or attend the next blood drive here on campus. These drives are held in various parts of campus, including the dorms. In fact, the next drive will be held in the Ogg Residence Hall in two weeks.

16 Please take this opportunity to save lives and make yourself feel like a million bucks. Give the ultimate gift—the gift of life. Donate blood!

My Crazy Aunt Sue

The aim of a commemorative speech is to pay tribute to a person, a group of people, an institution, or an idea. In the following student speech, the speaker commemorates her aunt Sue and her heroic battle against the debilitating disease of rheumatoid arthritis.

As you read the speech, notice that it is not a biography that simply recounts the details of aunt Sue's life. Instead, it focuses on her courage, her sense of humor, and her refusal to complain about her fate. The speaker provides enough details to make clear why her aunt is so commendable, but her ultimate purpose is to inspire the audience rather than to inform it. The speaker also uses vivid language, repetition, and parallel structure to give the speech the kind of formal tone appropriate for a commemorative speech.

In addition to reading this speech, you can view it in the online Media Library for this appendix at connectlucas.com.

connectlucas.com
View "My Crazy Aunt Sue" in the online Media Library for this appendix (Video Clip A3.6).

1 The strongest person I know cannot peel a potato. The strongest person I know has trouble putting on her makeup. The strongest person I know needs a special key holder to turn the key in her car's ignition.

2 For the past 15 years, my 47-year-old aunt Sue has been living with rheumatoid arthritis, a painfully debilitating disease in which the joints of the body become intensely inflamed due to the immune system's activity. Yet despite the daily torments of this disease, my aunt Sue is stronger than any woman or man I have ever met.

3 Not a moment passes that my aunt Sue is not confronted with this demon of a disease and reminded of her disability through the pills she must take and the pain she must endure. It hurts to stand, it hurts to walk, it hurts to sit. After an infinite number of failed medications, aunt Sue is now undergoing her most aggressive treatment, which includes weekly oral chemotherapy. After half a dozen surgeries, her frail body is in need of still more.

4 And yet despite all of this, I can't recall ever hearing her complain about her fate. After all the indignities and inconveniences her illness has thrown at her, my aunt Sue still finds the energy to devote much of her time not to herself, but to those less fortunate than her. This past Thanksgiving, for example, she helped organize a dinner for more than 500 poor and homeless people. My aunt Sue, who has her medications put in non-childproof containers so she can open them, helped coordinate a dinner for those in need.

5 The picture I have painted of my aunt Sue thus far is of a kind woman, a determined woman, a warmhearted woman whose own suffering seems inconsequential when compared to that of others. This is all completely true, but there is something else about my aunt Sue that makes me admire her so. Actually, it's what makes me love her as much as I do.

6 At five feet two inches, and 105 pounds, with the spunk of a teenager, she introduces herself as "Crazy Sue"—and sometimes I'd have to agree with her. Somehow she is able to approach this demonic disease with a sense of humor. And not just any sense of humor. My aunt Sue is one of the funniest people I know.

7 Years ago, when the disease began to hit her really hard, one of the attorneys at her law firm asked why she was limping. She told him she fell off a trapeze performing her weekend hobby—and he believed her! Following an ankle sprain and further complications, her ankle became deformed and the arch of her foot completely collapsed. Whereas most people would wallow in their misery, aunt Sue calls it her "cartoon foot."

8 My aunt Sue has made a positive impression on countless people throughout her life, but I hope she knows how much of an impression she has made on me—and how much I admire her.

9 I complain about trudging through the snow to class, but I'm walking pain free. I complain about driving my friends around town, but I'm steering the wheel pain free. I complain about the final exams I'll have to write, but I have the mobility in my wrist to write pain free. I have learned from my aunt Sue that I need to do a better job about being happy for the things that I have, rather than worrying about the not-so-perfect things in my life.

10 Aunt Sue may call herself crazy, but I call her phenomenal—a joy to be around and a reminder that having a physical disability in no way diminishes a person's spirit or inner beauty.

Photo Credits

Chapter 1

3: © Joel Gordon Photography; 7: © Tom Grill/IPN Stock; 11: © Jeff Mitchell/Reuters/Corbis; 15: © Abdelhak Senna/AFP/Getty Images; 19: © Photodisc/Getty Images; 24: Stefan Wermuth/Reuters/Landov

Chapter 2

29: © Jim Young/Reuters/Corbis; 33: © Tannen Maury/The Image Works; 36: © Dick Blume/Syracuse Newspapers/The Image Works; 39: The McGraw-Hill Companies, Inc./Erica S. Leeds, photographer; 43: © Roger L. Wollenberg/UPI/Newscom

Chapter 3

47: © Masterfile; 51: © Michael Newman/PhotoEdit, Inc.; 55: © Jacque Brund 2005/Design Conceptions; 59: © Jeff Jacobson/Redux

Appendix 1

63: Mannic Media/McGraw-Hill, Inc.

Chapter 4

75: © Chris Ware/The Image Works; 77: © Tom Smart/The New York Times/Redux; 84: © DLILLC/Corbis; 89: © Jose Luis Pelaez, Inc./Corbis

Chapter 5

95: Tim Shaffer/Reuters/Landov; 99: © Bob Daemmrich/The Image Works; 103: © Marwan Naamani/AFP/Getty Images; 109: AP Photo/The Greenwich Time, Bob Luckey; 113: © David Young-Wolff/PhotoEdit, Inc.

Chapter 6

119: George Shelley/ArtLife; 123: © Tetra Images/Getty Images; 127: AP Photo/Virginia Mayo; 133: © Rachel Epstein/PhotoEdit, Inc.; 137: © LWA-Sharie Kennedy Williams/Corbis

Chapter 7

141: © Lynn Goldsmith/Corbis; 145: AP Photo/Bebeto Matthews; 149: AP Photo/Christopher Pfuhl; 157: Mannic Media/McGraw-Hill, Inc.

Chapter 8

165: © RubberBall/Age Fotostock; 169: David Karp/Bloomberg News/Landov; 171: © Bill Aron/PhotoEdit, Inc.; 179: Kevin Lamarque/Reuters/Landov

Chapter 9

185: © Bob Daemmrich/The Image Works; 189: © Joel Gordon Photography; 191: © Digital Vision/Creatas; 193: © Henning Kaiser/AFP/Getty Images; 197: © Bernard Weil/Toronto Star/Age Fotostock; 199: © Peter Yates/Corbis

Chapter 10

207: © Joel Gordon Photography; 211: © Chris Stock Photography/Alamy; 217: AP Photo/Doug Mills

Chapter 11

223: © David Young-Wolff/PhotoEdit, Inc.; 225: Fred Prouser/Reuters/Landov; 229: AP Photo/Paul Franz; 231: © Lynn Goldsmith/Corbis; 237: © James Rulison/NewSport/Corbis

Chapter 12

243: AP Photo/Keystone/Martial Trezzini; 247: Joel Page/AP Photo; 251: © Patitucci Photo/Aurora Photos; 255: Fred Prouser/Reuters/Landov; 259: © AFP/Getty Images; 261: © Tim Wimborne/Reuters/Corbis

Chapter 13

267: © Andrea Mohin/The New York Times/Redux; 269: © Jim Zuckerman/Corbis; 275: Mannic Media/McGraw-Hill, Inc.

Appendix 2

285: © Creatas/Photolibrary; 290: Courtesy of The Library of Congress; 294: © Digital Vision/Alamy

Chapter 14

299: © David R. Frazier/The Image Works; 303: AP Photo/Harry Cabluck; 307: Claro Cortes IV/Reuters/Landov; 311: © Suzanne DeChillo/The New York Times/Redux; 315: Denkou Images/drr.net

Chapter 15

323: AP Photo/Paul Sakuma; 327: AP Photo/Rick Bowmer; 331: © Rainer Jensen/EPA/Corbis; 335: © Joel Gordon Photography; 339: © Mark Lewis/TSI/Getty Images; 343: © Ramin Talaie/Corbis

Chapter 16

351: Jamie Rector/Bloomberg News/Landov; 355: © Rachel Epstein/PhotoEdit, Inc.; 359: AP Photo/Dennis Cook; 365: © Tim Pannell/Corbis; 369: Steve Pope/Bloomberg News/Landov; 371: © Mariela Lombard/Zuma Press; 373: © Ramin Talaie/Corbis

Chapter 17

381: © David Young-Wolff/Alamy; 385: AP Photo/Daian Dovarganes; 389: © Scott London

Chapter 18

393: © moodboard/SuperStock; 396: © Corbis; 401: © Ryan McVay/Getty Images; 405: © Cow Studio - Mad/Photo Library

Notes

Chapter 1

[1] Pericles, quoted in Richard Whately, *Elements of Rhetoric*, 7th ed. (London: John W. Parker, 1846), p. 10.

[2] Albert R. Karr, "A Special News Report About Life on the Job and Trends Taking Shape There," *Wall Street Journal*, December 29, 1998, p. A1; Andrew A. Zekeri, "College Curriculum Competencies and Skills Former Students Found Essential to Their Careers," *College Student Journal*, 38 (2004), pp. 412–422.

[3] Stephanie Armour, "Failure to Communicate Costly for Companies," *USA Today*, April 30, 1998, p. 1B; Midge Costanza quoted in Sharon Nelson, "Address for Success," *Nation's Business* (February 1991), pp. 43–44.

[4] George A. Kennedy, *Comparative Rhetoric: An Historical and Cross-Cultural Introduction* (New York: Oxford University Press, 1998).

[5] For an excellent selection of works from the figures discussed in this and the previous paragraph, see Patricia Bizzell and Bruce Herzberg (eds.), *The Rhetorical Tradition: Readings from Classical Times to the Present*, 2nd ed. (New York: Bedford/St. Martin's, 2001).

[6] Geoffrey Brewer, "Snakes Top List of Americans' Fears," Gallup News Service, February 2001; Alex Blyth, "How to Get the Most Out of Public Speaking Training," *Training Magazine* (June 14, 2006), p. 7.

[7] Daniel Goleman, "Social Anxiety: New Focus Leads to Insights and Therapy," *New York Times*, December 18, 1984

[8] Cicero, *De Oratore*, trans. E. W. Sutton (Cambridge, MA: Harvard University Press, 1942), p. xxvi.

[9] Digby Jones, "Public Speaking Tests the Nerves of Most Directors," *Birmingham Post*, August 25, 2003.

[10] Quoted in Bert E. Bradley, *Fundamentals of Speech Communication: The Credibility of Ideas*, 6th ed. (Dubuque, IA: W. C. Brown, 1991), p. 36.

[11] Elayne Synder, *Speak for Yourself—With Confidence* (New York: New American Library, 1983), p. 113.

[12] Sharon Aschaiek, "Conquer Your Fear of Public Speaking," *Toronto Sun*, March 16, 2005.

[13] A number of studies have shown that taking a public speaking course is effective in reducing stage fright. See, for example, Ralph R. Behnke and Chris R. Sawyer, "Public Speaking Anxiety as a Function of Sensitization and Habituation Processes," *Communication Education*, 53 (2004), 164–173.

[14] Lilly Walters, *Secrets of Successful Speakers* (New York: McGraw-Hill, 1993), pp. 32–36.

[15] See Steven Ungerleider, *Mental Training for Peak Performance*, rev. ed. (Emmaus, PA: Rodale Books, 2005).

[16] Joe Ayres, Tim Hopf, and Debbie M. Ayres, "Visualization and Performance Visualization: Applications, Evidence, and Speculation," in John A. Daly, James C. McCroskey, Joe Ayres, Tim Hopf, and Debbie M. Ayres (eds.), *Avoiding Communication: Shyness, Reticence, and Communication Apprehension*, 2nd ed. (Cresskill, NJ: Hampton Press, 1997), pp. 401–422.

[17] Dick Cavett, quoted in Steve Allen, *How to Make a Speech* (New York: McGraw-Hill, 1986), p. 10.

[18] For more detail on the ideas in this paragraph, see Michael T. Motley, *Overcoming Your Fear of Public Speaking: A Proven Method* (Boston: Houghton Mifflin, 1998).

[19] Chris R. Sawyer and Ralph R. Behnke, "Reduction in Public Speaking State Anxiety During Performance as a Function of Sensitization Processes," *Communication Quarterly*, 50 (2002), 110–121.

[20] For more detail on the dimensions of critical thinking, see M. Neil Browne and Stuart M. Keeley, *Asking the Right Questions: A Guide to Critical Thinking*, 8th ed. (Upper Saddle River, NJ: Pearson/Prentice-Hall, 2007).

[21] For the transference of critical thinking skills from public speaking to other activities, see Mike Allen, Sandra Berkowitz, Steve Hunt, and Allen Louden, "A Meta-Analysis of the Impact of Forensics and Communication Education on Critical Thinking," *Communication Education*, 48 (1999), 18–30.

[22] For other models of the speech communication process, see Stephen W. Littlejohn and Karen A. Foss, *Theories of Human Communication*, 8th ed. (Belmont, CA: Thomson/Wadsworth, 2008); Em Griffin, *A First Look at Communication Theory*, 7th ed. (New York: McGraw-Hill, 2009).

[23] John Elson, "The Great Migration," *Time* (Fall 1993), p. 30; Melville quoted in Ronald Takaki, *A Different Mirror: A History of Multicultural America* (Boston: Little, Brown, 1993), p. 427.

[24] See Michael Barone, *The New Americans: How the Melting Pot Can Work Again* (New York: Regnery, 2001).

[25] Ben J. Wattenberg, *The First Universal Nation: Leading Indicators and Ideas About the Surge of America in the 1990s* (New York: Free Press, 1991). For a more theoretical perspective, see Stephen B. Croft, "Rethinking Nationality in the Context of Globalization," *Communication Theory*, 14 (2004), 78–96.

[26] William B. Gudykunst and Young Yun Kim, *Communicating with Strangers: An Approach to Intercultural Communication*, 4th ed. (New York: McGraw-Hill, 2003), p. 4.

[27] For more detail on gestures and other aspects of intercultural communication, see Fred E. Jandt, *An Introduction to Intercultural Communication: Identities in a Global Community*, 5th ed. (Thousand Oaks, CA: Sage, 2007).

[28] Adapted from Roger E. Axtell (ed.), *Do's and Taboos Around the World*, 3rd ed. (New York: John Wiley and Sons, 1993), p. 41.

[29]Myron W. Lustig and Jolene Koester, *Intercultural Competence: Interpersonal Communication Across Cultures*, 5th ed. (Boston: Allyn and Bacon, 2006), pp. 145–148.

[30]For a comprehensive review of scholarship on multiculturalism and communication, see William B. Gudykunst and Bella Moody (eds.), *Handbook of International and Intercultural Communication*, 2nd ed. (Thousand Oaks, CA: Sage, 2002).

Chapter 2

[1]Richard L. Johannesen, Kathleen S. Valde, and Karen E. Whedbee, *Ethics in Human Communication*, 6th ed. (Prospect Heights, IL: Waveland Press, 2008), p. 14.

[2]Johannesen, Valde, and Whedbee, *Ethics in Human Communication*, p. 13.

[3]See, for example, Vincent Ryan Ruggiero, *Thinking Critically About Ethical Issues*, 6th ed. (New York: McGraw-Hill, 2008).

[4]Haig A. Bosmajian, *The Language of Oppression* (Lanham, MD: University Press of America, 1983), p. 5.

[5]See Steven J. Heyman, *Free Speech and Human Dignity* (New Haven, CT: Yale University Press, 2008).

[6]Thomas L. Tedford and Dale A. Herbeck, *Freedom of Speech in the United States*, 5th ed. (State College, PA: Strata Publishing, 2005), pp. 179–185.

[7]Kenneth Blanchard and Norman Vincent Peale, *The Power of Ethical Management* (New York: Ballantine Books, 1988), p. 64.

[8]Joseph Gibaldi, *MLA Handbook for Writers of Research Papers*, 6th ed. (New York: Modern Language Association of America, 2003), p. 66.

[9]Merry Firschein, "School Chief Calls Speech 'An Error in Judgment,'" *The Record*, June 2, 2007; "Superintendent's Speech Stirs Talk of Plagiarism," *New York Times*, June 2, 2007; Merry Firschein, "Teachers Worried About Boss's Last Year," *The Record*, June 13, 2007.

[10]Bruce Perry, *Malcolm: The Life of the Man Who Changed Black America* (Tarrytown, NY: Station Hill, 1991), p. 380.

[11]The credo is available at www.natcom.org/nca/Template2.asp?bid=374.

[12]See www.natcom.org/nca/Template2.asp?bid=374.

Chapter 3

[1]Larry Barker and Kittie Watson, *Listen Up: What You've Never Heard About the Other Half of Every Conversation* (New York: St. Martin's, 2001), p. 5.

[2]Michael P. Nichols, *The Lost Art of Listening* (New York: Guilford, 1995).

[3]See Lyman K. Steil and Richard K. Bommelje, *Listening Leaders: The Ten Golden Rules to Listen, Lead, and Succeed* (Edina, MN: Beaver's Pond Press, 2004).

[4]Beverly Davenport Sypher, Robert N. Bostrom, and Joy Hart Seibert, "Listening, Communication Abilities, and Success at Work," *Journal of Business Communication*, 26 (1989), 293–303.

[5]See the studies cited by Andrew D. Wolvin and Carolyn Gwynn Coakley, "A Survey of the Status of Listening Training in Some Fortune 500 Corporations," *Communication Education*, 40 (1991), 153.

[6]Wolvin and Coakley, "Survey of the Status of Listening Training," 152–162.

[7]See, for example, Rick Bommelje, John M. Houston, and Robert Smither, "Personality Characteristics of Effective Listeners: A Five-Factor Perspective," *International Journal of Listening*, 17 (2003), 32–46.

[8]Andrew W. Wolvin and Carolyn Gwynn Coakley, *Listening*, 5th ed. (Dubuque, IA: Brown and Benchmark, 1995), pp. 223–396.

[9]For more on this point, see Virginia O'Keefe, *Developing Critical Thinking: The Speaking/Listening Connection* (Portsmouth, NH: Boynton/Cook, 1999).

[10]Judi Brownell, *Listening: Attitudes, Principles, and Skills*, 3rd ed. (Boston, MA: Pearson/Allyn and Bacon, 2006), p. 86.

[11]Louis Nizer, *My Life in Court* (New York: Doubleday, 1961), pp. 297–298.

[12]Adapted from Lyman K. Steil, Larry L. Barker, and Kittie W. Watson, *Effective Listening* (Reading, MA: Addison-Wesley, 1983).

[13]George H. Putnam, *Abraham Lincoln* (New York: Putnam, 1909), pp. 44–45.

[14]M. Scott Peck, *The Road Less Traveled: A New Psychology of Love, Traditional Values, and Spiritual Growth*, 25th anniversary ed. (New York: Touchstone Books, 2003), p. 127.

[15]Robert Ingram, "Sound Solutions for Rising Healthcare Costs," *Vital Speeches*, 79 (2006), 746–751.

[16]See Ralph G. Nichols and Leonard A. Stevens, *Are You Listening?* (New York: McGraw-Hill, 1957), pp. 113–114. This classic work still has much of value to say about its subject.

[17]See, for example, Robert L. Williams and Alan C. Eggert, "Notetaking in College Classes: Student Patterns and Instructional Strategies," *Journal of General Education*, 51 (2002), 173–199.

[18]For one study that confirms the multiple benefits of note taking, see B. Scott Titsworth and Kenneth A. Kiewra, "Spoken Organizational Lecture Cues and Student Notetaking as Facilitators of Student Learning," *Contemporary Educational Psychology*, 29 (2004), 447–461.

Chapter 5

[1]Seeing the speech classroom as a real audience is also important because it engages students in a form of rhetorical activity that is vital to participatory democracy. See Rosa A. Eberly, "Rhetoric and the Anti-Logos Doughball: Teaching Deliberating Bodies the Practices of Participatory Democracy," *Rhetoric and Public Affairs*, 5 (2002), 296.

[2]Quoted in Halford R. Ryan, "Harry Emerson Fosdick," in Bernard K. Duffy and Halford R. Ryan (eds.), *American Orators of the Twentieth Century* (New York: Greenwood Press, 1987), p. 148.

[3]Saul Alinsky, *Rules for Radicals* (New York: Random House, 1971), p. 81.

[4]For a broader discussion of gender issues in communication, see Julia T. Wood, *Gendered Lives: Communication, Gender, and Culture*, 8th ed. (Belmont, CA: Thomson Wadsworth, 2009); Diana K. Ivy and Phil Backlund, *Exploring GenderSpeak: Personal Effectiveness in Gender Communication*, 4th ed. (Boston, MA: Pearson/Allyn and Bacon, 2008).

[5]"Ferraro's Flub," *New York Daily News*, March 12, 2008.

[6]Diana L. Eck, *A New Religious America* (New York: Harper-Collins, 2001), p. 4.

[7]Research shows that speakers are usually more persuasive when they attempt to refute opposing arguments rather than ignoring them. See Richard M. Perloff, *The Dynamics of Persuasion: Communication and Attitudes in the 21st Century,* 3rd ed. (New York: Lawrence Erlbaum Associates, 2008), pp. 249–250.

Chapter 6

[1]For more detail on Internet research, see Maura D. Shaw, *Mastering Online Research: A Comprehensive Guide* (Cincinnati, OH: Writer's Digest Books, 2007); Randolph Hock, *The Extreme Searcher's Internet Handbook: A Guide for the Serious Researcher,* 2nd ed. (Medford, NJ: Cyber-Age Books, 2007).

[2]These criteria are adapted from Sheridan Libraries, "Evaluating Information Found on the Internet," *Johns Hopkins University.* Web. July 5, 2008.

[3]For more information on conducting research interviews, see John Brady, *The Interviewer's Handbook, A Guerrilla Guide: Techniques for Reporters and Writers* (Waukesha, WI: Writer Books, 2004). Charles J. Stewart and William B. Cash, Jr., *Interviewing: Principles and Practices,* 12th ed. (New York: McGraw-Hill, 2008), provides insight on various interview types and situations.

[4]For an interesting study that confirms the extent to which the process of researching and developing speeches can affect the beliefs and attitudes of student speakers, see Barbara Mae Gayle, "Transformations in a Civil Discourse Public Speaking Class: Speakers' and Listeners' Attitude Change," *Communication Education,* 53 (2004), 174–184.

[5]For more on the principles and practice of academic research, see Wayne C. Booth, Gregory G. Colomb, and Joseph M. Williams, *The Craft of Research,* 3rd ed. (Chicago: University of Chicago Press, 2008).

Chapter 7

[1]See, for example, Nurit Tal-Or, David S. Boninger, Amir Poran, and Faith Gleicher, "Counterfactual Thinking as a Mechanism in Narrative Persuasion," *Human Communication Research,* 30 (2004), 301–328.

[2]I would like to thank *21st Century* and *China Daily* for permission to include this excerpt from Sun Yan's speech in the online Media Library for this edition of *The Art of Public Speaking.*

[3]Elliot Aronson, *The Social Animal,* 10th ed. (New York: Worth, 2008), pp. 92–93.

[4]This point was made by James A. Winans in his classic *Speech-Making* (New York: Appleton-Century-Crofts, 1922), p. 141.

[5]Over the years, there has been much debate over whether statistics or examples have more impact on listeners. For a recent study that addresses this subject, see Enny Das, Peter Kerkhof, and Joyce Kuiper, "Improving the Effectiveness of Fundraising Messages: The Impact of Charity Goal Attainment, Message Framing, and Evidence on Persuasion," *Journal of Applied Communication Research,* 36 (2008), pp. 161–175.

[6]Joel Best, *More Damned Lies and Statistics: How Numbers Confuse Public Issues* (Berkeley: University of California Press, 2004), provides a fascinating look at the use and misuse of statistics. For a more technical approach, see Neil J. Salkind, *Statistics for People Who (Think They) Hate Statistics,* 3rd ed. (Thousand Oaks, CA: Sage, 2008).

[7]Bob Papper, "A Run for the Money," *RTNDA Communicator,* 62 (May/June 2008), pp. 17–19.

[8]M. Allen, R. Bruflat, R. Fucilla, M. Kramer, S. McKellips, D. J. Ryan, and M. Spiegelhoff, "Testing the Persuasiveness of Evidence: Combining Narrative and Statistical Forms," *Communication Research Reports,* 17 (2000), 331–336.

[9]For research confirming the importance of citing sources when presenting evidence, see Rodney A. Reynolds and J. Lynn Reynolds, "Evidence," in James Price Dillard and Michael Pfau (eds.), *The Persuasion Handbook: Developments in Theory and Practice* (Thousand Oaks, CA: Sage, 2002), pp. 429–430.

[10]See Richard M. Perloff, *The Dynamics of Persuasion: Communication and Attitudes in the 21st Century,* 3rd ed. (New York: Lawrence Erlbaum, 2008), pp. 251–254.

Chapter 8

[1]Ernest C. Thompson, "An Experimental Investigation of the Relative Effectiveness of Organizational Structure in Oral Communication," *Southern Speech Journal,* 26 (1960), pp. 59–69.

[2]Harry Sharp, Jr., and Thomas McClung, "Effects of Organization on the Speaker's Ethos," *Speech Monographs,* 33 (1966), pp. 182–183.

[3]For recent studies, see B. Scott Titsworth, "Students' Notetaking: The Effects of Teacher Immediacy and Clarity," *Communication Education,* 53 (2004), pp. 305–320; Joseph L. Chesebro, "Effects of Teacher Clarity and Nonverbal Immediacy on Student Learning, Receiver Apprehension, and Affect," *Communication Education,* 52 (2003), pp. 135–147.

Chapter 9

[1]Judith S. Kaye, "Gathering Dreams and Giving Them Life," *Vital Speeches,* 73 (2007), pp. 239–242.

[2]Robert S. Mueller III, "Child Pornography and the Internet: Protecting the Most Vulnerable Among Us," *Vital Speeches,* 73 (2007), pp. 45–47.

[3]Dorothy Sarnoff, *Speech Can Change Your Life* (Garden City, NY: Doubleday, 1970), p. 189.

[4]Sarnoff, *Speech Can Change Your Life,* p. 190.

Chapter 10

[1]Robert T. Oliver, *History of Public Speaking in America* (Boston: Allyn and Bacon, 1965), p. 143.

[2]Oliver, *History of Public Speaking,* p. 145.

Chapter 11

[1]Dorothy Sarnoff, *Speech Can Change Your Life* (New York: Doubleday, 1970), p. 71.

[2]Annmarie Mungo, "A Child Is Born," *Winning Orations, 1980* (Mankato, MN: Interstate Oratorical Association, 1980), pp. 49–50.

[3]Adapted from Richard Conniff, "You Never Know What the Fire Ant Is Going to Do Next," *Smithsonian,* July 1990, p. 49.

[4]Edward Bliss, Jr. (ed.)., *In Search of Light: The Broadcasts of Edward R. Murrow, 1938–1961* (New York: Knopf, 1967), p. 276.

[5]William Safire, *On Language* (New York: Times Books, 1980), p. xiv.

[6]Rosalie Maggio, *Talking About People: A Guide to Fair and Accurate Language* (Phoenix, AZ: Oryx Press, 1997), p. 26.

Chapter 12

[1]Irving Bartlett, *Wendell Phillips: Boston Brahmin* (Boston: Beacon Press, 1961), p. 192.

[2]A. Craig Baird, *Rhetoric: A Philosophical Inquiry* (New York: Ronald Press, 1965), p. 207.

[3]Daniel J. O'Keefe, *Persuasion: Theory and Research,* 2nd ed. (Thousand Oaks, CA: Sage, 2002), p. 185.

[4]James Joyce, "Chamber Music XXXV," from *Collected Poems,* ed. Harry Levin (New York: Viking, 1946–1947). Reprinted by permission of Penguin Putnam, Inc.

[5]Dorothy Sarnoff, *Speech Can Change Your Life* (Garden City, NY: Doubleday, 1970), p. 73.

[6]For more detail, see Walt Wolfram and Ben Ward (eds.), *American Voices: How Dialects Differ from Coast to Coast* (Malden, MA: Blackwell, 2006).

[7]For a more detailed guide on vocal communication, consult Lyle V. Mayer, *Fundamentals of Voice and Diction,* 14th ed. (New York: McGraw-Hill, 2008).

[8]See Mark L. Knapp and Judith A. Hall, *Nonverbal Communication in Human Interaction,* 6th ed. (Belmont, CA: Wadsworth, 2006), pp. 12–15.

[9]Richard M. Perloff, *The Dynamics of Persuasion: Communication and Attitudes in the 21st Century,* 3rd ed. (New York: Lawrence Erlbaum, 2008), pp. 235–239.

[10]For more on managing question-and-answer sessions, consult Thomas F. Calcagni, *Tough Questions—Good Answers: Taking Control of Any Interview* (Sterling, VA: Capital Books, 2008).

Chapter 13

[1]For a compendium of research on this subject, see Richard E. Mayer (ed.), *Cambridge Handbook of Multimedia Learning* (New York: Cambridge University Press, 2005).

[2]Douglas R. Vogel, Gary W. Dickson, and John A Lehman, *Persuasion and the Role of Visual Presentation Support: The UM/3M Study* (Minneapolis: University of Minnesota School of Management, 1986).

[3]See Stephen Few, *Show Me the Numbers: Designing Tables and Graphs to Enlighten* (Oakland, CA: Analytics Press, 2004), for an authoritative look at the art of statistical graphics.

[4]For research on this point, see Richard E. Mayer and Cheryl I. Johnson, "Revising the Redundancy Principle in Multimedia Learning," *Journal of Educational Psychology,* 100 (2008), pp. 380–386.

[5]Claudyne Wilder, *The Presentations Kit: 10 Steps for Selling Your Ideas,* rev. ed. (New York: Wiley, 1994), p. 101.

[6]Adapted from Eric A. Walker, "About the 'Death' of an Engineer," *Centre Daily Times,* April 25, 1972.

[7]For additional information on the effective use of visual aids, see Garr Reynolds, *Presentation Zen: Simple Ideas on Presentation and Delivery* (Berkeley, CA: New Riders Press, 2008).

Appendix

[1]Joe Downing and Cecile Garmon, "Teaching Students in the Basic Course How to Use Presentation Software," *Communication Education,* 50 (2002), p. 219; Linda Mahin, "PowerPoint Pedagogy," *Business Communication Quarterly,* 67 (2004), pp. 219–222.

[2]Herbert W. Lovelace, "The Medium Is More Than the Message," *Informationweek.com* (July 16, 2001), p. 74.

[3]See, for example, David G. Levasseur and J. Kanan Sawyer, "Pedagogy Meets PowerPoint: A Research Review of the Effects of Computer-Generated Slides in the Classroom," *Review of Communication,* 6 (2006), pp. 101–123.

[4]For more information, check the Copyright and Image Management Web site (www.utsystem.edu/ogc/ intellectualproperty/image.htm#elec) and the Copyright Basics page (www.library.wisc.edu/copyright/basics.html).

Chapter 14

[1]John R. Johnson and Nancy Szczupakiewicz, "The Public Speaking Course: Is It Preparing Students with Work-Related Public Speaking Skills?" *Communication Education,* 36 (1987), pp. 131–137; Andrew D. Wolvin and Diana Corley, "The Technical Speech Communication Course; A View from the Field," *Association for Communication Administration Bulletin,* 49 (1984), pp. 83–91.

[2]Richard E. Mayer, Sherry Fennell, Lindsay Farmer, and Julie Campbell, "A Personalization Effect in Multimedia Learning: Students Learn Better When Words Are in Conversational Style Rather Than Formal Style," *Journal of Educational Psychology,* 96 (2004), pp. 389–395.

[3]Joseph Conrad, "Youth: A Narrative," in Samuel Hynes (ed.), *Collected Stories of Joseph Conrad* (Hopewell, NJ: Ecco Press, 1991), p. 166.

[4]James Humes, *Roles Speakers Play* (New York: Harper and Row, 1976), p. 25.

Chapter 15

[1]There are many competing definitions of persuasion. Mine is drawn from Gerald R. Miller, "On Being Persuaded: Some Basic Distinctions," in James Price Dillard and Michael Pfau (eds.), *The Persuasion Handbook: Developments in Theory and Practice* (Thousand Oaks, CA: Sage, 2002), pp. 3–16.

[2]Amanda Bennett, "Economics + Meeting = A Zillion Causes and Effects," *The Wall Street Journal,* January 10, 1995, B1.

[3]See Richard L. Johannesen, Kathleen S. Valde, and Karen E. Whedbee, *Ethics in Human Communication,* 6th ed. (Prospect Heights, IL: Waveland Press, 2008), for a full look at communication ethics.

[4]Adapted from Herbert W. Simons, *Persuasion in Society* (Thousand Oaks, CA: Sage, 2001), p. 30.

[5]This view of the interaction between speaker and listener reflects cognitive processing models of persuasion in general and the Elaboration Likelihood Model in particular. For a concise explanation of the latter, see Em Griffin, *A First Look at Communication Theory,* 7th ed. (New York: McGraw-Hill, 2009), pp. 193–204.

[6]There is a great deal of research confirming the need for persuasive speakers to answer potential objections to their arguments. See, for example, Chasu An and

Michael Pfau, "The Efficacy of Inoculation in Televised Political Debates," *Journal of Communication,* 54 (2004), 421–436.

[7]For a superb look at the research on courtroom persuasion, see John C. Reinard, "Persuasion in the Legal Setting," in Dillard and Pfau, *Persuasion Handbook,* pp. 543–602.

[8]Richard M. Perloff, *The Dynamics of Persuasion: Communication and Attitudes in the 21st Century,* 3rd ed. (New York: Lawrence Erlbaum, 2008), pp. 355–357.

[9]Daniel J. O'Keefe, *Persuasion: Theory and Research,* 2nd ed. (Thousand Oaks, CA: Sage, 2002), pp. 218–219.

[10]See, for example, Amber Marie Reinhart, Heather M. Marshall, Thomas Hugh Feeley, and Frank Tutzauer, "The Persuasive Effects of Message Framing in Organ Donation: The Mediating Role of Psychological Reactance," *Communication Monographs,* 74 (2007), pp. 229–255.

Chapter 16

[1]James C. McCroskey, *An Introduction to Rhetorical Communication,* 9th ed. (Boston: Allyn and Bacon, 2006), pp. 84–96.

[2]Edward L. Fink, Deborah A. Cai, Stan A. Kaplowitz, Sungeun Chung, Mark A. Van Dyke, and Jeong-Nam Kim, "The Semantics of Social Influence: Threats vs. Persuasion," *Communication Monographs,* 70 (2003), pp. 295–316.

[3]Richard M. Perloff, *The Dynamics of Persuasion: Communication and Attitudes in the 21st Century,* 3rd ed. (New York: Lawrence Erlbaum, 2008), pp. 283–285.

[4]See, for example, Chasu An and Michael Pfau, "The Efficacy of Inoculation in Televised Debates," *Journal of Communication,* 54 (2004), pp. 421–436.

[5]John C. Reinard, "The Empirical Study of the Persuasive Effects of Evidence: The Status after Fifty Years of Research," *Human Communication Research,* 15 (1988), pp. 37–38.

[6]See, for example, Michael T. Stephenson, "Examining Adolescents' Responses to Antimarijuana PSAs," *Human Communication Research,* 29 (2003), pp. 343–369.

[7]Rodney A. Reynolds and J. Lynn Reynolds, "Evidence," in James Price Dillard and Michael Pfau (eds.), *The Persuasion Handbook: Developments in Theory and Practice* (Thousand Oaks, CA: Sage, 2002), pp. 429–430.

[8]Daniel J. O'Keefe, *Persuasion: Theory and Research,* 2nd ed. (Thousand Oaks, CA: Sage, 2002), pp. 216–218.

[9]Adapted from James C. Humes, *A Speaker's Treasury of Anecdotes About the Famous* (New York: Harper and Row, 1978), p. 131.

[10]In classical systems of logic, reasoning from particular facts to a general conclusion was known as induction. Contemporary logicians, however, have redefined induction as any instance of reasoning in which the conclusion follows from its premises with probability. regardless of whether the reasoning moves from specific instances to a general conclusion or from a general premise to a specific conclusion. In this scheme, reasoning from specific instances is one kind of inductive argument—as are causal reasoning and analogical reasoning. See, for example, Howard Kahane and Nancy Cavender, *Logic and Contemporary Rhetoric: The Use of Reason in Everyday Life,* 10th ed. (Belmont, CA: Thomson Wadsworth, 2006).

[11]Lionel Ruby, *The Art of Making Sense* (Philadelphia: Lippincott, 1954), p. 261.

[12]In classical systems of logic, reasoning from a general premise to a specific conclusion was known as deduction. But just as contemporary logicians have redefined induction (see note 10), they have redefined deduction as any instance of reasoning in which the conclusion follows from its premises with certainty. Some deductive arguments move from general premises to a specific conclusion, but others move from specific premises to a general conclusion. Many speech textbooks confuse reasoning from principle, which is one form of deduction, with deductive reasoning in general.

[13]For more on fallacies and methods of reasoning, see Douglas Walton, *Informal Logic: A Pragmatic Approach,* 2nd ed. (Cambridge: Cambridge University Press, 2008).

[14]H. E. Butler (trans.), *The Institutio Oratoria of Quintilian* (Cambridge, MA: Harvard University Press, 1961), IV, p. 141.

[15]George Campbell, *The Philosophy of Rhetoric,* ed. Lloyd F. Bitzer (Carbondale, IL: Southern Illinois University Press, 1988), p. 77.

[16]Research on fear appeals, for example, has demonstrated that messages devoted exclusively to arousing fear in the audience are usually less effective than messages that combine fear appeals with reasonable explanations of how to eliminate or cope with the source of fear. For an excellent review of that research, see Perloff, *Dynamics of Persuasion,* pp. 263–280.

Chapter 17

[1]James C. Humes, *Roles Speakers Play* (New York: Harper and Row, 1976), p. 8.

[2]For both speeches, see "Remarks by President Clinton and President Nelson Mandela at Presentation of the Congressional Gold Medal to President Nelson Mandela," September 23, 1998. (*http://clinton4.nara.gov/WII/New/html/19980923-977.html*) January 28, 2003.

[3]Humes, *Roles Speakers Play,* pp. 33–34, 36.

Chapter 18

[1]Gloria J. Galanes and Katherine Adams, *Effective Group Discussion: Theory and Practice,* 12th ed. (New York: McGraw-Hill, 2007), pp. 285–287.

[2]See Charlan Jeanne Nemeth and Jack A. Goncalo, "Influence and Persuasion in Small Groups," in Timothy C. Brock and Melanie C. Green (eds.), *Persuasion: Psychological Insights and Perspectives*, 2nd ed. (Thousand Oaks, CA: Sage, 2005), pp. 171–194, for a helpful review of scholarship on this subject.

[3]Dennis S. Gouran, "Leadership as the Art of Counteractive Influence in Decision-Making and Problem-Solving Groups," in Randy Y. Hirokawa, Robert S. Cathcart, Larry A. Samovar, and Linda D. Henman (eds.), *Small Group Communication: Theory and Practice,* 8th ed. (Los Angeles: Roxbury, 2003), pp. 172–198.

[4]See, for example, Andrew J. Flanagin, Hee Sun Park, and David R. Seibold, "Group Performance and Collaborative Technology: A Longitudinal and Multilevel Analysis of Information Quality, Contribution Equity, and

Members' Satisfaction in Computer-Mediated Groups," *Communication Monographs,* 71 (2004), 352–372.

[5]For more on dealing with conflict in small groups, see Scott A. Myers and Carolyn Anderson, *The Fundamentals of Small Group Communication* (Los Angeles: Sage, 2008), pp. 199–215.

[6]Charles Pavitt and Kelly K. Johnson, "Scheidel and Crowell Revisited: A Descriptive Study of Group Proposal Sequencing," *Communication Monographs,* 69 (2002), 19–32.

[7]For research on this subject, see Michele H. Jackson and Marshall Scott Poole, "Idea-Generation in Naturally Occurring Contexts: Complex Appropriation of Simple Group Procedure," *Human Communication Research,* 29 (2003), 560–591.

[8]For further reading on research in small-group communication, see Marshall Scott Poole and Andrea B. Hollingshead (eds.), *Theories of Small Groups: Interdisciplinary Perspectives* (Thousand Oaks, CA: Sage, 2005).

[9]For more information on small-group oral presentations, see Katherine Adams and Gloria J. Galanes, *Communicating in Groups: Applications and Skills,* 7th ed. (New York: McGraw-Hill, 2009), pp. 314–335.

Index